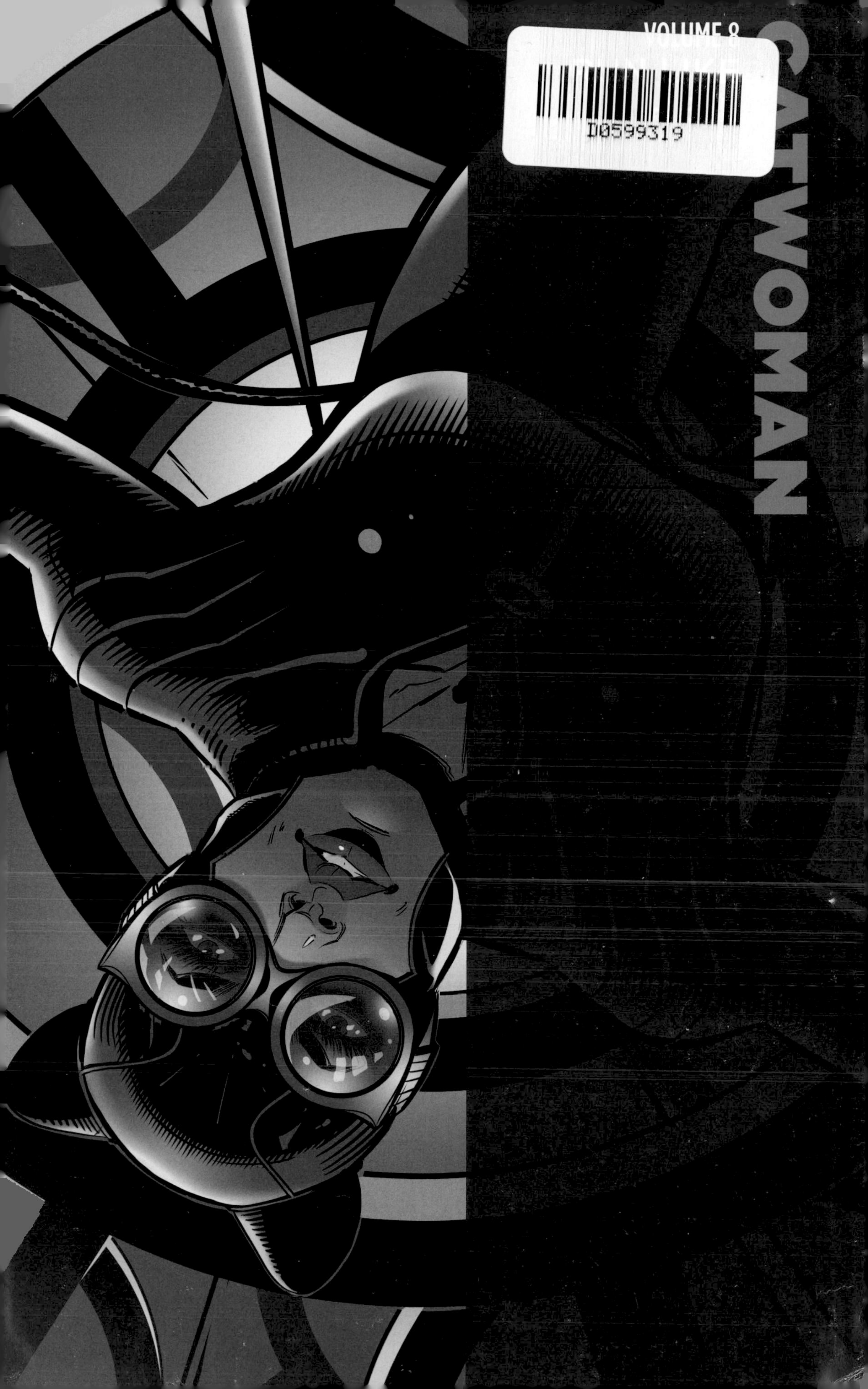
VOLUME 8
CATWOMAN

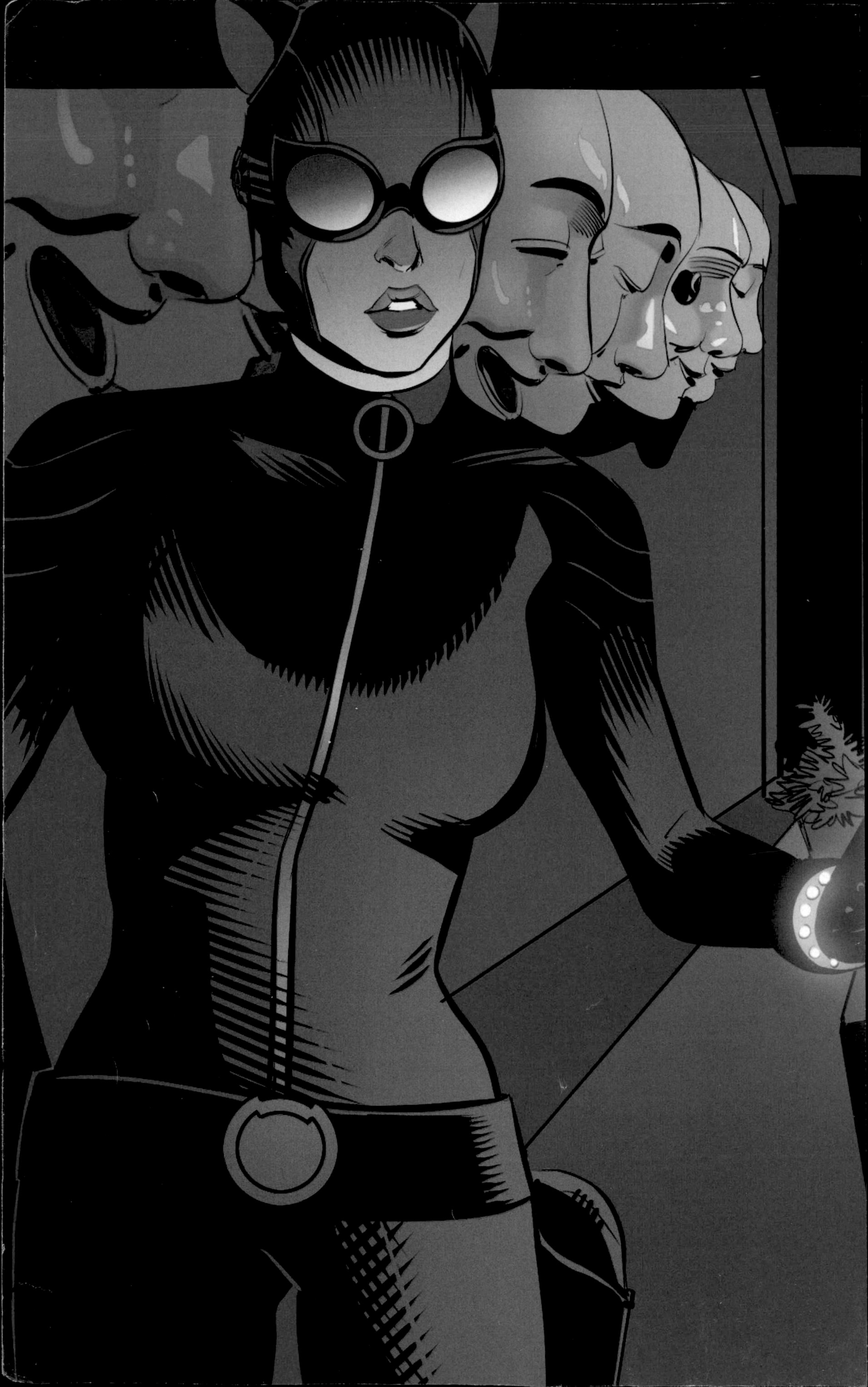

CATWOMAN

VOLUME 8
RUN LIKE HELL

WRITER
FRANK TIERI

ARTISTS
INAKI MIRANDA
GERALDO BORGES
ELIA BONETTI
POP MHAN
GIUSEPPE CAFARO
DAN PANOSIAN
ALEX KONAT
JAY LEISTEN
STEVE PUGH

COLORISTS
EVA DE LA CRUZ
BLOND
BETH SOTELO
JOHN STARR

LETTERER
TRAVIS LANHAM

SERIES & COLLECTION
COVER ARTIST
JOSH MIDDLETON

REBECCA TAYLOR and DAVID WOHL Editors – Original Series
JEB WOODARD Group Editor – Collected Editions
STEVE COOK Design Director – Books
DAMIAN RYLAND Publication Design

BOB HARRAS Senior VP – Editor-in-Chief, DC Comics

DIANE NELSON President
DAN DiDIO and JIM LEE Co-Publishers
GEOFF JOHNS Chief Creative Officer
AMIT DESAI Senior VP – Marketing & Global Franchise Management
NAIRI GARDINER Senior VP – Finance
SAM ADES VP – Digital Marketing
BOBBIE CHASE VP – Talent Development
MARK CHIARELLO Senior VP – Art, Design & Collected Editions
JOHN CUNNINGHAM VP – Content Strategy
ANNE DePIES VP – Strategy Planning & Reporting
DON FALLETTI VP – Manufacturing Operations
LAWRENCE GANEM VP – Editorial Administration & Talent Relations
ALISON GILL Senior VP – Manufacturing & Operations
HANK KANALZ Senior VP – Editorial Strategy & Administration
JAY KOGAN VP – Legal Affairs
DEREK MADDALENA Senior VP – Sales & Business Development
JACK MAHAN VP – Business Affairs
DAN MIRON VP – Sales Planning & Trade Development
NICK NAPOLITANO VP – Manufacturing Administration
CAROL ROEDER VP – Marketing
EDDIE SCANNELL VP – Mass Account & Digital Sales
COURTNEY SIMMONS Senior VP – Publicity & Communications
JIM (SKI) SOKOLOWSKI VP – Comic Book Specialty & Newsstand Sales
SANDY YI Senior VP – Global Franchise Management

CATWOMAN VOLUME 8: RUN LIKE HELL

DC Comics, 2900 West Alameda Ave., Burbank, CA 91505
Printed by RR Donnelley, Salem, VA, USA. 9/9/16. First Printing.
ISBN: 978-1-4012-6486-4

Library of Congress Cataloging-in-Publication Data is available.

PEFC Certified

Printed on paper from
sustainably managed
forests and controlled
sources

PEFC™
PEFC/29-31-75   www.pefc.org

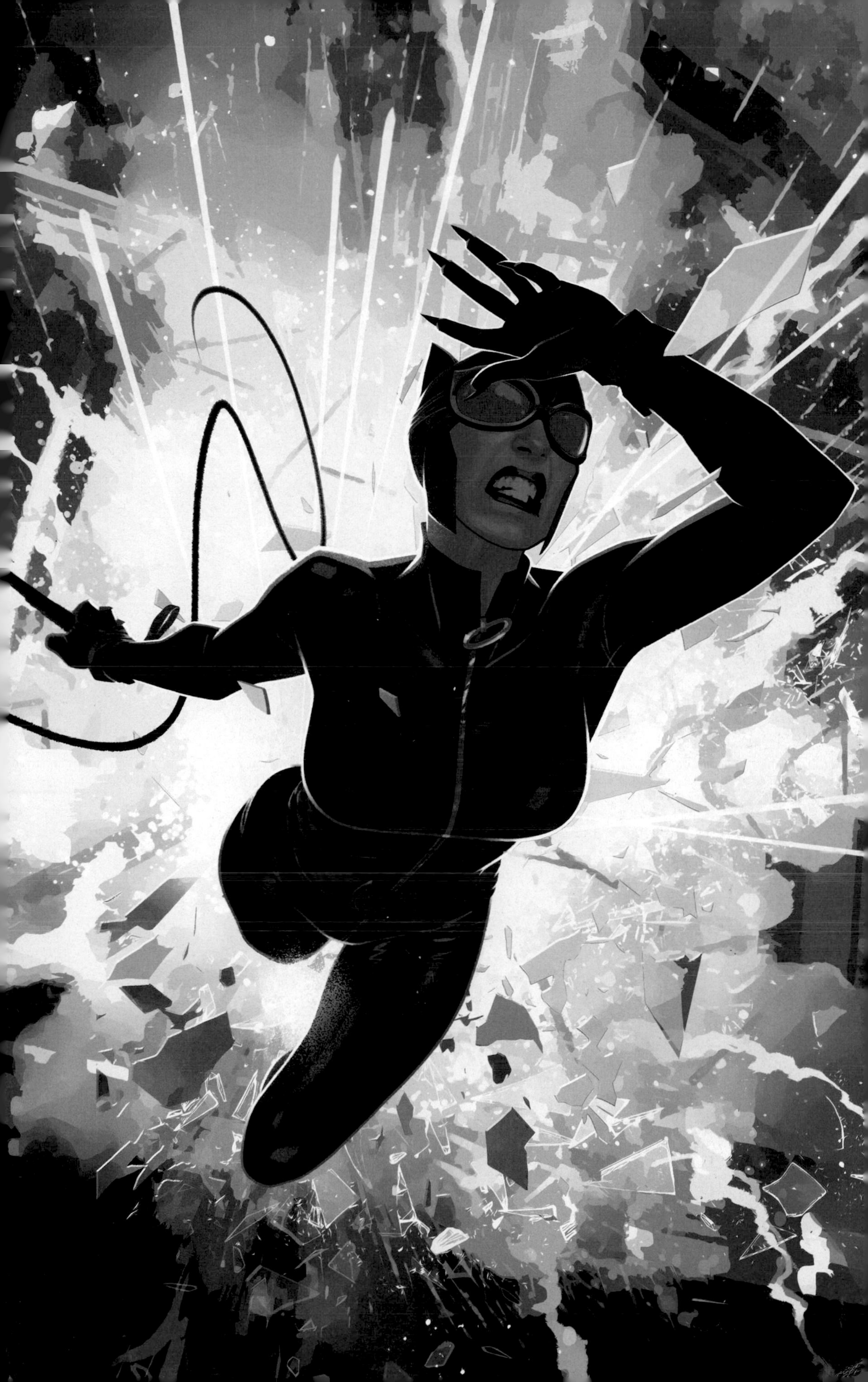

RUN LIKE HELL, PART ONE

FRANK TIERI writer **INAKI MIRANDA** artist **EVA DE LA CRUZ** colorist **TRAVIS LANHAM** letterer **JOSH MIDDLETON** cover

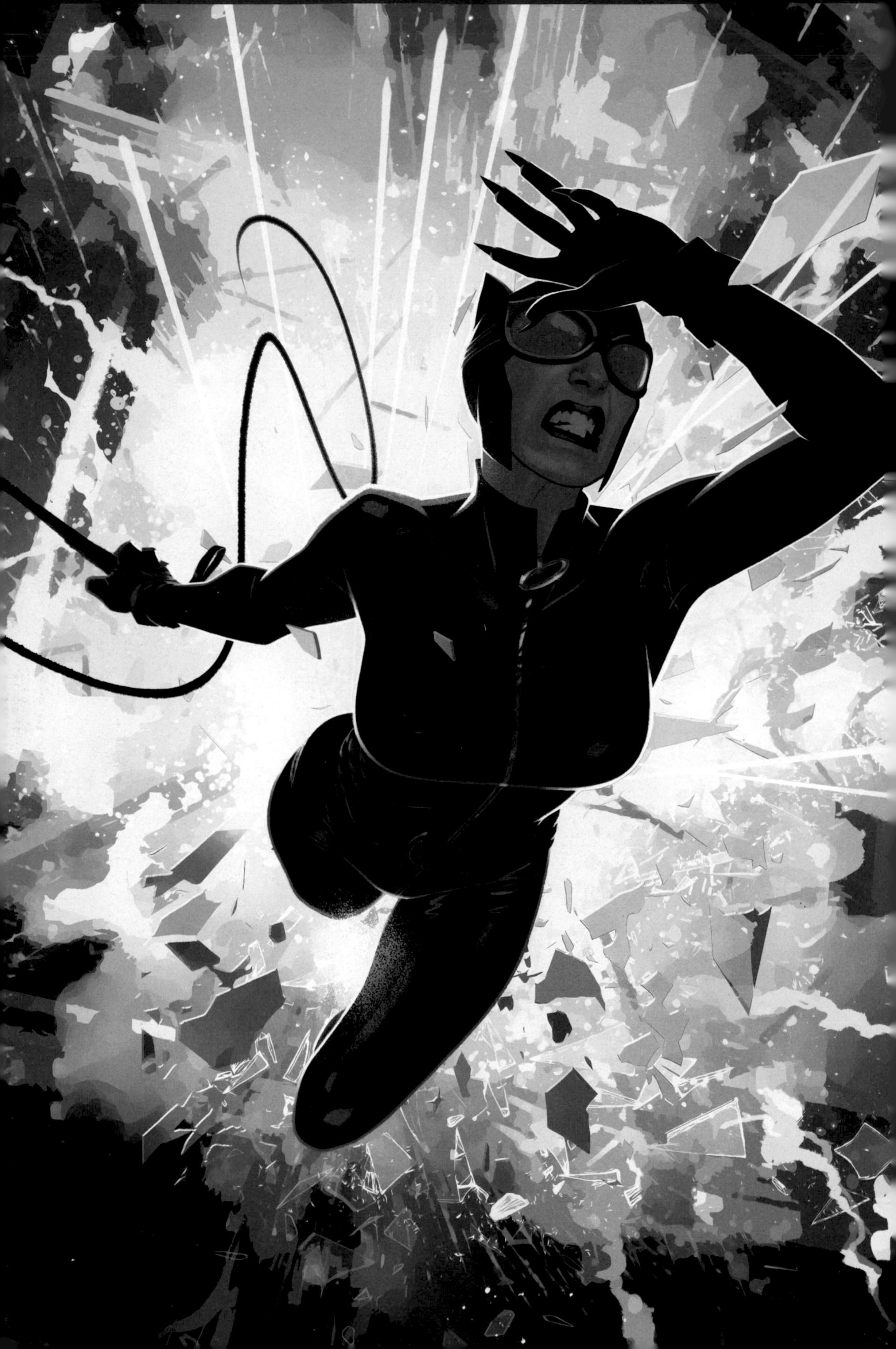

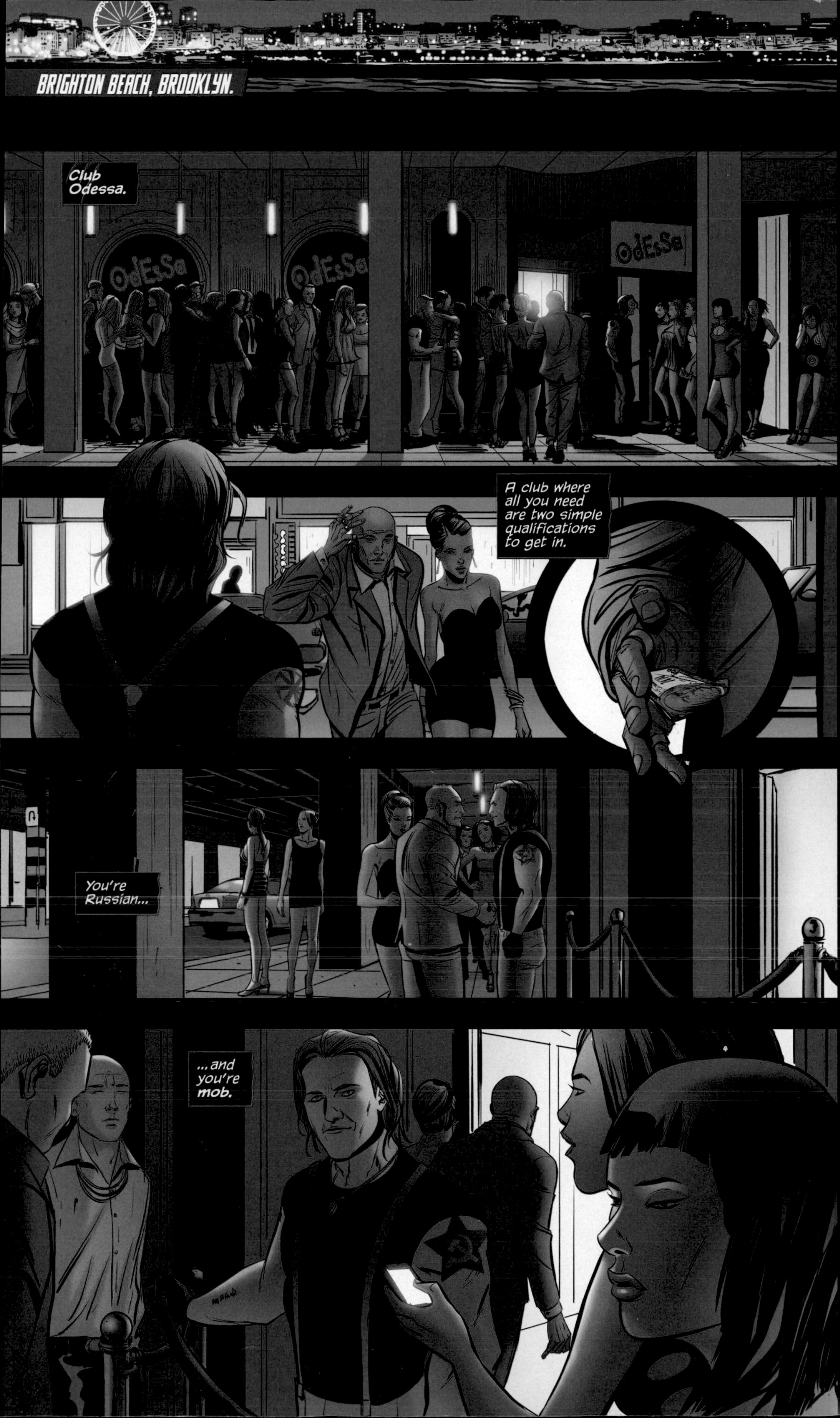
BRIGHTON BEACH, BROOKLYN.
Club Odessa.
A club where all you need are two simple qualifications to get in.
You're Russian...
...and you're mob.

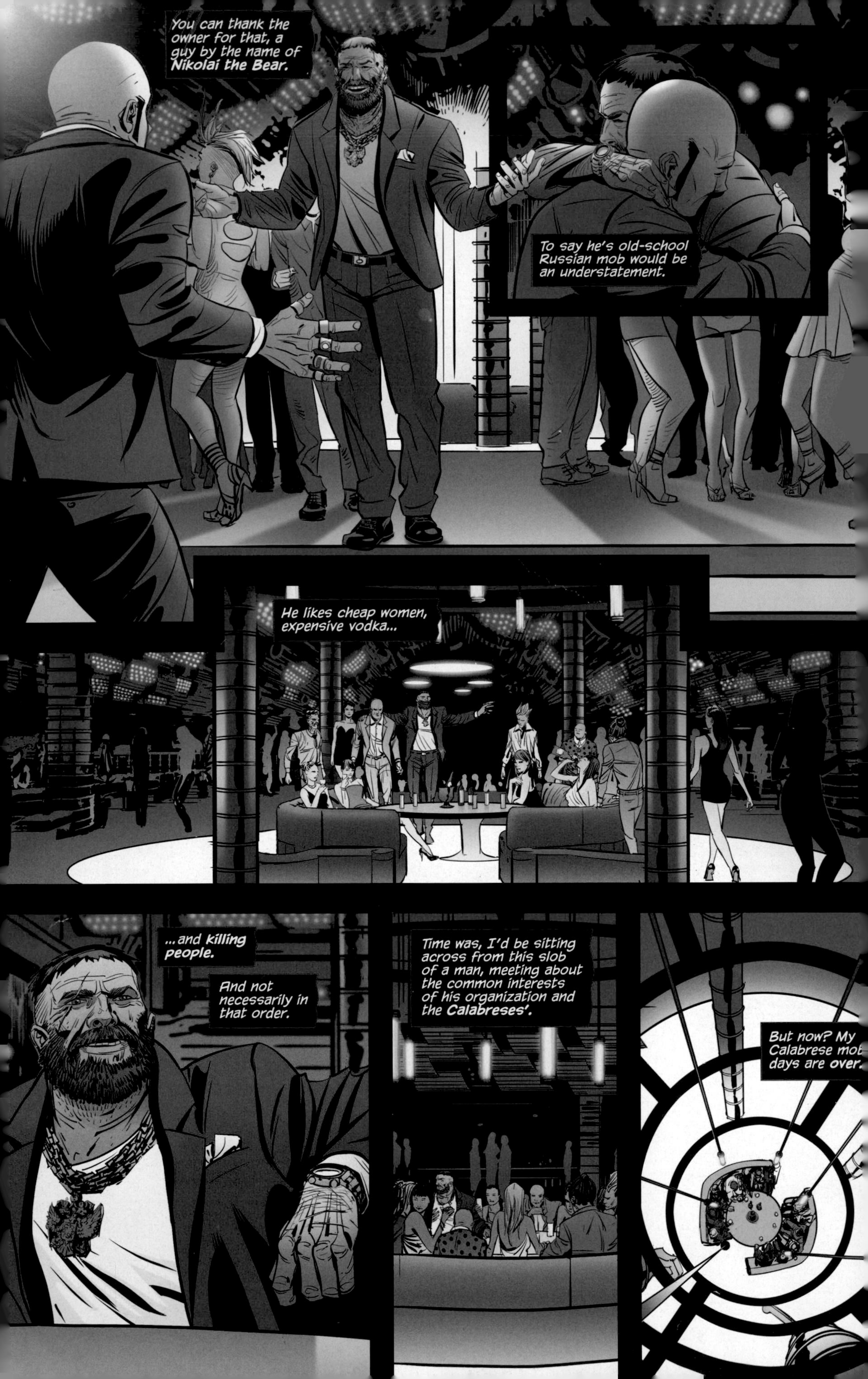
You can thank the owner for that, a guy by the name of Nikolai the Bear.
To say he's old-school Russian mob would be an understatement.
He likes cheap women, expensive vodka...
...and killing people.
And not necessarily in that order.
Time was, I'd be sitting across from this slob of a man, meeting about the common interests of his organization and the Calabreses'.
But now? My Calabrese mob days are over.

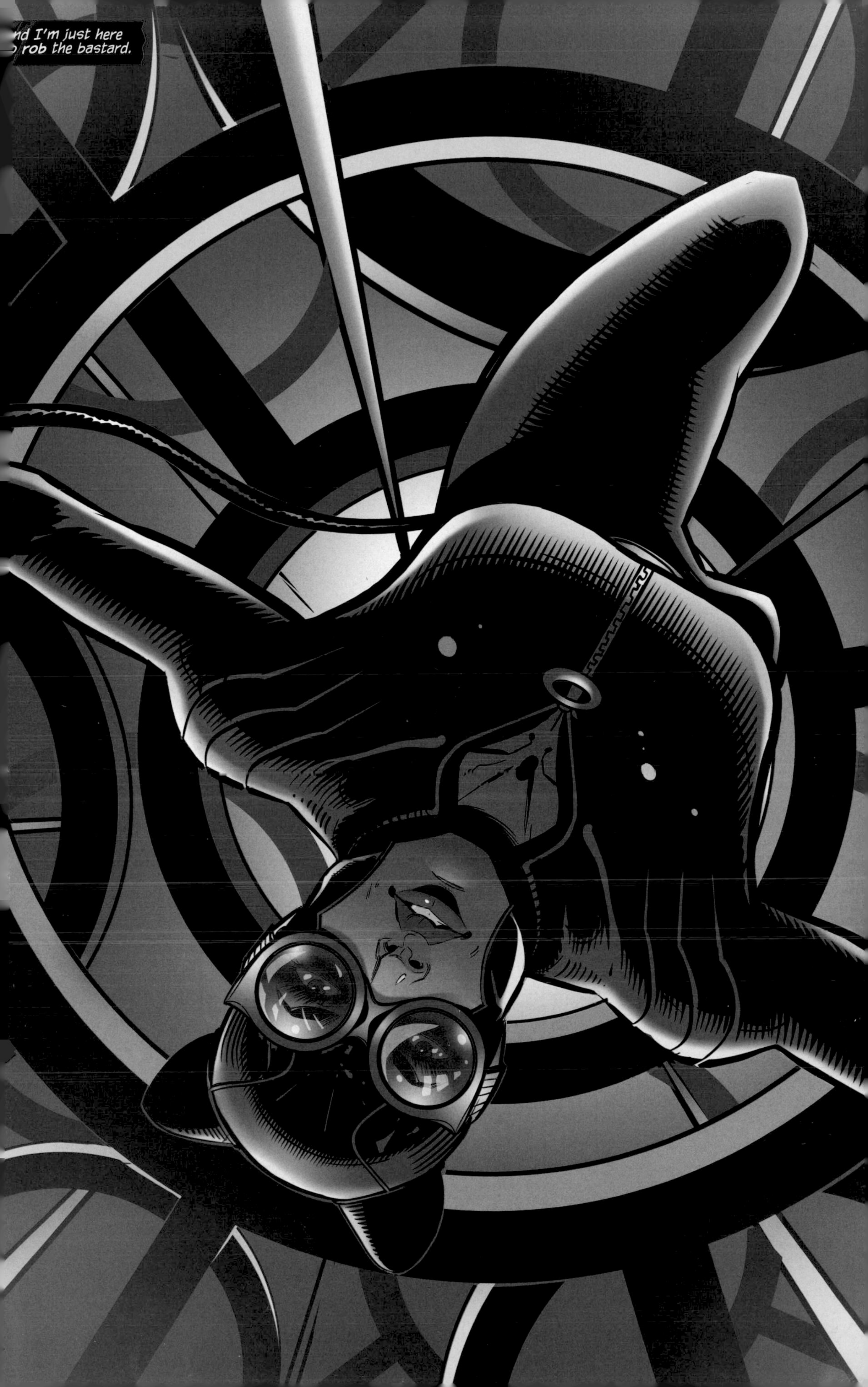
nd I'm just here
o rob the bastard.

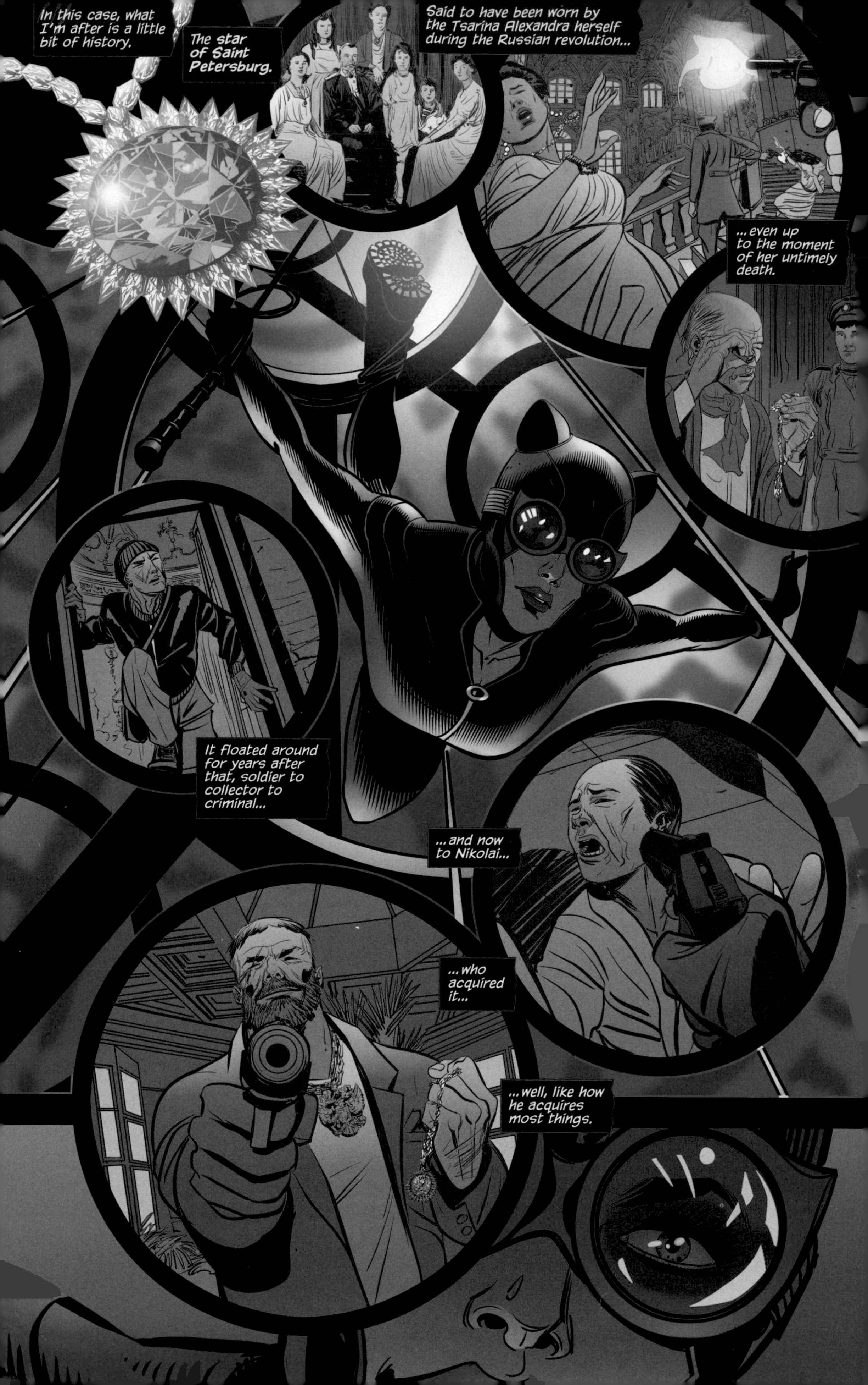

In this case, what I'm after is a little bit of history.
The star of Saint Petersburg.
Said to have been worn by the Tsarina Alexandra herself during the Russian revolution...
...even up to the moment of her untimely death.
It floated around for years after that, soldier to collector to criminal...
...and now to Nikolai...
...who acquired it...
...well, like how he acquires most things.

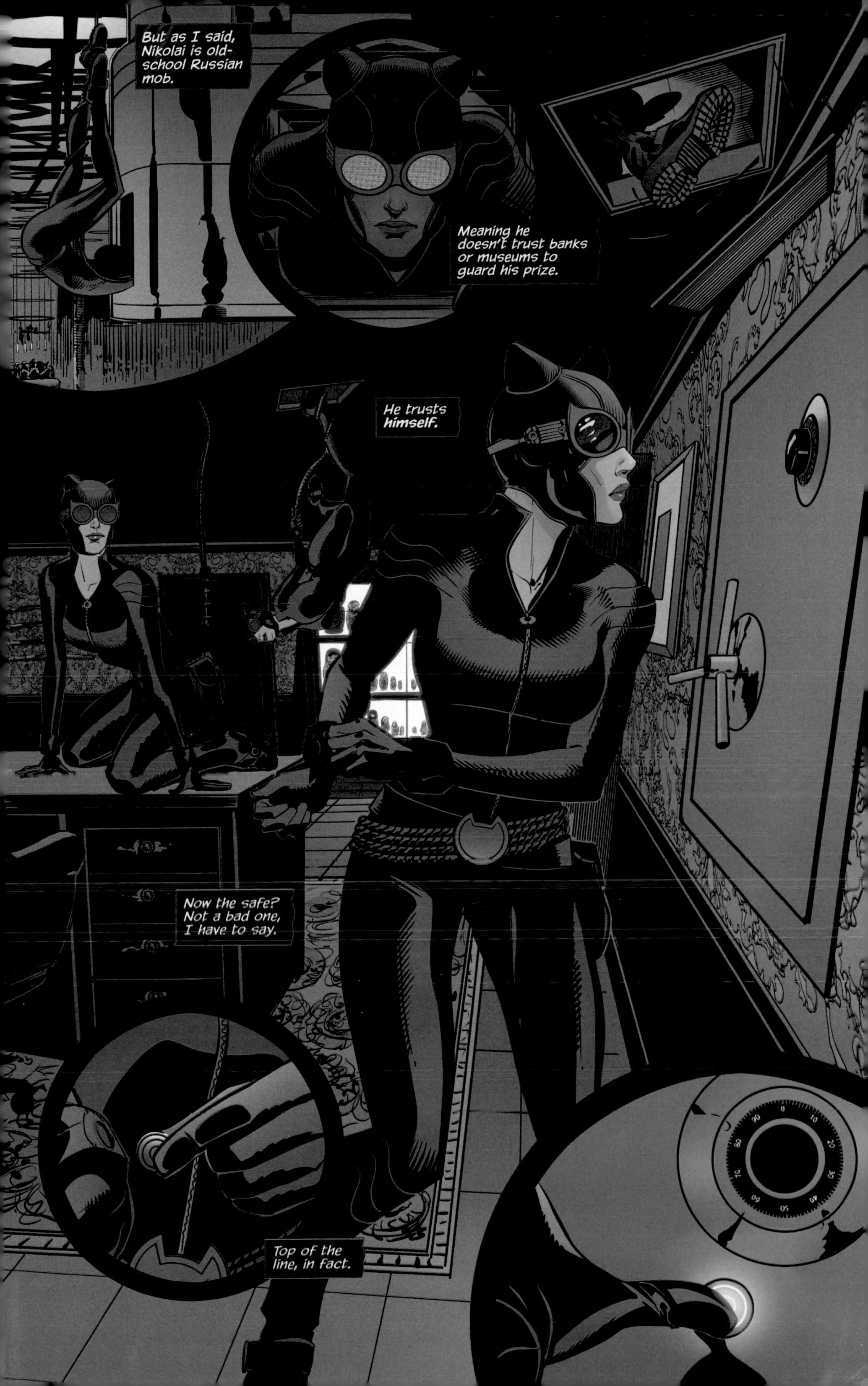
But as I said, Nikolai is old-school Russian mob.
Meaning he doesn't trust banks or museums to guard his prize.
He trusts **himself.**
Now the safe? Not a bad one, I have to say.
Top of the line, in fact.

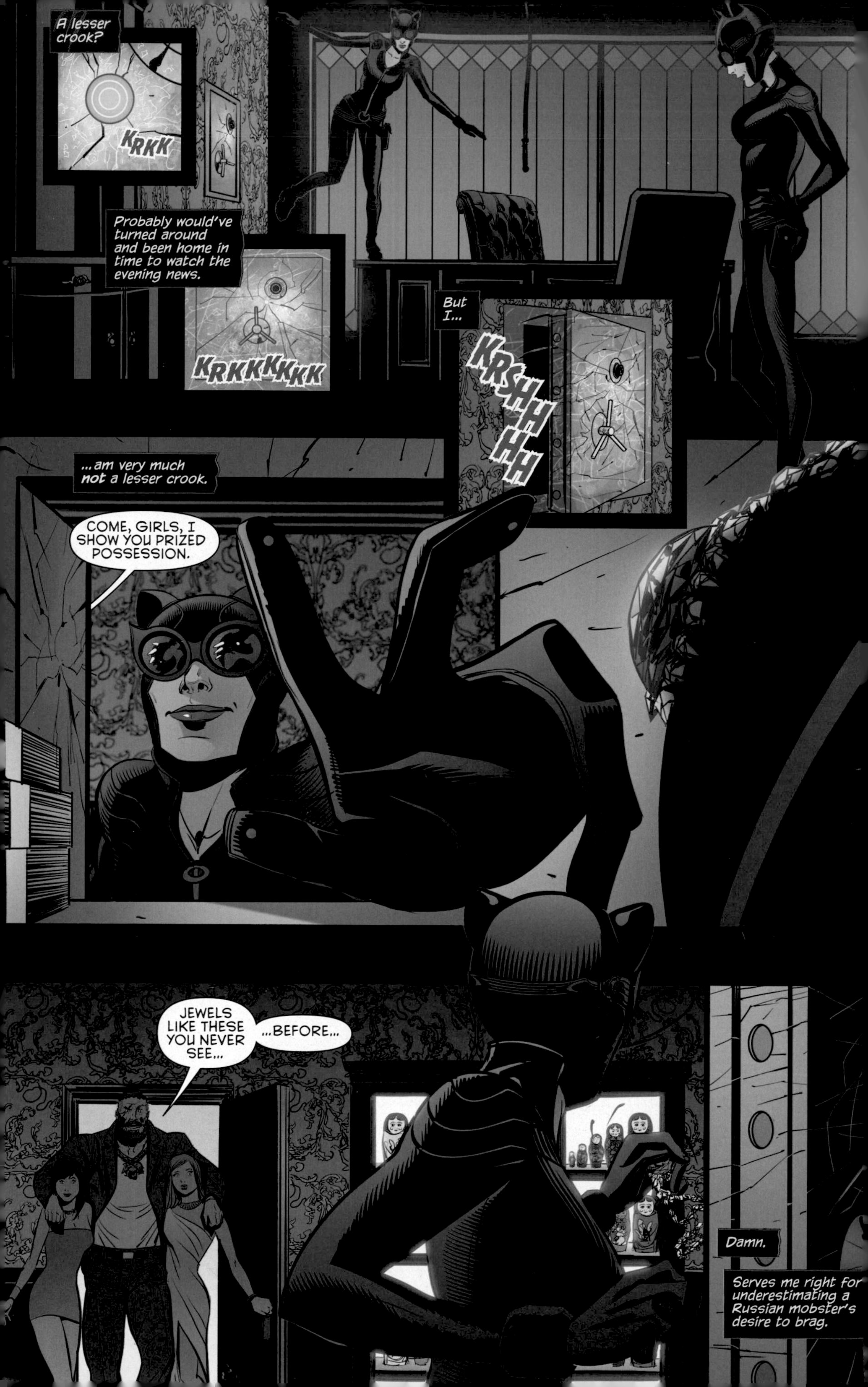
A lesser crook?
KRKK
Probably would've turned around and been home in time to watch the evening news.
KRKKKKKKK
But I...
KRSHHHHH
...am very much not a lesser crook.
COME, GIRLS, I SHOW YOU PRIZED POSSESSION.
JEWELS LIKE THESE YOU NEVER SEE...
...BEFORE...
Damn.
Serves me right for underestimating a Russian mobster's desire to brag.

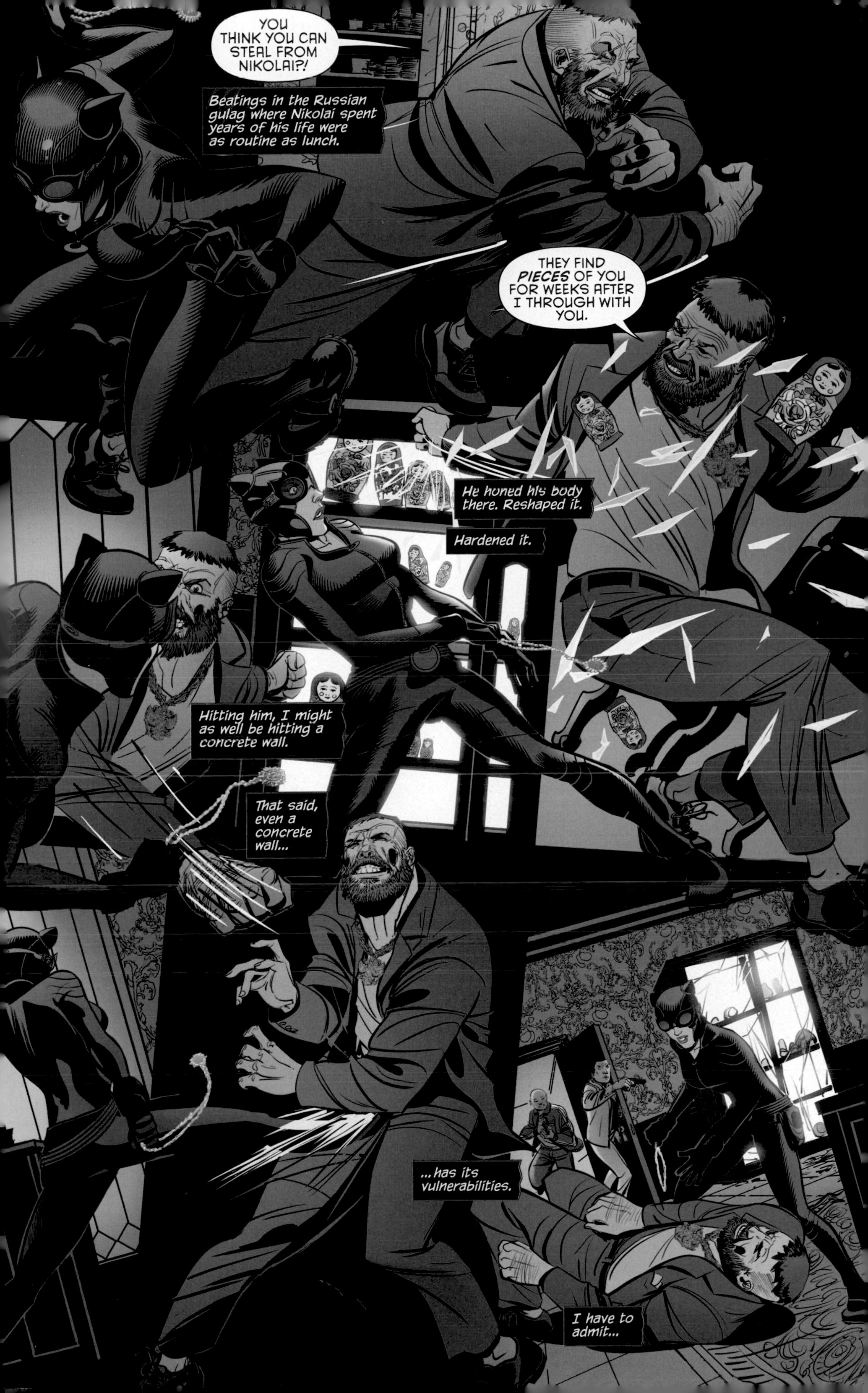

YOU THINK YOU CAN STEAL FROM NIKOLAI?!
Beatings in the Russian gulag where Nikolai spent years of his life were as routine as lunch.
THEY FIND PIECES OF YOU FOR WEEKS AFTER I THROUGH WITH YOU.
He honed his body there. Reshaped it.
Hardened it.
Hitting him, I might as well be hitting a concrete wall.
That said, even a concrete wall...
...has its vulnerabilities.
I have to admit...

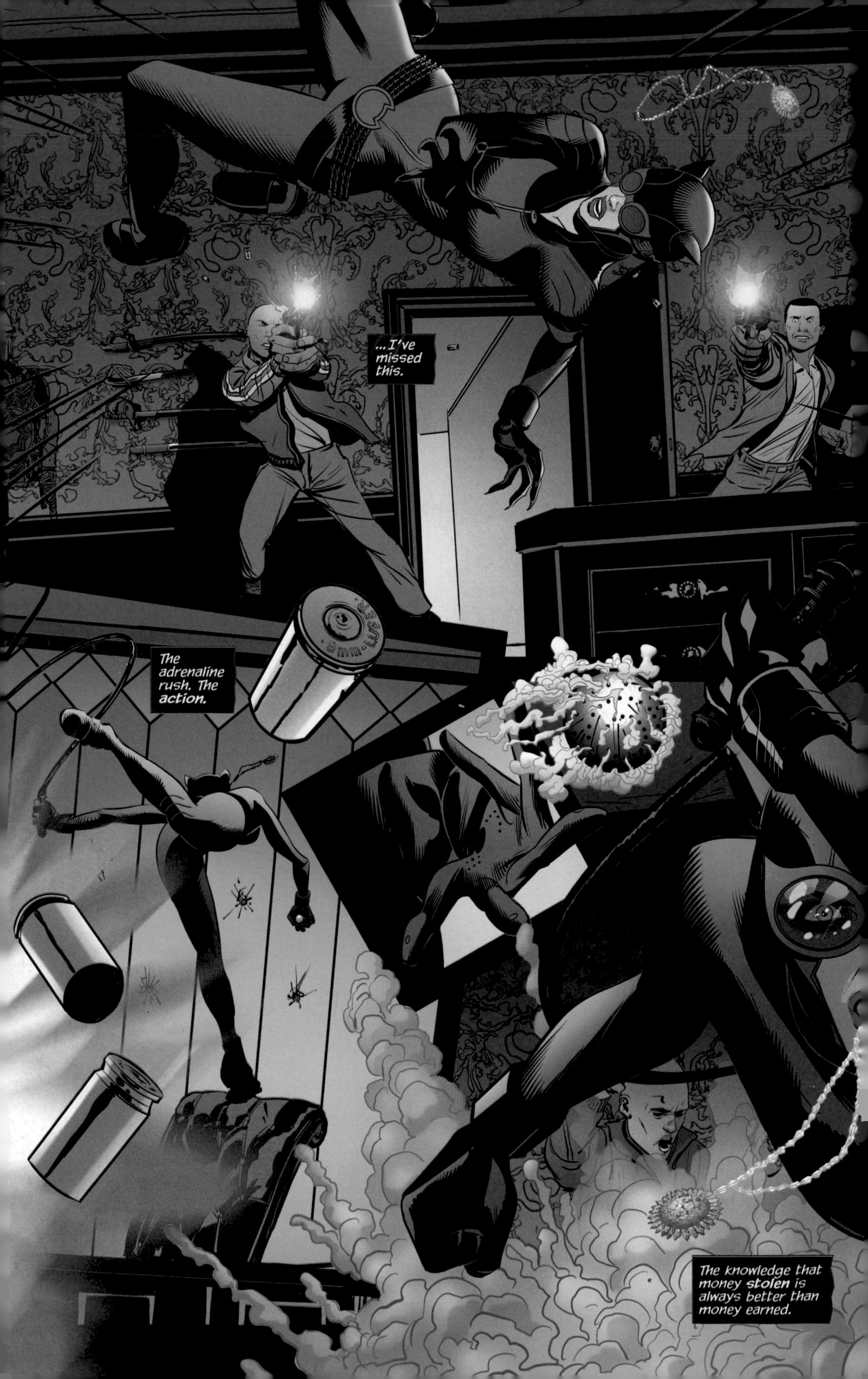
...I've missed this.
The adrenaline rush. The action.
The knowledge that money stolen is always better than money earned.

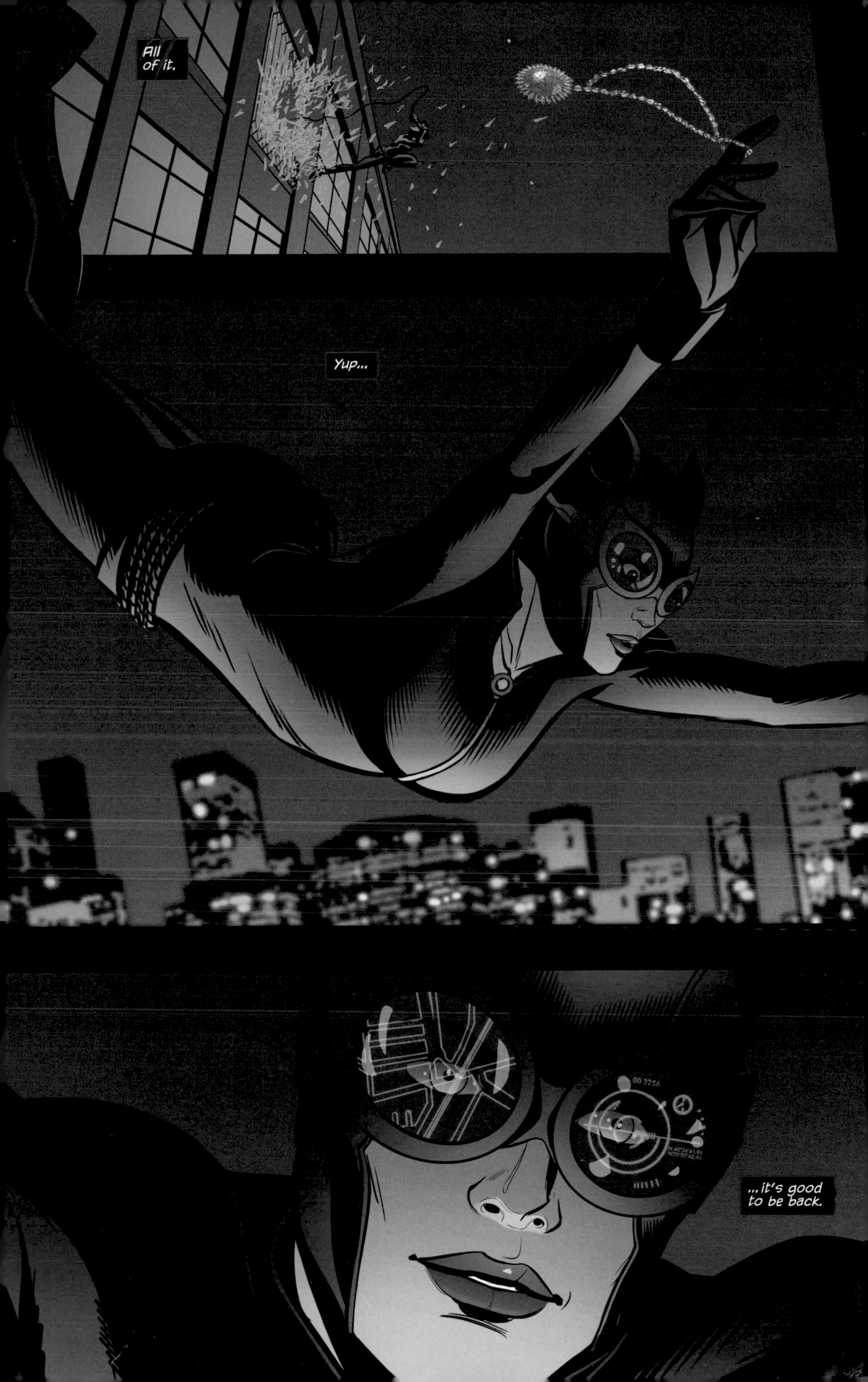
All of it.
Yup...
...it's good to be back.

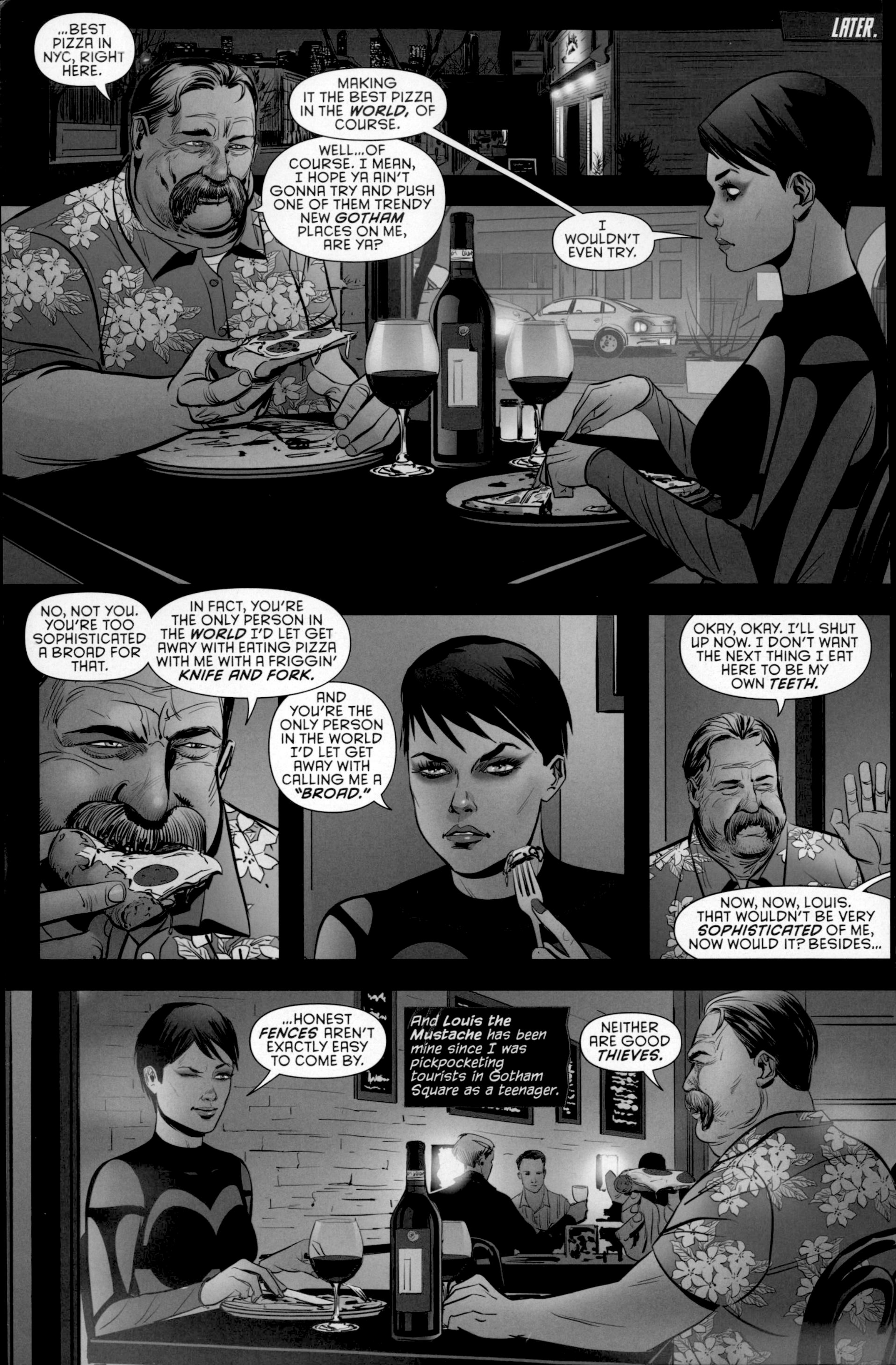
LATER.
...BEST PIZZA IN NYC, RIGHT HERE.
MAKING IT THE BEST PIZZA IN THE WORLD, OF COURSE.
WELL...OF COURSE. I MEAN, I HOPE YA AIN'T GONNA TRY AND PUSH ONE OF THEM TRENDY NEW GOTHAM PLACES ON ME, ARE YA?
I WOULDN'T EVEN TRY.
NO, NOT YOU. YOU'RE TOO SOPHISTICATED A BROAD FOR THAT.
IN FACT, YOU'RE THE ONLY PERSON IN THE WORLD I'D LET GET AWAY WITH EATING PIZZA WITH ME WITH A FRIGGIN' KNIFE AND FORK.
AND YOU'RE THE ONLY PERSON IN THE WORLD I'D LET GET AWAY WITH CALLING ME A "BROAD."
OKAY, OKAY. I'LL SHUT UP NOW. I DON'T WANT THE NEXT THING I EAT HERE TO BE MY OWN TEETH.
NOW, NOW, LOUIS. THAT WOULDN'T BE VERY SOPHISTICATED OF ME, NOW WOULD IT? BESIDES...
...HONEST FENCES AREN'T EXACTLY EASY TO COME BY.
And Louis the Mustache has been mine since I was pickpocketing tourists in Gotham Square as a teenager.
NEITHER ARE GOOD THIEVES.

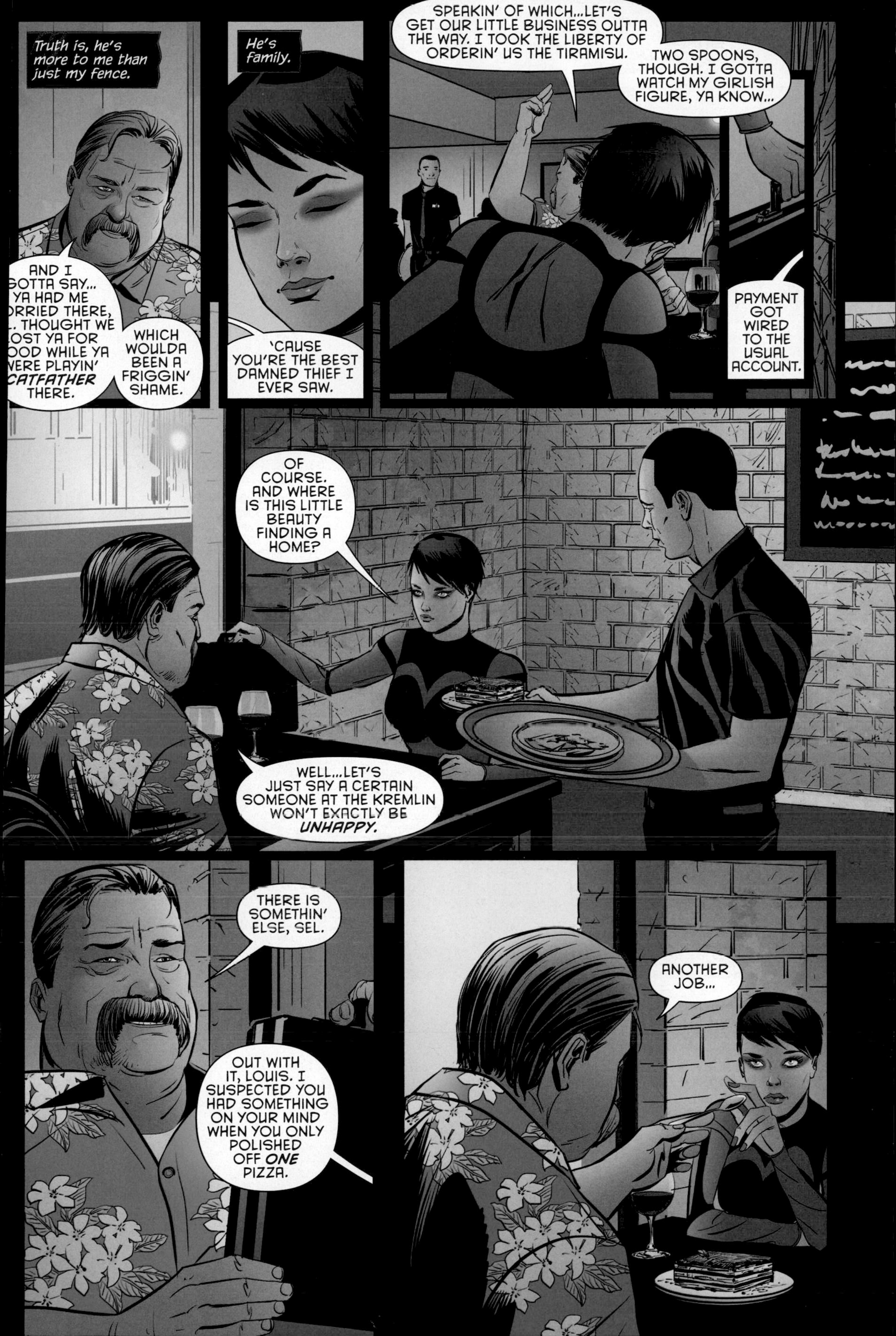

Truth is, he's more to me than just my fence.
AND I GOTTA SAY... YA HAD ME ORRIED THERE, L. THOUGHT WE OST YA FOR OOD WHILE YA VERE PLAYIN' *CATFATHER* THERE.
WHICH WOULDA BEEN A FRIGGIN' SHAME.
He's family.
'CAUSE YOU'RE THE BEST DAMNED THIEF I EVER SAW.
SPEAKIN' OF WHICH...LET'S GET OUR LITTLE BUSINESS OUTTA THE WAY. I TOOK THE LIBERTY OF ORDERIN' US THE TIRAMISU.
TWO SPOONS, THOUGH. I GOTTA WATCH MY GIRLISH FIGURE, YA KNOW...
PAYMENT GOT WIRED TO THE USUAL ACCOUNT.
OF COURSE. AND WHERE IS THIS LITTLE BEAUTY FINDING A HOME?
WELL...LET'S JUST SAY A CERTAIN SOMEONE AT THE KREMLIN WON'T EXACTLY BE *UNHAPPY.*
THERE IS SOMETHIN' ELSE, SEL.
OUT WITH IT, LOUIS. I SUSPECTED YOU HAD SOMETHING ON YOUR MIND WHEN YOU ONLY POLISHED OFF *ONE* PIZZA.
ANOTHER JOB...

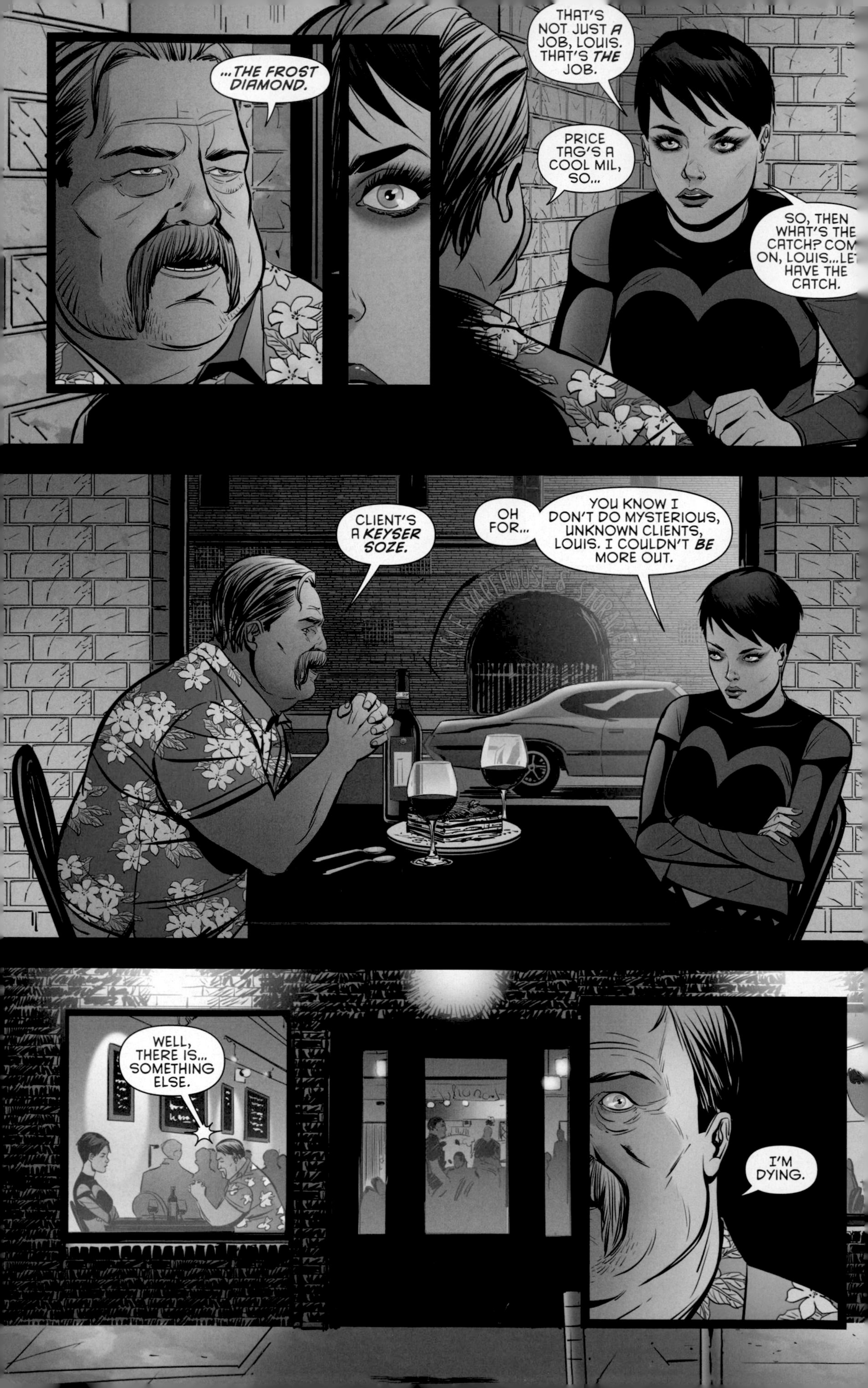
...THE FROST DIAMOND.
THAT'S NOT JUST A JOB, LOUIS. THAT'S THE JOB.
PRICE TAG'S A COOL MIL, SO...
SO, THEN WHAT'S THE CATCH? COME ON, LOUIS...LET'S HAVE THE CATCH.
CLIENT'S A KEYSER SOZE.
OH FOR...
YOU KNOW I DON'T DO MYSTERIOUS, UNKNOWN CLIENTS, LOUIS. I COULDN'T BE MORE OUT.
WELL, THERE IS... SOMETHING ELSE.
I'M DYING.

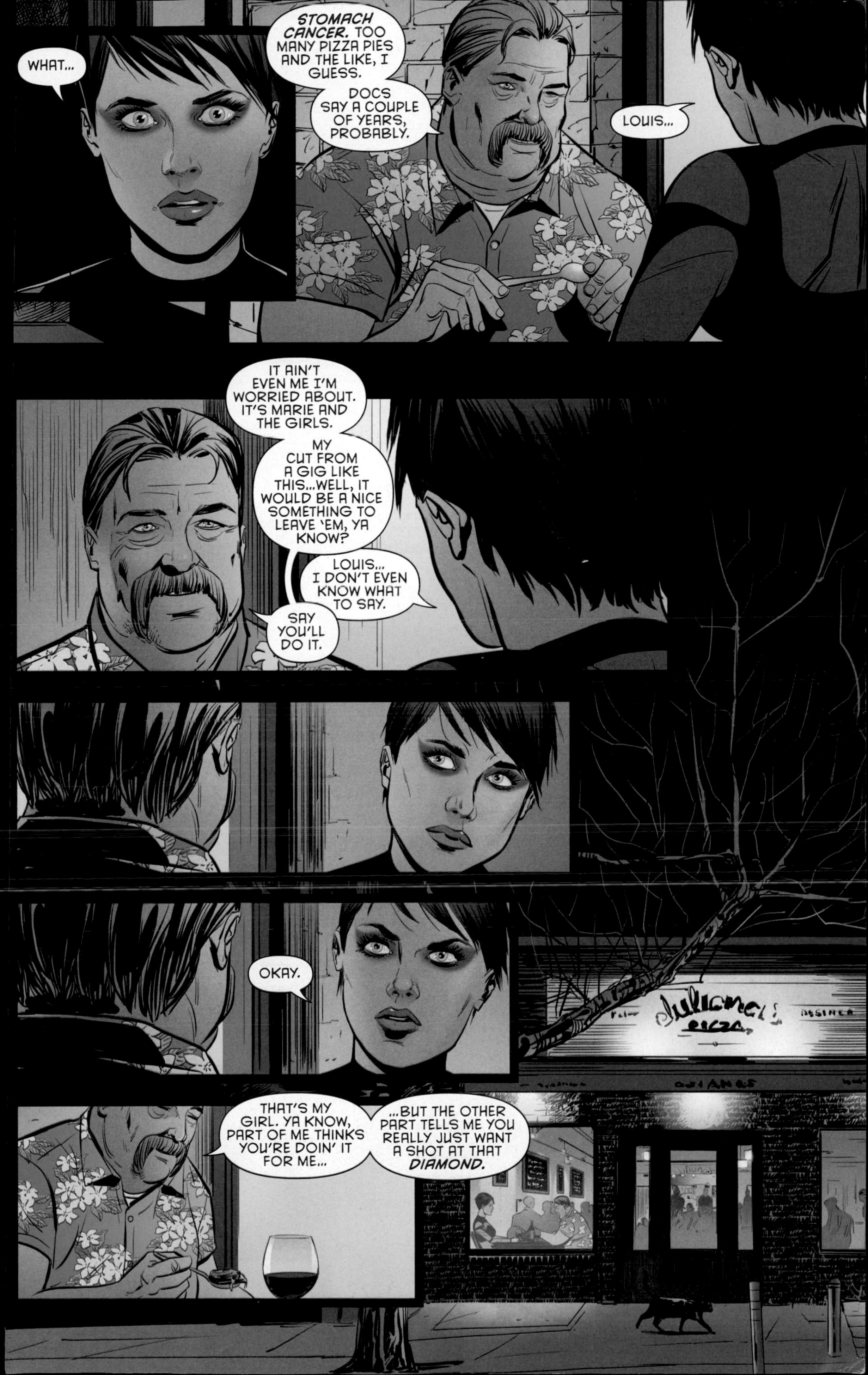

WHAT...
STOMACH CANCER. TOO MANY PIZZA PIES AND THE LIKE, I GUESS.
DOCS SAY A COUPLE OF YEARS, PROBABLY.
LOUIS...
IT AIN'T EVEN ME I'M WORRIED ABOUT. IT'S MARIE AND THE GIRLS.
MY CUT FROM A GIG LIKE THIS...WELL, IT WOULD BE A NICE SOMETHING TO LEAVE 'EM, YA KNOW?
LOUIS... I DON'T EVEN KNOW WHAT TO SAY.
SAY YOU'LL DO IT.
OKAY.
THAT'S MY GIRL. YA KNOW, PART OF ME THINKS YOU'RE DOIN' IT FOR ME...
...BUT THE OTHER PART TELLS ME YOU REALLY JUST WANT A SHOT AT THAT DIAMOND.

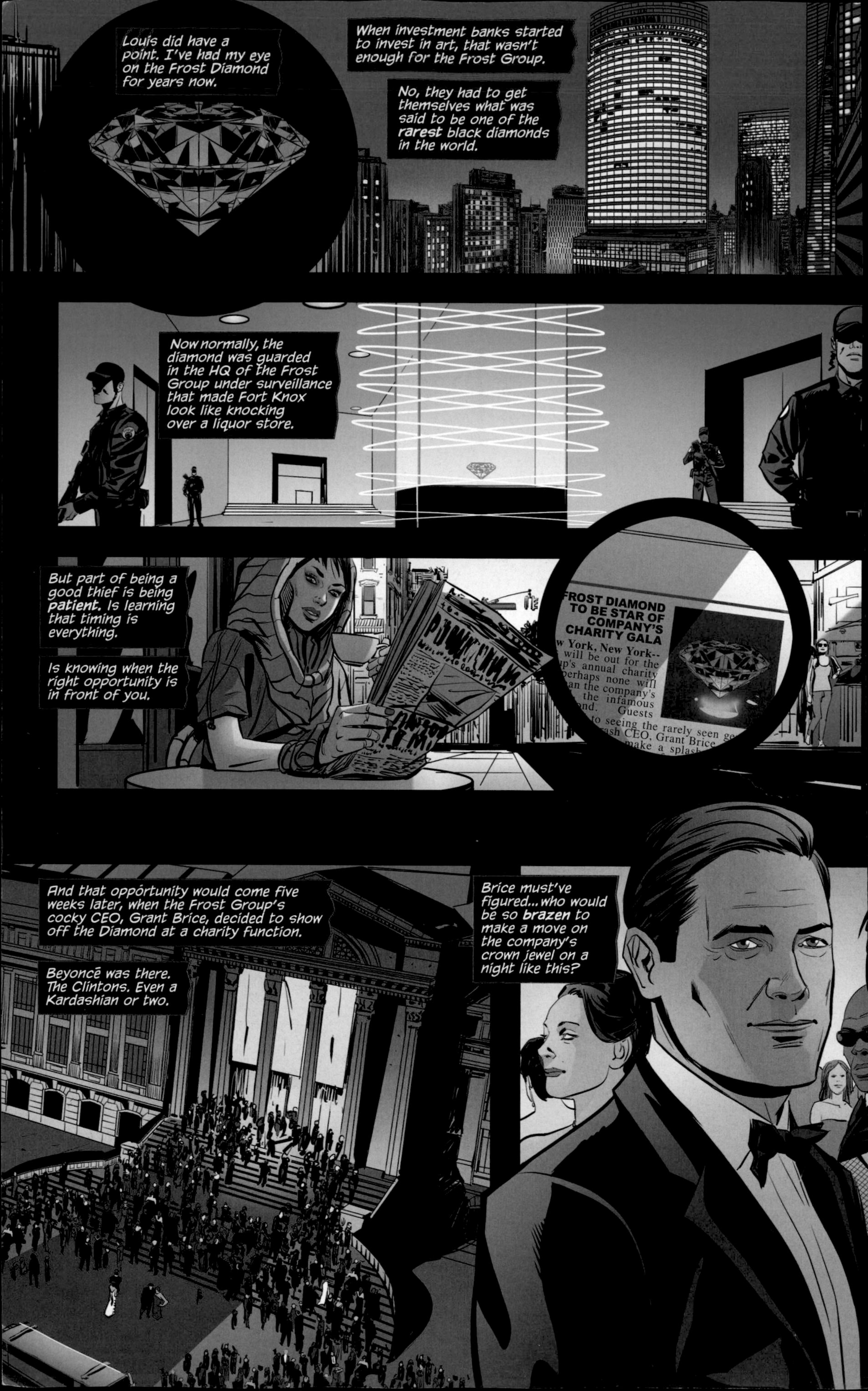

Louis did have a point. I've had my eye on the Frost Diamond for years now.
When investment banks started to invest in art, that wasn't enough for the Frost Group.
No, they had to get themselves what was said to be one of the **rarest** black diamonds in the world.
Now normally, the diamond was guarded in the HQ of the Frost Group under surveillance that made Fort Knox look like knocking over a liquor store.
But part of being a good thief is being **patient.** Is learning that timing is everything.
Is knowing when the right opportunity is in front of you.
FROST DIAMOND TO BE STAR OF COMPANY'S CHARITY GALA
w York, New York--
will be out for the
p's annual charity
perhaps none will
an the company's
the infamous
ond. Guests
to seeing the rarely seen ge
ash CEO, Grant Brice
make a splash
And that opportunity would come five weeks later, when the Frost Group's cocky CEO, Grant Brice, decided to show off the Diamond at a charity function.
Beyoncé was there. The Clintons. Even a Kardashian or two.
Brice must've figured...who would be so **brazen** to make a move on the company's crown jewel on a night like this?

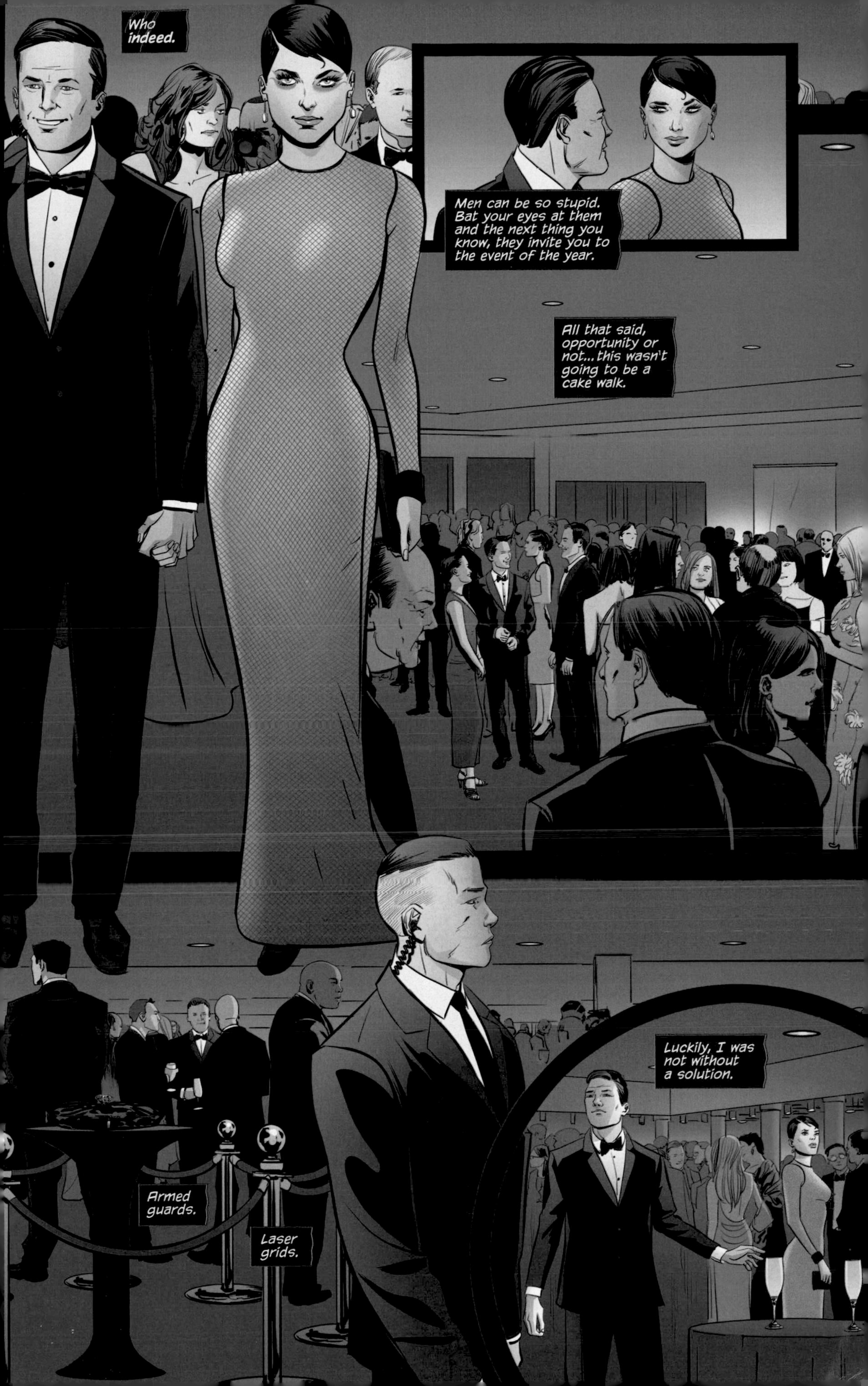
Who indeed.
Men can be so stupid. Bat your eyes at them and the next thing you know, they invite you to the event of the year.
All that said, opportunity or not...this wasn't going to be a cake walk.
Armed guards.
Laser grids.
Luckily, I was not without a solution.

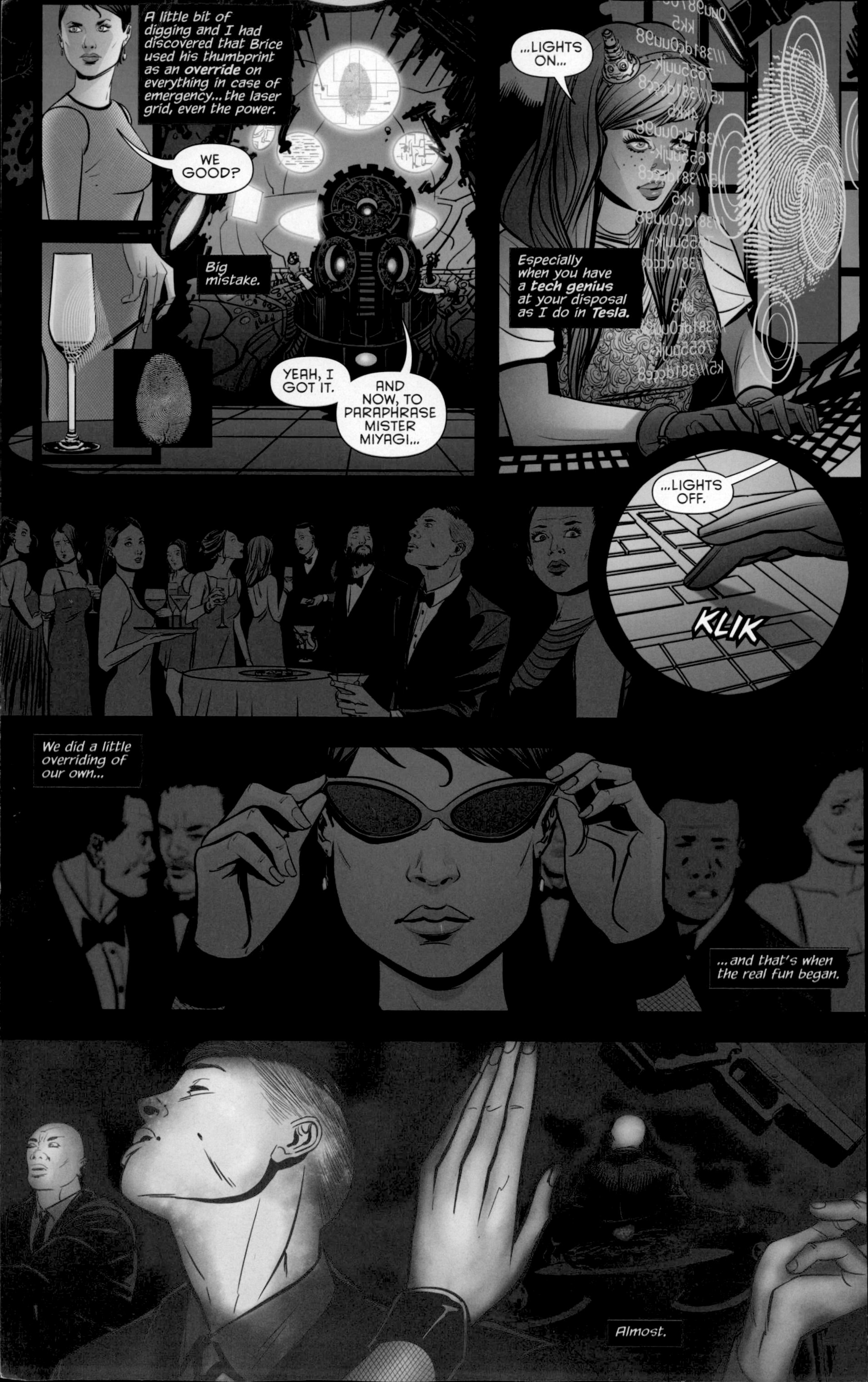
A little bit of digging and I had discovered that Brice used his thumbprint as an **override** on everything in case of emergency...the laser grid, even the power.
WE GOOD?
Big mistake.
YEAH, I GOT IT.
AND NOW, TO PARAPHRASE MISTER MIYAGI...
...LIGHTS ON...
Especially when you have a **tech genius** at your disposal as I do in **Tesla.**
...LIGHTS OFF.
KLIK
We did a little overriding of our own...
...and that's when the real fun began.
Almost.

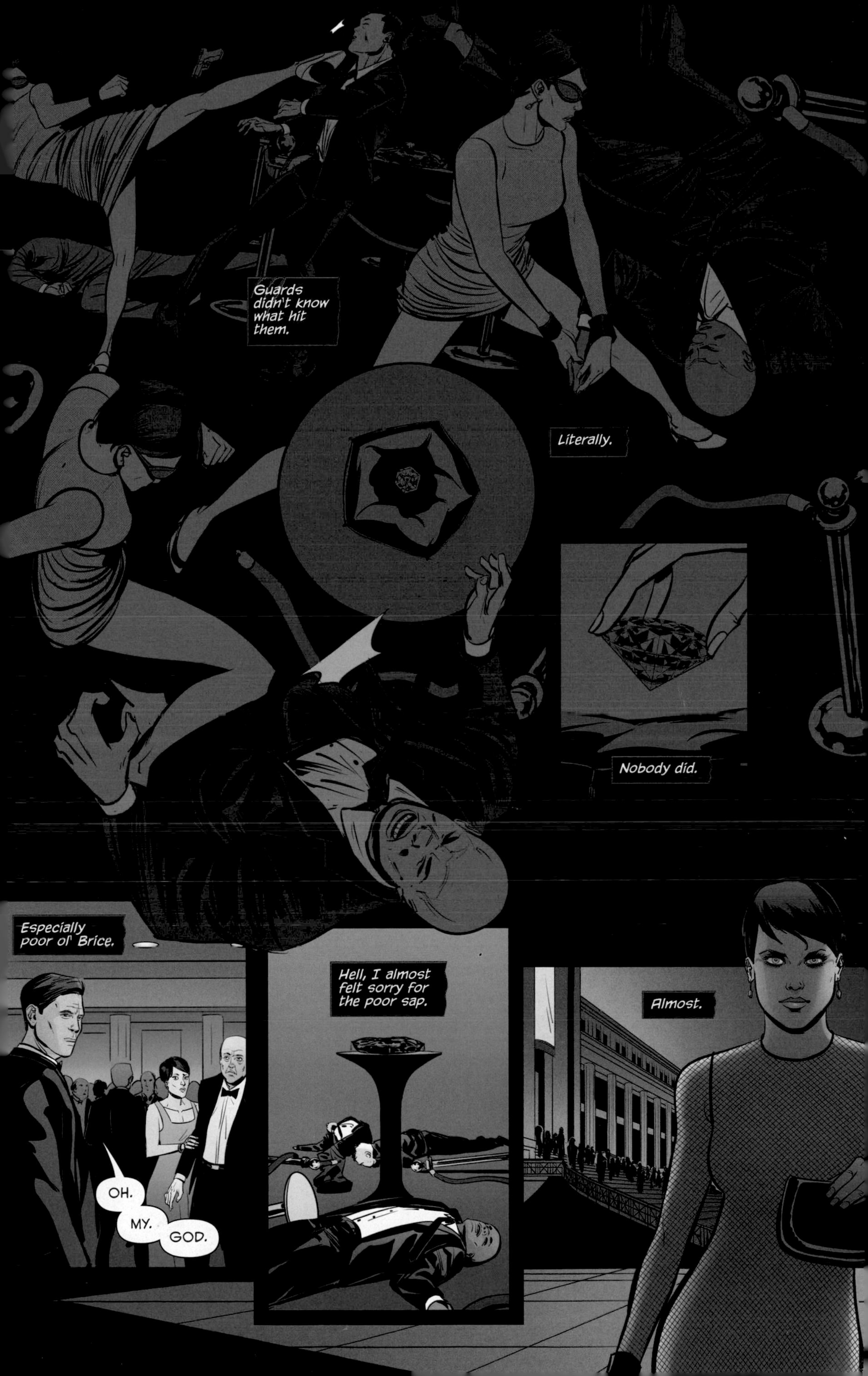
Guards didn't know what hit them.
Literally.
Nobody did.
Especially poor ol' Brice.
OH.
MY.
GOD.
Hell, I almost felt sorry for the poor sap.
Almost.

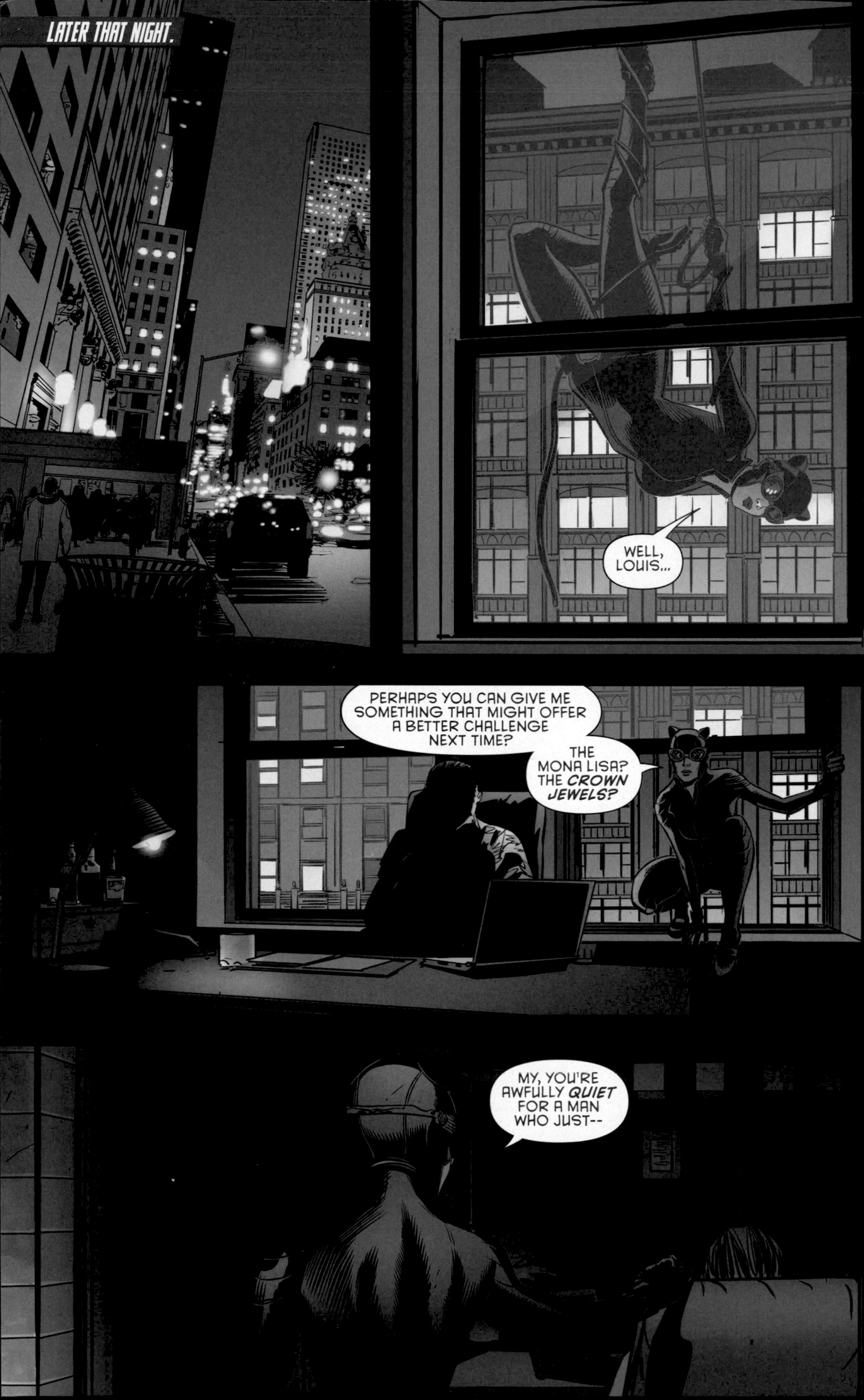
LATER THAT NIGHT.
WELL, LOUIS...
PERHAPS YOU CAN GIVE ME SOMETHING THAT MIGHT OFFER A BETTER CHALLENGE NEXT TIME?
THE MONA LISA? THE CROWN JEWELS?
MY, YOU'RE AWFULLY QUIET FOR A MAN WHO JUST--

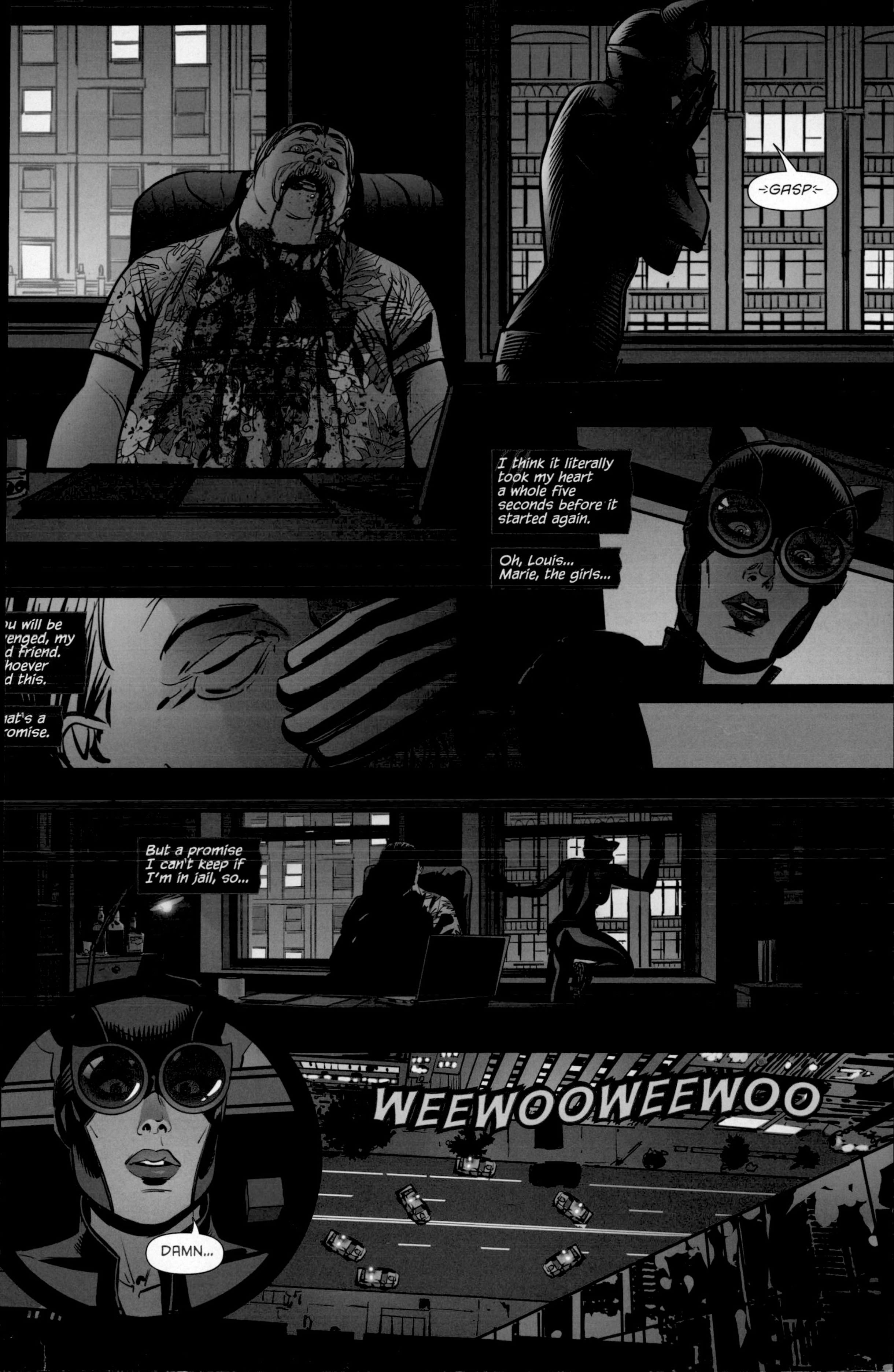

-GASP-
I think it literally took my heart a whole five seconds before it started again.
Oh, Louis... Marie, the girls...
ou will be enged, my d friend. hoever d this.
at's a romise.
But a promise I can't keep if I'm in jail, so...
WEEWOOWEEWOO
DAMN...

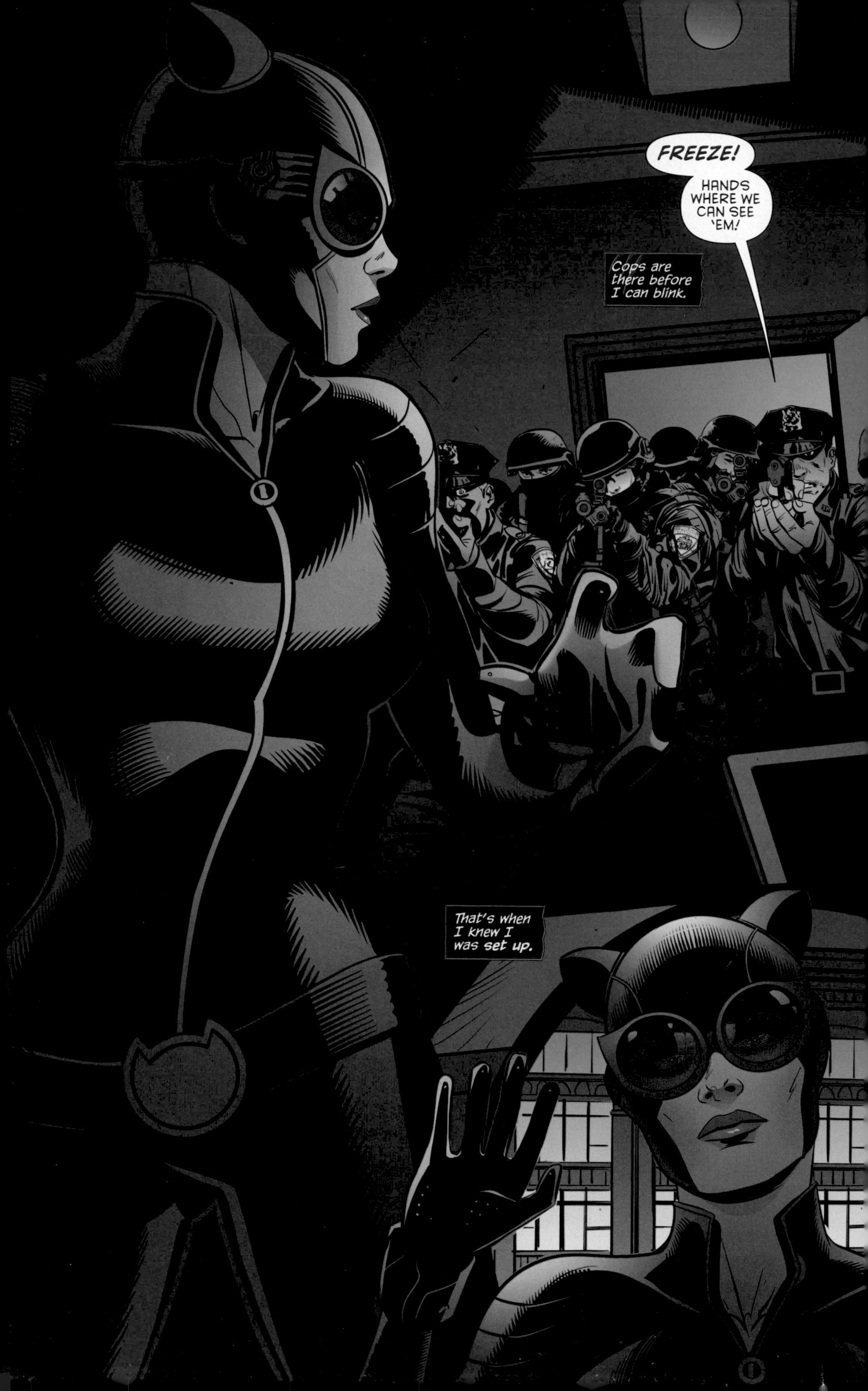
FREEZE!
HANDS WHERE WE CAN SEE 'EM!
Cops are there before I can blink.
That's when I knew I was set up.

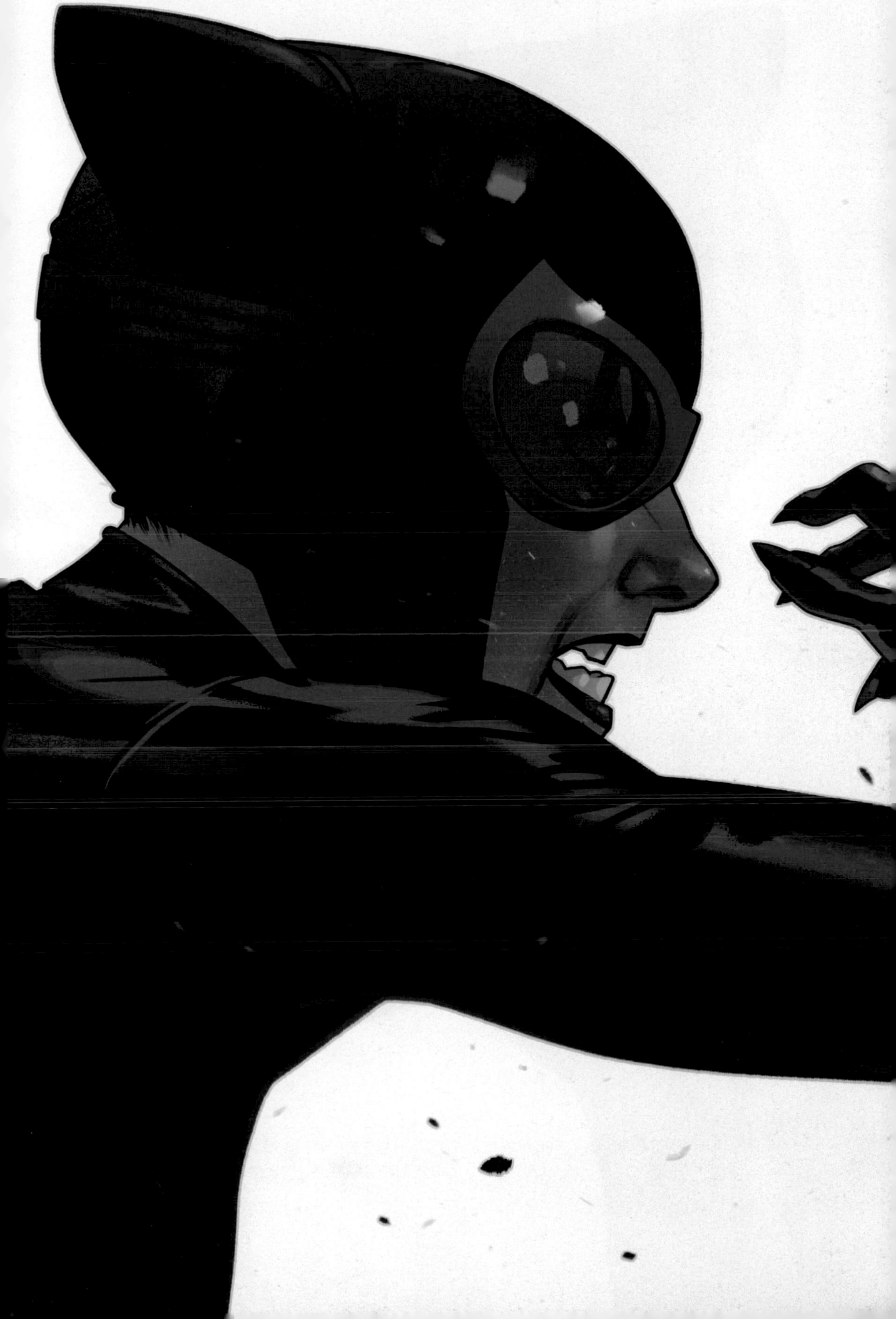

RUN LIKE HELL, PART TWO

FRANK TIERI writer **INAKI MIRANDA** artist **EVA DE LA CRUZ** colorist **TRAVIS LANHAM** letterer **JOSH MIDDLETON** cover

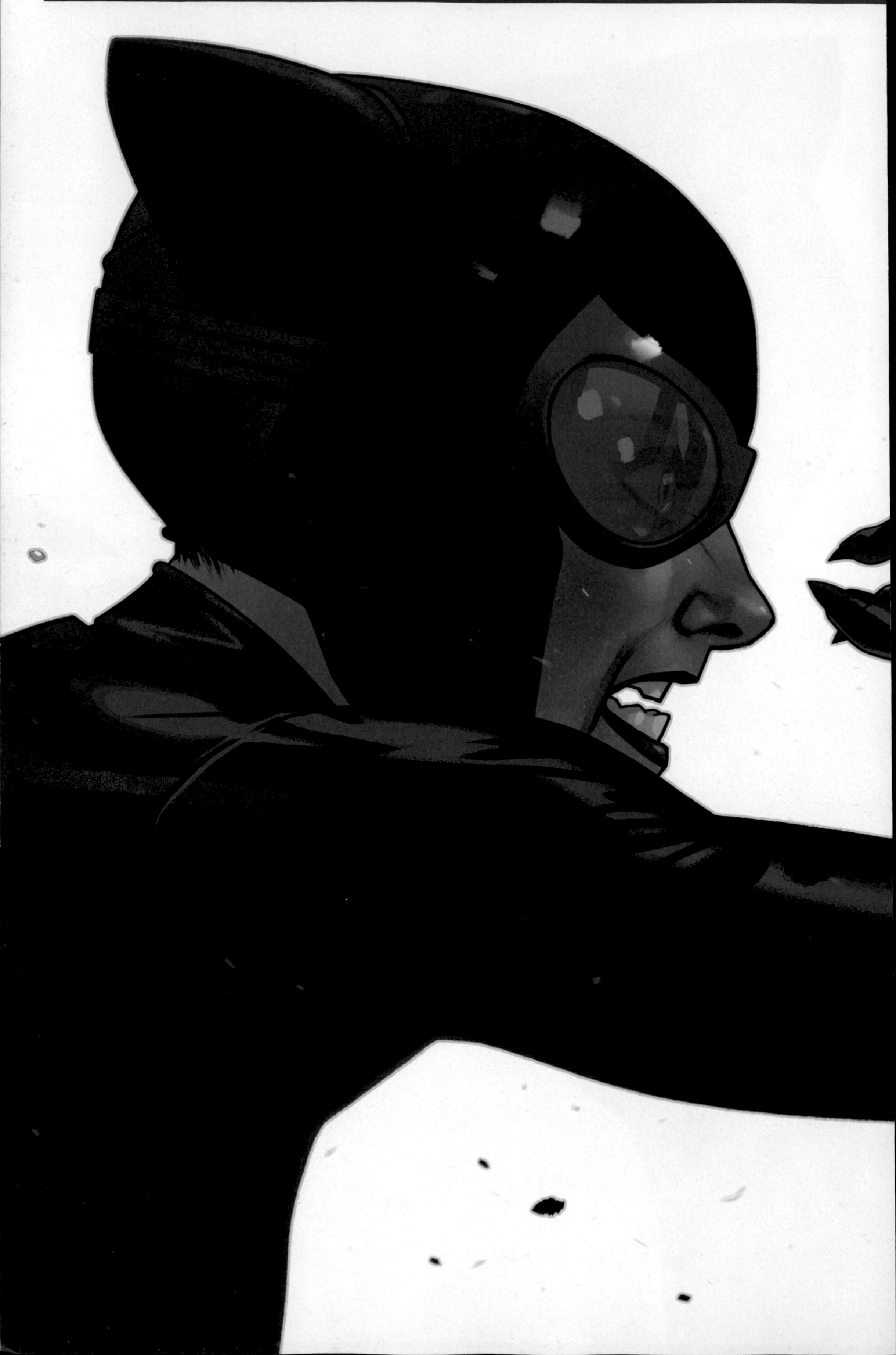

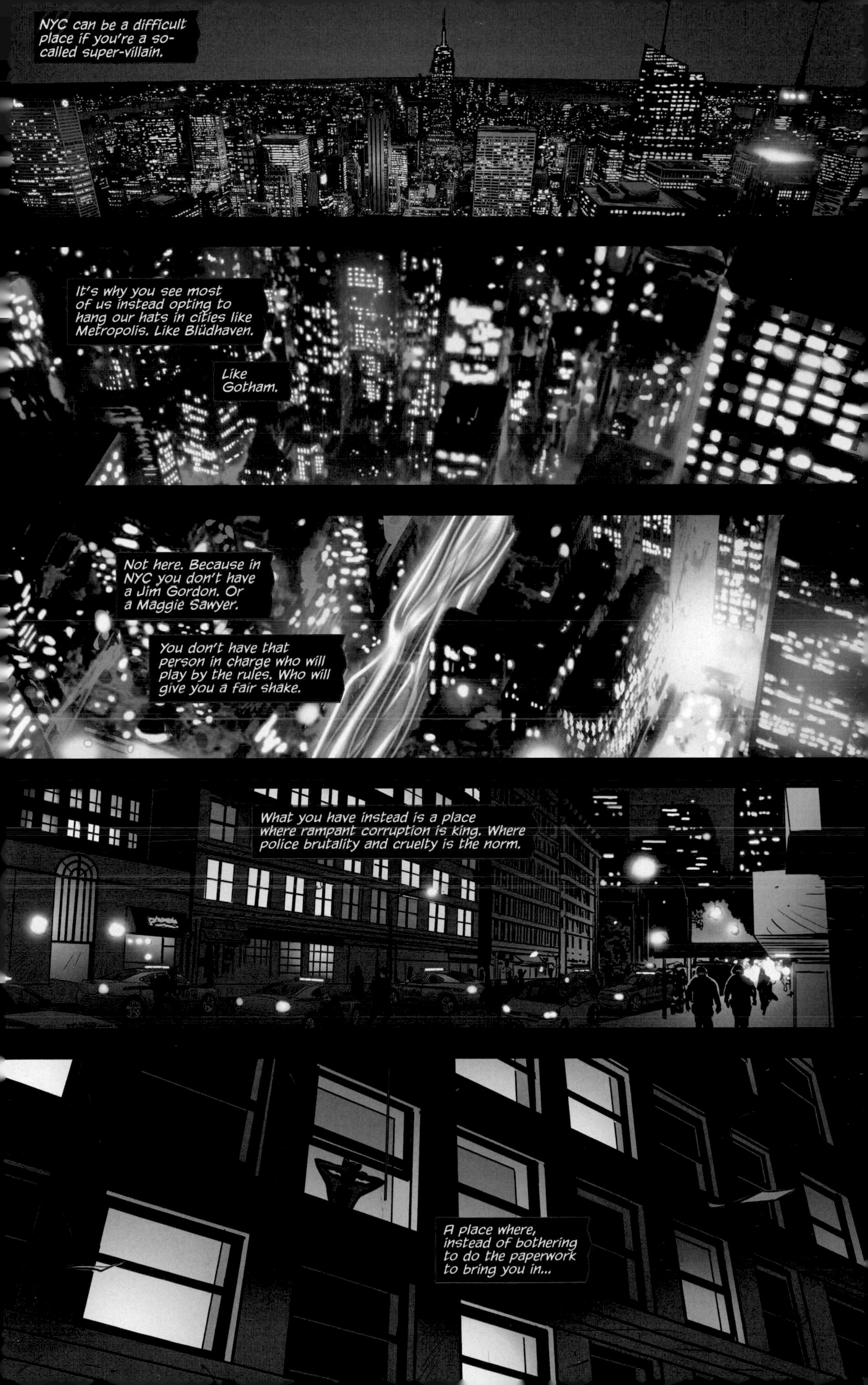

NYC can be a difficult place if you're a so-called super-villain.
It's why you see most of us instead opting to hang our hats in cities like Metropolis. Like Blüdhaven.
Like Gotham.
Not here. Because in NYC you don't have a Jim Gordon. Or a Maggie Sawyer.
You don't have that person in charge who will play by the rules. Who will give you a fair shake.
What you have instead is a place where rampant corruption is king. Where police brutality and cruelty is the norm.
A place where, instead of bothering to do the paperwork to bring you in...

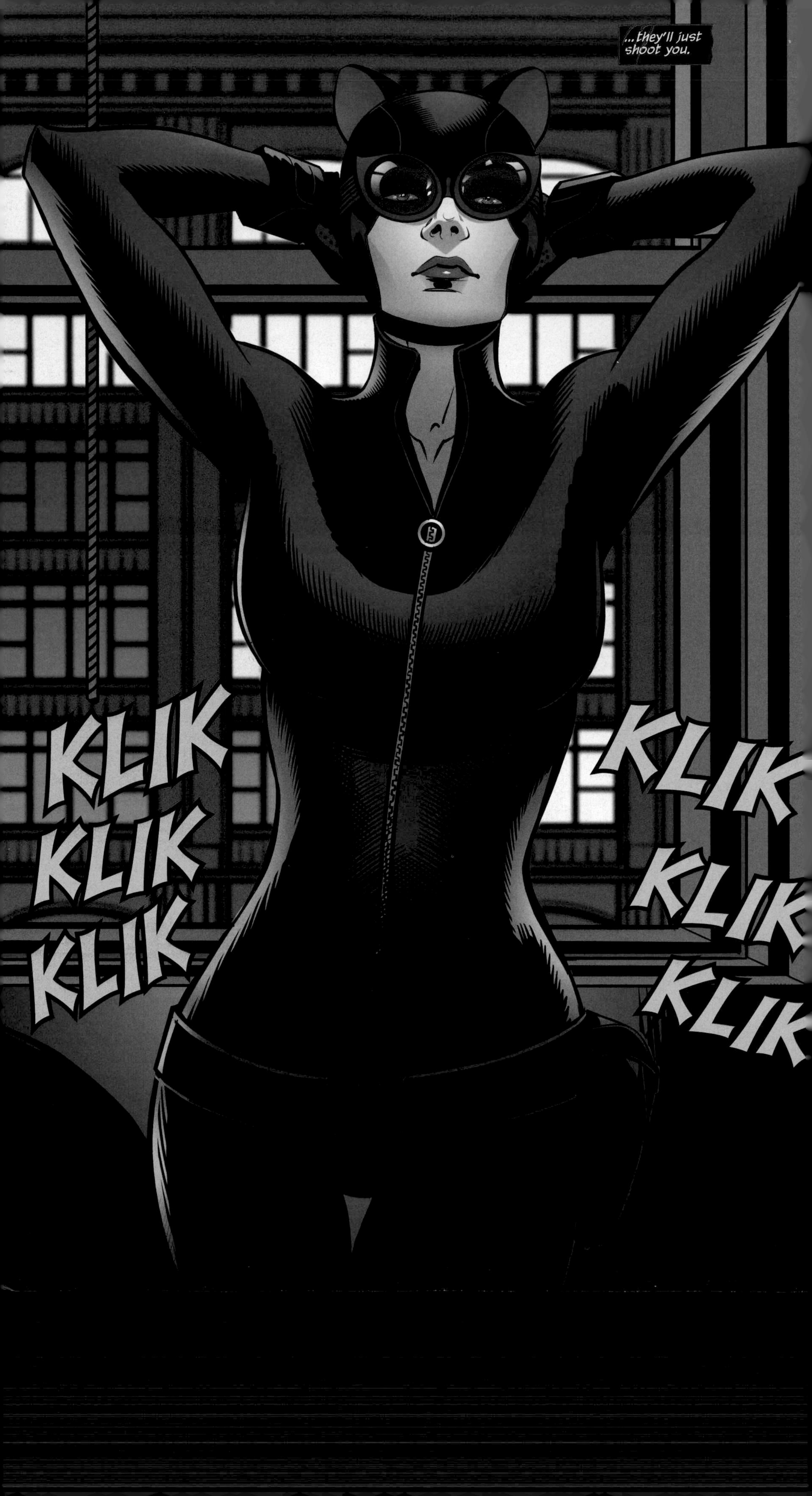
...they'll just shoot you.
KLIK KLIK KLIK
KLIK KLIK KLIK

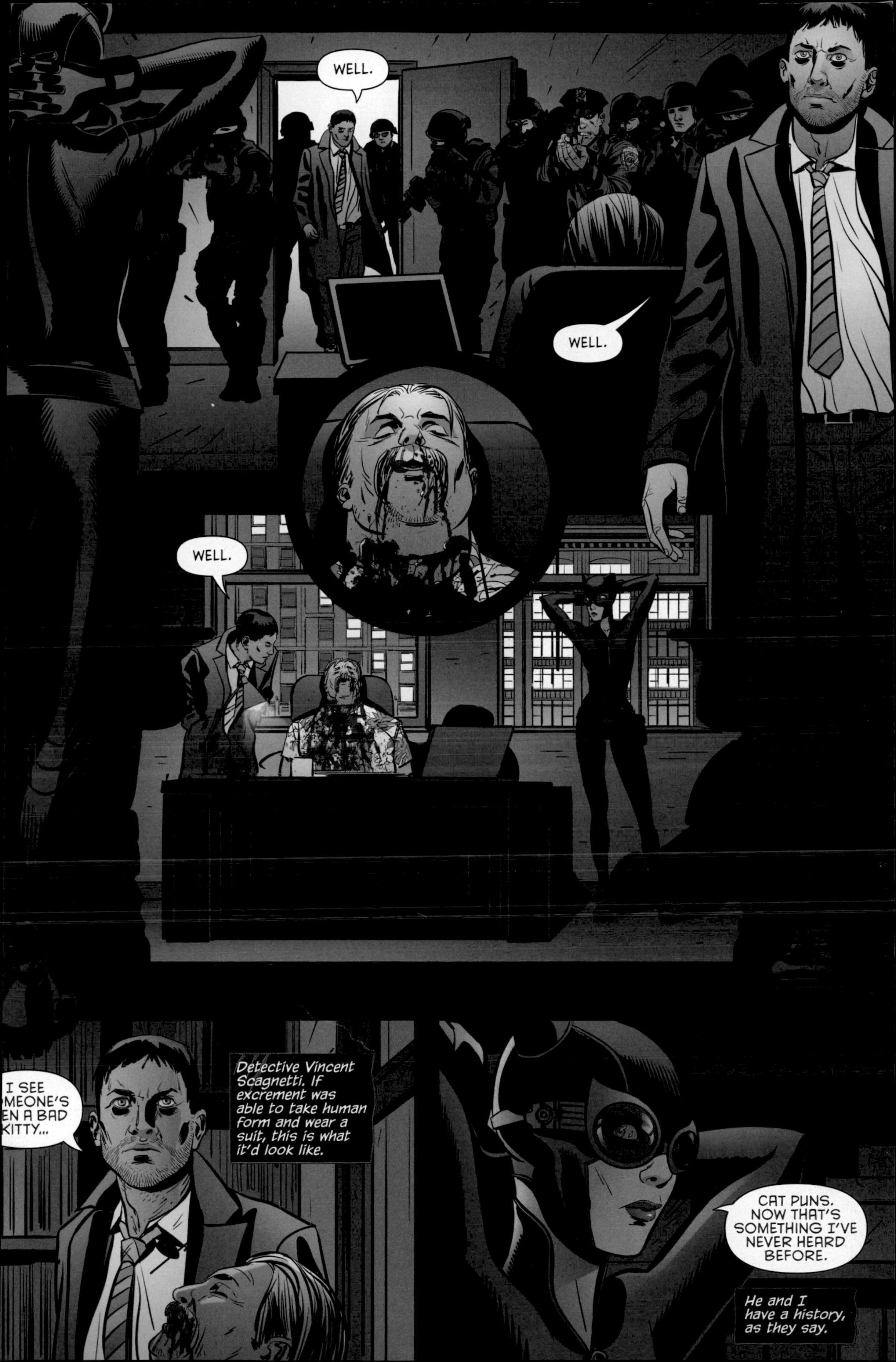

WELL.
WELL.
WELL.
I SEE MEONE'S EN A BAD KITTY...
Detective Vincent Scagnetti. If excrement was able to take human form and wear a suit, this is what it'd look like.
CAT PUNS. NOW THAT'S SOMETHING I'VE NEVER HEARD BEFORE.
He and I have a history, as they say.

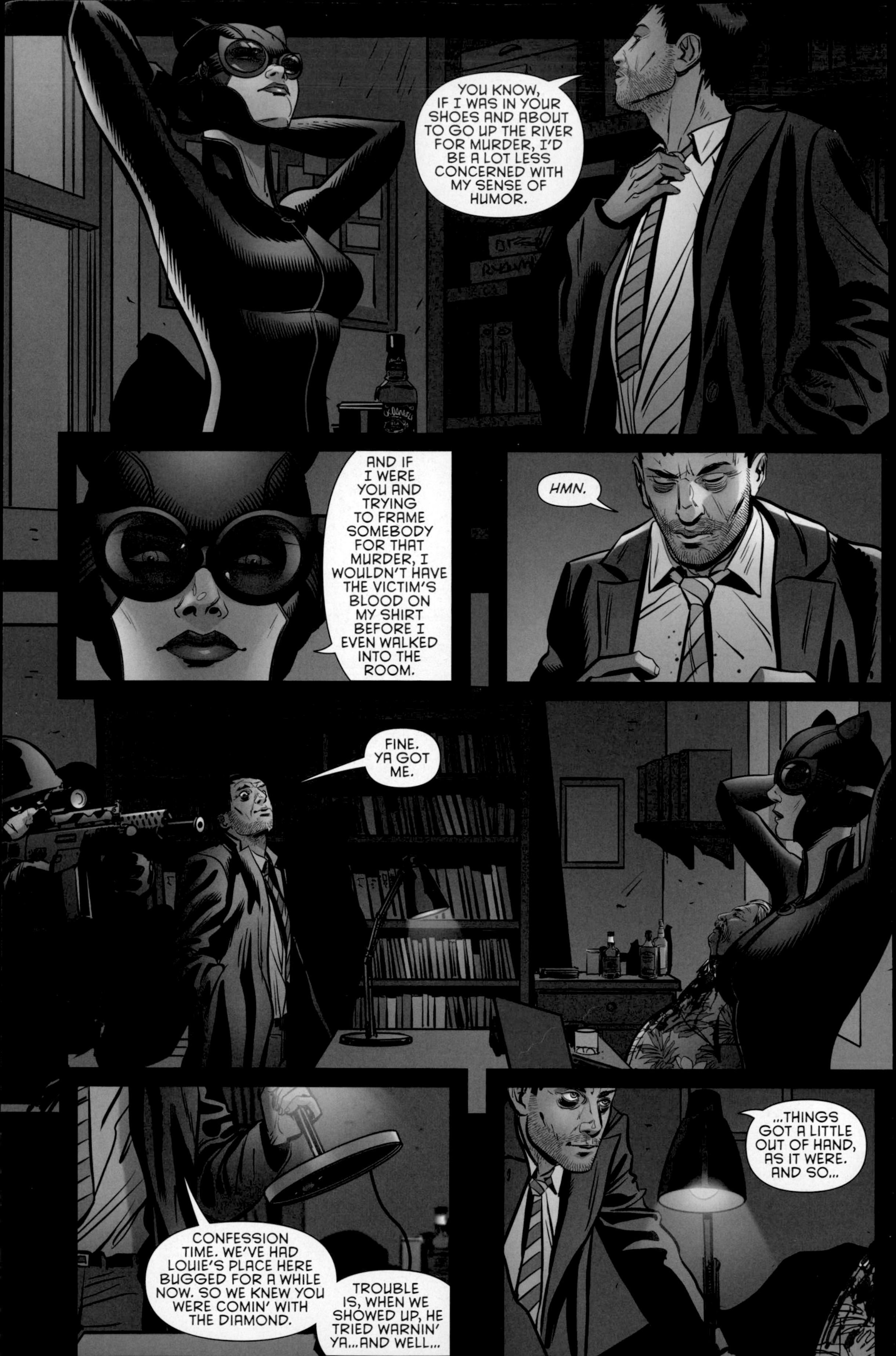
YOU KNOW, IF I WAS IN YOUR SHOES AND ABOUT TO GO UP THE RIVER FOR MURDER, I'D BE A LOT LESS CONCERNED WITH MY SENSE OF HUMOR.
AND IF I WERE YOU AND TRYING TO FRAME SOMEBODY FOR THAT MURDER, I WOULDN'T HAVE THE VICTIM'S BLOOD ON MY SHIRT BEFORE I EVEN WALKED INTO THE ROOM.
HMN.
FINE. YA GOT ME.
CONFESSION TIME. WE'VE HAD LOUIE'S PLACE HERE BUGGED FOR A WHILE NOW. SO WE KNEW YOU WERE COMIN' WITH THE DIAMOND.
TROUBLE IS, WHEN WE SHOWED UP, HE TRIED WARNIN' YA...AND WELL...
...THINGS GOT A LITTLE OUT OF HAND, AS IT WERE. AND SO...

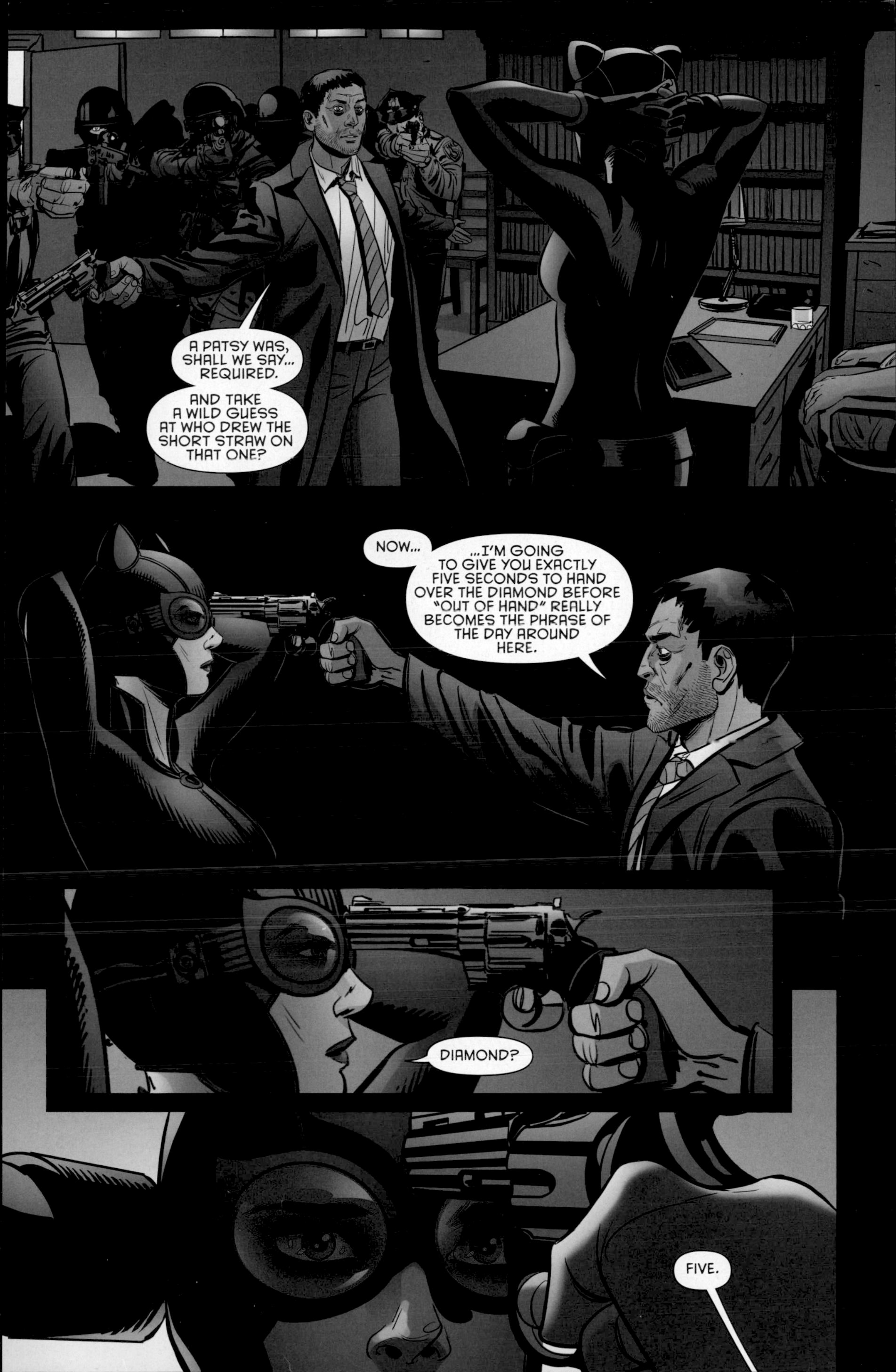
A PATSY WAS, SHALL WE SAY... REQUIRED.
AND TAKE A WILD GUESS AT WHO DREW THE SHORT STRAW ON THAT ONE?
NOW...
...I'M GOING TO GIVE YOU EXACTLY FIVE SECONDS TO HAND OVER THE DIAMOND BEFORE "OUT OF HAND" REALLY BECOMES THE PHRASE OF THE DAY AROUND HERE.
DIAMOND?
FIVE.

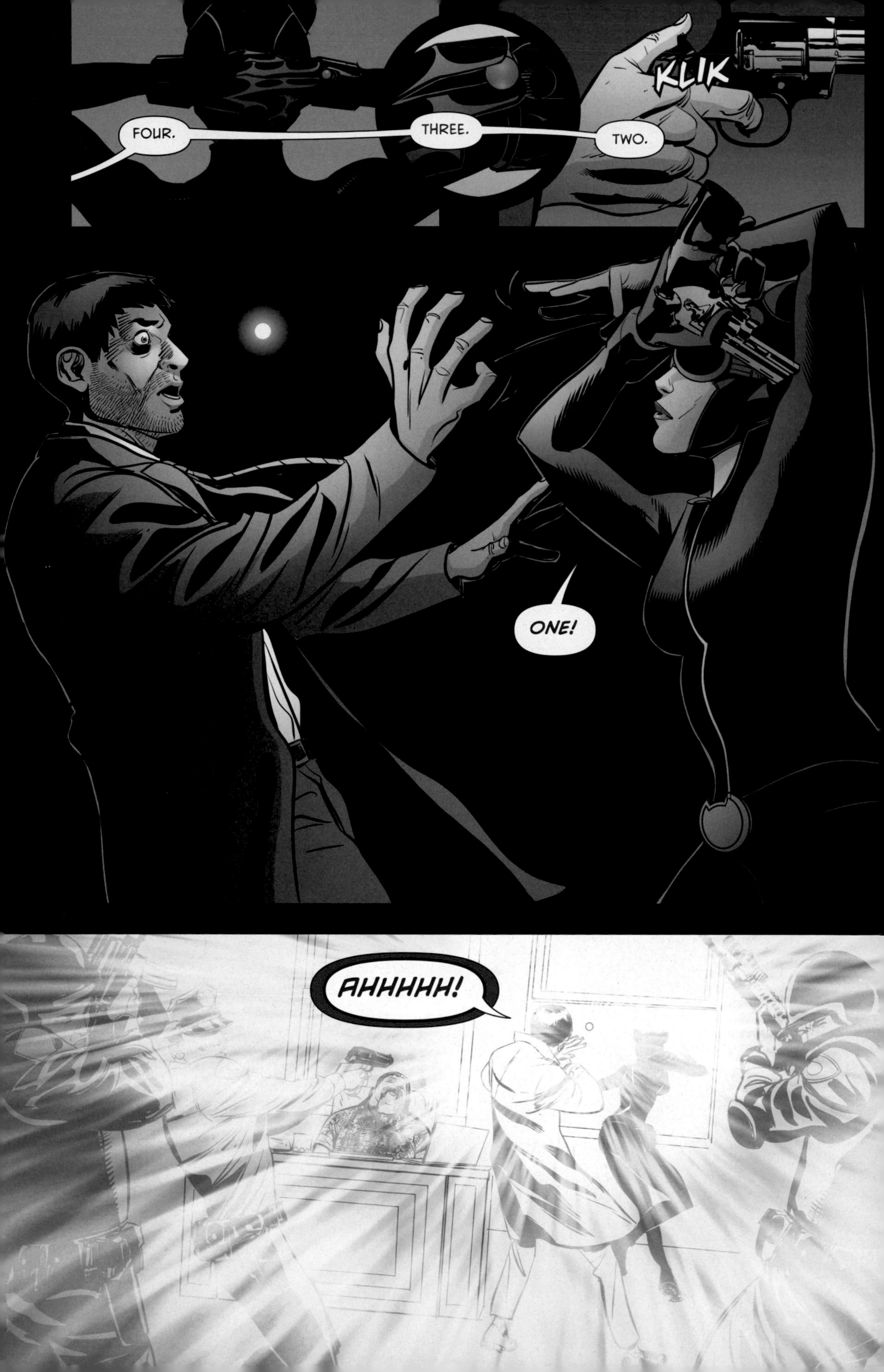
KLIK
FOUR.
THREE.
TWO.
ONE!
AHHHHH!

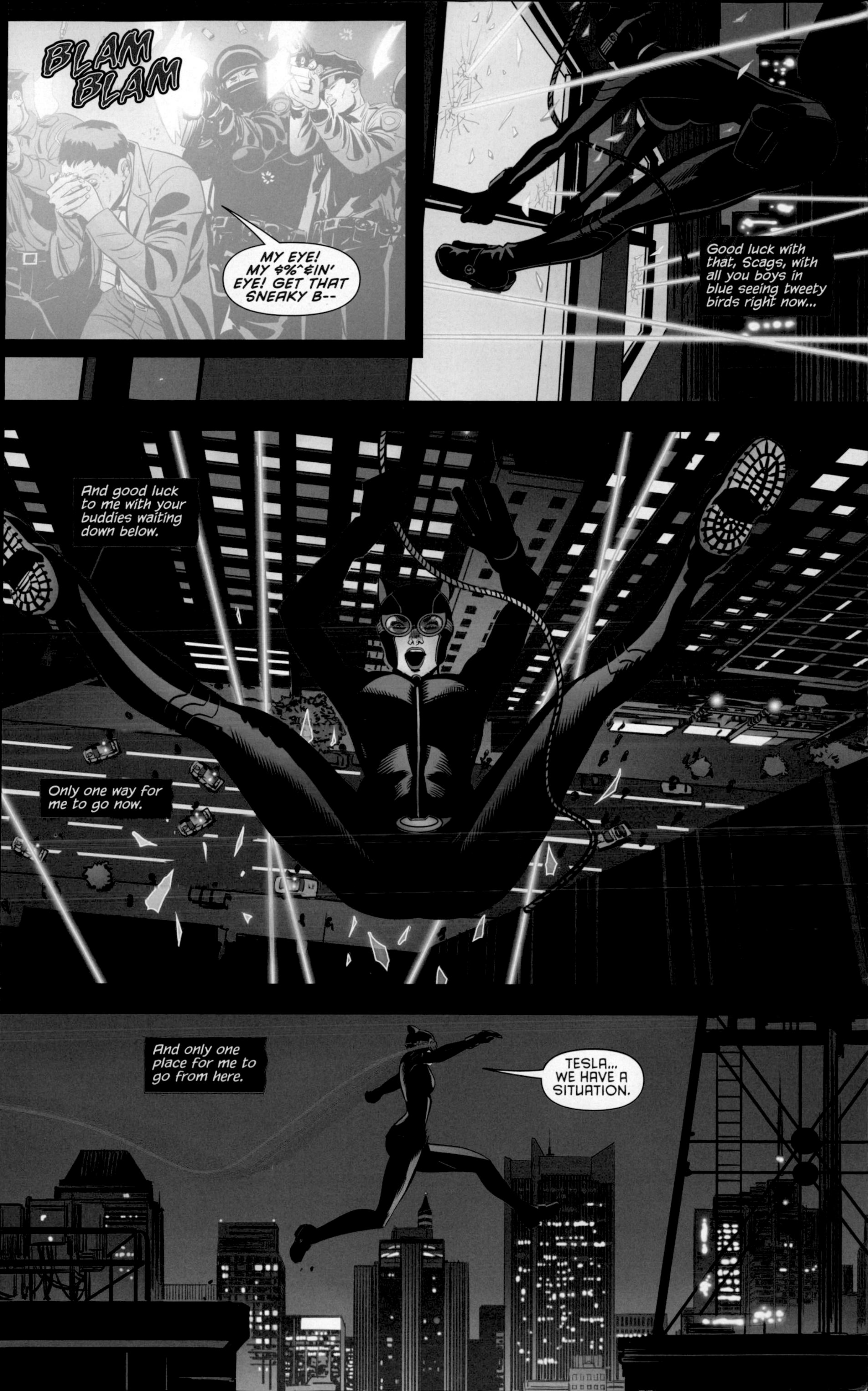
BLAM BLAM
MY EYE! MY $%^&IN' EYE! GET THAT SNEAKY B--
Good luck with that, Scags, with all you boys in blue seeing tweety birds right now...
And good luck to me with your buddies waiting down below.
Only one way for me to go now.
And only one place for me to go from here.
TESLA... WE HAVE A SITUATION.

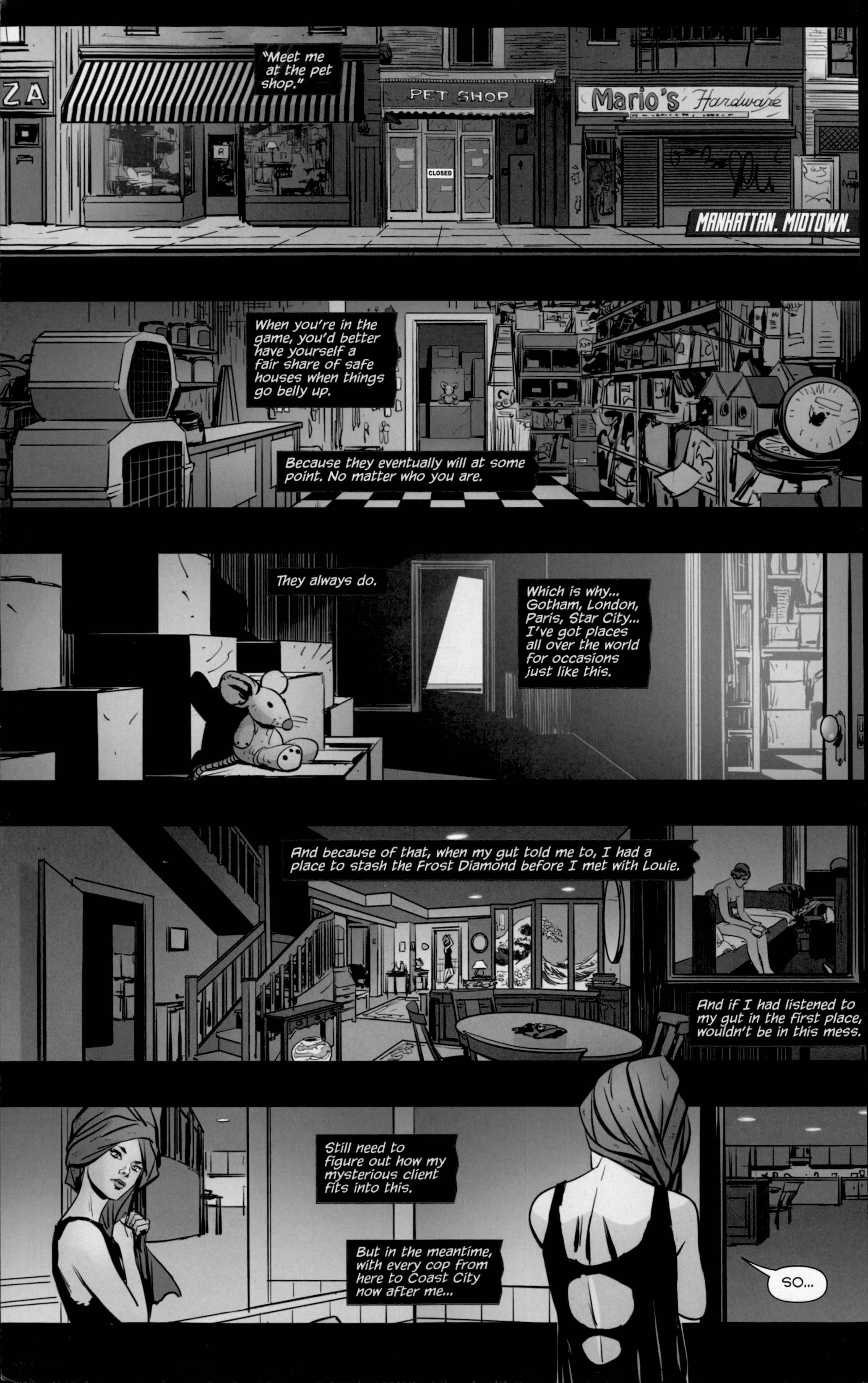
ZA
"Meet me at the pet shop."
PET SHOP
CLOSED
Mario's Hardware
MANHATTAN. MIDTOWN.
When you're in the game, you'd better have yourself a fair share of safe houses when things go belly up.
Because they eventually will at some point. No matter who you are.
They always do.
Which is why... Gotham, London, Paris, Star City... I've got places all over the world for occasions just like this.
And because of that, when my gut told me to, I had a place to stash the Frost Diamond before I met with Louie.
And if I had listened to my gut in the first place, wouldn't be in this mess.
Still need to figure out how my mysterious client fits into this.
But in the meantime, with every cop from here to Coast City now after me...
SO...

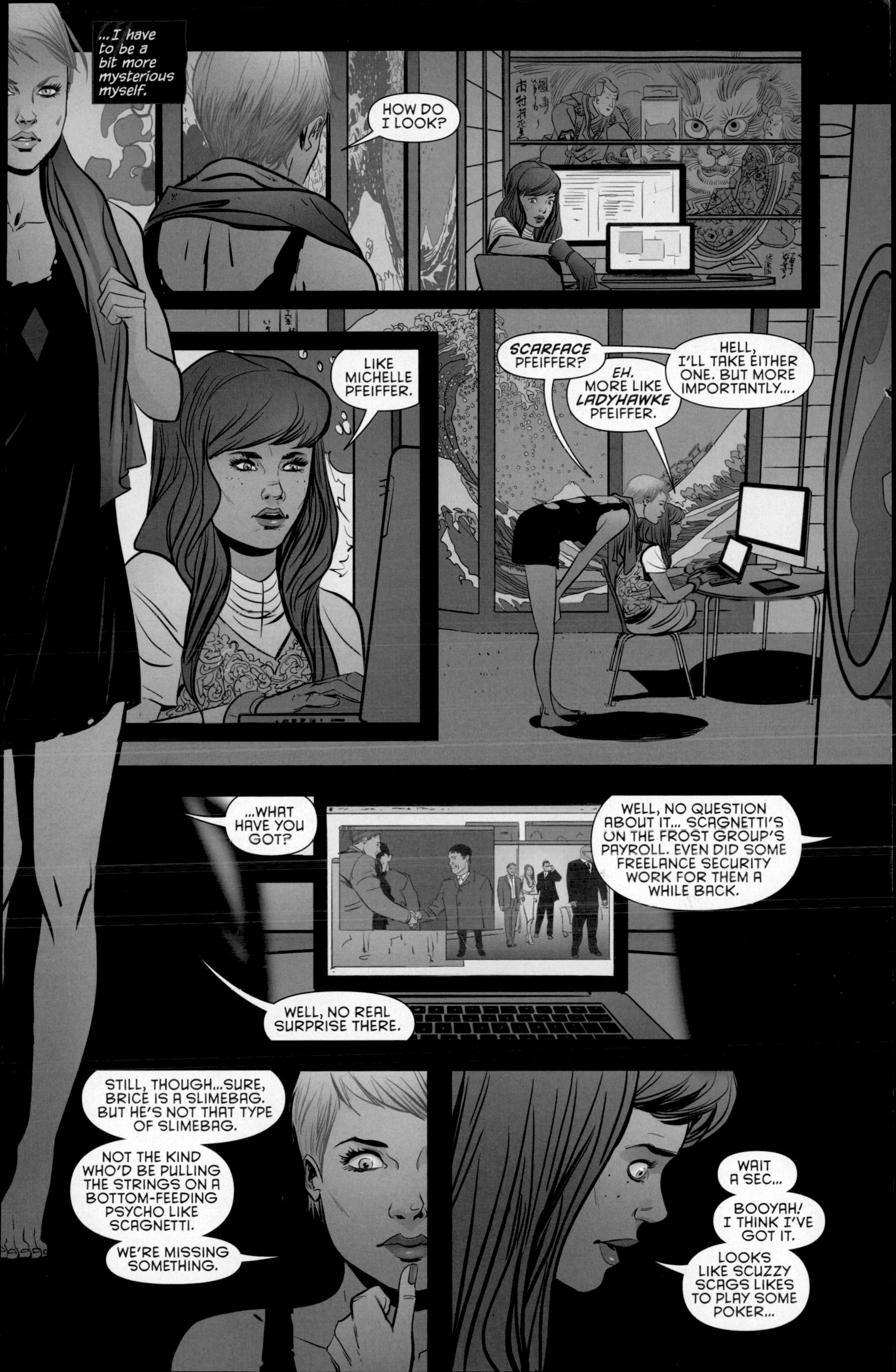
...I have to be a bit more mysterious myself.
HOW DO I LOOK?
LIKE MICHELLE PFEIFFER.
SCARFACE PFEIFFER?
EH. MORE LIKE LADYHAWKE PFEIFFER.
HELL, I'LL TAKE EITHER ONE. BUT MORE IMPORTANTLY....
...WHAT HAVE YOU GOT?
WELL, NO QUESTION ABOUT IT... SCAGNETTI'S ON THE FROST GROUP'S PAYROLL. EVEN DID SOME FREELANCE SECURITY WORK FOR THEM A WHILE BACK.
WELL, NO REAL SURPRISE THERE.
STILL, THOUGH...SURE, BRICE IS A SLIMEBAG. BUT HE'S NOT THAT TYPE OF SLIMEBAG.
NOT THE KIND WHO'D BE PULLING THE STRINGS ON A BOTTOM-FEEDING PSYCHO LIKE SCAGNETTI.
WE'RE MISSING SOMETHING.
WAIT A SEC...
BOOYAH! I THINK I'VE GOT IT.
LOOKS LIKE SCUZZY SCAGS LIKES TO PLAY SOME POKER...

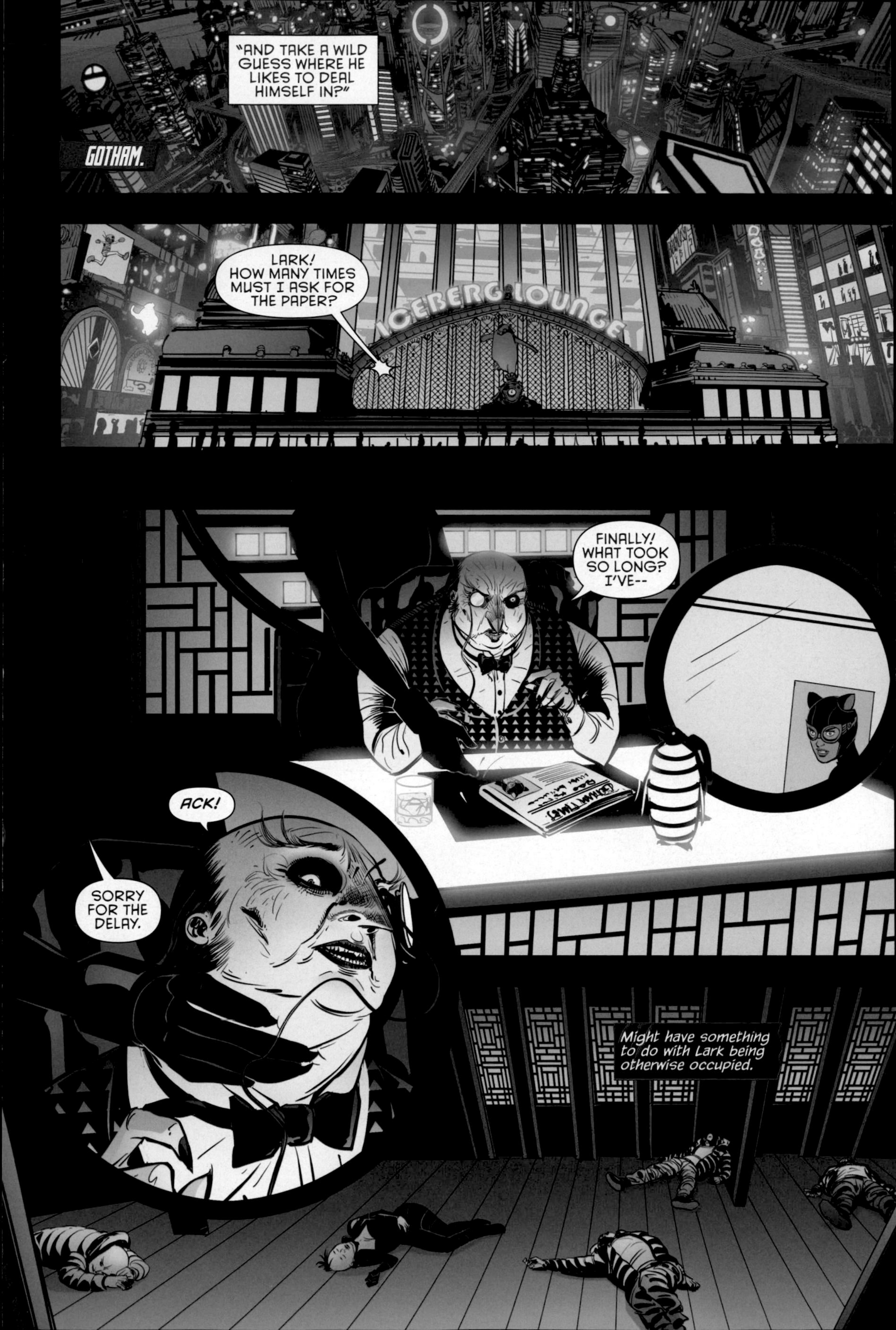
"AND TAKE A WILD GUESS WHERE HE LIKES TO DEAL HIMSELF IN?"
GOTHAM.
LARK! HOW MANY TIMES MUST I ASK FOR THE PAPER?
ICEBERG LOUNGE
FINALLY! WHAT TOOK SO LONG? I'VE--
ACK!
SORRY FOR THE DELAY.
Might have something to do with Lark being otherwise occupied.

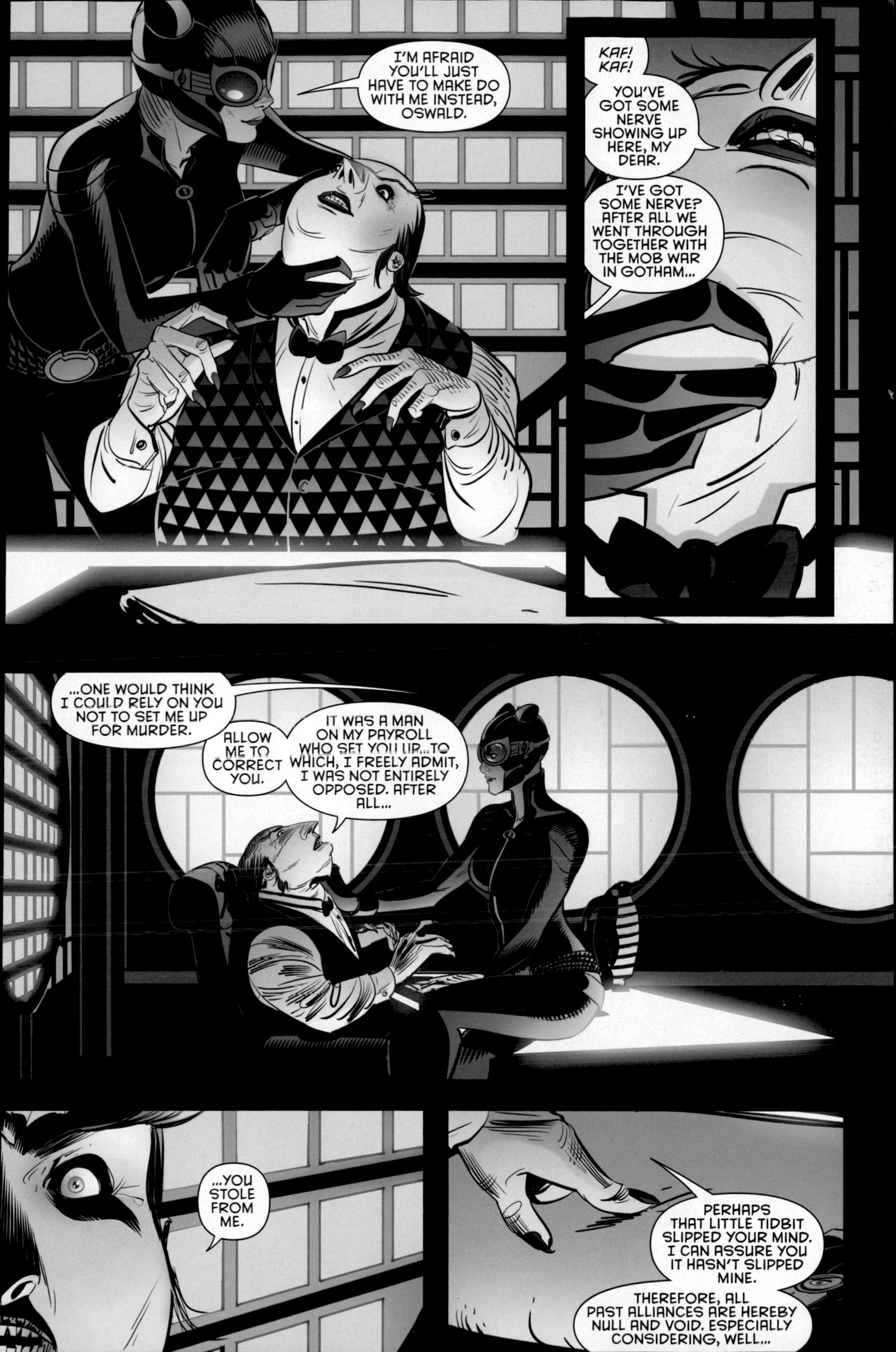
I'M AFRAID YOU'LL JUST HAVE TO MAKE DO WITH ME INSTEAD, OSWALD.
KAF! KAF!
YOU'VE GOT SOME NERVE SHOWING UP HERE, MY DEAR.
I'VE GOT SOME NERVE? AFTER ALL WE WENT THROUGH TOGETHER WITH THE MOB WAR IN GOTHAM...
...ONE WOULD THINK I COULD RELY ON YOU NOT TO SET ME UP FOR MURDER.
ALLOW ME TO CORRECT YOU.
IT WAS A MAN ON MY PAYROLL WHO SET YOU UP...TO WHICH, I FREELY ADMIT, I WAS NOT ENTIRELY OPPOSED. AFTER ALL...
...YOU STOLE FROM ME.
PERHAPS THAT LITTLE TIDBIT SLIPPED YOUR MIND. I CAN ASSURE YOU IT HASN'T SLIPPED MINE.
THEREFORE, ALL PAST ALLIANCES ARE HEREBY NULL AND VOID. ESPECIALLY CONSIDERING, WELL...

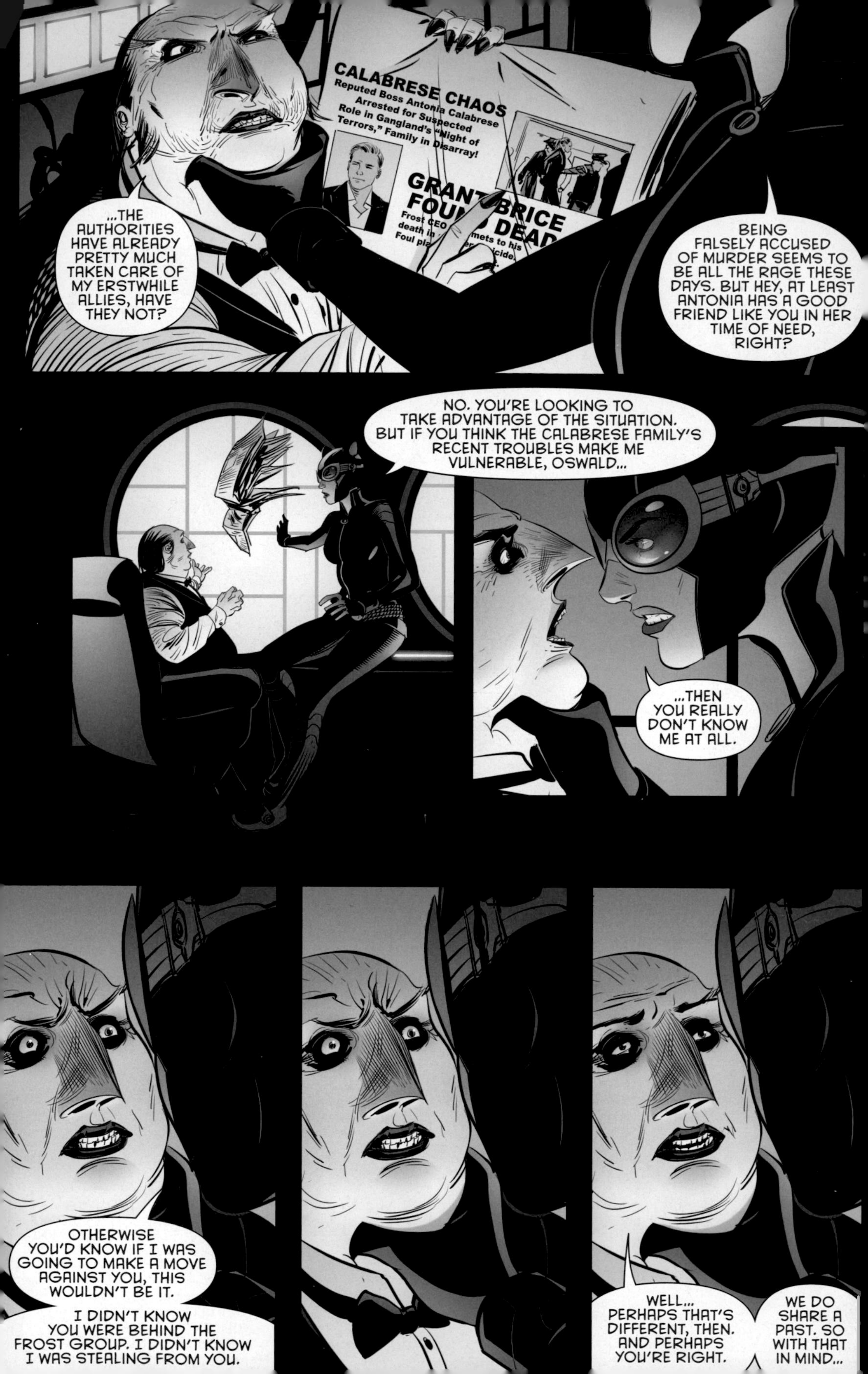
CALABRESE CHAOS
Reputed Boss Antonia Calabrese Arrested for Suspected Role in Gangland's "Night of Terrors," Family in Disarray!
GRANT BRICE FOU DEAD
Frost CEO
...THE AUTHORITIES HAVE ALREADY PRETTY MUCH TAKEN CARE OF MY ERSTWHILE ALLIES, HAVE THEY NOT?
BEING FALSELY ACCUSED OF MURDER SEEMS TO BE ALL THE RAGE THESE DAYS. BUT HEY, AT LEAST ANTONIA HAS A GOOD FRIEND LIKE YOU IN HER TIME OF NEED, RIGHT?
NO. YOU'RE LOOKING TO TAKE ADVANTAGE OF THE SITUATION. BUT IF YOU THINK THE CALABRESE FAMILY'S RECENT TROUBLES MAKE ME VULNERABLE, OSWALD...
...THEN YOU REALLY DON'T KNOW ME AT ALL.
OTHERWISE YOU'D KNOW IF I WAS GOING TO MAKE A MOVE AGAINST YOU, THIS WOULDN'T BE IT.
I DIDN'T KNOW YOU WERE BEHIND THE FROST GROUP. I DIDN'T KNOW I WAS STEALING FROM YOU.
WELL... PERHAPS THAT'S DIFFERENT, THEN. AND PERHAPS YOU'RE RIGHT.
WE DO SHARE A PAST. SO WITH THAT IN MIND...

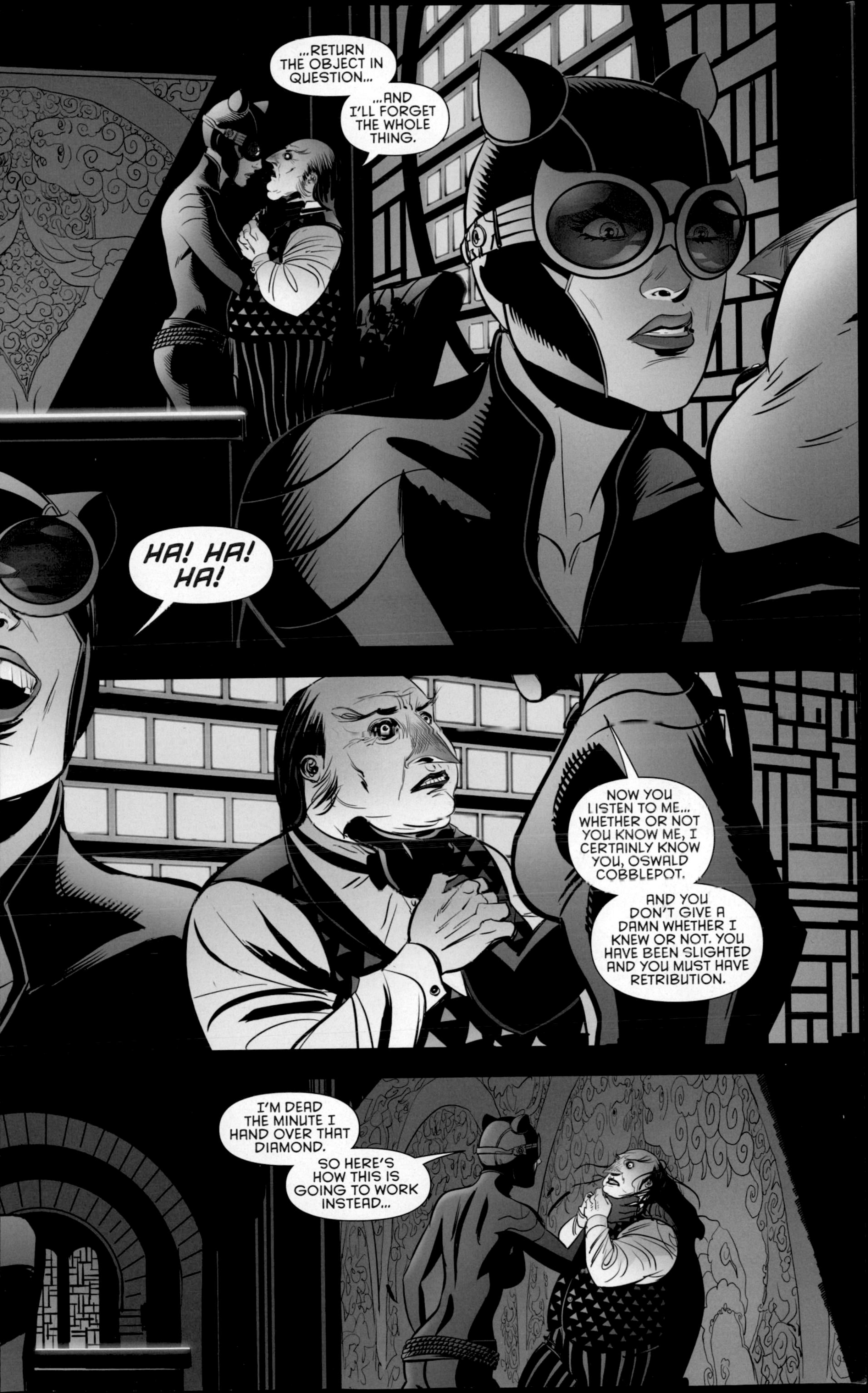
...RETURN THE OBJECT IN QUESTION...
...AND I'LL FORGET THE WHOLE THING.
HA! HA! HA!
NOW YOU LISTEN TO ME... WHETHER OR NOT YOU KNOW ME, I CERTAINLY KNOW YOU, OSWALD COBBLEPOT.
AND YOU DON'T GIVE A DAMN WHETHER I KNEW OR NOT. YOU HAVE BEEN SLIGHTED AND YOU MUST HAVE RETRIBUTION.
I'M DEAD THE MINUTE I HAND OVER THAT DIAMOND.
SO HERE'S HOW THIS IS GOING TO WORK INSTEAD...

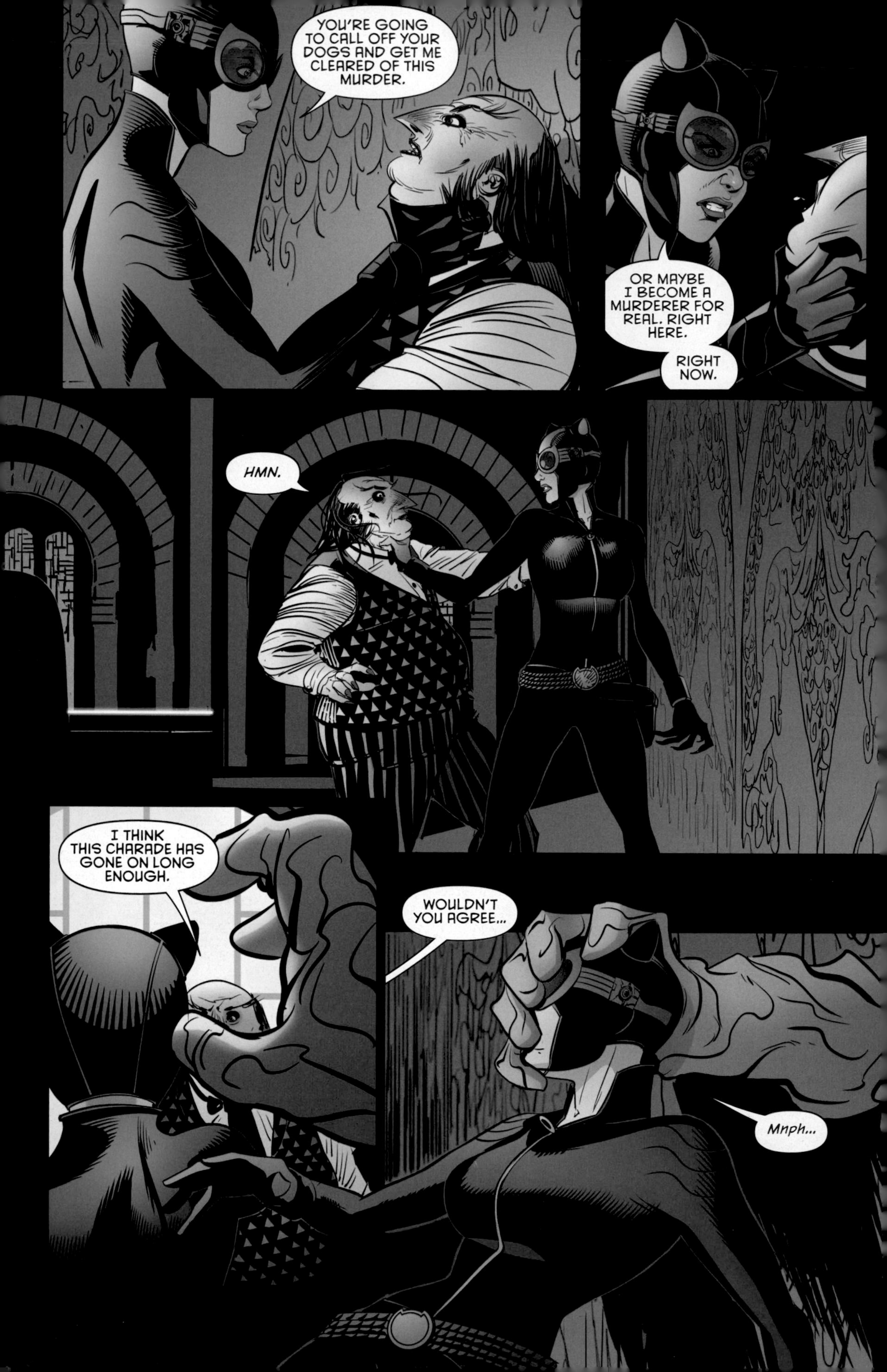
YOU'RE GOING TO CALL OFF YOUR DOGS AND GET ME CLEARED OF THIS MURDER.
OR MAYBE I BECOME A MURDERER FOR REAL. RIGHT HERE.
RIGHT NOW.
HMN.
I THINK THIS CHARADE HAS GONE ON LONG ENOUGH.
WOULDN'T YOU AGREE...
Mnph...

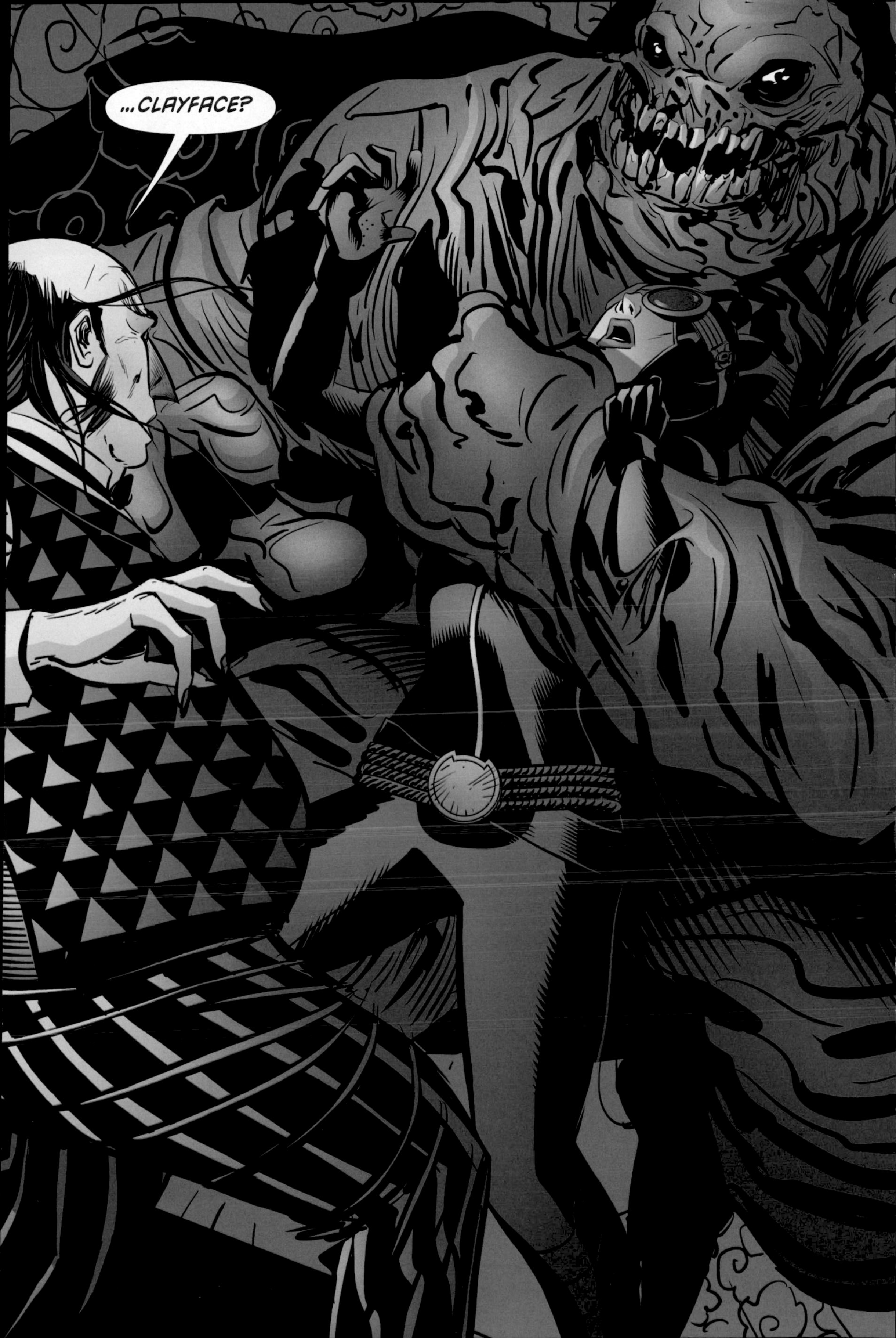
...CLAYFACE?

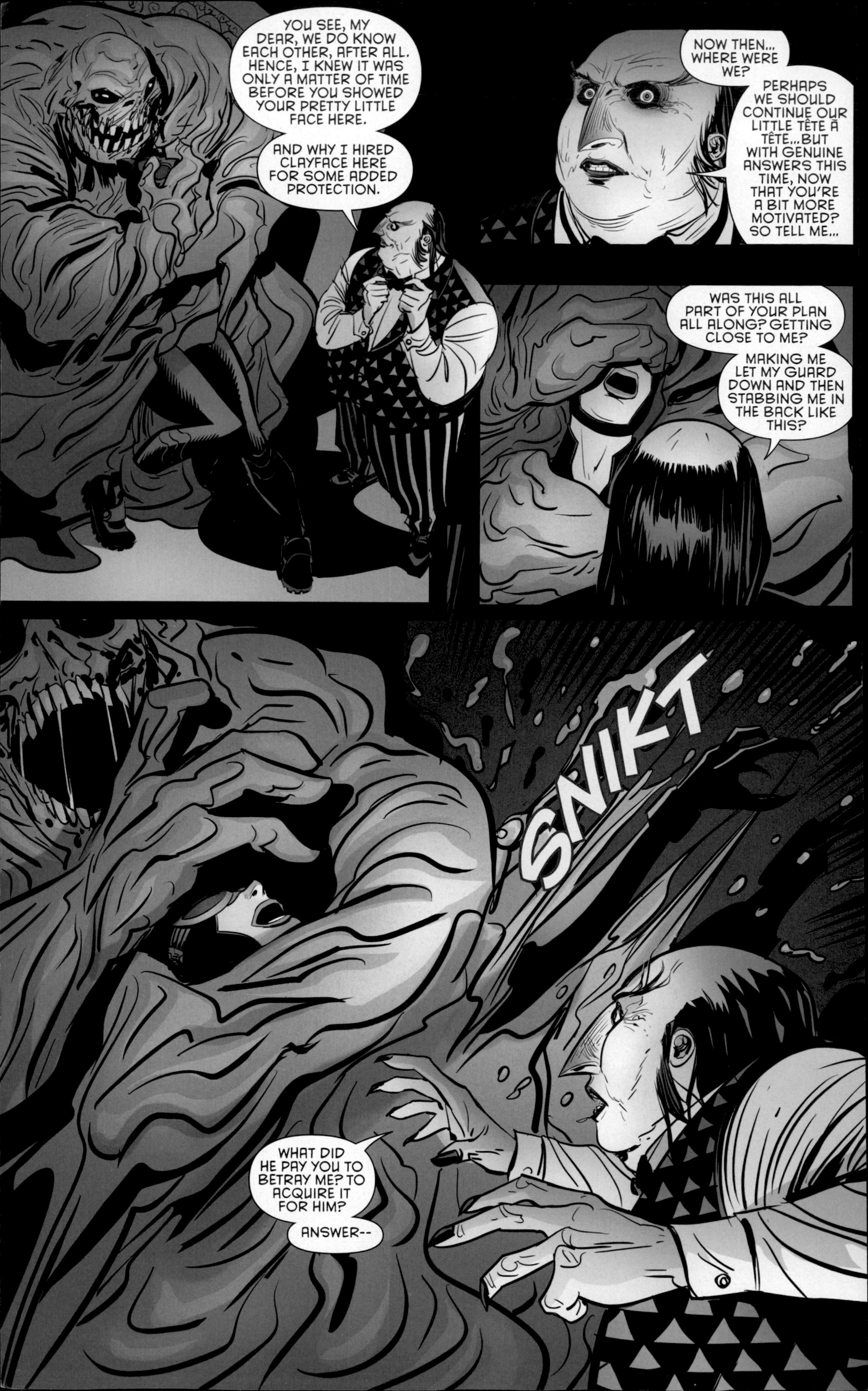
YOU SEE, MY DEAR, WE DO KNOW EACH OTHER, AFTER ALL. HENCE, I KNEW IT WAS ONLY A MATTER OF TIME BEFORE YOU SHOWED YOUR PRETTY LITTLE FACE HERE.
AND WHY I HIRED CLAYFACE HERE FOR SOME ADDED PROTECTION.
NOW THEN... WHERE WERE WE?
PERHAPS WE SHOULD CONTINUE OUR LITTLE TÊTE À TÊTE...BUT WITH GENUINE ANSWERS THIS TIME, NOW THAT YOU'RE A BIT MORE MOTIVATED? SO TELL ME...
WAS THIS ALL PART OF YOUR PLAN ALL ALONG? GETTING CLOSE TO ME?
MAKING ME LET MY GUARD DOWN AND THEN STABBING ME IN THE BACK LIKE THIS?
SNIKT
WHAT DID HE PAY YOU TO BETRAY ME? TO ACQUIRE IT FOR HIM?
ANSWER--

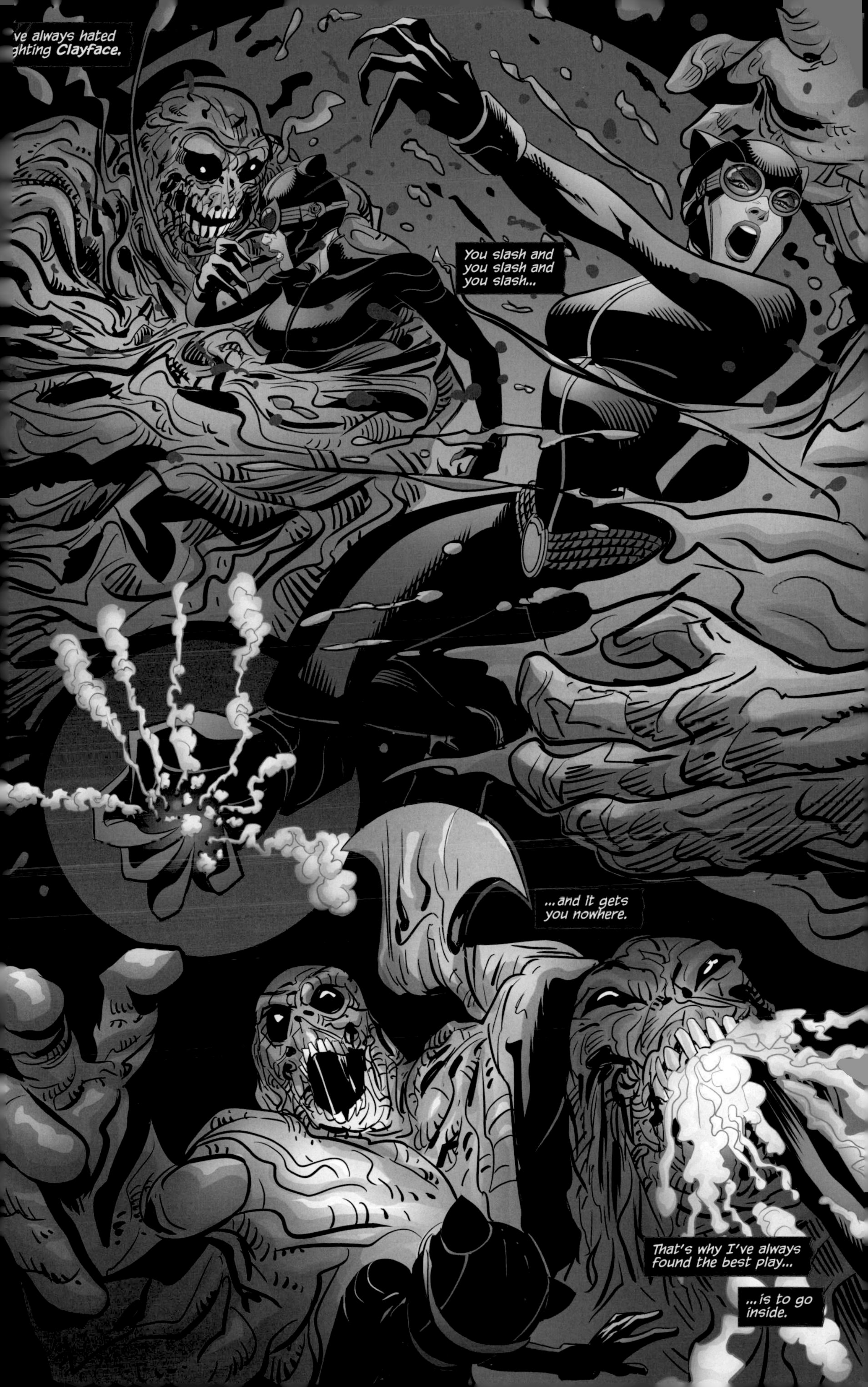

've always hated
ghting Clayface.
You slash and you slash and you slash...
...and it gets you nowhere.
That's why I've always found the best play...
...is to go inside.

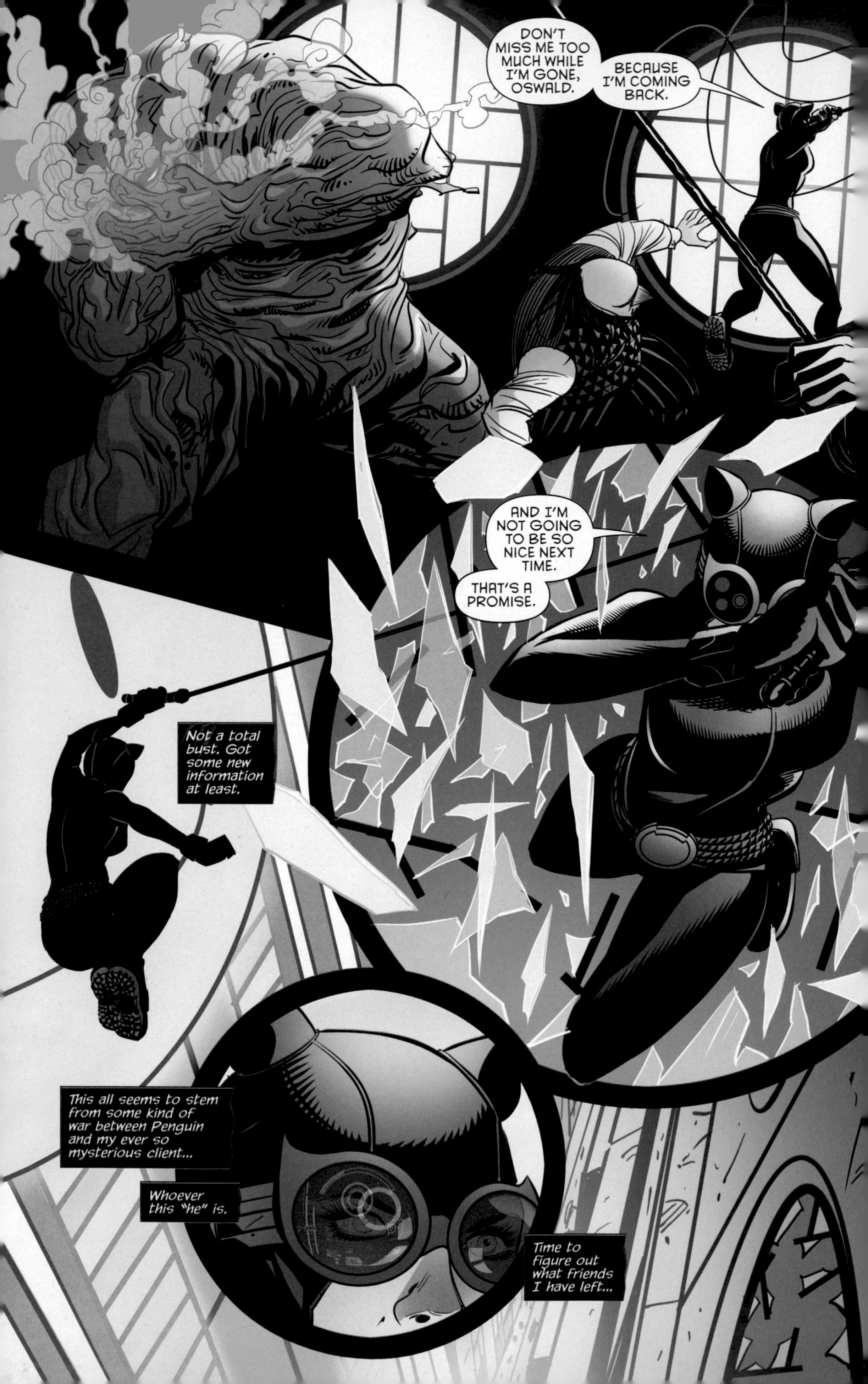
DON'T MISS ME TOO MUCH WHILE I'M GONE, OSWALD.
BECAUSE I'M COMING BACK.
AND I'M NOT GOING TO BE SO NICE NEXT TIME.
THAT'S A PROMISE.
Not a total bust. Got some new information at least.
This all seems to stem from some kind of war between Penguin and my ever so mysterious client...
Whoever this "he" is.
Time to figure out what friends I have left...

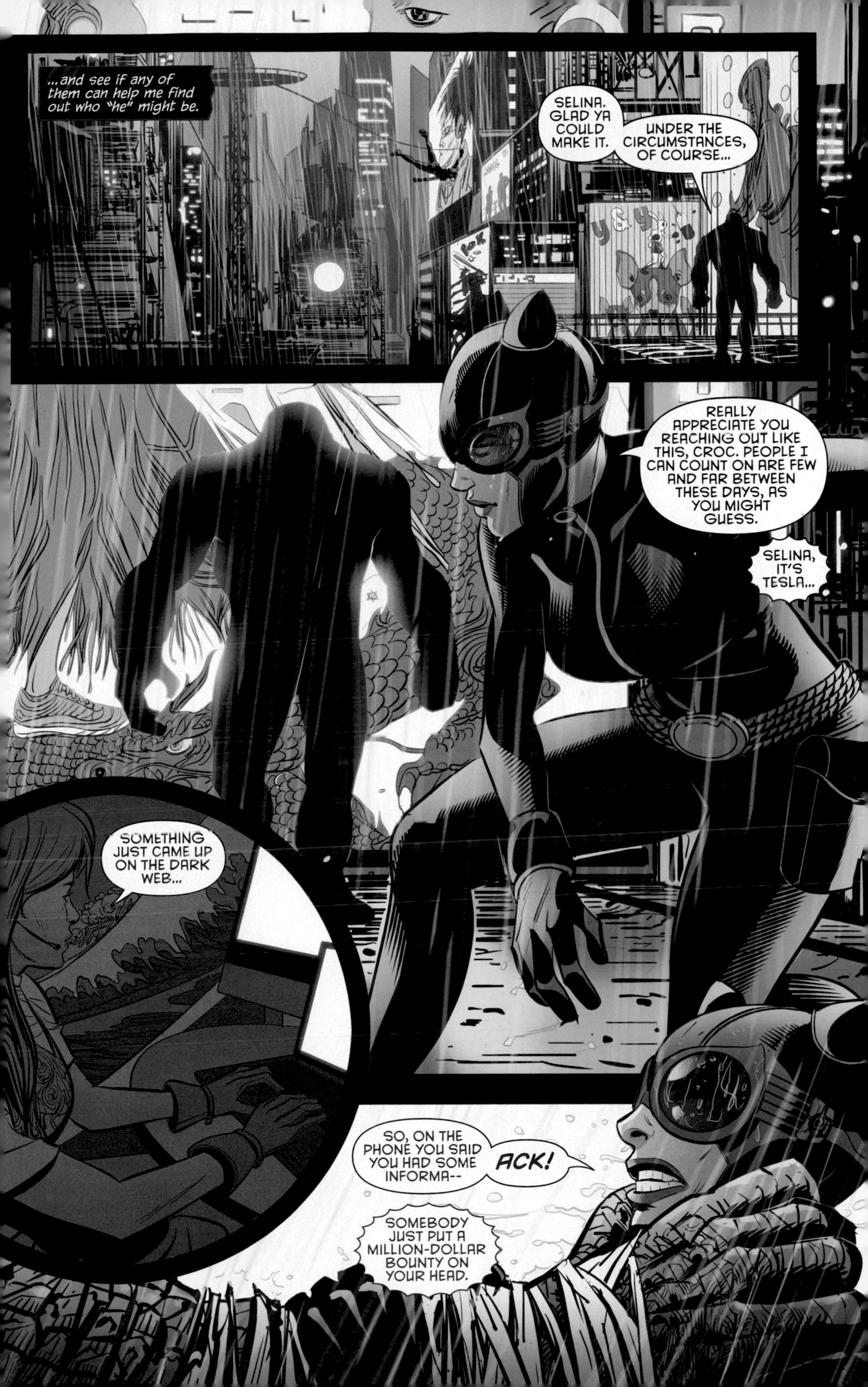

...and see if any of them can help me find out who "he" might be.
SELINA. GLAD YA COULD MAKE IT.
UNDER THE CIRCUMSTANCES, OF COURSE...
REALLY APPRECIATE YOU REACHING OUT LIKE THIS, CROC. PEOPLE I CAN COUNT ON ARE FEW AND FAR BETWEEN THESE DAYS, AS YOU MIGHT GUESS.
SELINA, IT'S TESLA...
SOMETHING JUST CAME UP ON THE DARK WEB...
SO, ON THE PHONE YOU SAID YOU HAD SOME INFORMA--
ACK!
SOMEBODY JUST PUT A MILLION-DOLLAR BOUNTY ON YOUR HEAD.

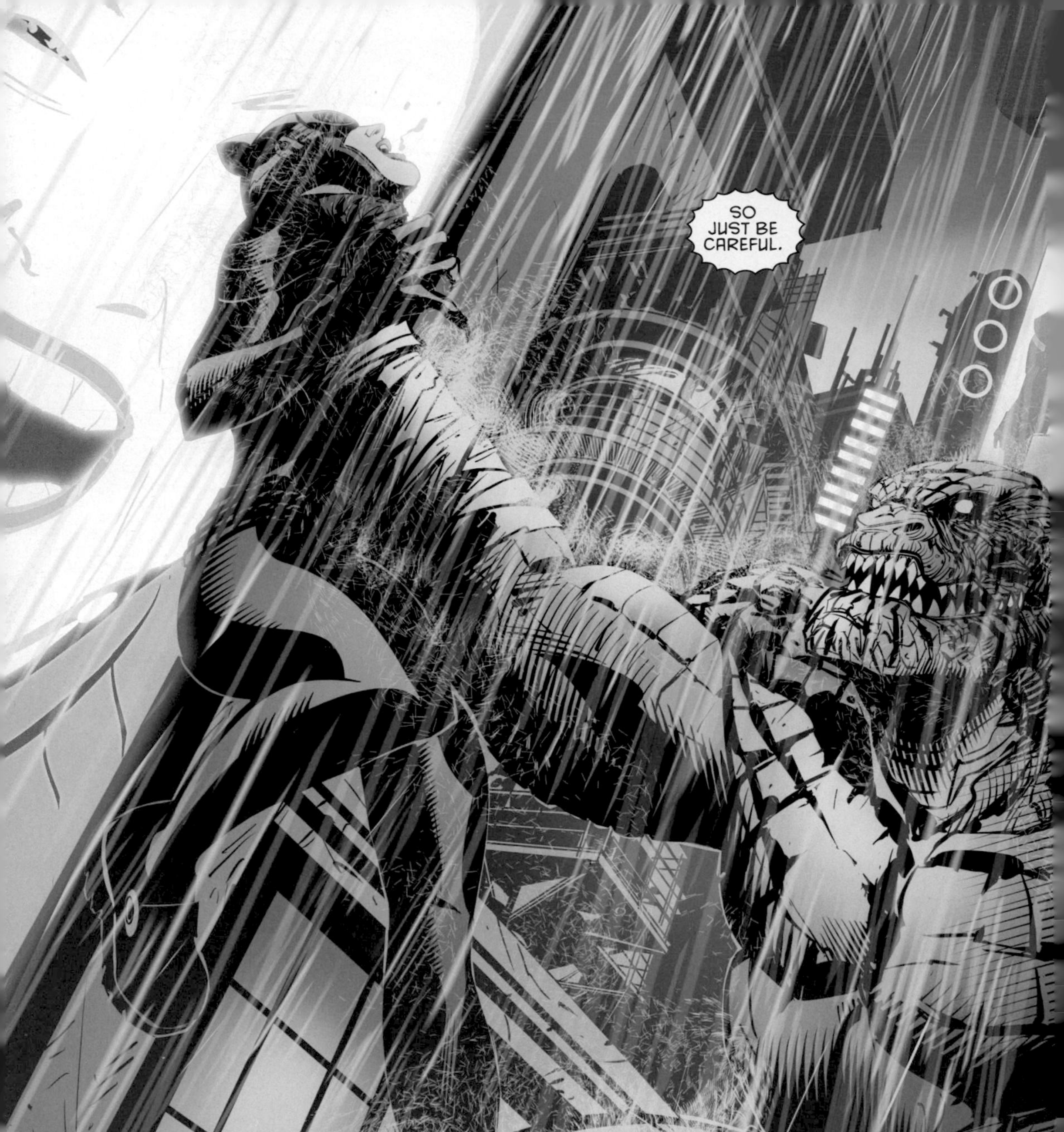
SO JUST BE CAREFUL.

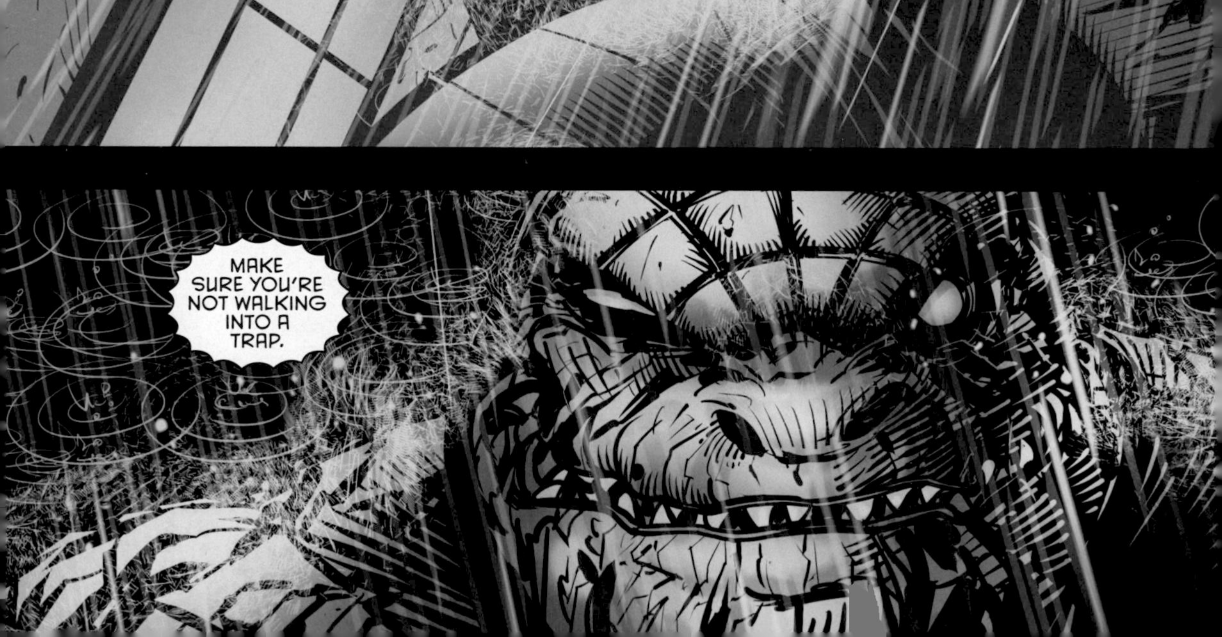
MAKE SURE YOU'RE NOT WALKING INTO A TRAP.

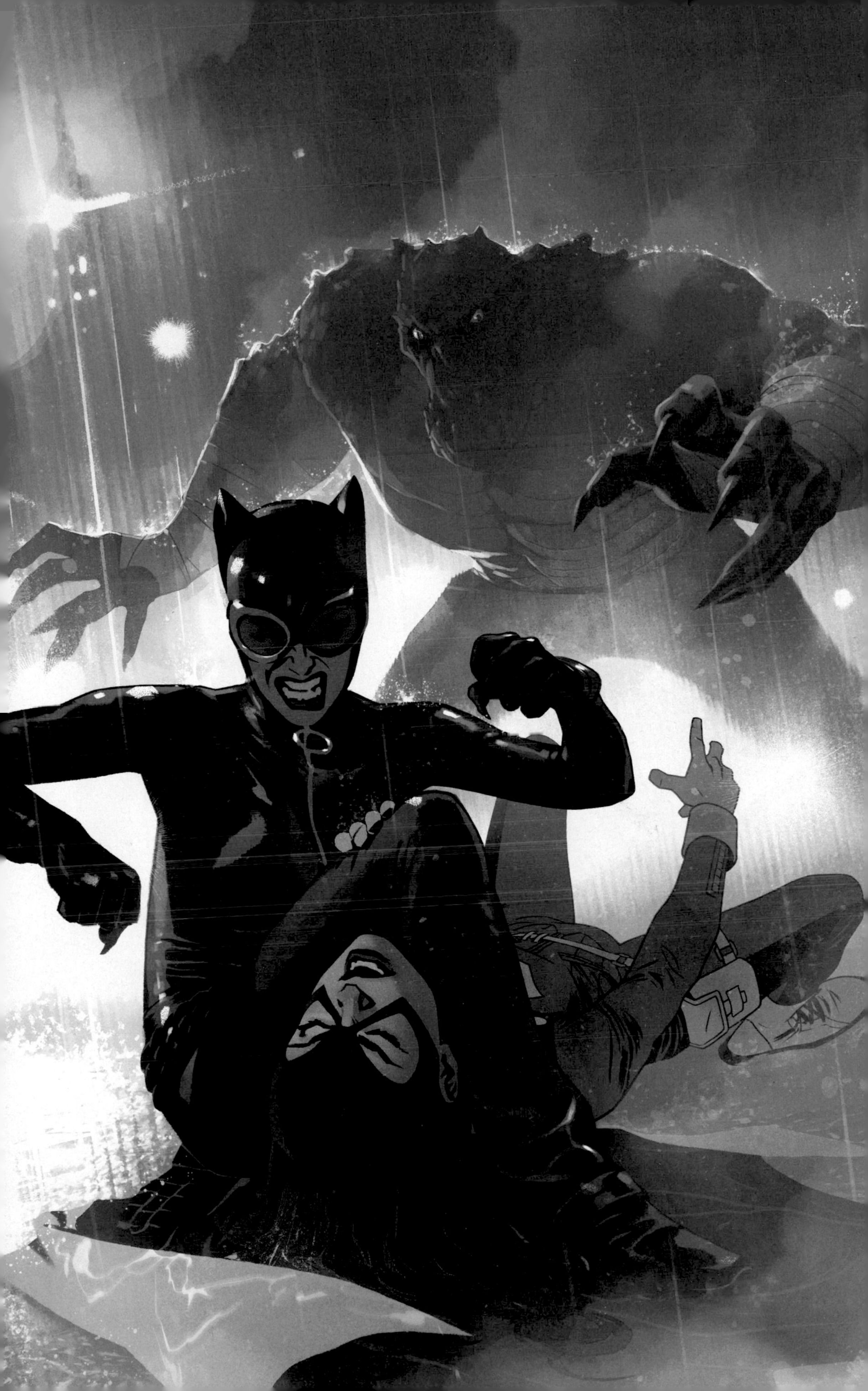

RUN LIKE HELL, PART THREE

FRANK TIERI writer **INAKI MIRANDA** artist **EVA DE LA CRUZ** colorist **TRAVIS LANHAM** letterer **JOSH MIDDLETON** cover

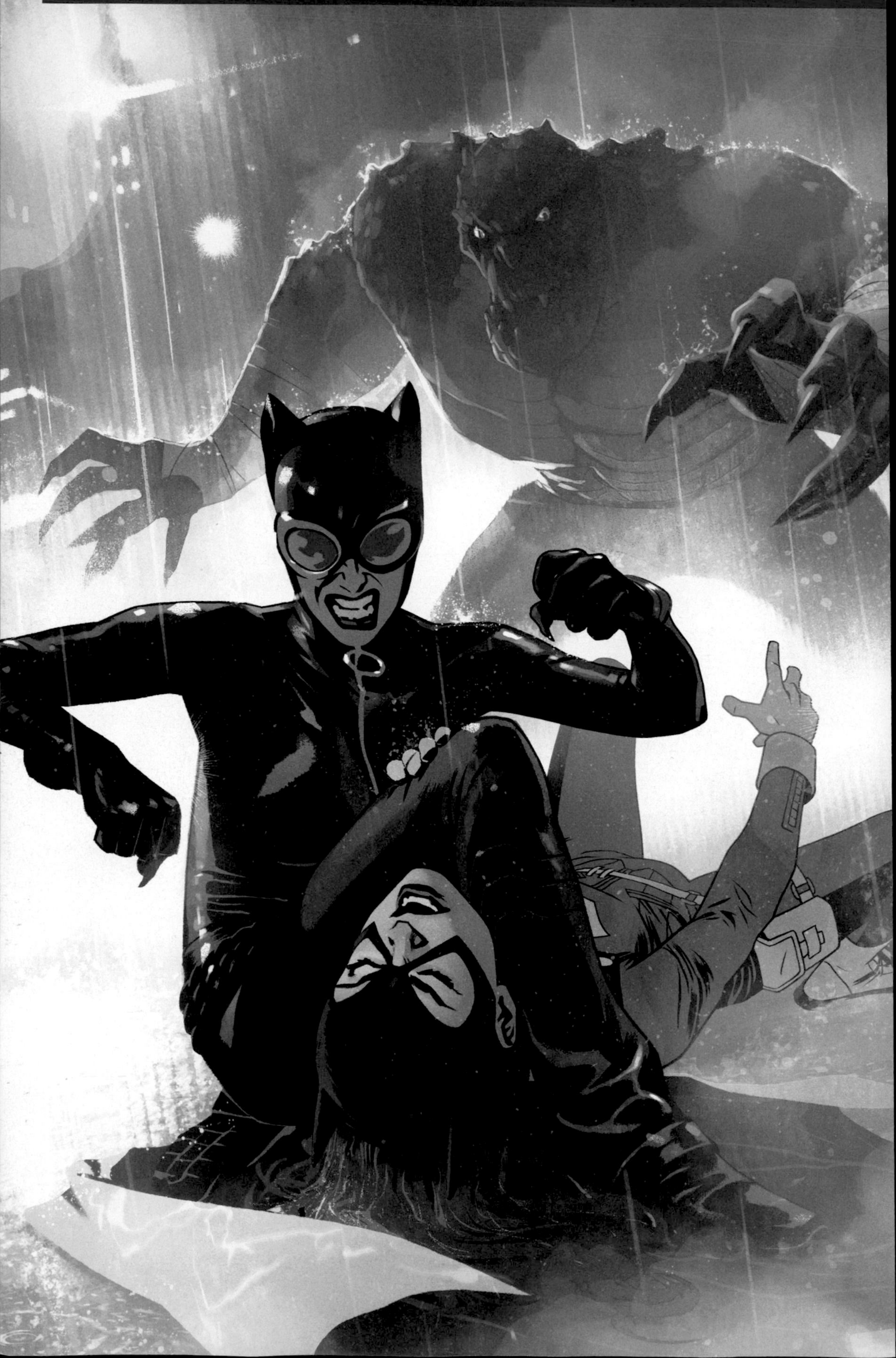

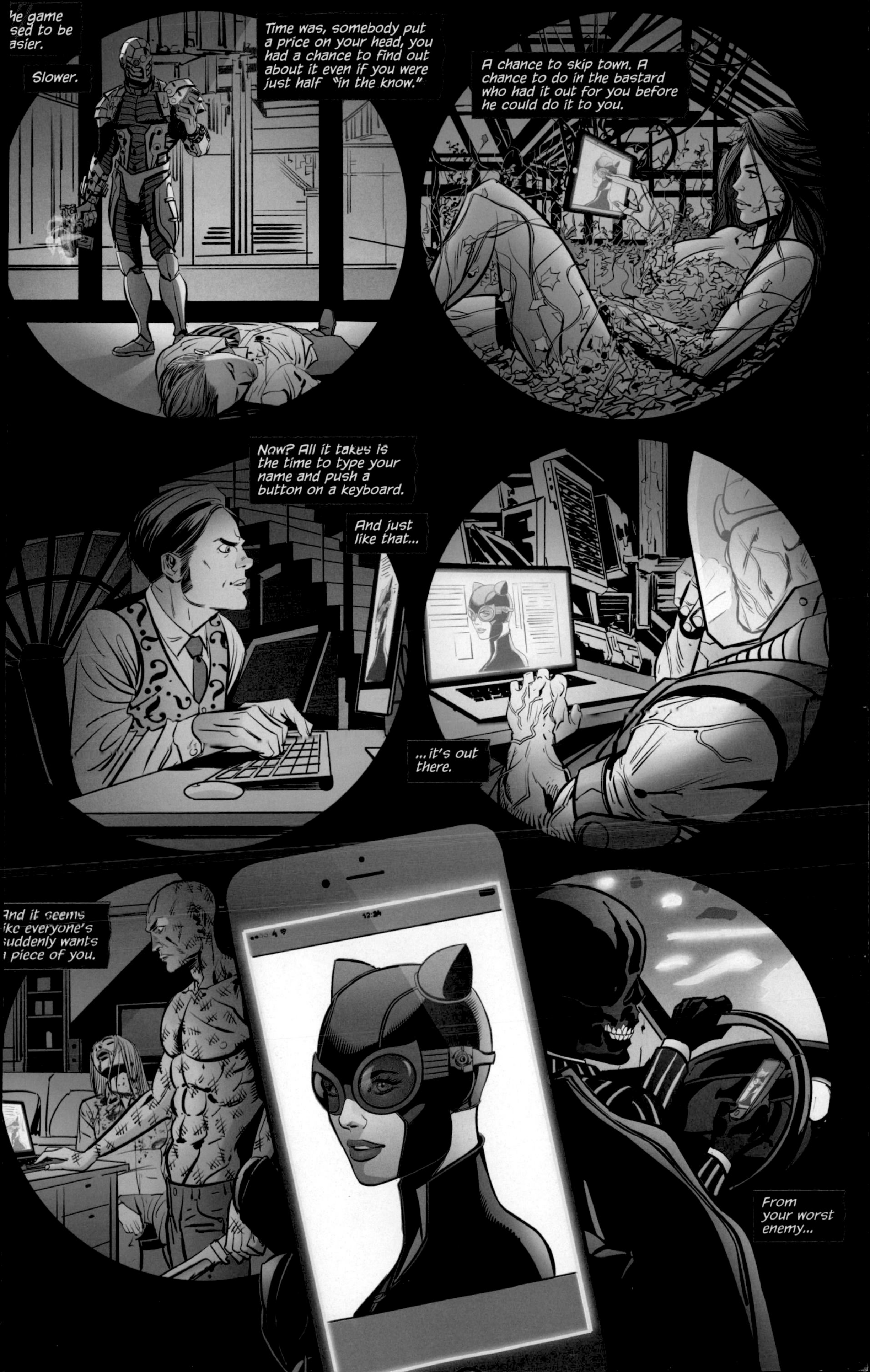

he game
sed to be
asier.
Slower.
Time was, somebody put a price on your head, you had a chance to find out about it even if you were just half "in the know."
A chance to skip town. A chance to do in the bastard who had it out for you before he could do it to you.
Now? All it takes is the time to type your name and push a button on a keyboard.
And just like that...
...it's out there.
And it seems
ike everyone's
uddenly wants
piece of you.
From your worst enemy...

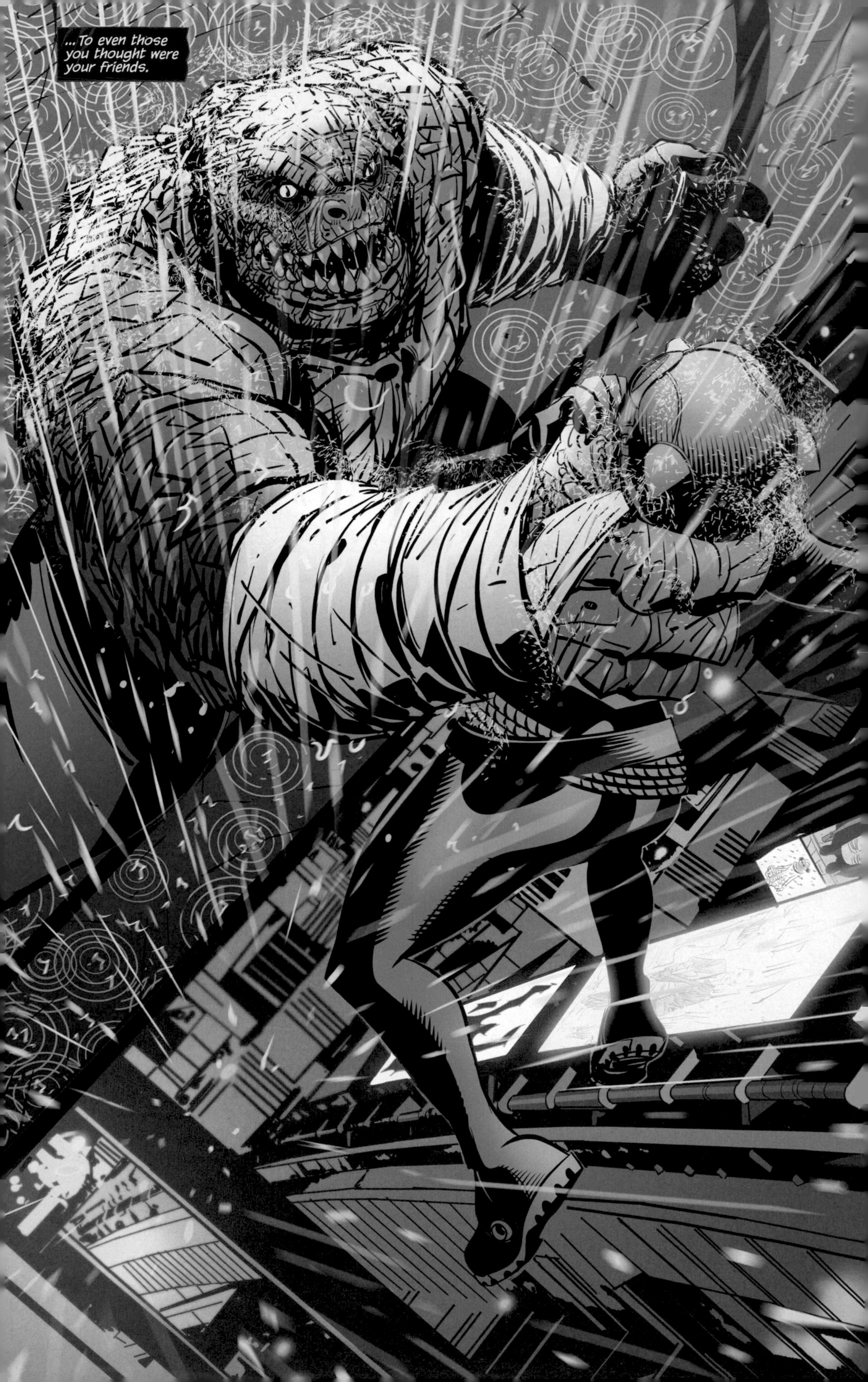
...To even those you thought were your friends.

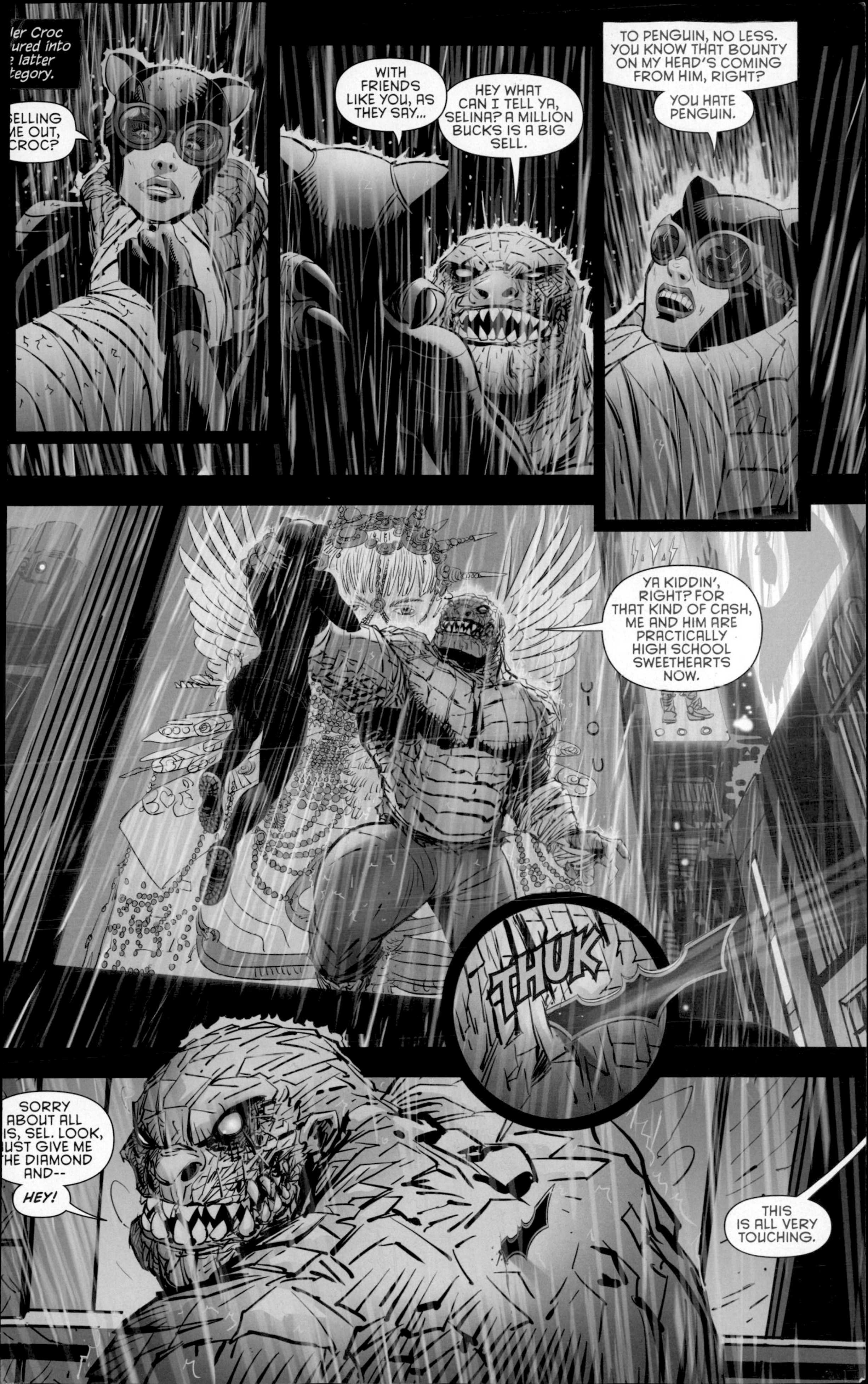

ler Croc ured into e latter tegory.
SELLING ME OUT, CROC?
WITH FRIENDS LIKE YOU, AS THEY SAY...
HEY WHAT CAN I TELL YA, SELINA? A MILLION BUCKS IS A BIG SELL.
TO PENGUIN, NO LESS. YOU KNOW THAT BOUNTY ON MY HEAD'S COMING FROM HIM, RIGHT?
YOU HATE PENGUIN.
YA KIDDIN', RIGHT? FOR THAT KIND OF CASH, ME AND HIM ARE PRACTICALLY HIGH SCHOOL SWEETHEARTS NOW.
THUK
SORRY ABOUT ALL IS, SEL. LOOK, UST GIVE ME HE DIAMOND AND--
HEY!
THIS IS ALL VERY TOUCHING.

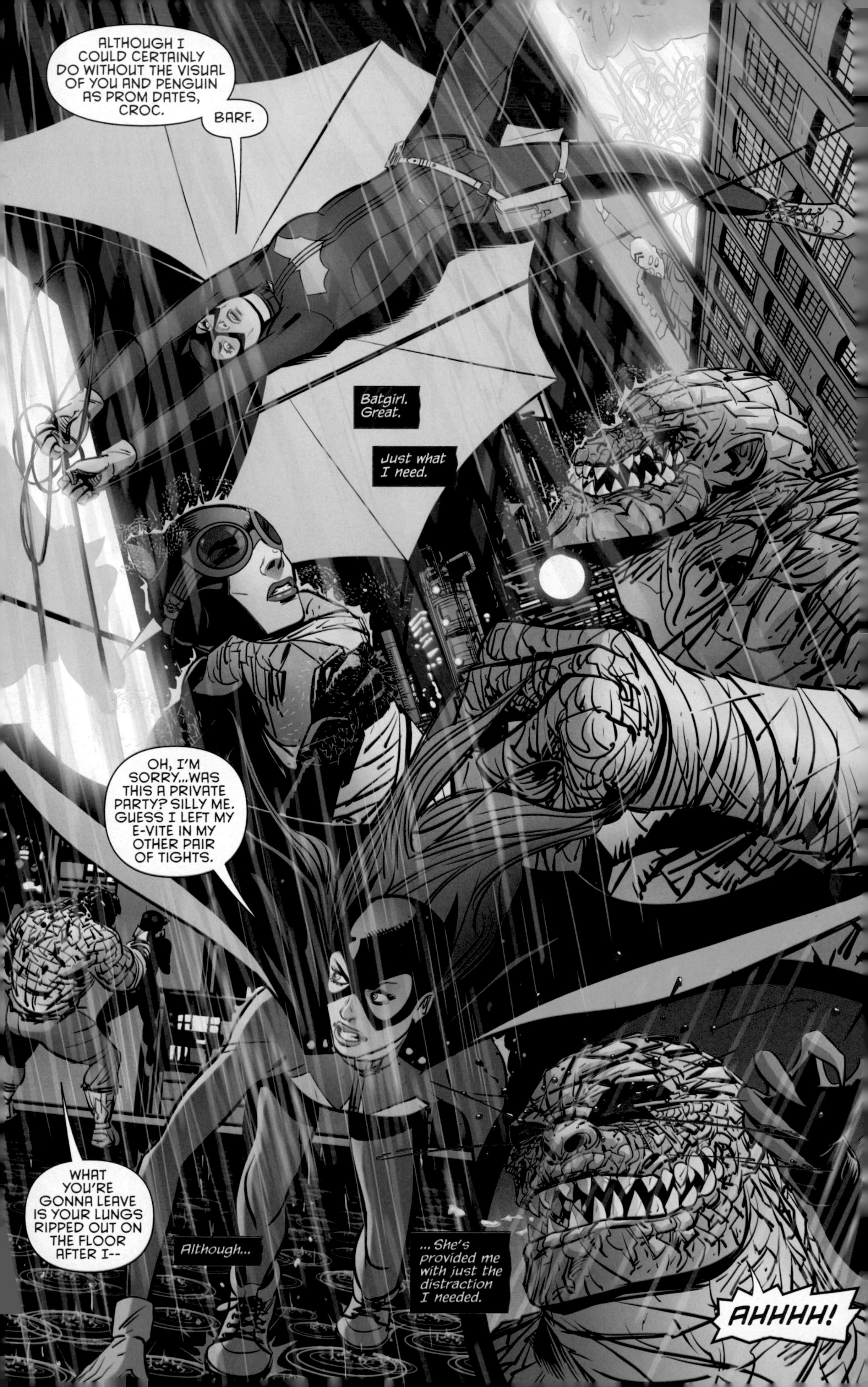
ALTHOUGH I COULD CERTAINLY DO WITHOUT THE VISUAL OF YOU AND PENGUIN AS PROM DATES, CROC.
BARF.
Batgirl. Great.
Just what I need.
OH, I'M SORRY...WAS THIS A PRIVATE PARTY? SILLY ME. GUESS I LEFT MY E-VITE IN MY OTHER PAIR OF TIGHTS.
WHAT YOU'RE GONNA LEAVE IS YOUR LUNGS RIPPED OUT ON THE FLOOR AFTER I--
Although...
...She's provided me with just the distraction I needed.
AHHHH!

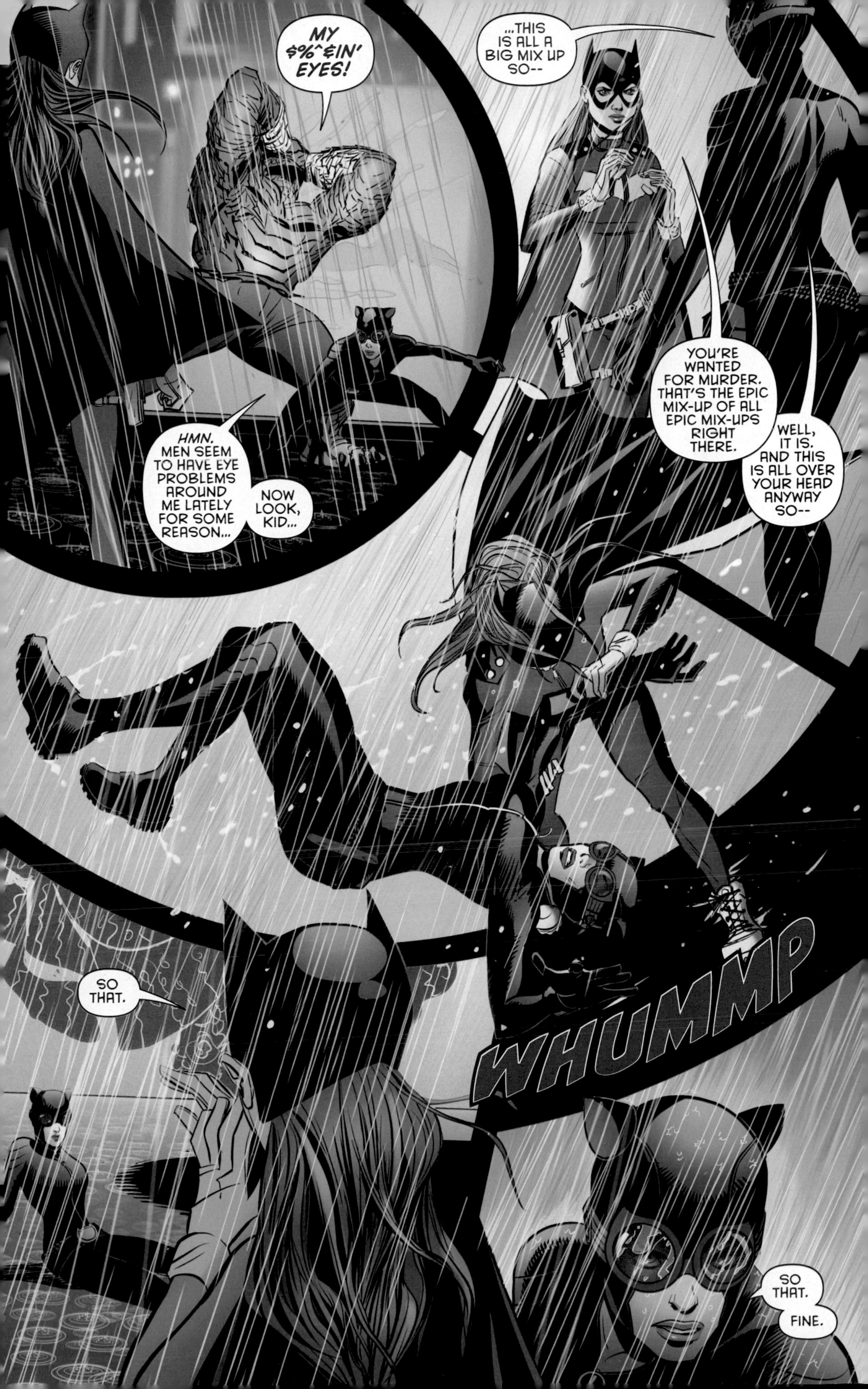

MY $%^&IN' EYES!
HMN. MEN SEEM TO HAVE EYE PROBLEMS AROUND ME LATELY FOR SOME REASON...
NOW LOOK, KID...
...THIS IS ALL A BIG MIX UP SO--
YOU'RE WANTED FOR MURDER. THAT'S THE EPIC MIX-UP OF ALL EPIC MIX-UPS RIGHT THERE.
WELL, IT IS. AND THIS IS ALL OVER YOUR HEAD ANYWAY SO--
WHUMMMP
SO THAT.
SO THAT.
FINE.

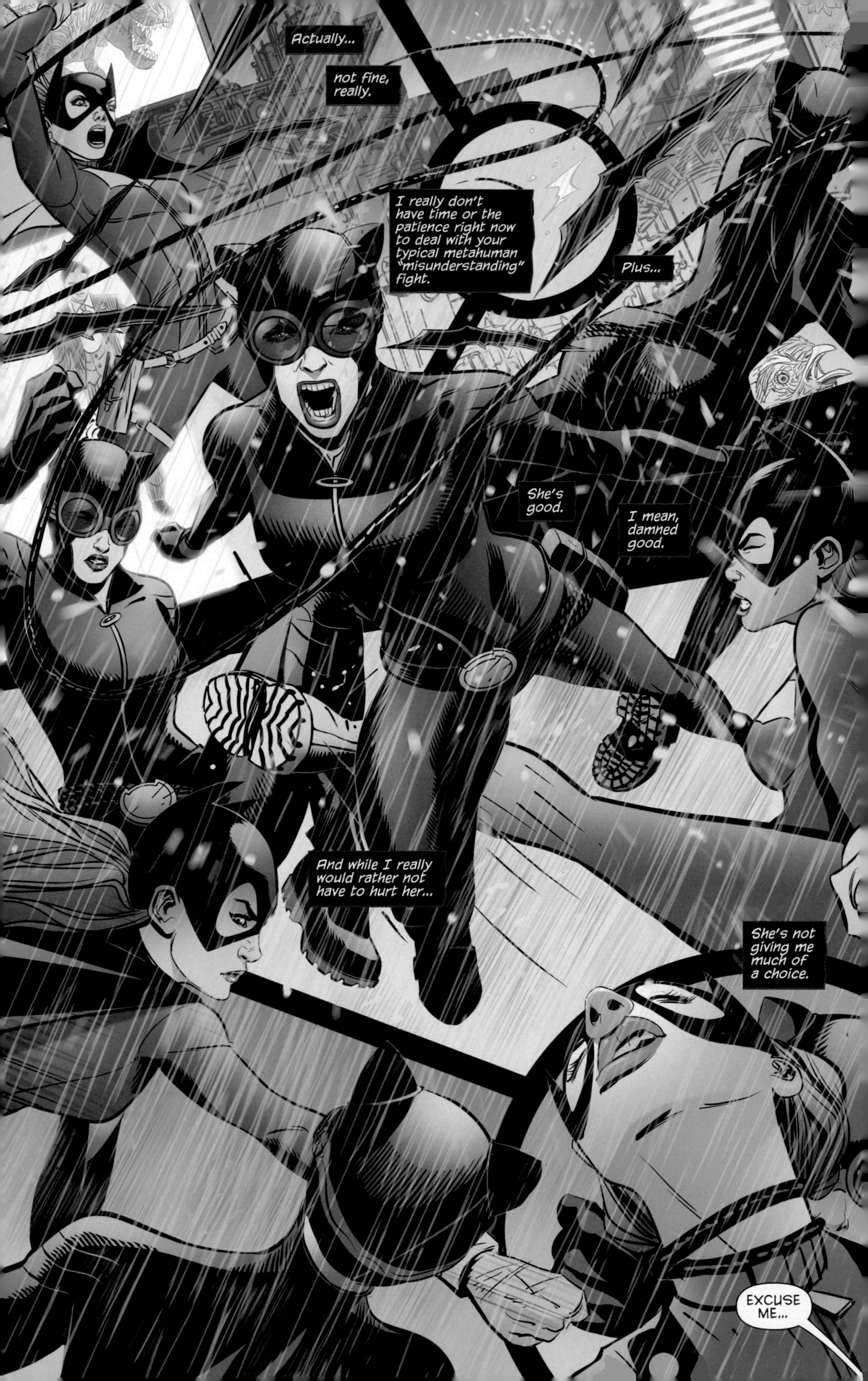
Actually...
not fine, really.
I really don't have time or the patience right now to deal with your typical metahuman "misunderstanding" fight.
Plus...
She's good.
I mean, damned good.
And while I really would rather not have to hurt her...
She's not giving me much of a choice.
EXCUSE ME...

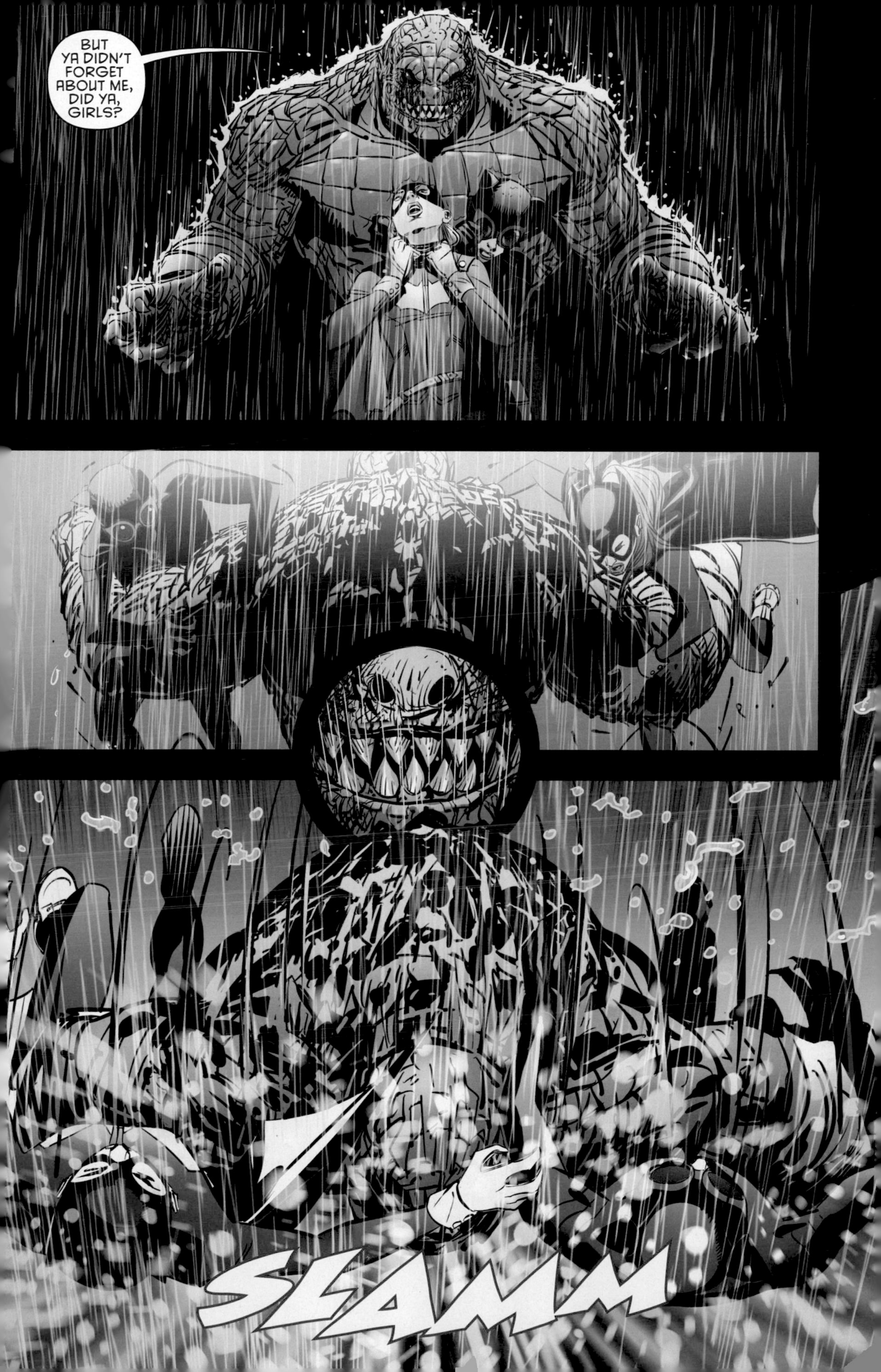
BUT YA DIDN'T FORGET ABOUT ME, DID YA, GIRLS?
SLAMM

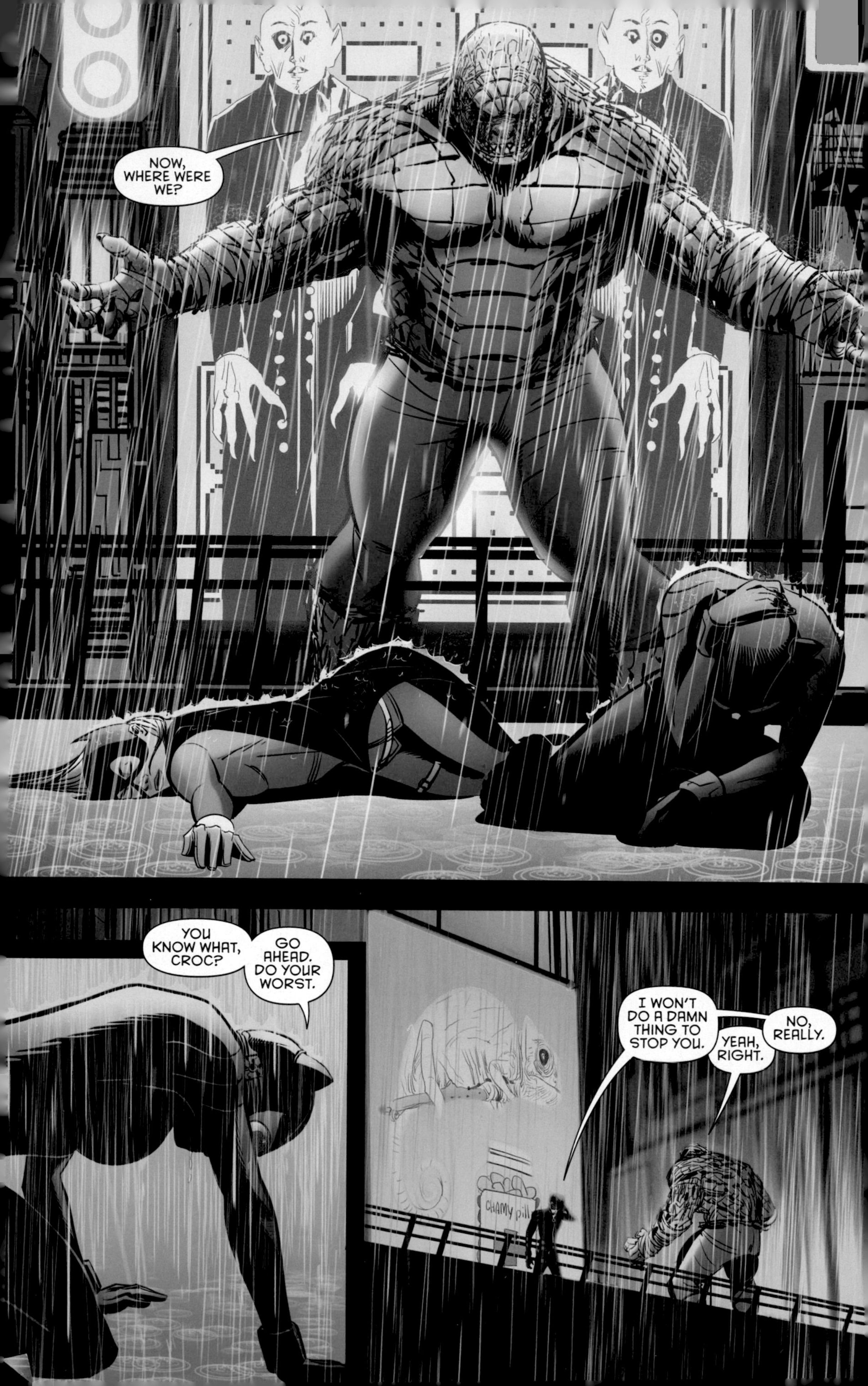
NOW, WHERE WERE WE?
YOU KNOW WHAT, CROC?
GO AHEAD. DO YOUR WORST.
I WON'T DO A DAMN THING TO STOP YOU.
YEAH, RIGHT.
NO, REALLY.
CHAMY pill

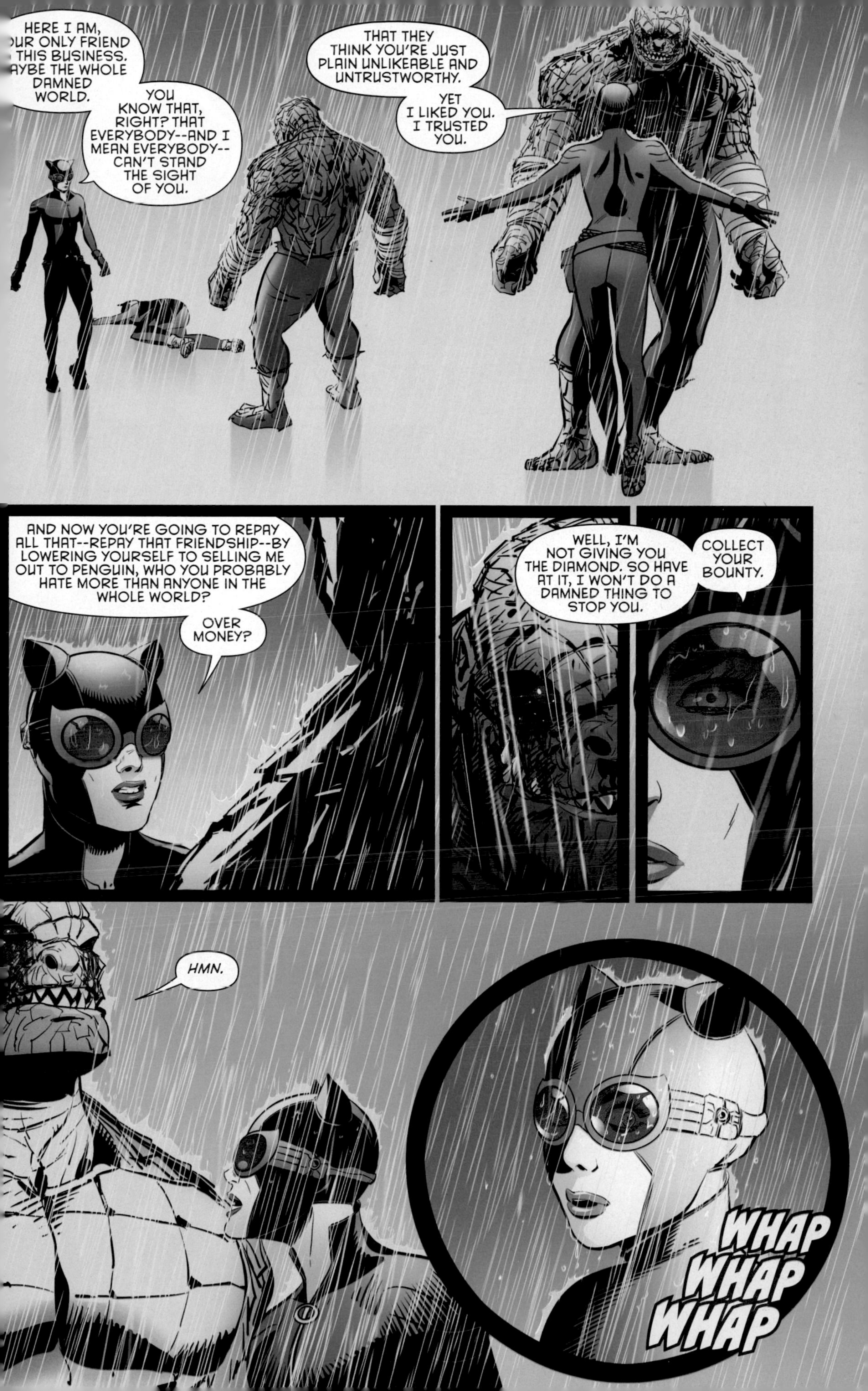
HERE I AM, OUR ONLY FRIEND THIS BUSINESS. AYBE THE WHOLE DAMNED WORLD.
YOU KNOW THAT, RIGHT? THAT EVERYBODY--AND I MEAN EVERYBODY--CAN'T STAND THE SIGHT OF YOU.
THAT THEY THINK YOU'RE JUST PLAIN UNLIKEABLE AND UNTRUSTWORTHY.
YET I LIKED YOU. I TRUSTED YOU.
AND NOW YOU'RE GOING TO REPAY ALL THAT--REPAY THAT FRIENDSHIP--BY LOWERING YOURSELF TO SELLING ME OUT TO PENGUIN, WHO YOU PROBABLY HATE MORE THAN ANYONE IN THE WHOLE WORLD?
OVER MONEY?
WELL, I'M NOT GIVING YOU THE DIAMOND. SO HAVE AT IT, I WON'T DO A DAMNED THING TO STOP YOU.
COLLECT YOUR BOUNTY.
HMN.
WHAP
WHAP
WHAP

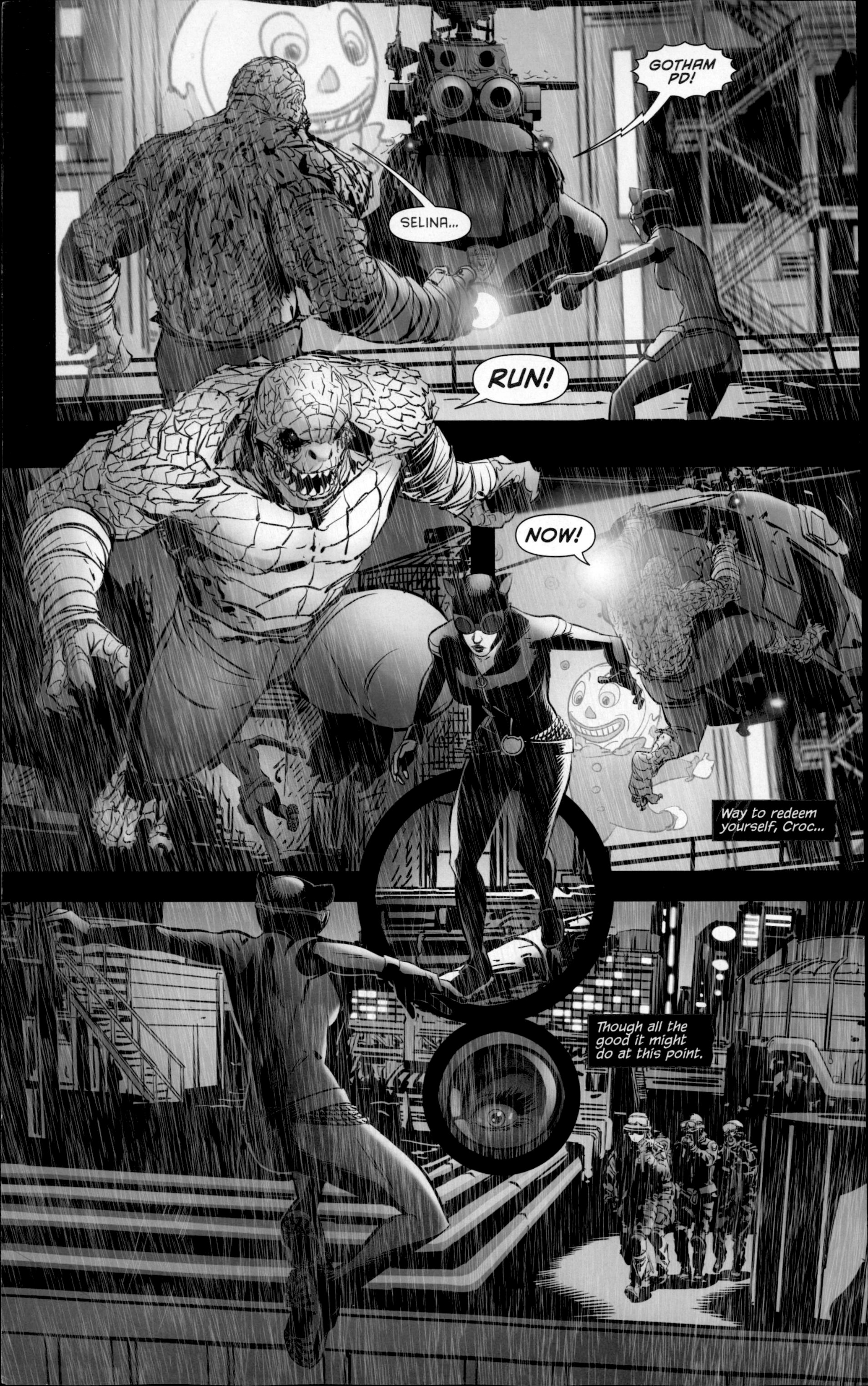
GOTHAM PD!
SELINA...
RUN!
NOW!
Way to redeem yourself, Croc...
Though all the good it might do at this point.

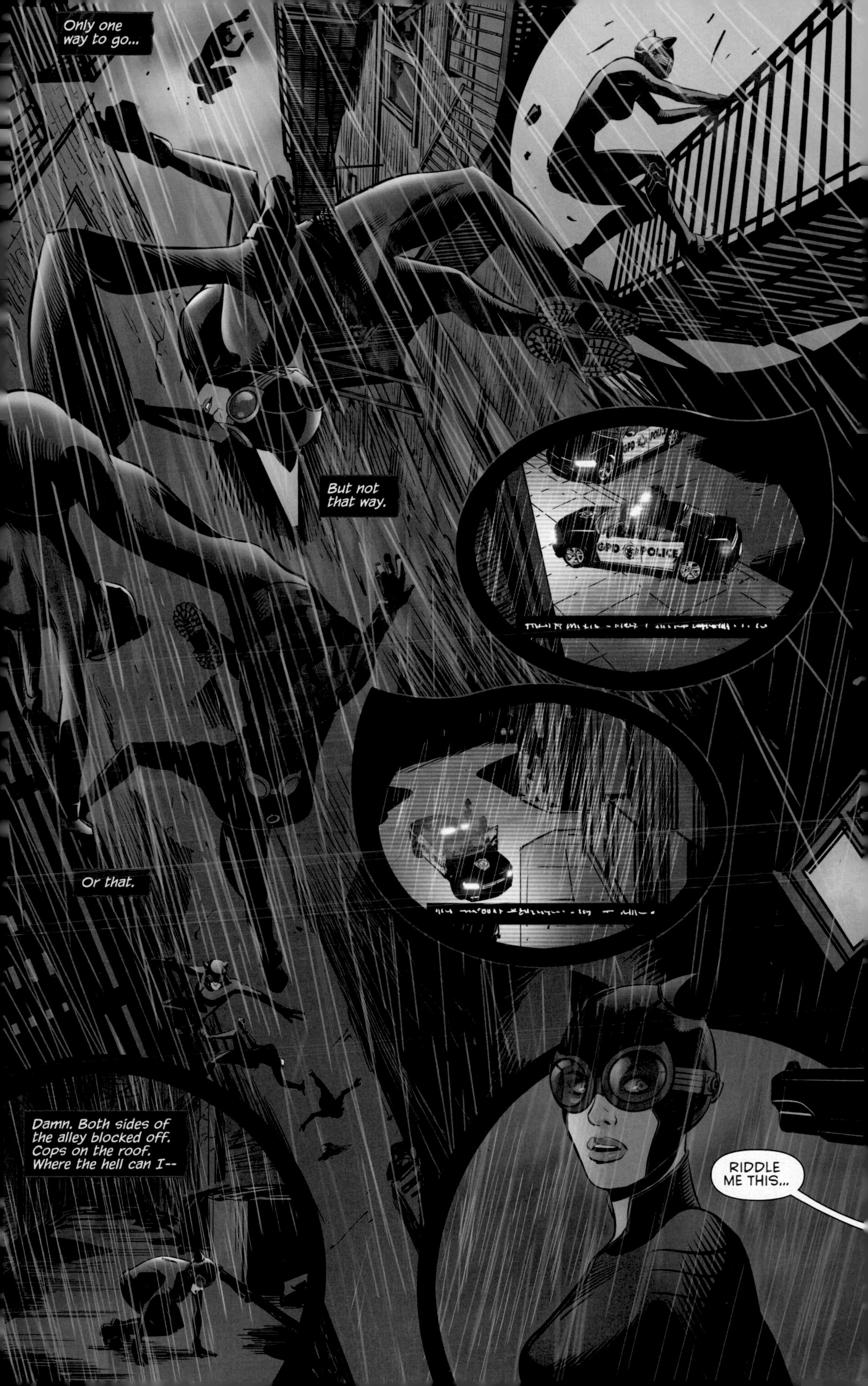
Only one way to go...
But not that way.
Or that.
Damn. Both sides of the alley blocked off. Cops on the roof. Where the hell can I--
RIDDLE ME THIS...

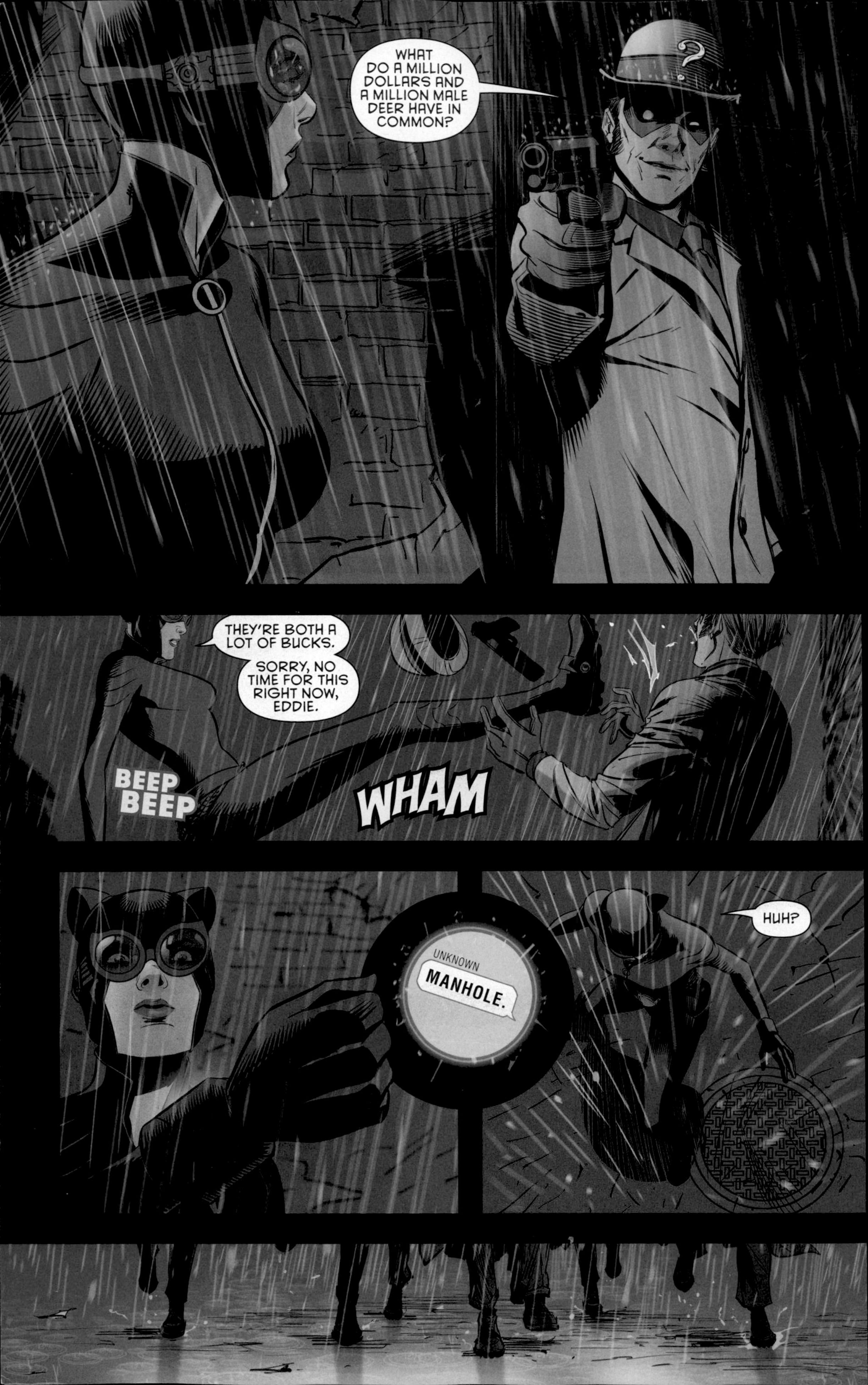
WHAT DO A MILLION DOLLARS AND A MILLION MALE DEER HAVE IN COMMON?
THEY'RE BOTH A LOT OF BUCKS.
SORRY, NO TIME FOR THIS RIGHT NOW, EDDIE.
BEEP BEEP
WHAM
UNKNOWN
MANHOLE.
HUH?

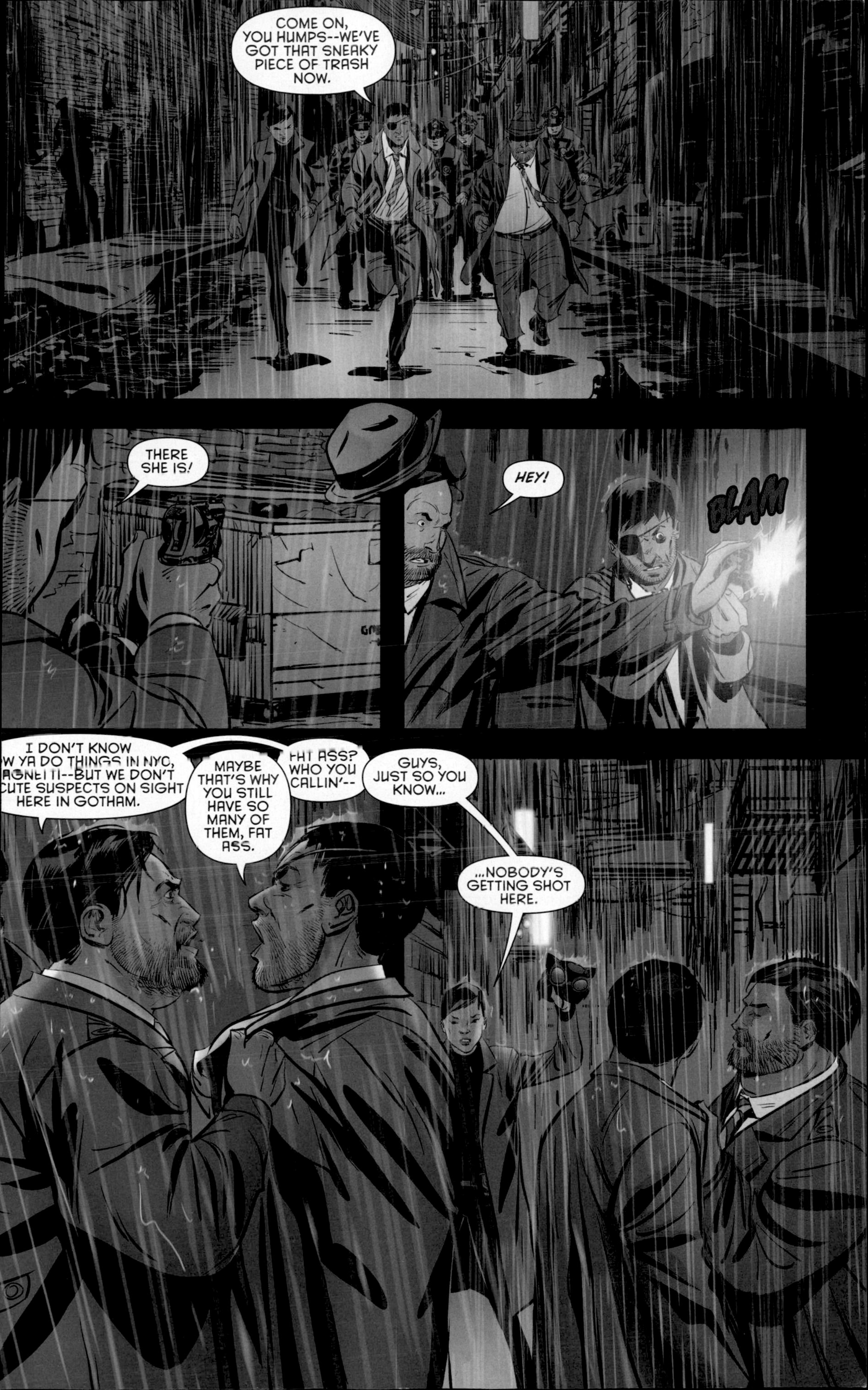
COME ON, YOU HUMPS--WE'VE GOT THAT SNEAKY PIECE OF TRASH NOW.
THERE SHE IS!
HEY!
BLAM
I DON'T KNOW W YA DO THINGS IN NYC, AGNETTI--BUT WE DON'T CUTE SUSPECTS ON SIGHT HERE IN GOTHAM.
MAYBE THAT'S WHY YOU STILL HAVE SO MANY OF THEM, FAT ASS.
FAT ASS? WHO YOU CALLIN'--
GUYS, JUST SO YOU KNOW...
...NOBODY'S GETTING SHOT HERE.

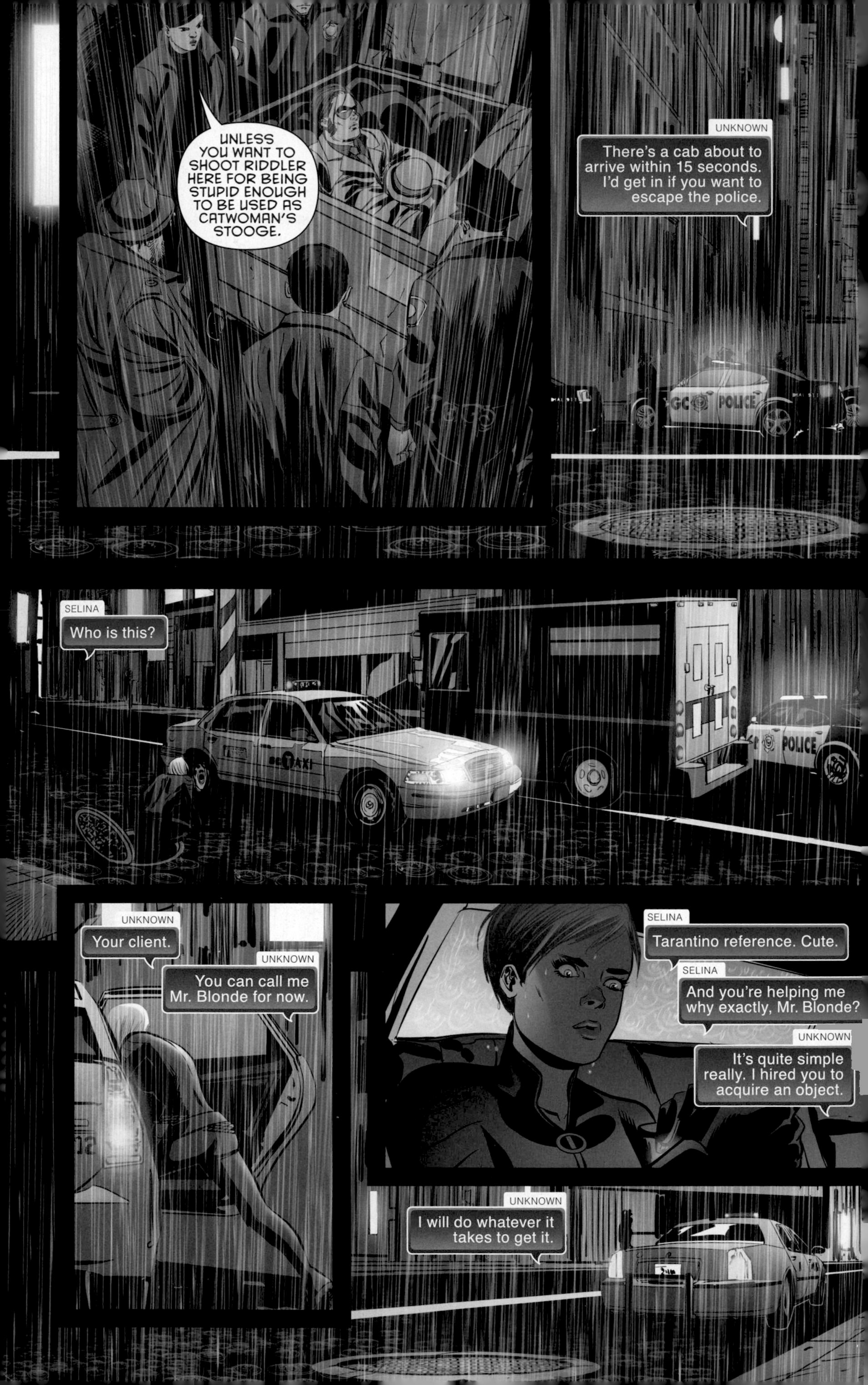
UNLESS YOU WANT TO SHOOT RIDDLER HERE FOR BEING STUPID ENOUGH TO BE USED AS CATWOMAN'S STOOGE.
UNKNOWN
There's a cab about to arrive within 15 seconds. I'd get in if you want to escape the police.
GCPD POLICE
SELINA
Who is this?
TAXI
POLICE
UNKNOWN
Your client.
UNKNOWN
You can call me Mr. Blonde for now.
SELINA
Tarantino reference. Cute.
SELINA
And you're helping me why exactly, Mr. Blonde?
UNKNOWN
It's quite simple really. I hired you to acquire an object.
UNKNOWN
I will do whatever it takes to get it.

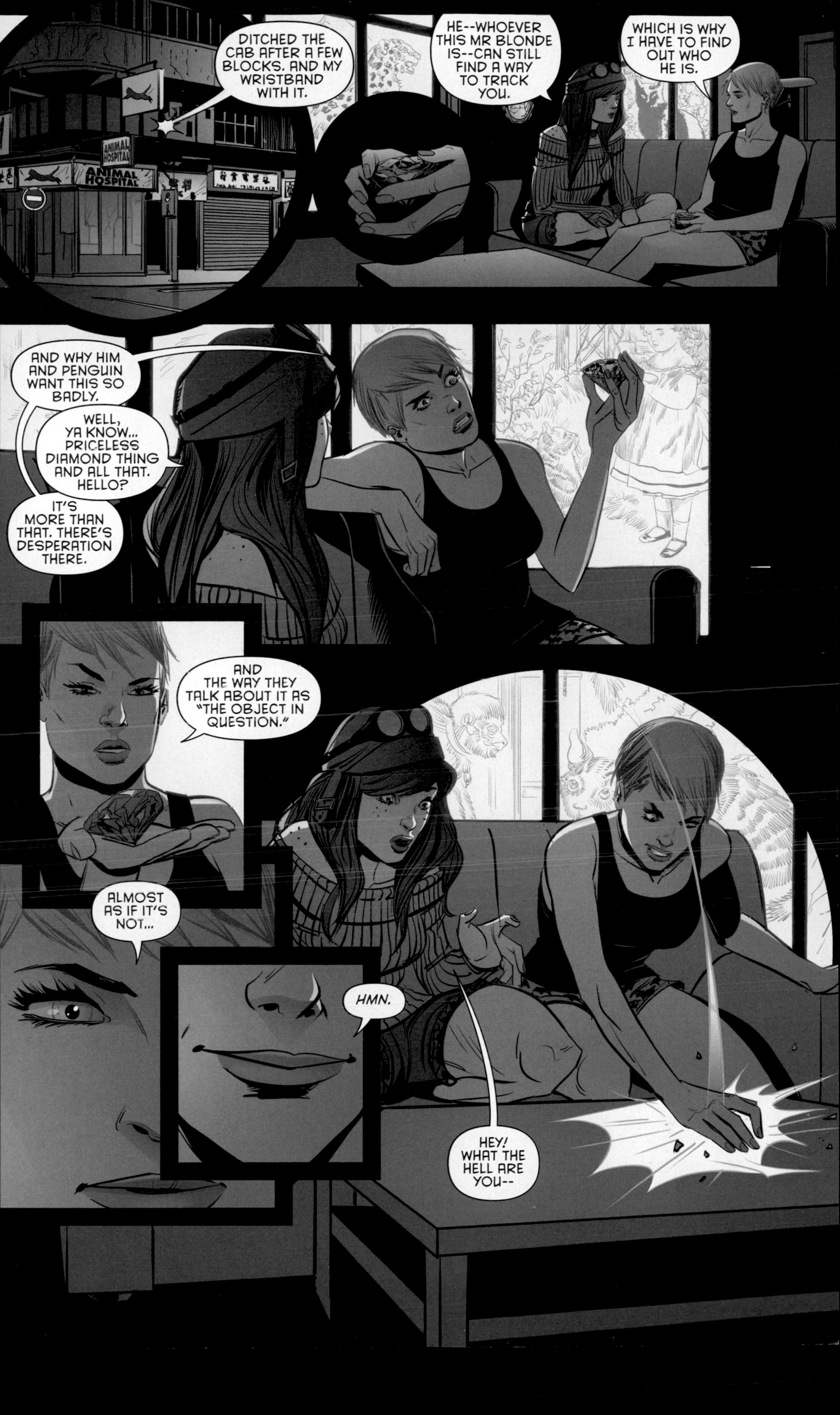
ANIMAL HOSPITAL
ANIMAL HOSPITAL
DITCHED THE CAB AFTER A FEW BLOCKS. AND MY WRISTBAND WITH IT.
HE--WHOEVER THIS MR BLONDE IS--CAN STILL FIND A WAY TO TRACK YOU.
WHICH IS WHY I HAVE TO FIND OUT WHO HE IS.
AND WHY HIM AND PENGUIN WANT THIS SO BADLY.
WELL, YA KNOW... PRICELESS DIAMOND THING AND ALL THAT. HELLO?
IT'S MORE THAN THAT. THERE'S DESPERATION THERE.
AND THE WAY THEY TALK ABOUT IT AS "THE OBJECT IN QUESTION."
ALMOST AS IF IT'S NOT...
HMN.
HEY! WHAT THE HELL ARE YOU--

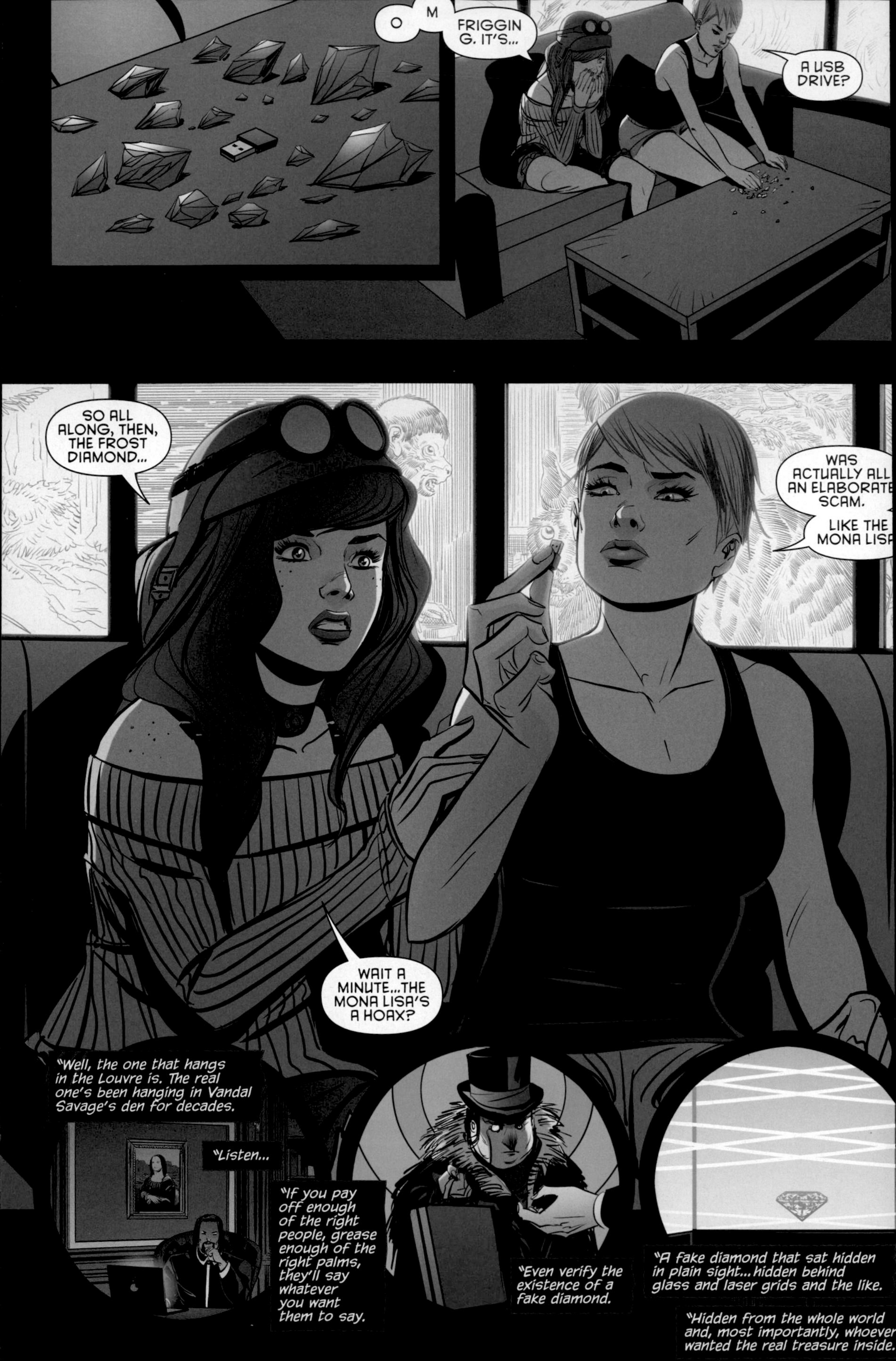
O M
FRIGGIN G. IT'S...
A USB DRIVE?
SO ALL ALONG, THEN, THE FROST DIAMOND...
WAS ACTUALLY ALL AN ELABORATE SCAM.
LIKE THE MONA LISA
WAIT A MINUTE...THE MONA LISA'S A HOAX?
"Well, the one that hangs in the Louvre is. The real one's been hanging in Vandal Savage's den for decades.
"Listen...
"If you pay off enough of the right people, grease enough of the right palms, they'll say whatever you want them to say.
"Even verify the existence of a fake diamond.
"A fake diamond that sat hidden in plain sight...hidden behind glass and laser grids and the like.
"Hidden from the whole world and, most importantly, whoever wanted the real treasure inside.

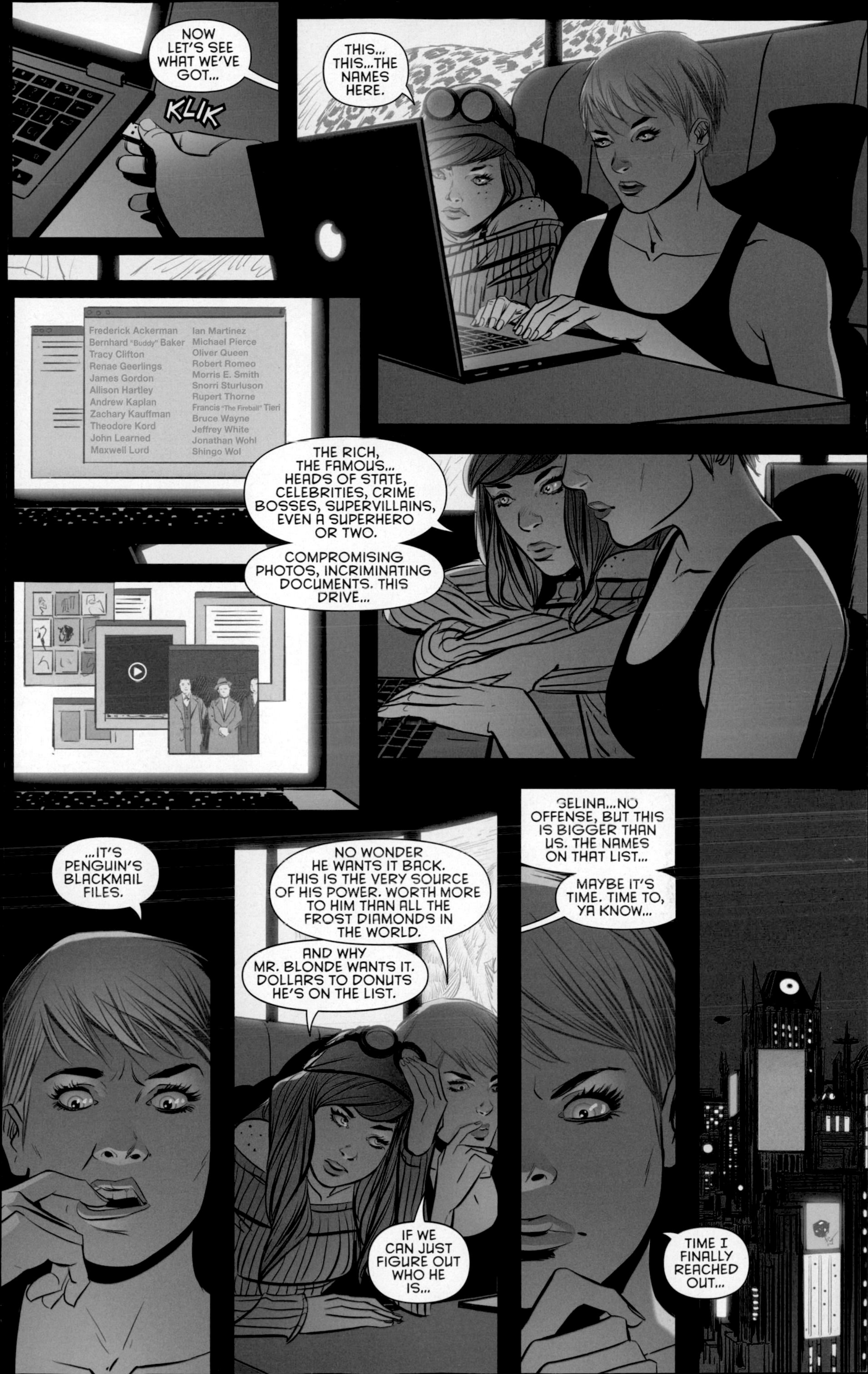

NOW LET'S SEE WHAT WE'VE GOT...
KLIK
THIS... THIS...THE NAMES HERE.
Frederick Ackerman
Bernhard "Buddy" Baker
Tracy Clifton
Renae Geerlings
James Gordon
Allison Hartley
Andrew Kaplan
Zachary Kauffman
Theodore Kord
John Learned
Maxwell Lord
Ian Martinez
Michael Pierce
Oliver Queen
Robert Romeo
Morris E. Smith
Snorri Sturluson
Rupert Thorne
Francis "The Fireball" Tieri
Bruce Wayne
Jeffrey White
Jonathan Wohl
Shingo Wol
THE RICH, THE FAMOUS... HEADS OF STATE, CELEBRITIES, CRIME BOSSES, SUPERVILLAINS, EVEN A SUPERHERO OR TWO.
COMPROMISING PHOTOS, INCRIMINATING DOCUMENTS. THIS DRIVE...
...IT'S PENGUIN'S BLACKMAIL FILES.
NO WONDER HE WANTS IT BACK. THIS IS THE VERY SOURCE OF HIS POWER. WORTH MORE TO HIM THAN ALL THE FROST DIAMONDS IN THE WORLD.
AND WHY MR. BLONDE WANTS IT. DOLLARS TO DONUTS HE'S ON THE LIST.
IF WE CAN JUST FIGURE OUT WHO HE IS...
SELINA...NO OFFENSE, BUT THIS IS BIGGER THAN US. THE NAMES ON THAT LIST...
MAYBE IT'S TIME. TIME TO, YA KNOW...
TIME I FINALLY REACHED OUT...

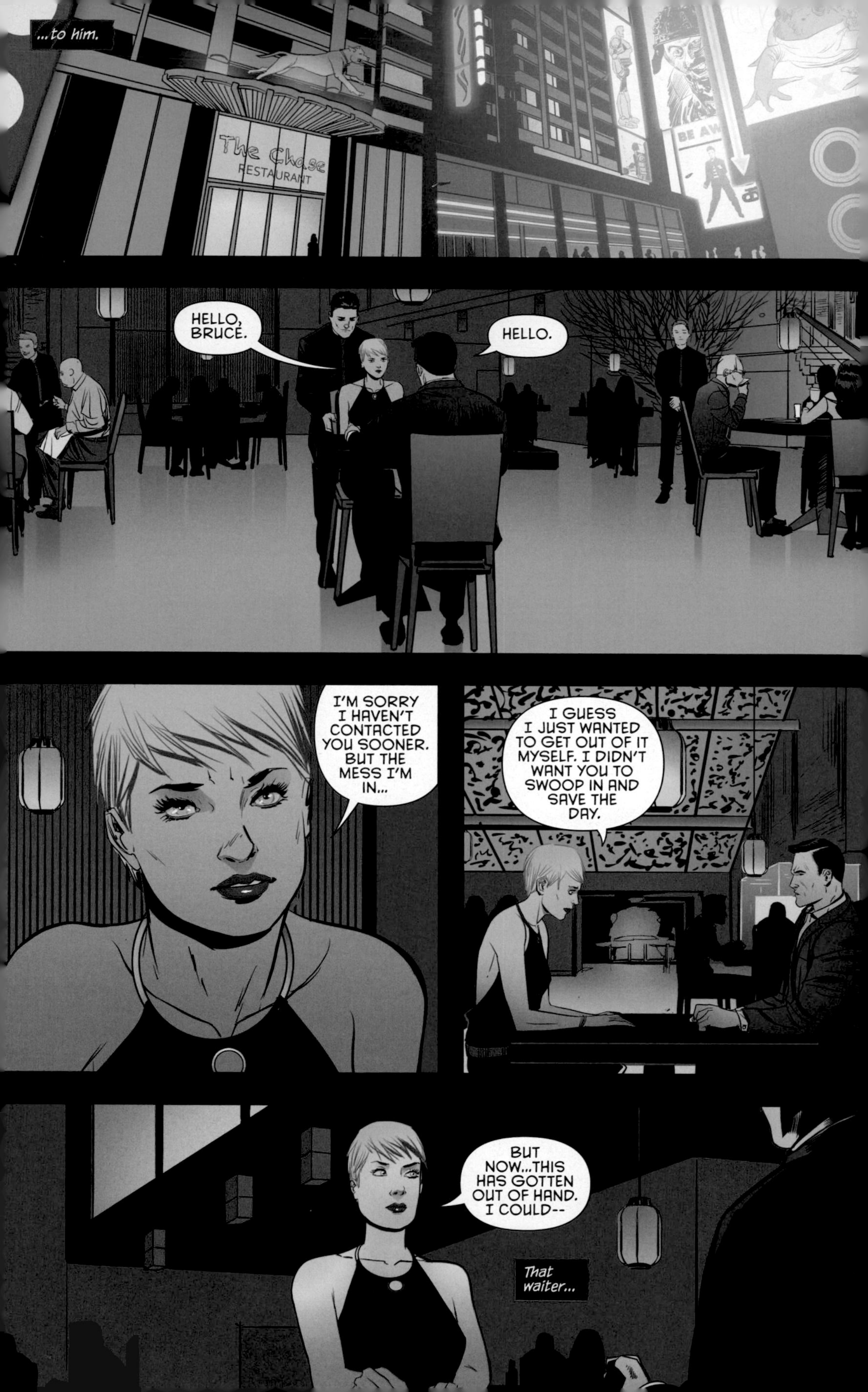
...to him.
The Chase RESTAURANT
HELLO, BRUCE.
HELLO.
I'M SORRY I HAVEN'T CONTACTED YOU SOONER. BUT THE MESS I'M IN...
I GUESS I JUST WANTED TO GET OUT OF IT MYSELF. I DIDN'T WANT YOU TO SWOOP IN AND SAVE THE DAY.
BUT NOW...THIS HAS GOTTEN OUT OF HAND. I COULD--
That waiter...

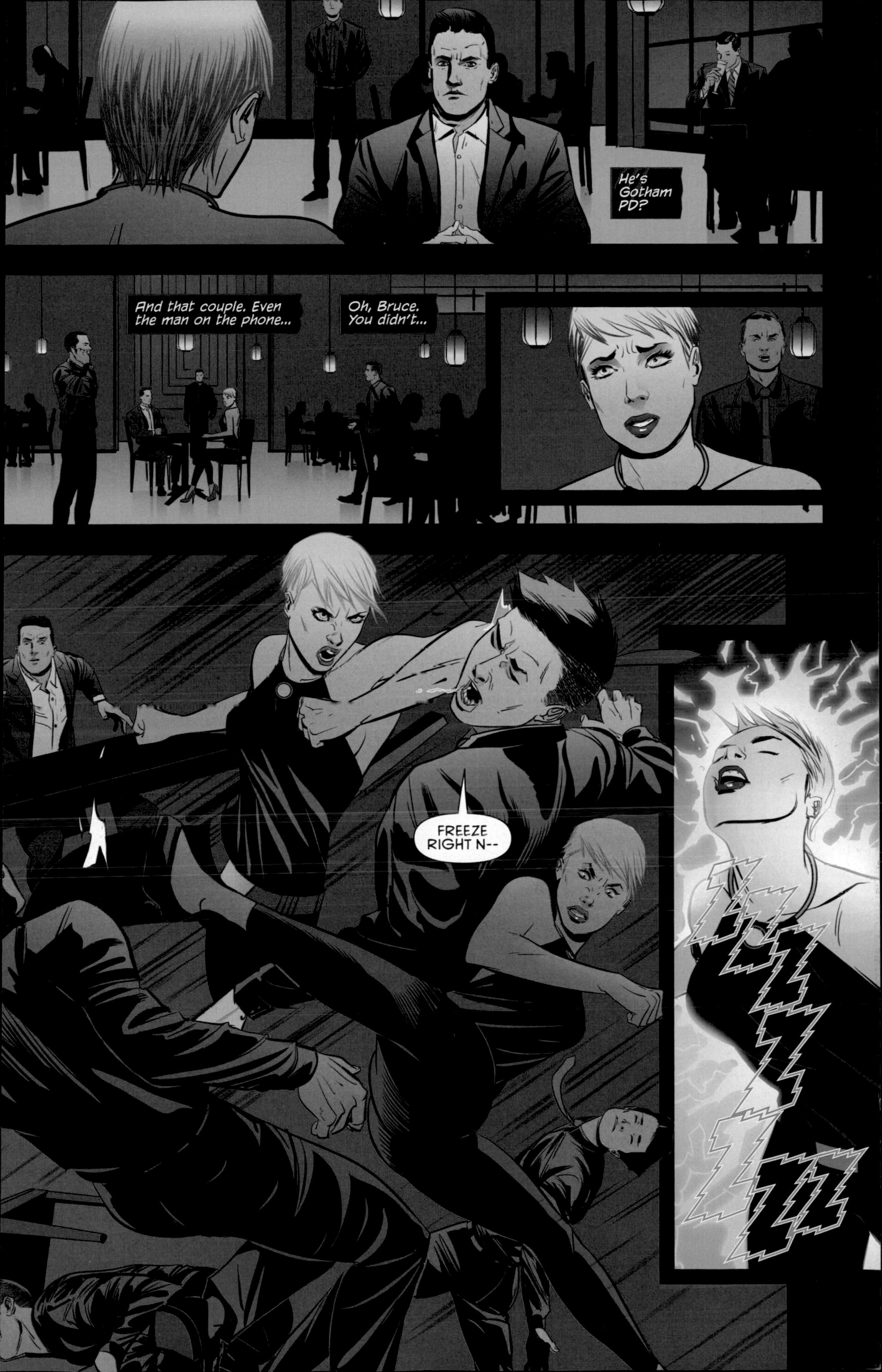
He's Gotham PD?
And that couple. Even the man on the phone...
Oh, Bruce. You didn't...
FREEZE RIGHT N--

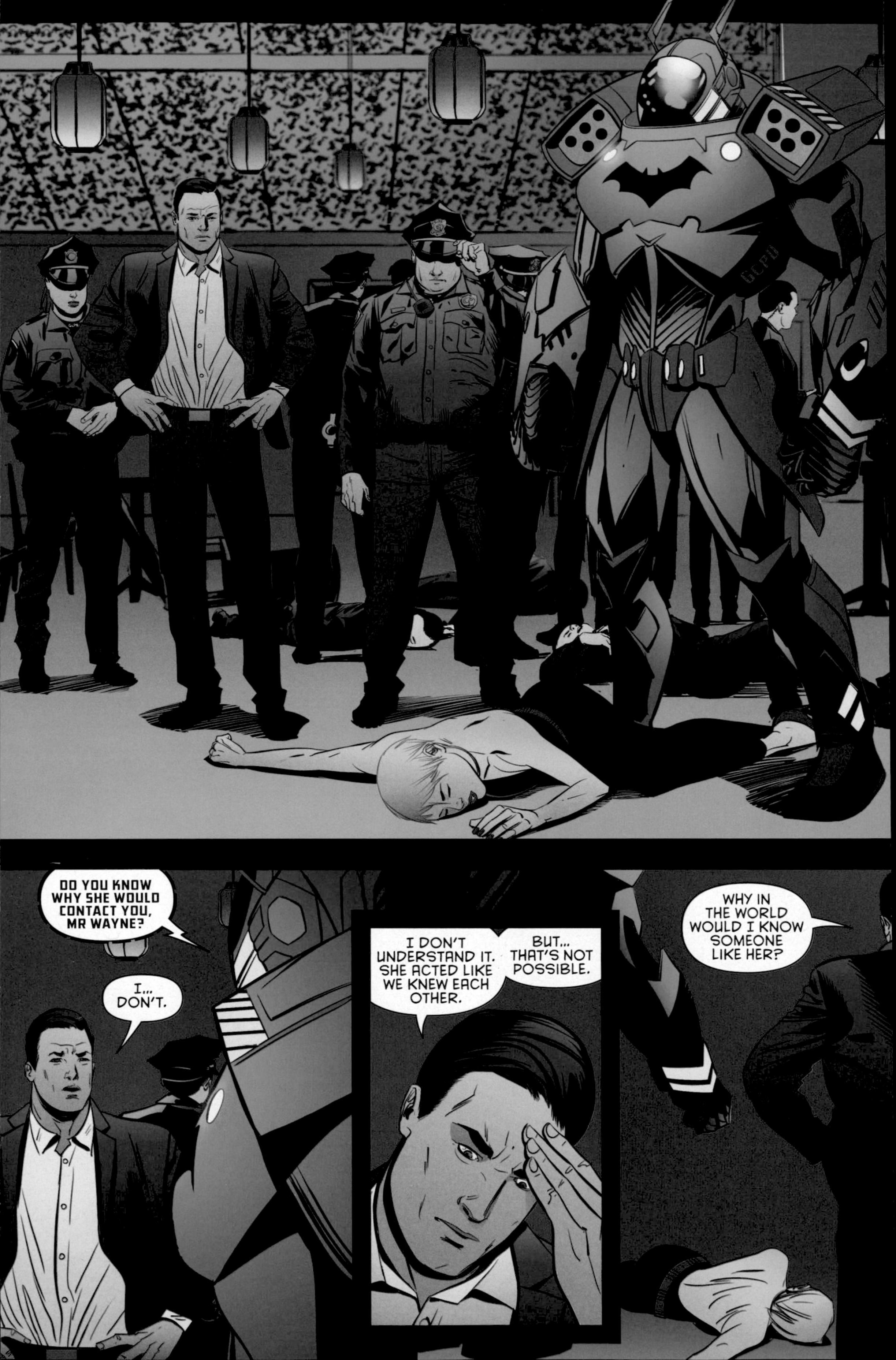
DO YOU KNOW WHY SHE WOULD CONTACT YOU, MR WAYNE?
I... DON'T.
I DON'T UNDERSTAND IT. SHE ACTED LIKE WE KNEW EACH OTHER.
BUT... THAT'S NOT POSSIBLE.
WHY IN THE WORLD WOULD I KNOW SOMEONE LIKE HER?

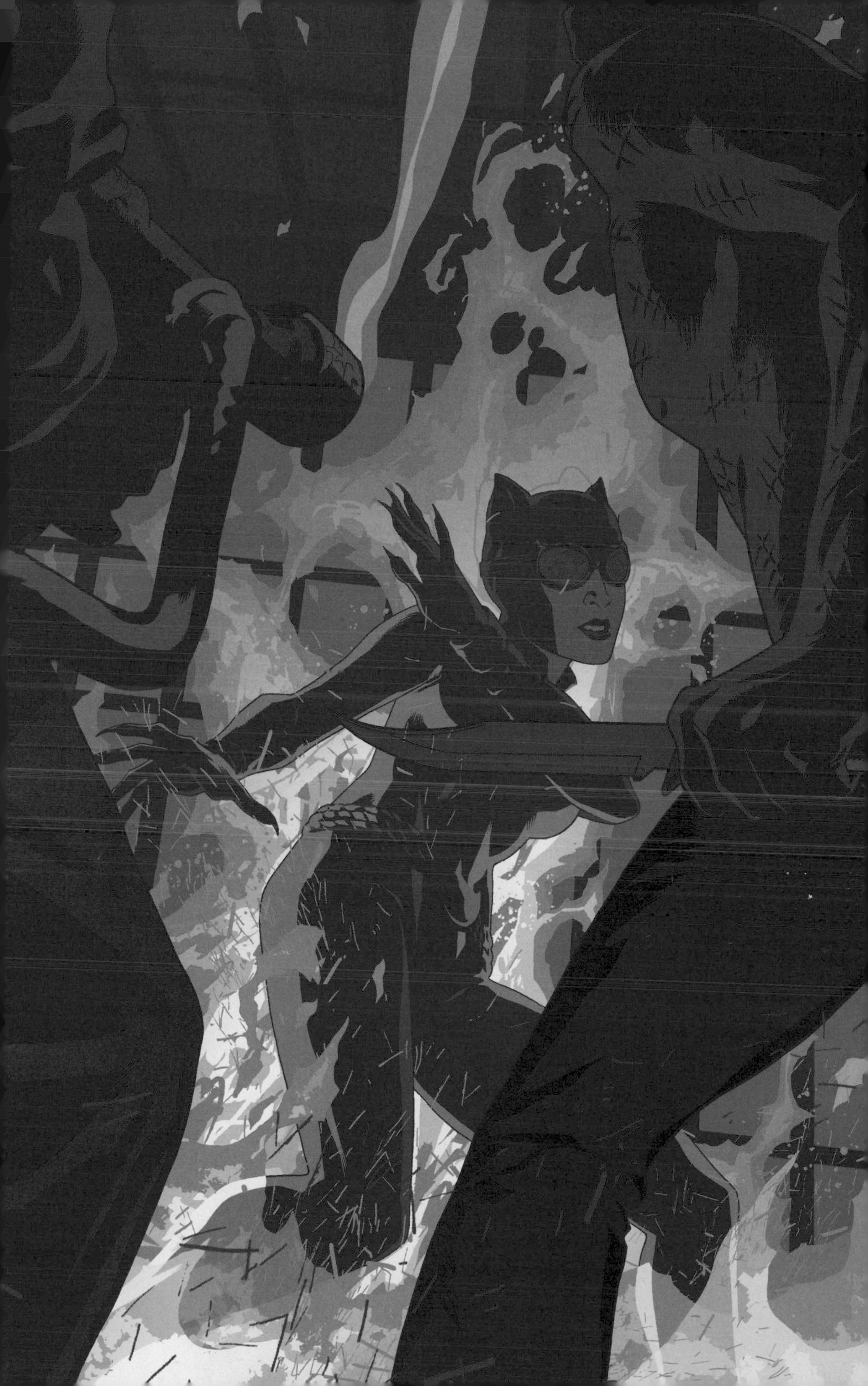

RUN LIKE HELL, PART FOUR
FRANK TIERI writer INAKI MIRANDA & GERALDO BORGES artists EVA DE LA CRUZ & BLOND colorists TRAVIS LANHAM letterer JOSH MIDDLETON cover

NIGHT AT THE MUSEUM
FRANK TIERI writer DAN PANOSIAN & ALEX KONAT pencillers DAN PANOSIAN & JAY LEISTEN inkers BLOND colorist TRAVIS LANHAM letterer

INTRUDER ALERT
FRANK TIERI writer STEVE PUGH artist BLOND colorist TRAVIS LANHAM letterer

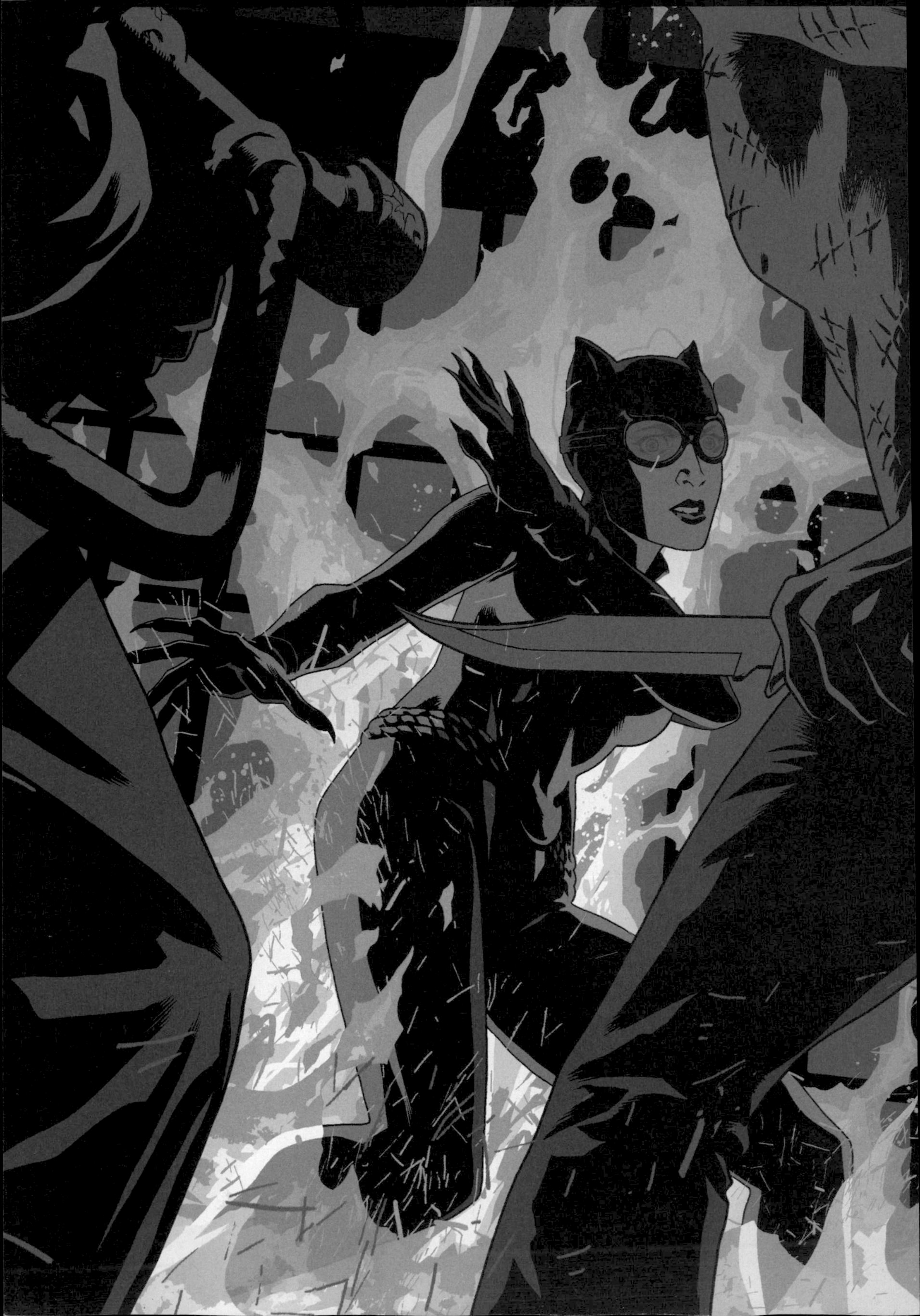

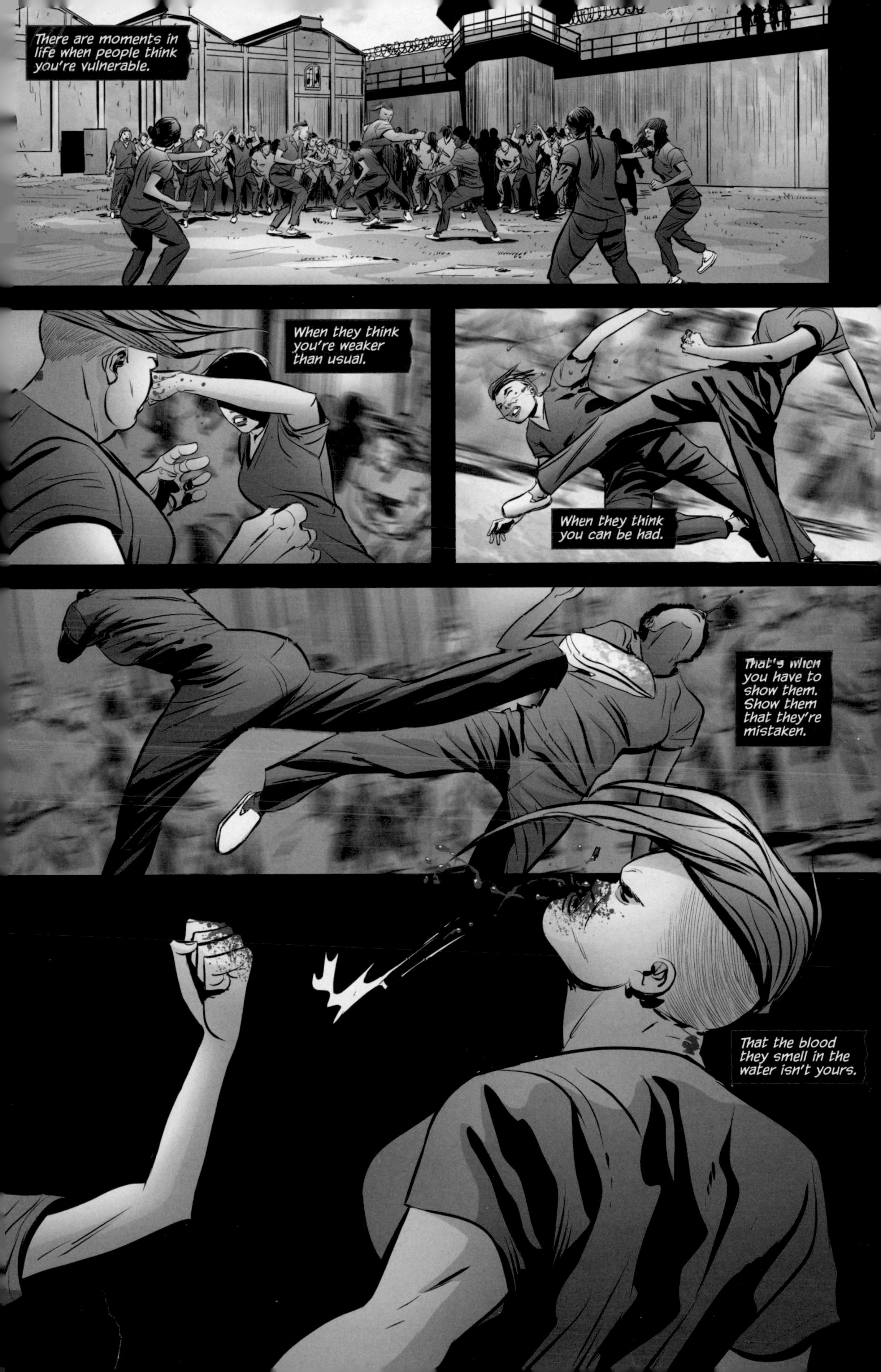
There are moments in life when people think you're vulnerable.
When they think you're weaker than usual.
When they think you can be had.
That's when you have to show them. Show them that they're mistaken.
That the blood they smell in the water isn't yours.

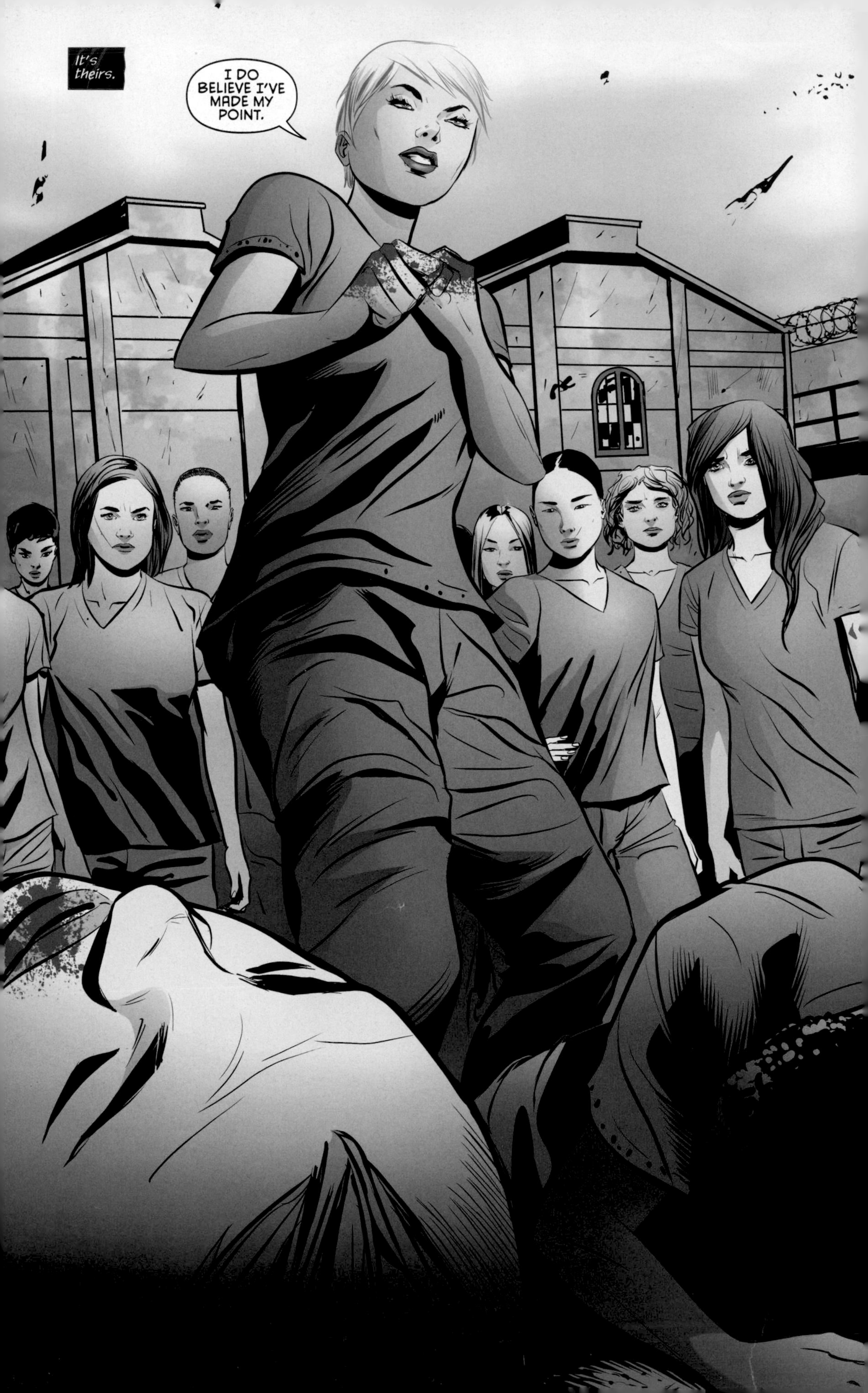
It's theirs.
I DO BELIEVE I'VE MADE MY POINT.

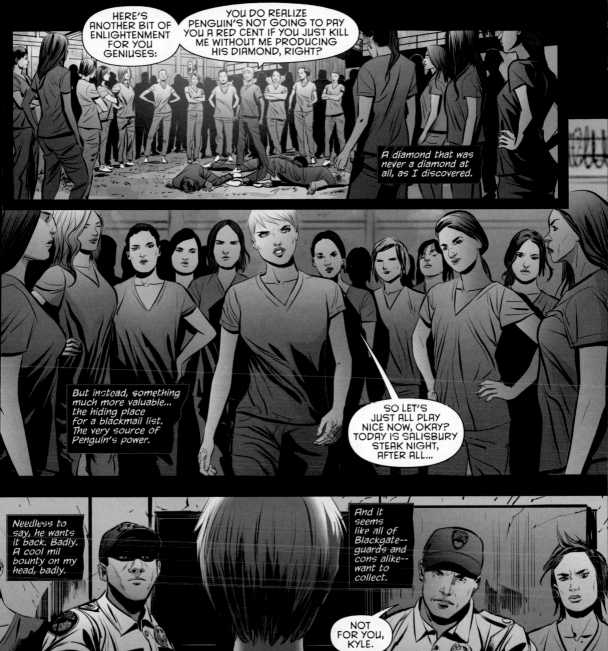

HERE'S ANOTHER BIT OF ENLIGHTENMENT FOR YOU GENIUSES:

YOU DO REALIZE PENGUIN'S NOT GOING TO PAY YOU A RED CENT IF YOU JUST KILL ME WITHOUT ME PRODUCING HIS DIAMOND, RIGHT?

A diamond that was never a diamond at all, as I discovered.

But instead, something much more valuable... the hiding place for a blackmail list. The very source of Penguin's power.

SO LET'S JUST ALL PLAY NICE NOW, OKAY? TODAY IS SALISBURY STEAK NIGHT, AFTER ALL...

Needless to say, he wants it back. Badly. A cool mil bounty on my head, badly.

And it seems like all of Blackgate-- guards and cons alike-- want to collect.

NOT FOR YOU, KYLE.

IT'S THE HOLE FOR YOU.

OH, YOU MEAN THE ONE PLACE IN THIS WHOLE DAMNED CESSPOOL WHERE I'M SAFE FROM CONS AND PAID-OFF GUARDS TRYING TO KILL ME?

OH NO, NO THAT. ANYTHING BUT THAT.

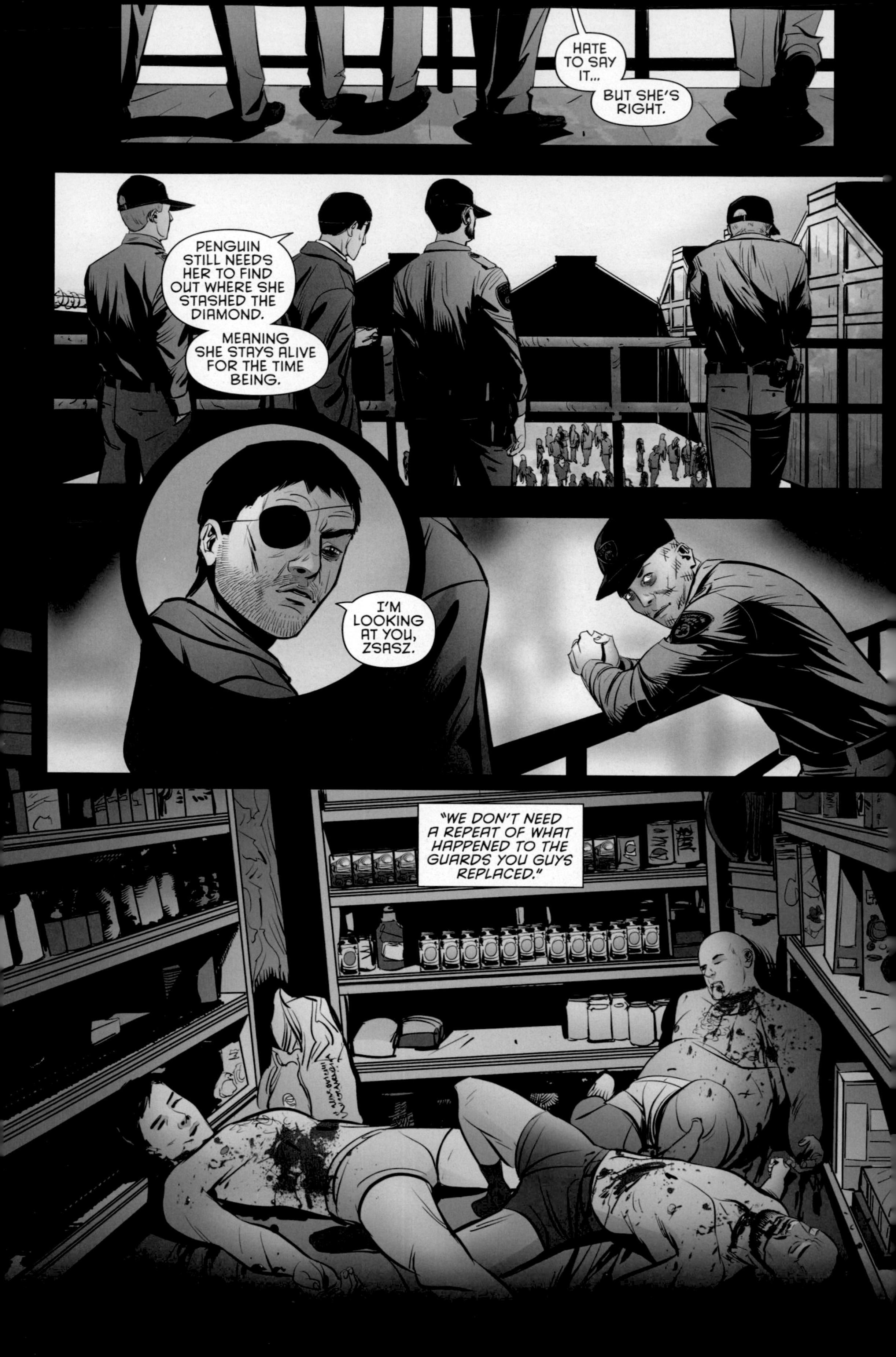
HATE TO SAY IT...
BUT SHE'S RIGHT.
PENGUIN STILL NEEDS HER TO FIND OUT WHERE SHE STASHED THE DIAMOND.
MEANING SHE STAYS ALIVE FOR THE TIME BEING.
I'M LOOKING AT YOU, ZSASZ.
"WE DON'T NEED A REPEAT OF WHAT HAPPENED TO THE GUARDS YOU GUYS REPLACED."

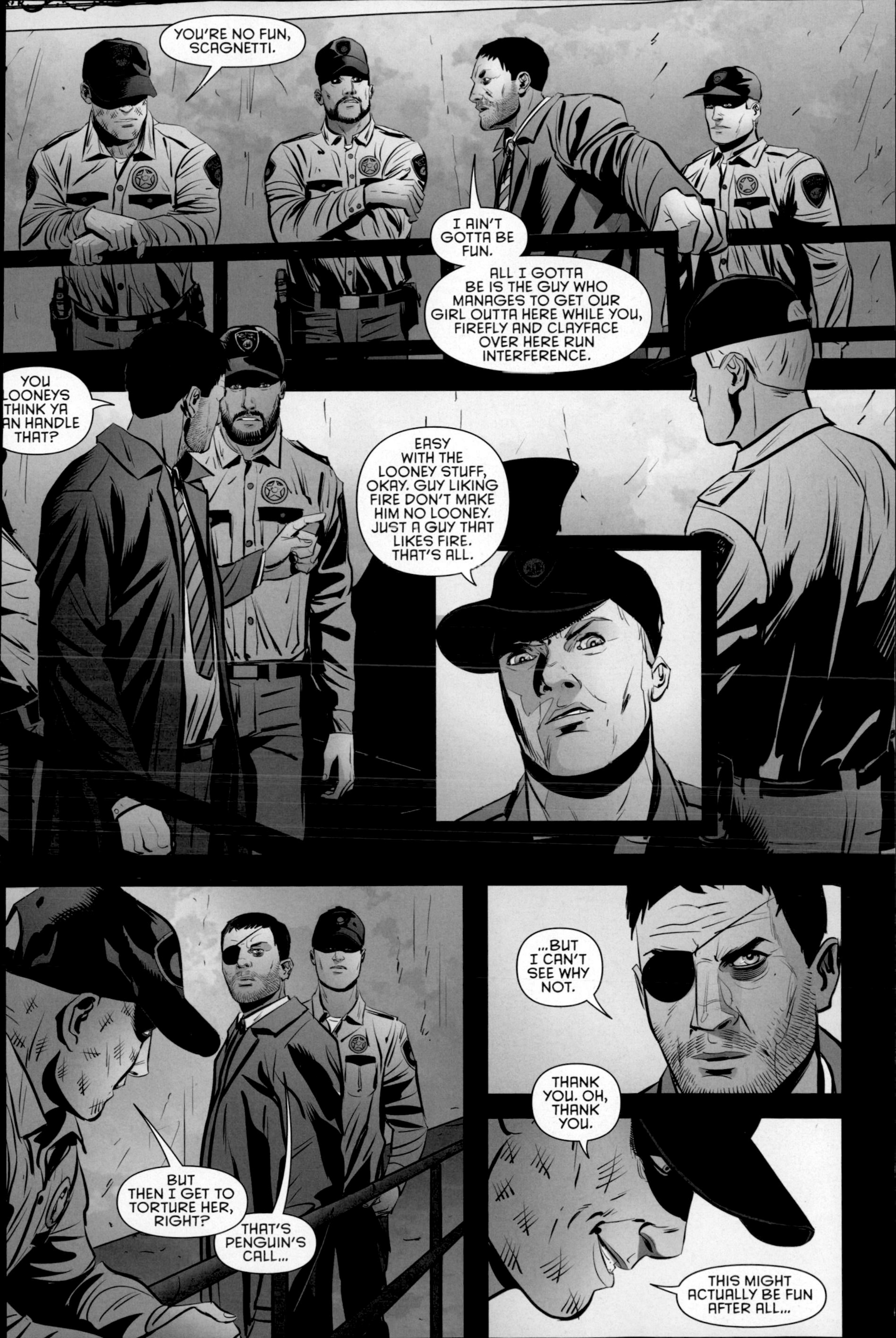
YOU'RE NO FUN, SCAGNETTI.
I AIN'T GOTTA BE FUN.
ALL I GOTTA BE IS THE GUY WHO MANAGES TO GET OUR GIRL OUTTA HERE WHILE YOU, FIREFLY AND CLAYFACE OVER HERE RUN INTERFERENCE.
YOU LOONEYS THINK YA AN HANDLE THAT?
EASY WITH THE LOONEY STUFF, OKAY. GUY LIKING FIRE DON'T MAKE HIM NO LOONEY. JUST A GUY THAT LIKES FIRE. THAT'S ALL.
BUT THEN I GET TO TORTURE HER, RIGHT?
THAT'S PENGUIN'S CALL...
...BUT I CAN'T SEE WHY NOT.
THANK YOU. OH, THANK YOU.
THIS MIGHT ACTUALLY BE FUN AFTER ALL...

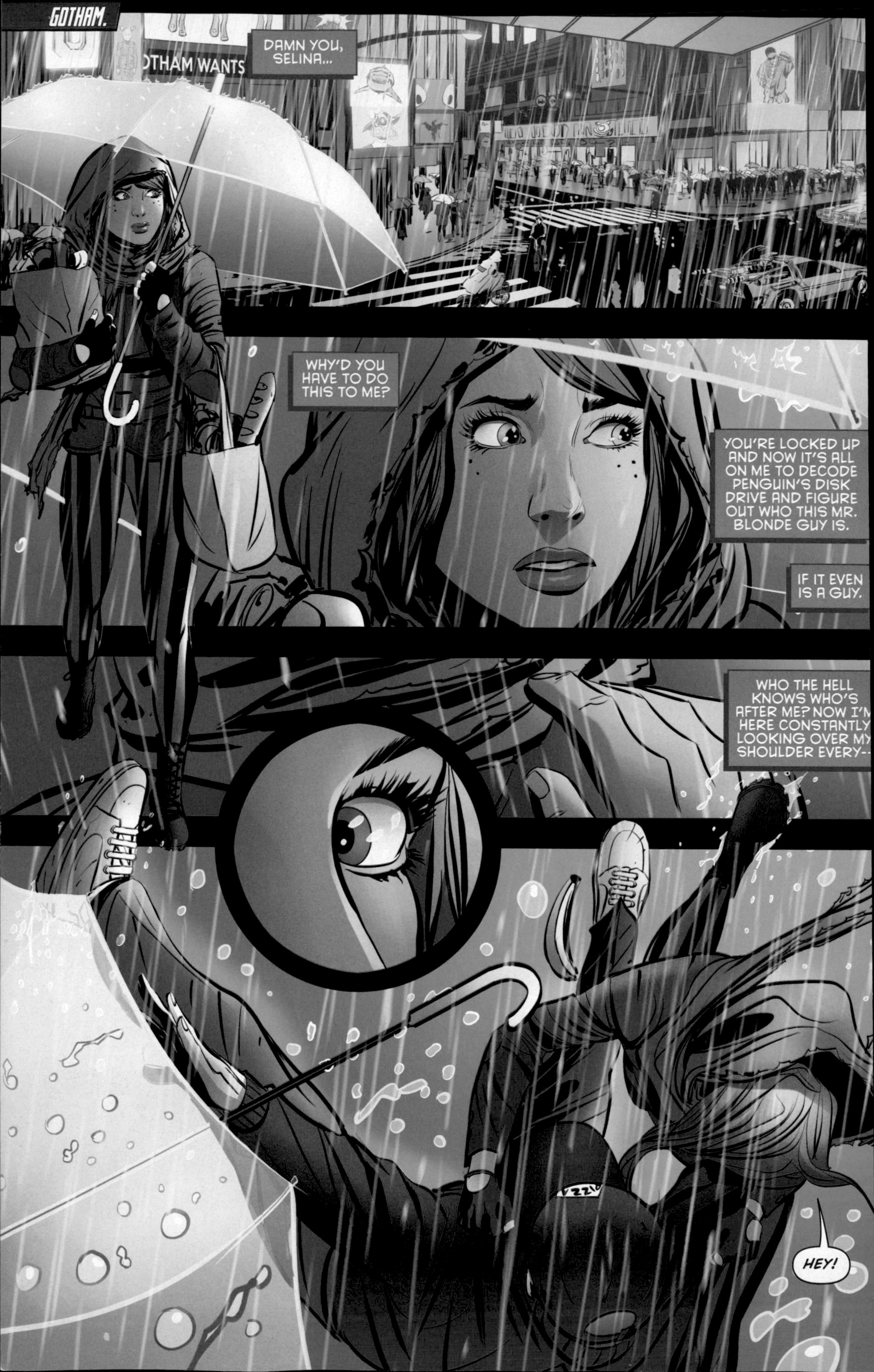
GOTHAM.
OTHAM WANTS
DAMN YOU, SELINA...
WHY'D YOU HAVE TO DO THIS TO ME?
YOU'RE LOCKED UP AND NOW IT'S ALL ON ME TO DECODE PENGUIN'S DISK DRIVE AND FIGURE OUT WHO THIS MR. BLONDE GUY IS.
IF IT EVEN IS A GUY.
WHO THE HELL KNOWS WHO'S AFTER ME? NOW I'M HERE CONSTANTLY LOOKING OVER MY SHOULDER EVERY--
HEY!

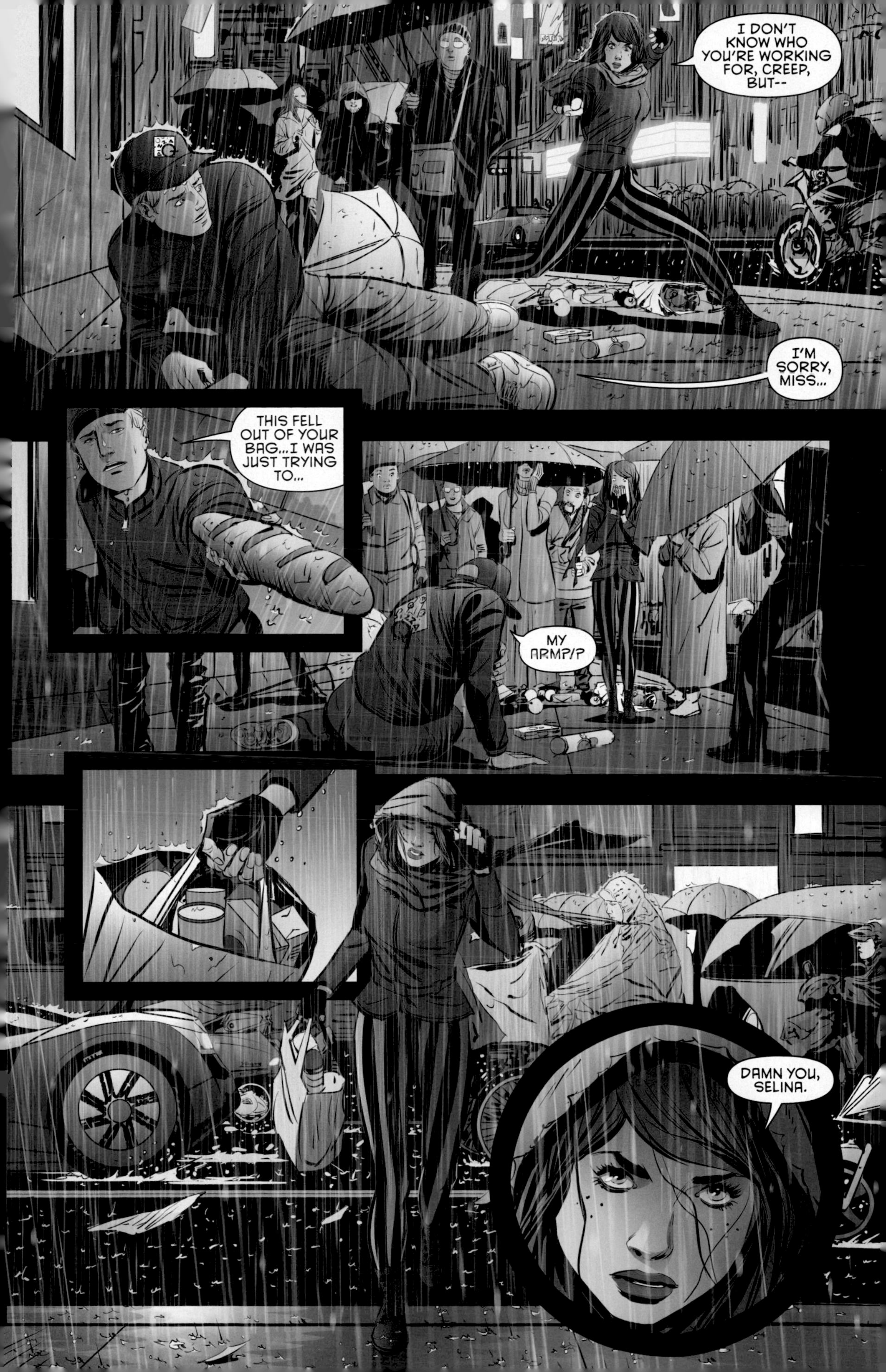
I DON'T KNOW WHO YOU'RE WORKING FOR, CREEP, BUT--
I'M SORRY, MISS...
THIS FELL OUT OF YOUR BAG...I WAS JUST TRYING TO...
MY ARM?!?
DAMN YOU, SELINA.

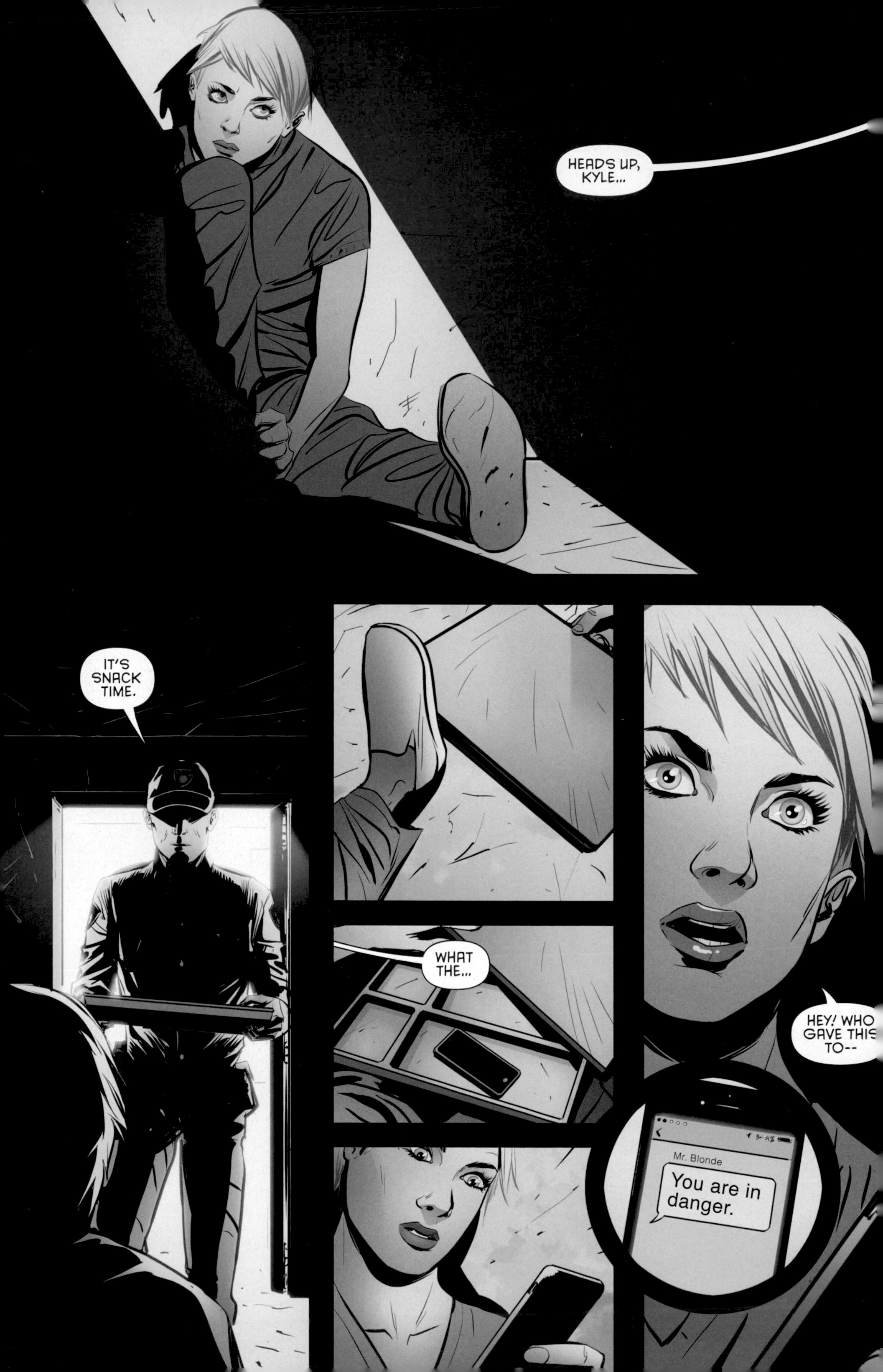
HEADS UP, KYLE...
IT'S SNACK TIME.
WHAT THE...
HEY! WHO GAVE THIS TO--
Mr. Blonde
You are in danger.

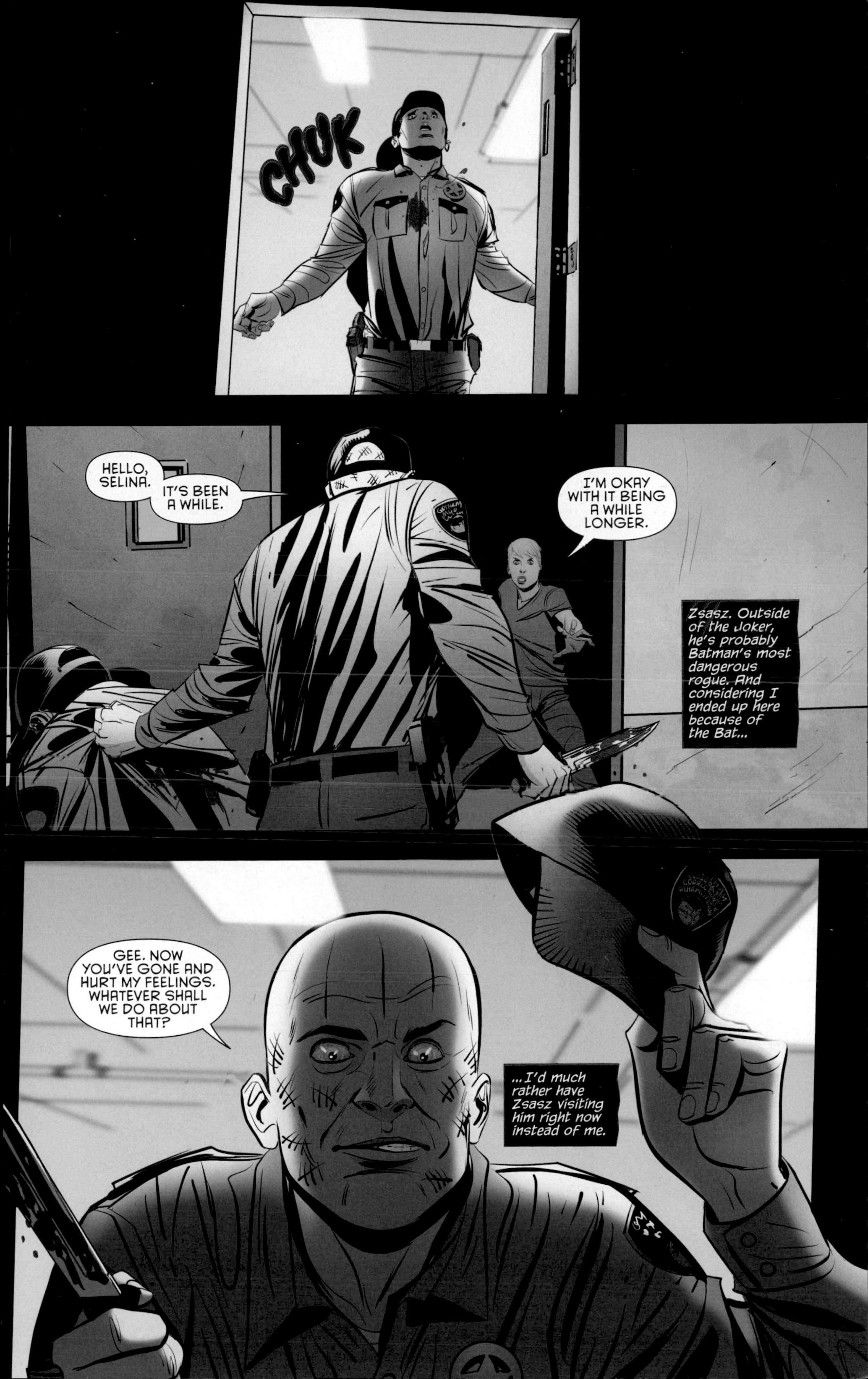
CHUK
HELLO, SELINA.
IT'S BEEN A WHILE.
I'M OKAY WITH IT BEING A WHILE LONGER.
Zsasz. Outside of the Joker, he's probably Batman's most dangerous rogue. And considering I ended up here because of the Bat...
GEE. NOW YOU'VE GONE AND HURT MY FEELINGS. WHATEVER SHALL WE DO ABOUT THAT?
...I'd much rather have Zsasz visiting him right now instead of me.

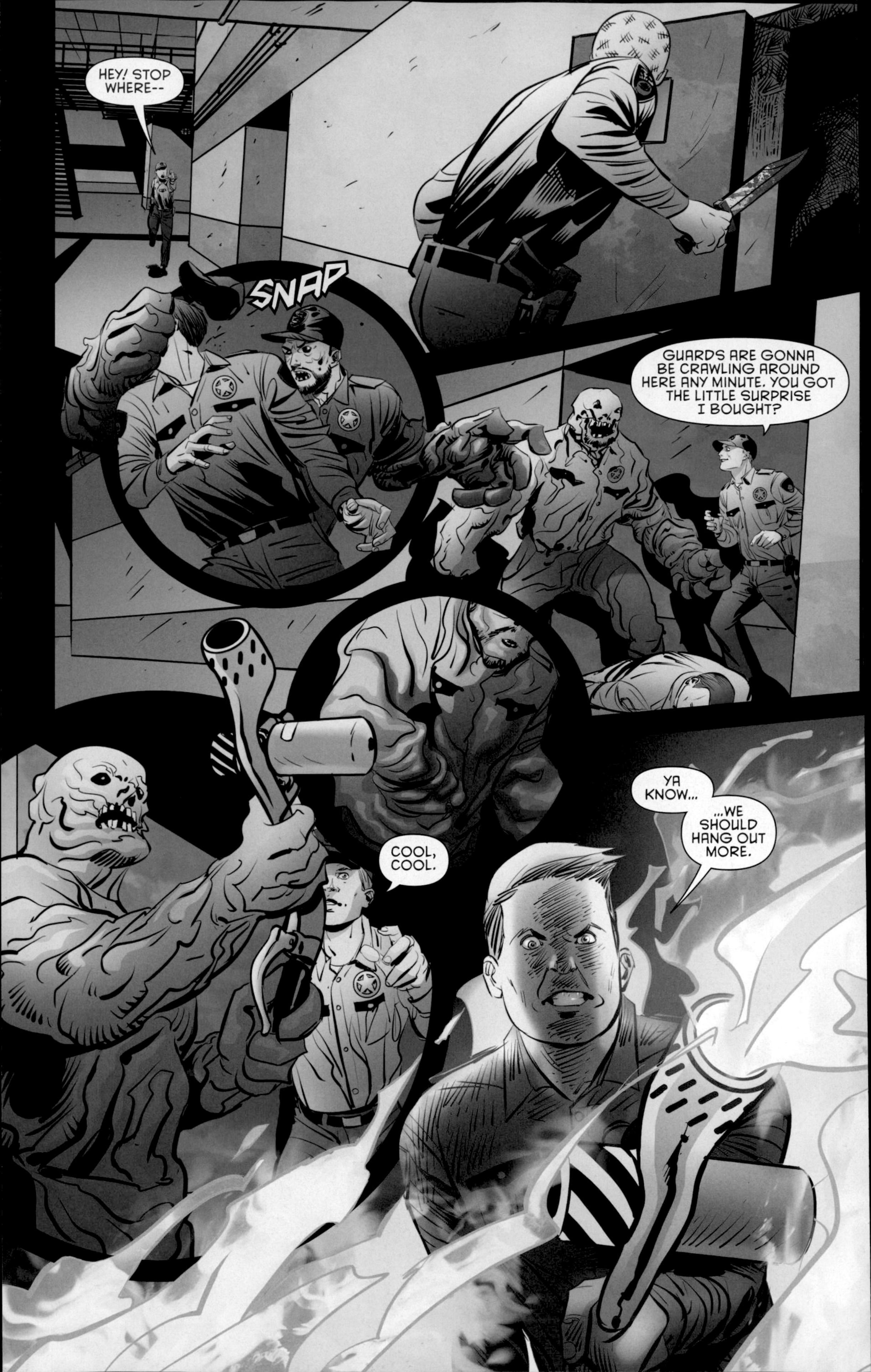
HEY! STOP WHERE--
SNAP
GUARDS ARE GONNA BE CRAWLING AROUND HERE ANY MINUTE. YOU GOT THE LITTLE SURPRISE I BOUGHT?
COOL, COOL.
YA KNOW...
...WE SHOULD HANG OUT MORE.

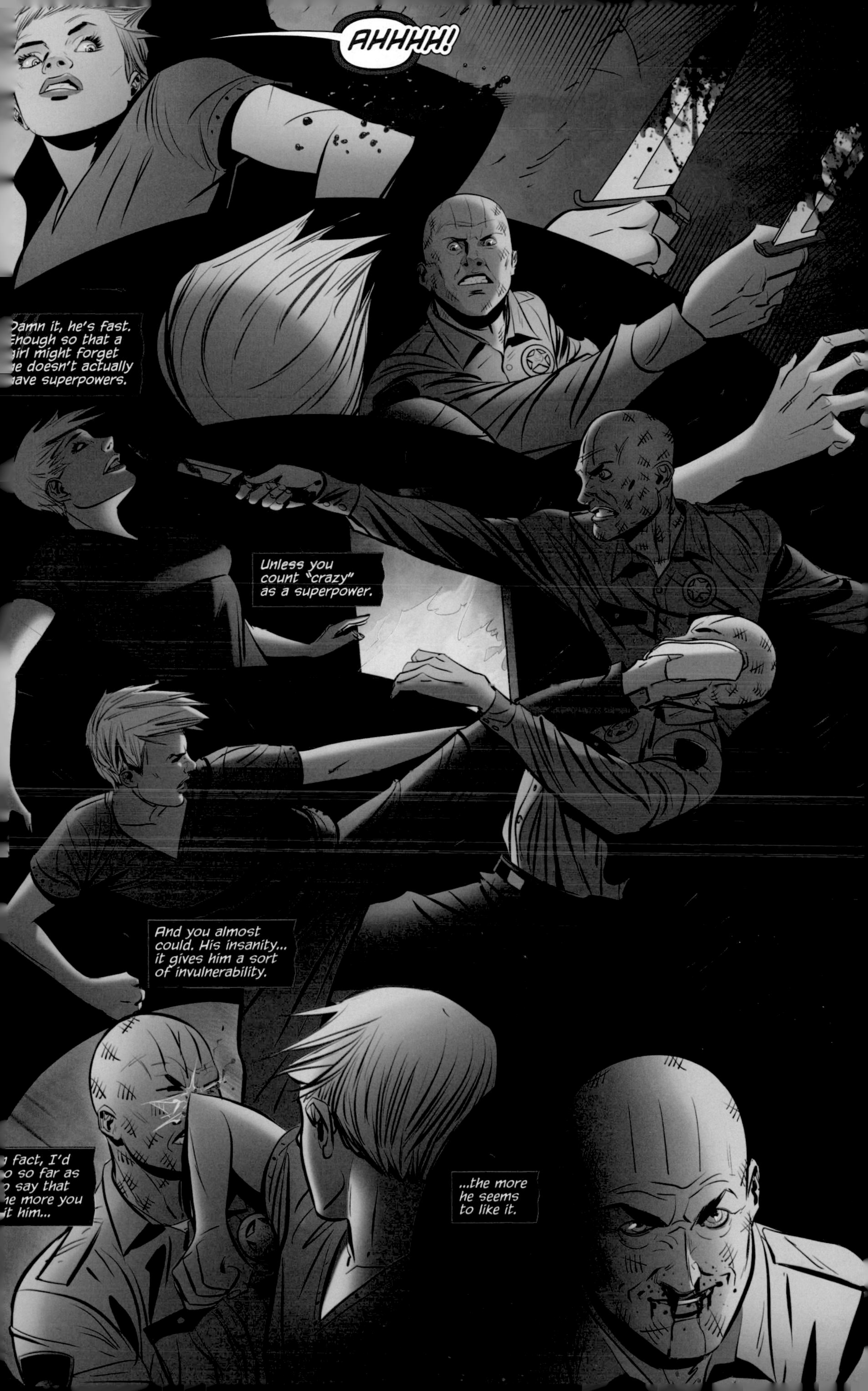
AHHHH!
Damn it, he's fast. Enough so that a girl might forget he doesn't actually have superpowers.
Unless you count "crazy" as a superpower.
And you almost could. His insanity... it gives him a sort of invulnerability.
fact, I'd o so far as o say that e more you it him...
...the more he seems to like it.

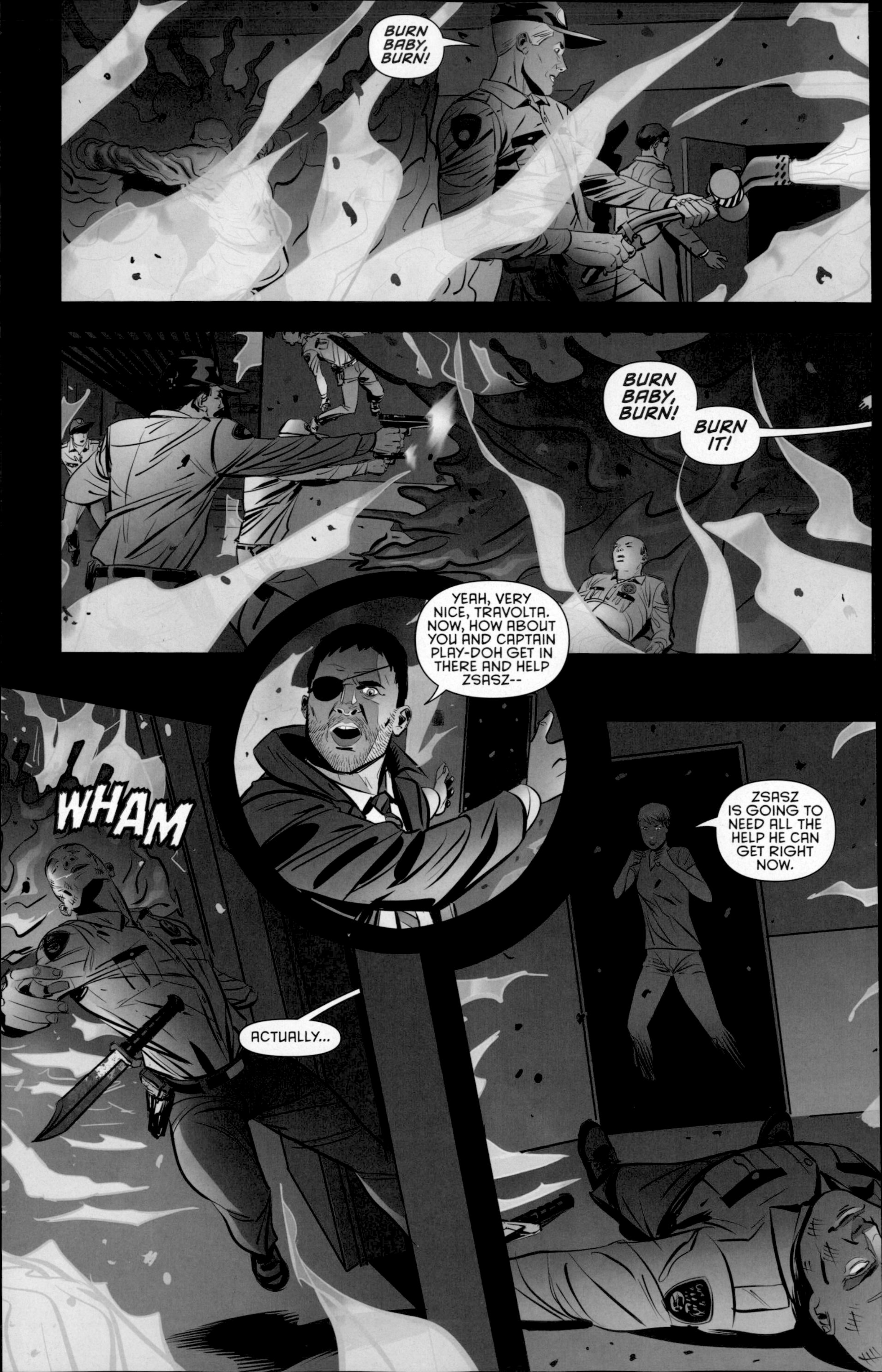
BURN BABY, BURN!
BURN BABY, BURN!
BURN IT!
YEAH, VERY NICE, TRAVOLTA. NOW, HOW ABOUT YOU AND CAPTAIN PLAY-DOH GET IN THERE AND HELP ZSASZ--
WHAM
ZSASZ IS GOING TO NEED ALL THE HELP HE CAN GET RIGHT NOW.
ACTUALLY...

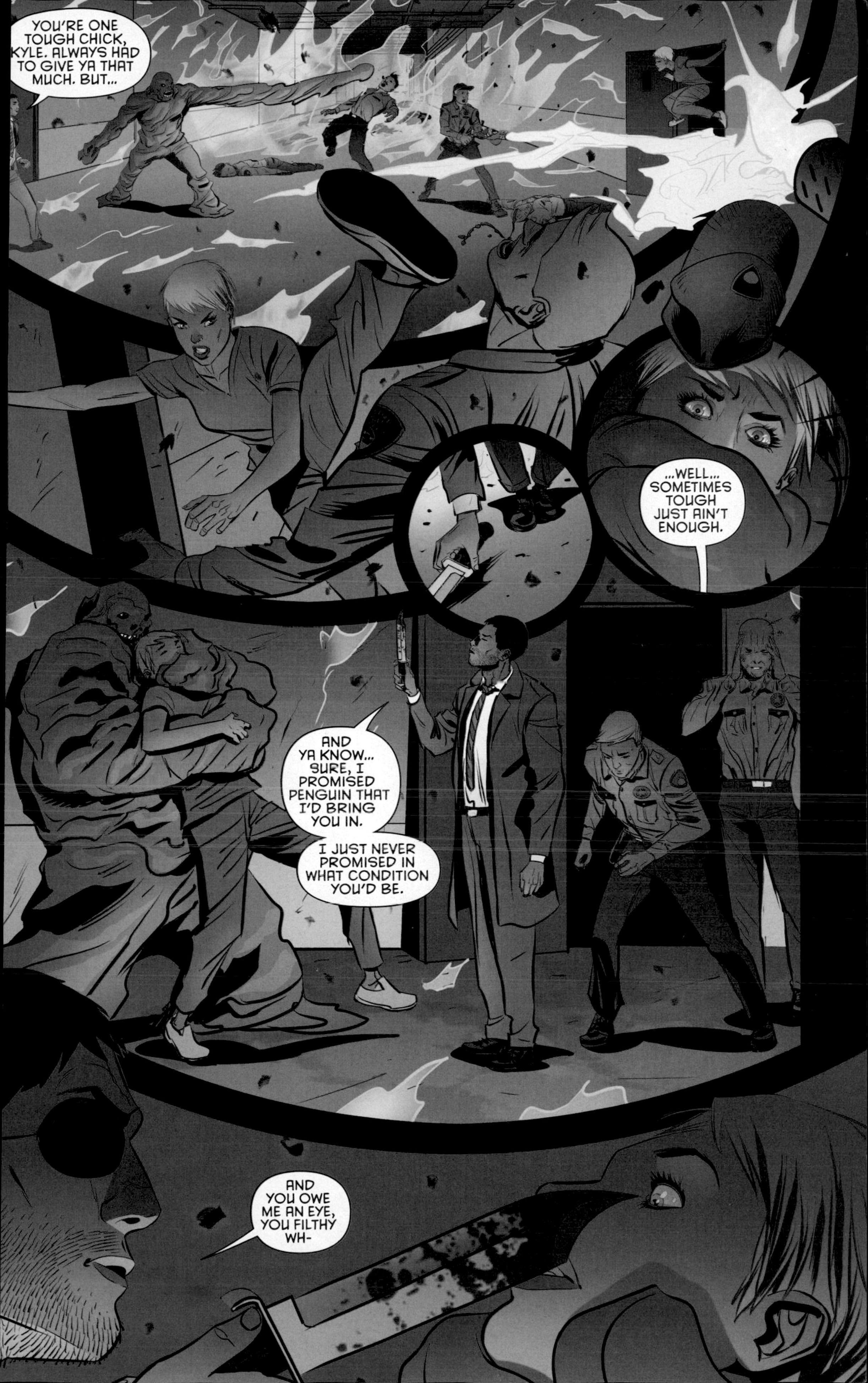
YOU'RE ONE TOUGH CHICK, KYLE. ALWAYS HAD TO GIVE YA THAT MUCH. BUT...
...WELL... SOMETIMES TOUGH JUST AIN'T ENOUGH.
AND YA KNOW... SURE, I PROMISED PENGUIN THAT I'D BRING YOU IN.
I JUST NEVER PROMISED IN WHAT CONDITION YOU'D BE.
AND YOU OWE ME AN EYE, YOU FILTHY WH-

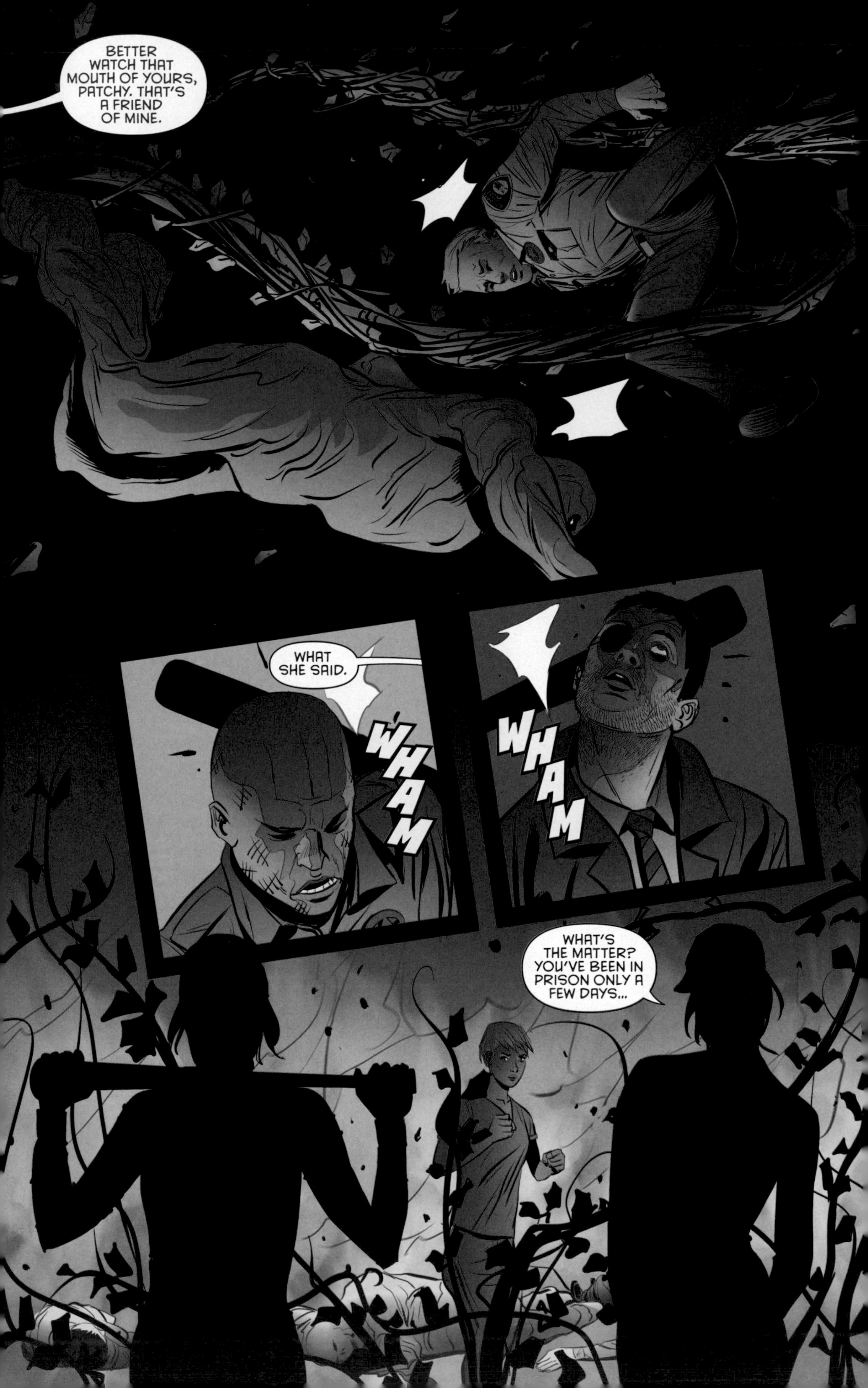
BETTER WATCH THAT MOUTH OF YOURS, PATCHY. THAT'S A FRIEND OF MINE.
WHAT SHE SAID.
WHAM
WHAM
WHAT'S THE MATTER? YOU'VE BEEN IN PRISON ONLY A FEW DAYS...

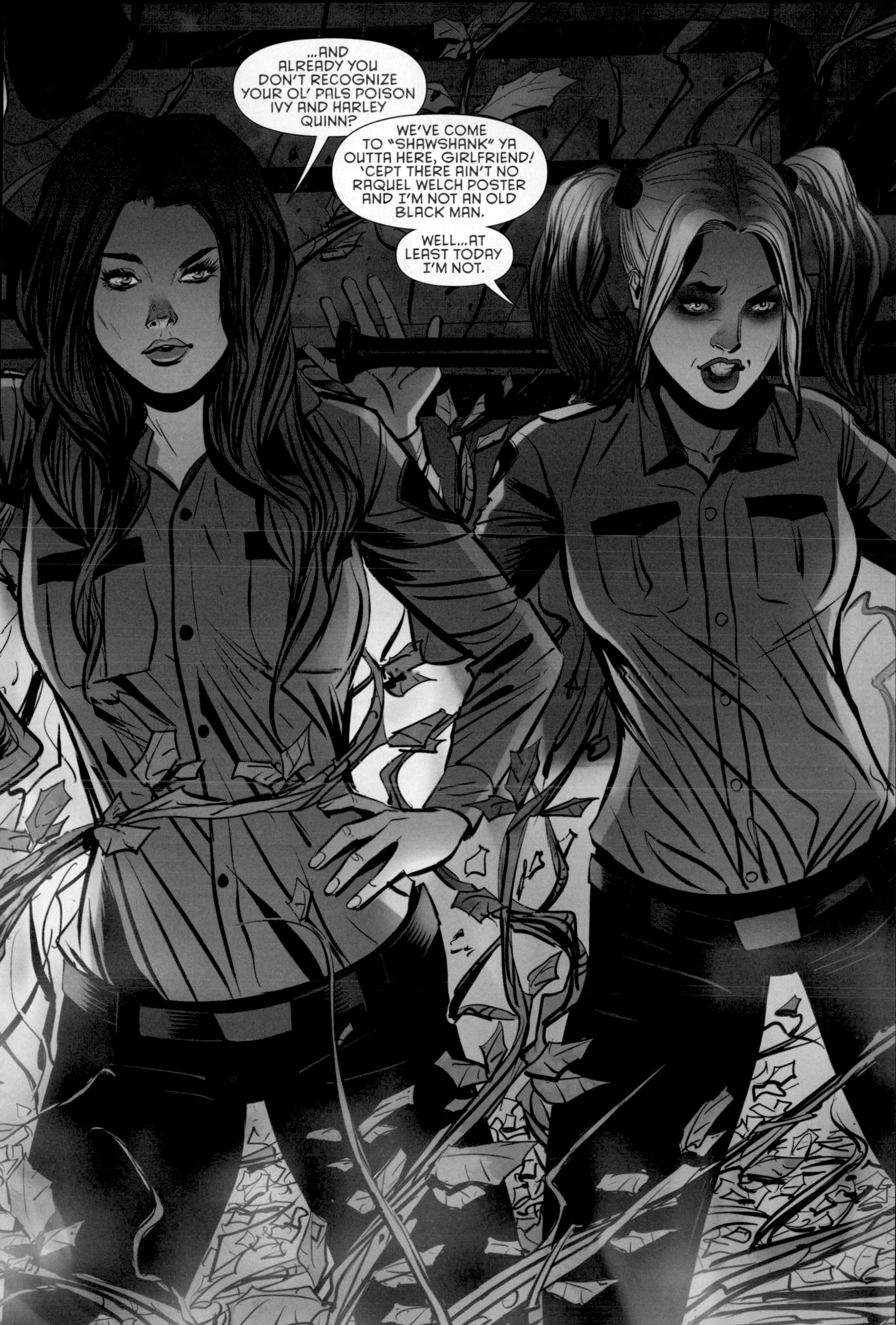
...AND ALREADY YOU DON'T RECOGNIZE YOUR OL' PALS POISON IVY AND HARLEY QUINN?
WE'VE COME TO "SHAWSHANK" YA OUTTA HERE, GIRLFRIEND! 'CEPT THERE AIN'T NO RAQUEL WELCH POSTER AND I'M NOT AN OLD BLACK MAN.
WELL...AT LEAST TODAY I'M NOT.

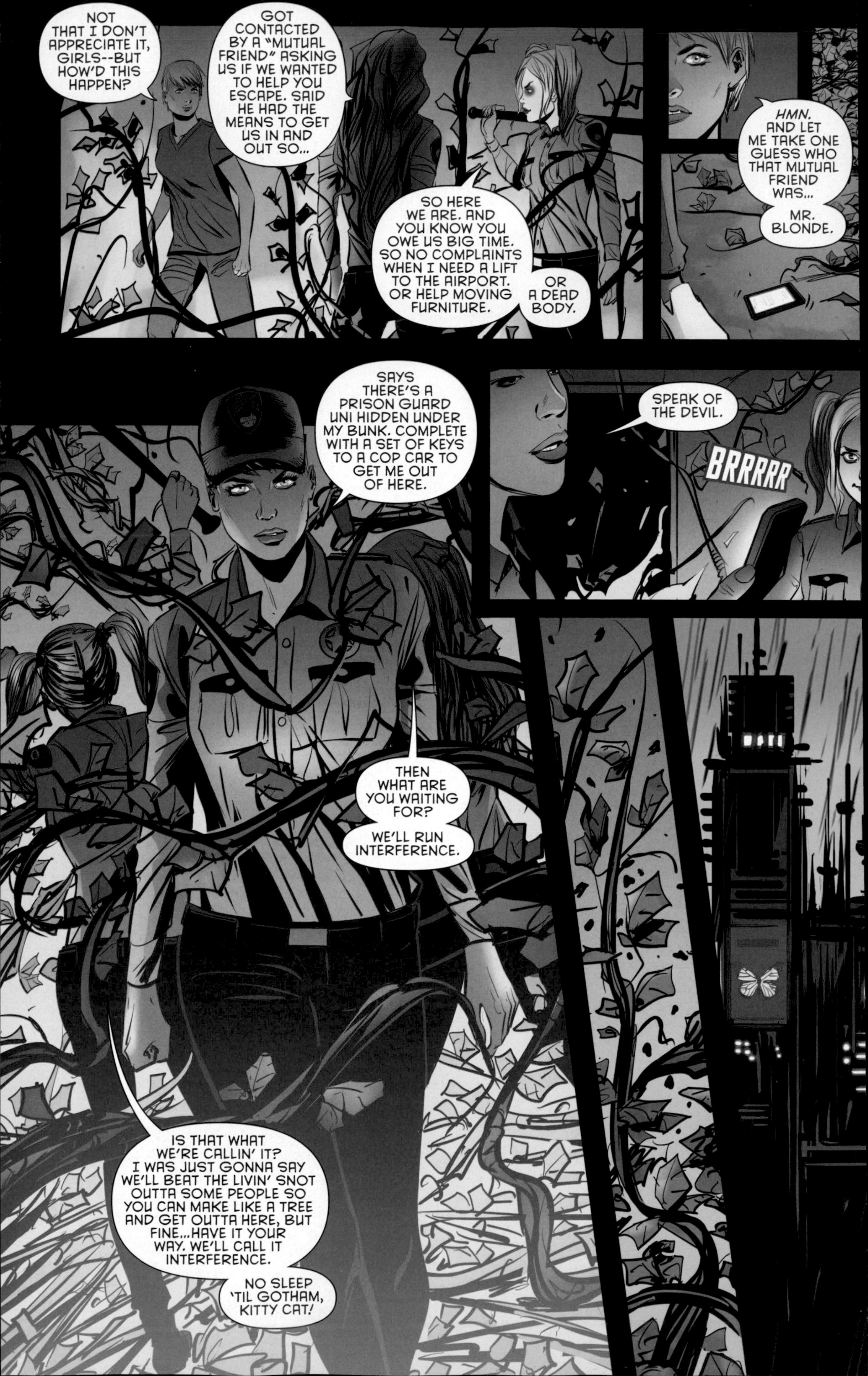
NOT THAT I DON'T APPRECIATE IT, GIRLS--BUT HOW'D THIS HAPPEN?
GOT CONTACTED BY A "MUTUAL FRIEND" ASKING US IF WE WANTED TO HELP YOU ESCAPE. SAID HE HAD THE MEANS TO GET US IN AND OUT SO...
SO HERE WE ARE. AND YOU KNOW YOU OWE US BIG TIME. SO NO COMPLAINTS WHEN I NEED A LIFT TO THE AIRPORT. OR HELP MOVING FURNITURE.
OR A DEAD BODY.
HMN. AND LET ME TAKE ONE GUESS WHO THAT MUTUAL FRIEND WAS...
MR. BLONDE.
SAYS THERE'S A PRISON GUARD UNI HIDDEN UNDER MY BUNK. COMPLETE WITH A SET OF KEYS TO A COP CAR TO GET ME OUT OF HERE.
SPEAK OF THE DEVIL.
BRRRRR
THEN WHAT ARE YOU WAITING FOR?
WE'LL RUN INTERFERENCE.
IS THAT WHAT WE'RE CALLIN' IT? I WAS JUST GONNA SAY WE'LL BEAT THE LIVIN' SNOT OUTTA SOME PEOPLE SO YOU CAN MAKE LIKE A TREE AND GET OUTTA HERE, BUT FINE...HAVE IT YOUR WAY. WE'LL CALL IT INTERFERENCE.
NO SLEEP 'TIL GOTHAM, KITTY CAT!

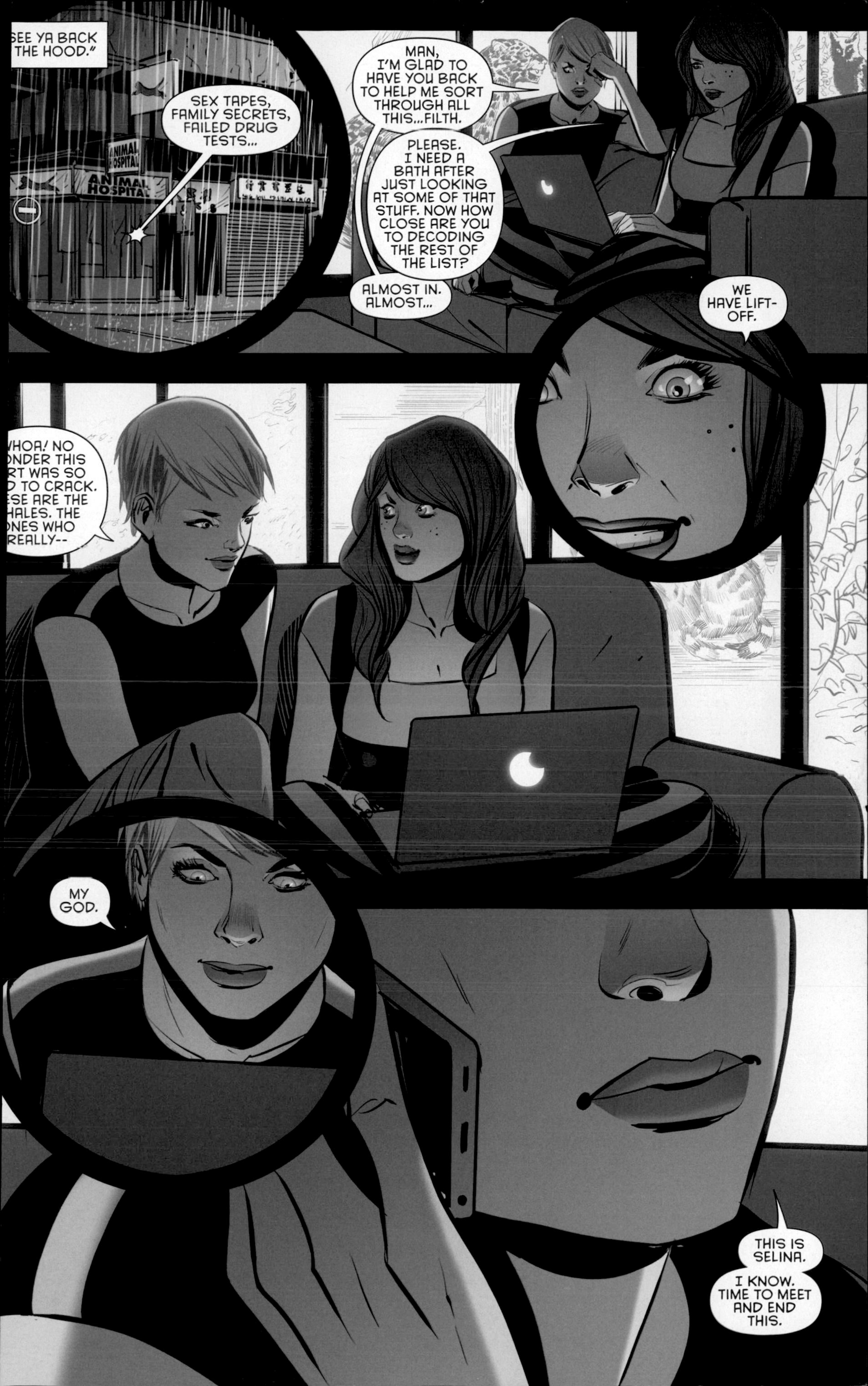

SEE YA BACK
THE HOOD."
SEX TAPES, FAMILY SECRETS, FAILED DRUG TESTS...
ANIMAL HOSPITAL
ANIMAL HOSPITAL
MAN, I'M GLAD TO HAVE YOU BACK TO HELP ME SORT THROUGH ALL THIS...FILTH.
PLEASE. I NEED A BATH AFTER JUST LOOKING AT SOME OF THAT STUFF. NOW HOW CLOSE ARE YOU TO DECODING THE REST OF THE LIST?
ALMOST IN. ALMOST...
WE HAVE LIFT-OFF.
MY GOD.
THIS IS SELINA.
I KNOW. TIME TO MEET AND END THIS.

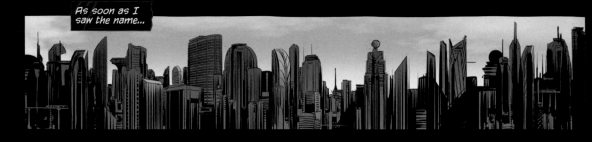

As soon as I saw the name...

I knew.

Hell, it might as well have been in flashing neon lights, it was so clear who it was.

Still...I don't like that it's him.

Considering he may in fact be the most dangerous man I've ever met.

In fact, on some level I'm even impressed Penguin would have the stones to go after him.

DECIDED YET, MISS?

YES...I'LL BE TAKING THE MOST EXPENSIVE BOTTLE OF CHAMPAGNE YOU HAVE.

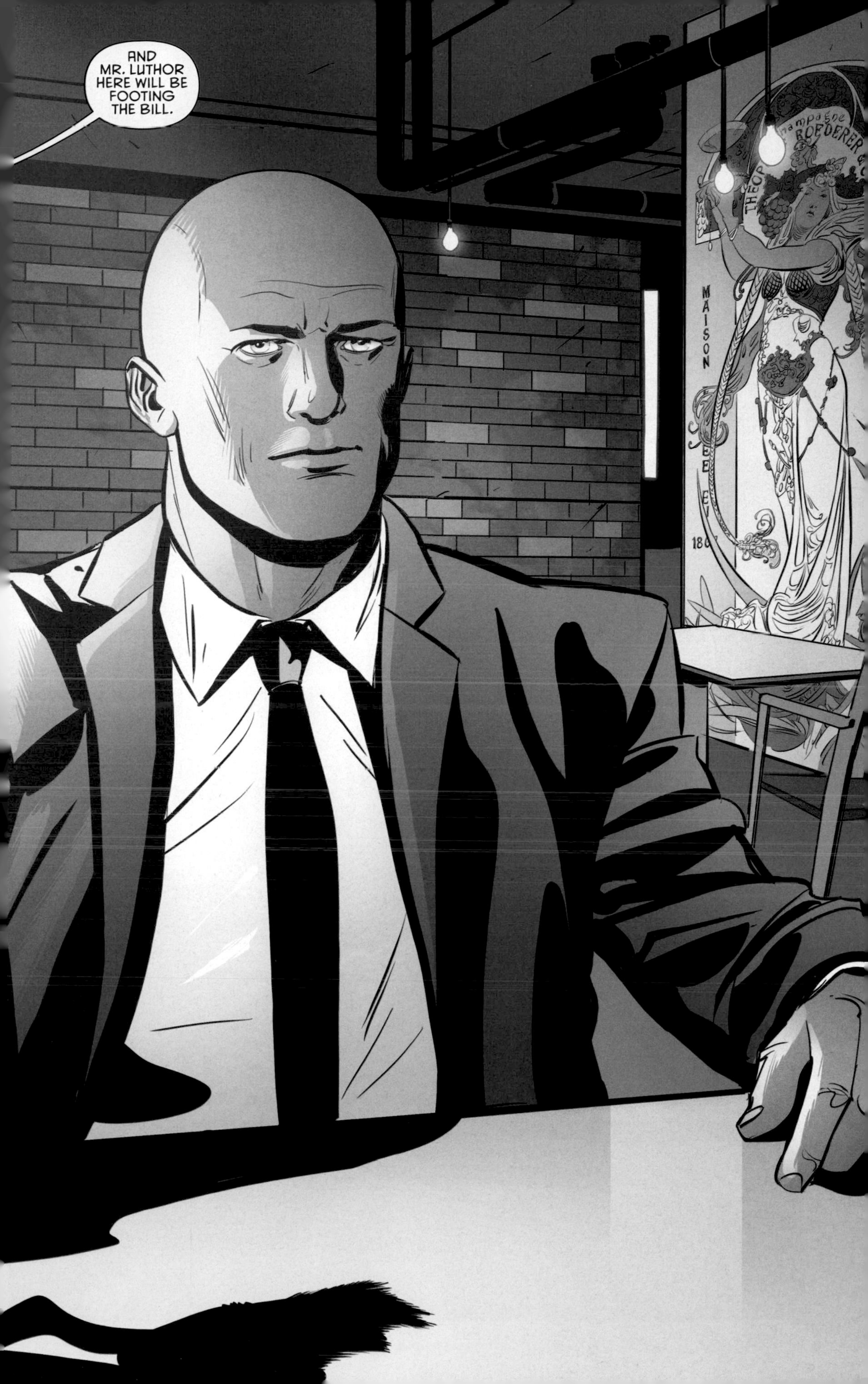
AND MR. LUTHOR HERE WILL BE FOOTING THE BILL.
ROEDERER
MAISON

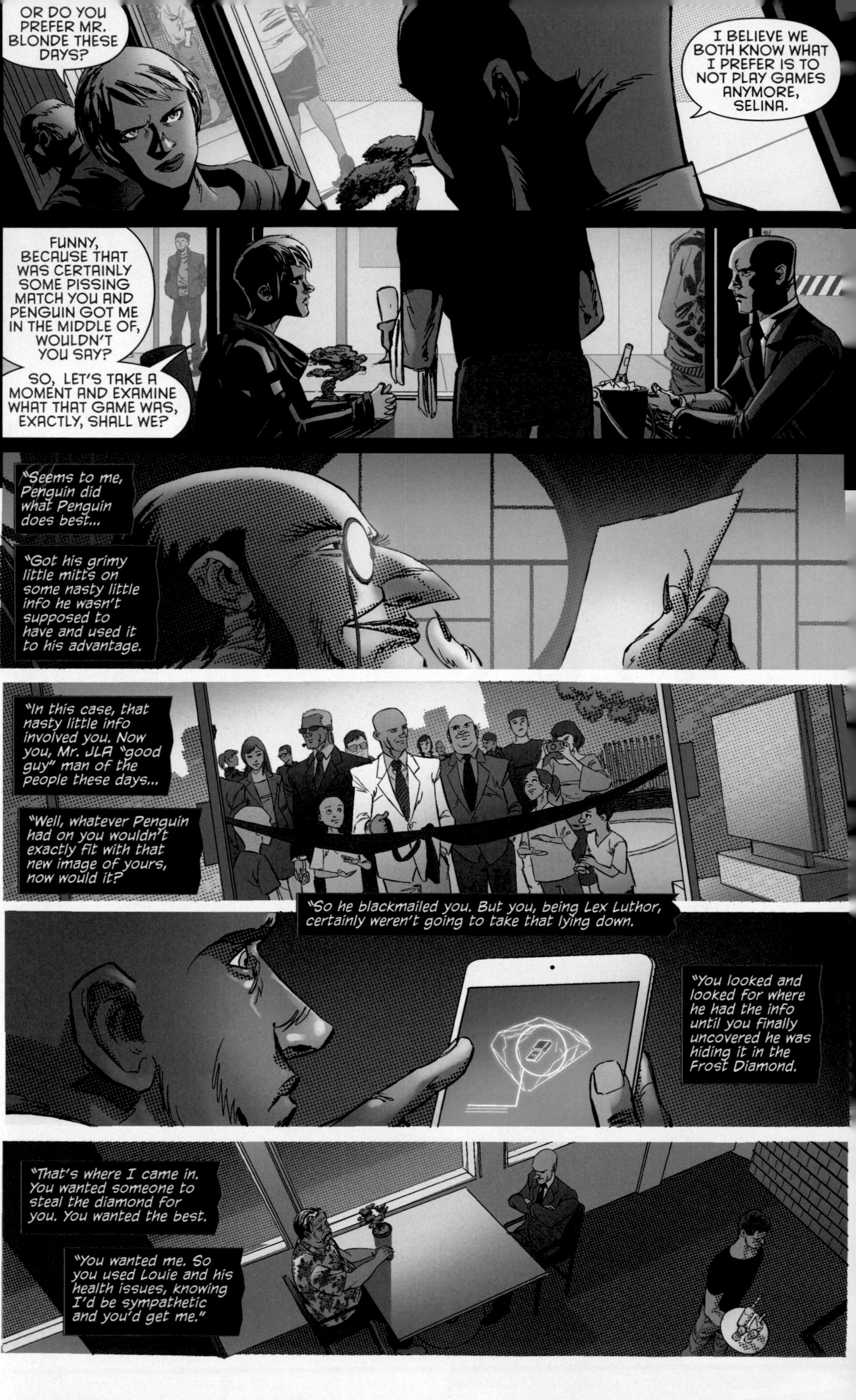
OR DO YOU PREFER MR. BLONDE THESE DAYS?
I BELIEVE WE BOTH KNOW WHAT I PREFER IS TO NOT PLAY GAMES ANYMORE, SELINA.
FUNNY, BECAUSE THAT WAS CERTAINLY SOME PISSING MATCH YOU AND PENGUIN GOT ME IN THE MIDDLE OF, WOULDN'T YOU SAY?
SO, LET'S TAKE A MOMENT AND EXAMINE WHAT THAT GAME WAS, EXACTLY, SHALL WE?
"Seems to me, Penguin did what Penguin does best...
"Got his grimy little mitts on some nasty little info he wasn't supposed to have and used it to his advantage.
"In this case, that nasty little info involved you. Now you, Mr. JLA "good guy" man of the people these days...
"Well, whatever Penguin had on you wouldn't exactly fit with that new image of yours, now would it?
"So he blackmailed you. But you, being Lex Luthor, certainly weren't going to take that lying down.
"You looked and looked for where he had the info until you finally uncovered he was hiding it in the Frost Diamond.
"That's where I came in. You wanted someone to steal the diamond for you. You wanted the best.
"You wanted me. So you used Louie and his health issues, knowing I'd be sympathetic and you'd get me."

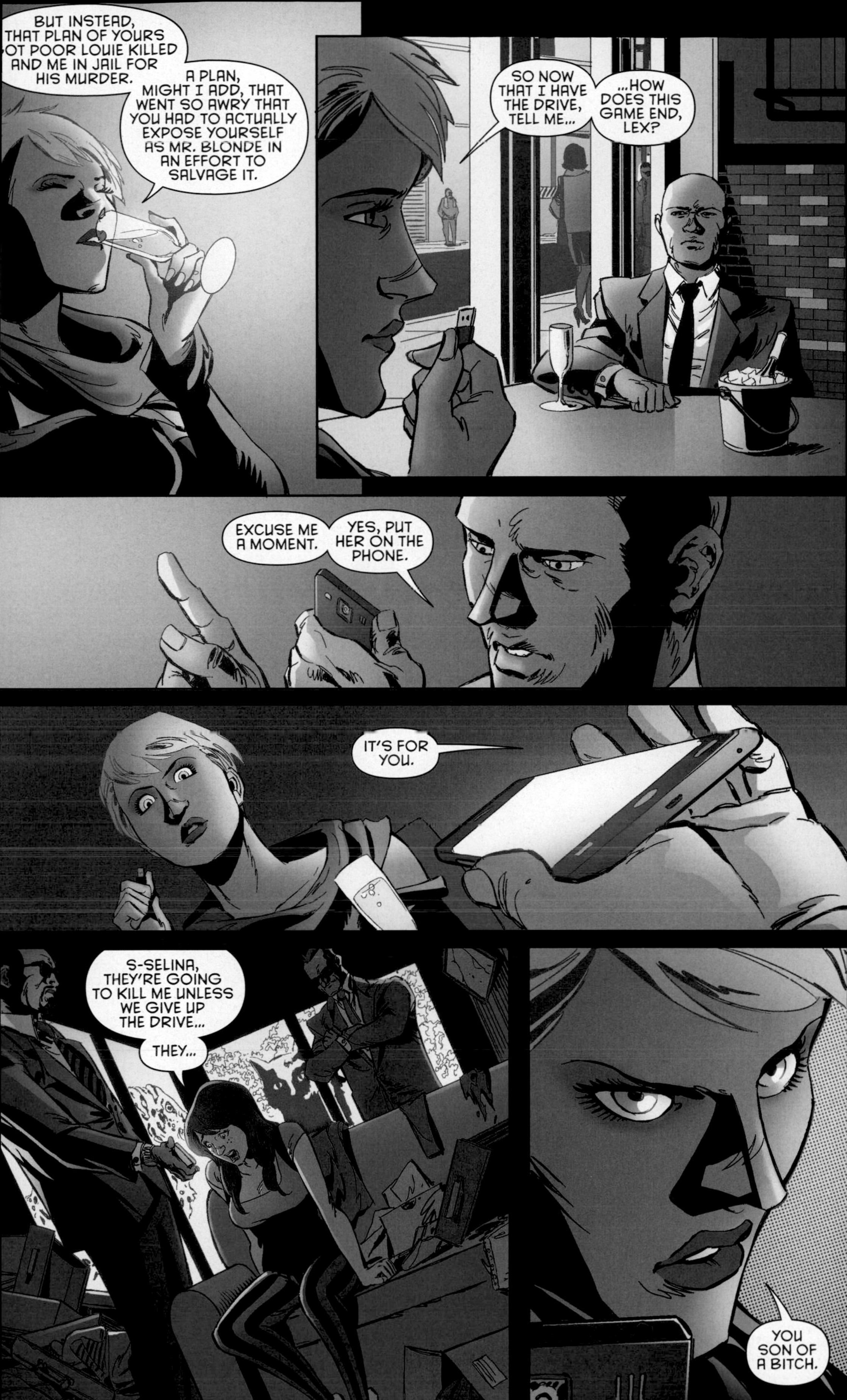
BUT INSTEAD, THAT PLAN OF YOURS GOT POOR LOUIE KILLED AND ME IN JAIL FOR HIS MURDER.
A PLAN, MIGHT I ADD, THAT WENT SO AWRY THAT YOU HAD TO ACTUALLY EXPOSE YOURSELF AS MR. BLONDE IN AN EFFORT TO SALVAGE IT.
SO NOW THAT I HAVE THE DRIVE, TELL ME...
...HOW DOES THIS GAME END, LEX?
EXCUSE ME A MOMENT.
YES, PUT HER ON THE PHONE.
IT'S FOR YOU.
S-SELINA, THEY'RE GOING TO KILL ME UNLESS WE GIVE UP THE DRIVE...
THEY...
YOU SON OF A BITCH.

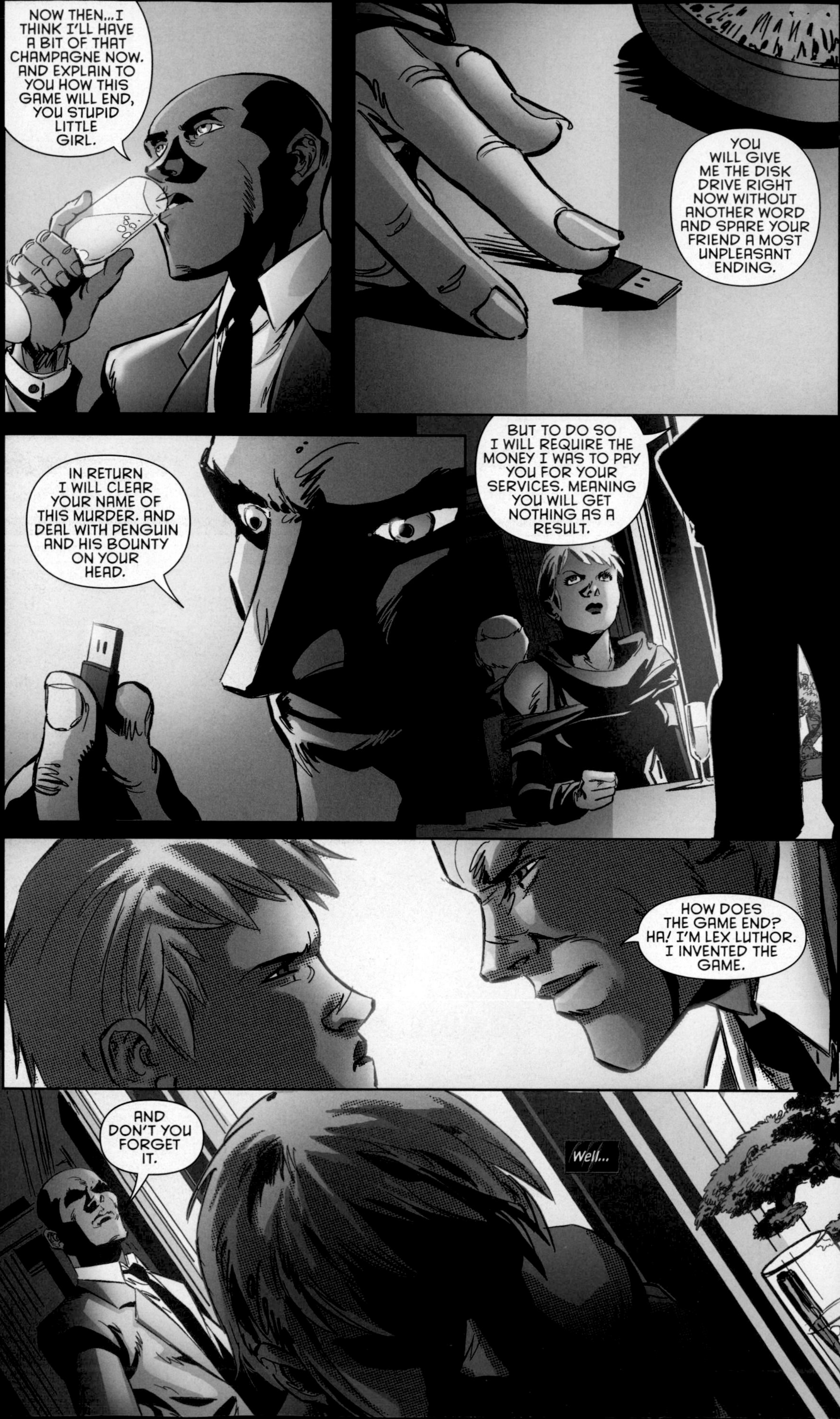

NOW THEN...I THINK I'LL HAVE A BIT OF THAT CHAMPAGNE NOW. AND EXPLAIN TO YOU HOW THIS GAME WILL END, YOU STUPID LITTLE GIRL.
YOU WILL GIVE ME THE DISK DRIVE RIGHT NOW WITHOUT ANOTHER WORD AND SPARE YOUR FRIEND A MOST UNPLEASANT ENDING.
IN RETURN I WILL CLEAR YOUR NAME OF THIS MURDER. AND DEAL WITH PENGUIN AND HIS BOUNTY ON YOUR HEAD.
BUT TO DO SO I WILL REQUIRE THE MONEY I WAS TO PAY YOU FOR YOUR SERVICES. MEANING YOU WILL GET NOTHING AS A RESULT.
HOW DOES THE GAME END? HA! I'M LEX LUTHOR. I INVENTED THE GAME.
AND DON'T YOU FORGET IT.
Well...

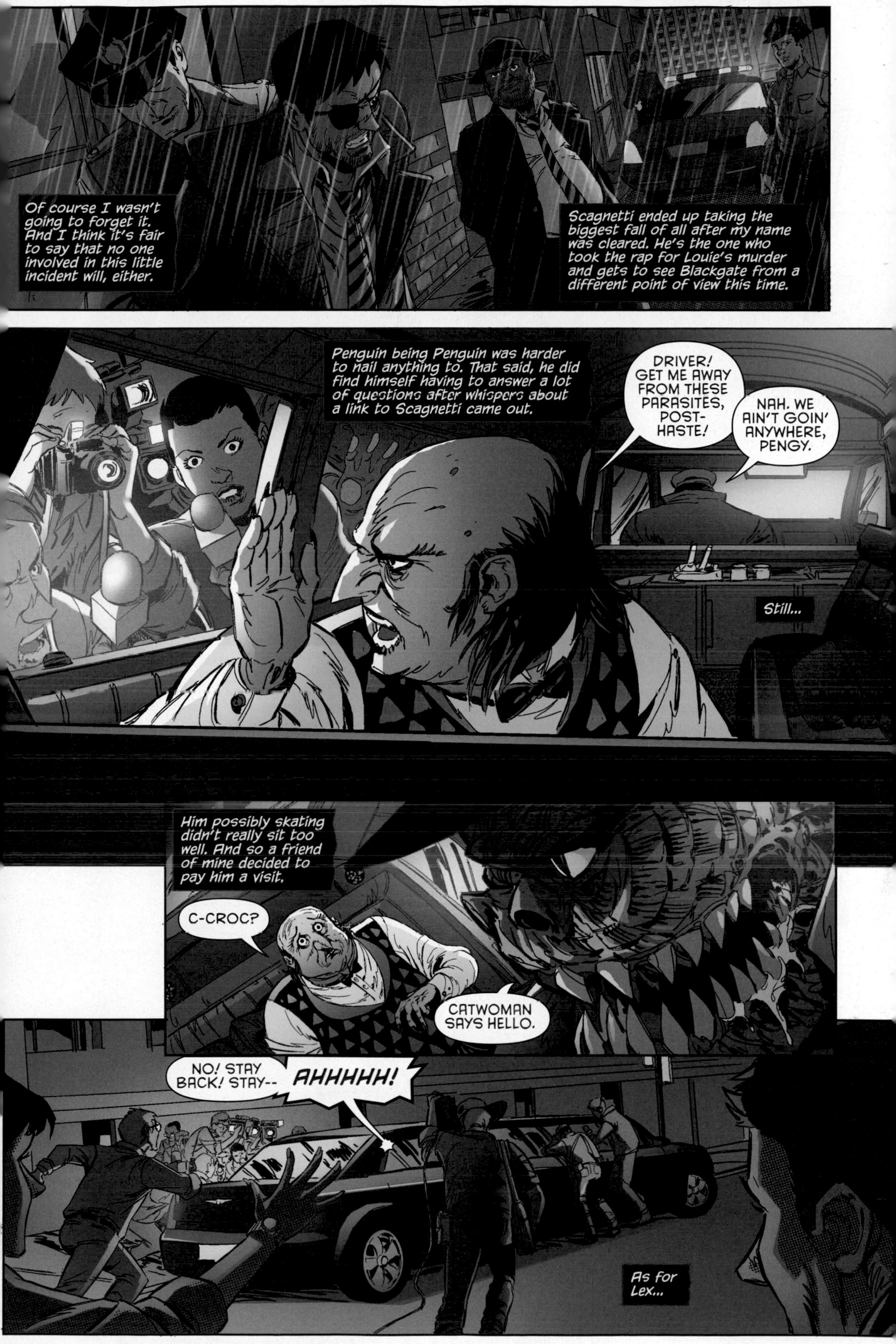
Of course I wasn't going to forget it. And I think it's fair to say that no one involved in this little incident will, either.
Scagnetti ended up taking the biggest fall of all after my name was cleared. He's the one who took the rap for Louie's murder and gets to see Blackgate from a different point of view this time.
Penguin being Penguin was harder to nail anything to. That said, he did find himself having to answer a lot of questions after whispers about a link to Scagnetti came out.
DRIVER! GET ME AWAY FROM THESE PARASITES, POST-HASTE!
NAH. WE AIN'T GOIN' ANYWHERE, PENGY.
Still...
Him possibly skating didn't really sit too well. And so a friend of mine decided to pay him a visit.
C-CROC?
CATWOMAN SAYS HELLO.
NO! STAY BACK! STAY--
AHHHHH!
As for Lex...

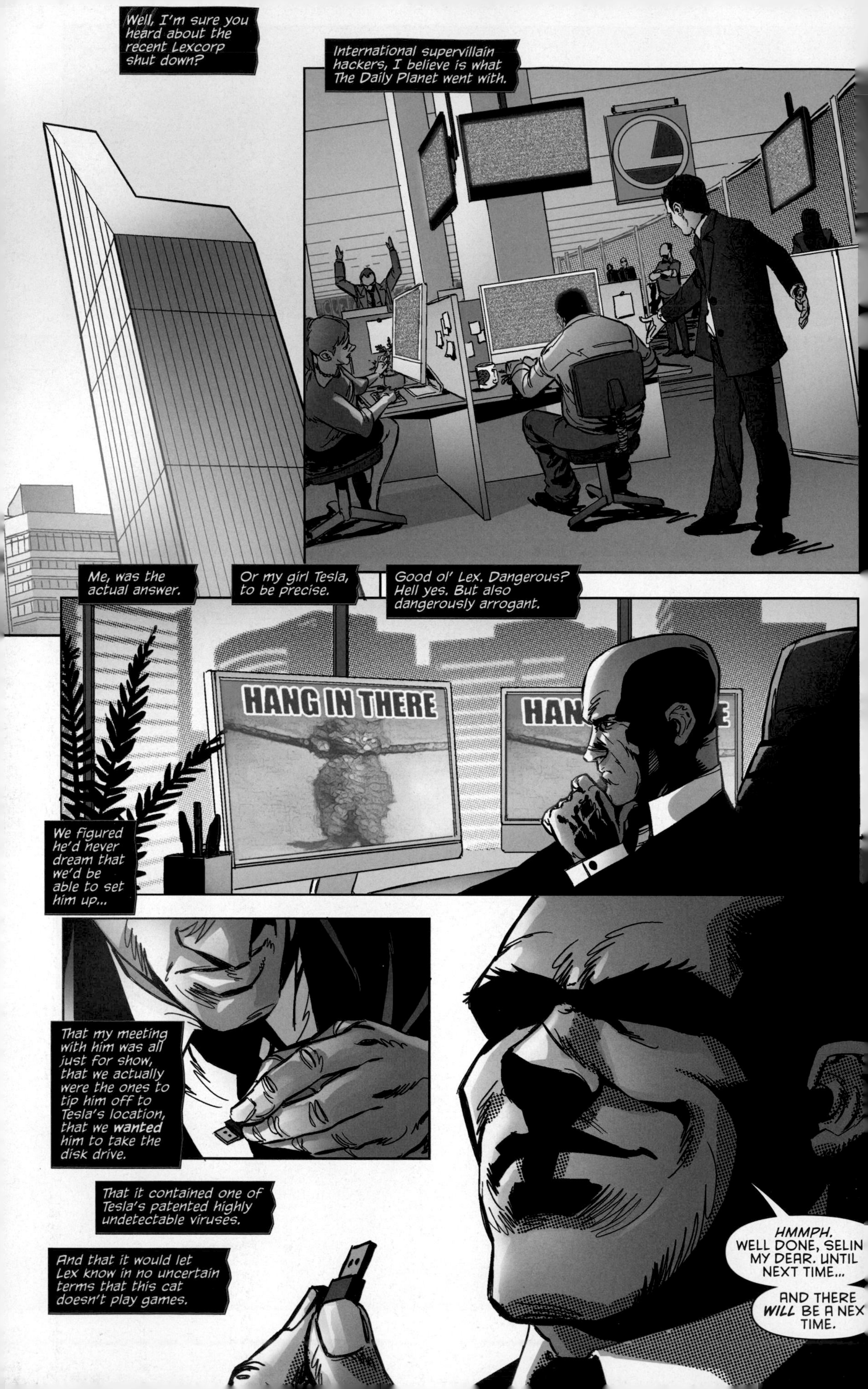
Well, I'm sure you heard about the recent Lexcorp shut down?
International supervillain hackers, I believe is what The Daily Planet went with.
Me, was the actual answer.
Or my girl Tesla, to be precise.
Good ol' Lex. Dangerous? Hell yes. But also dangerously arrogant.
HANG IN THERE
We figured he'd never dream that we'd be able to set him up...
That my meeting with him was all just for show, that we actually were the ones to tip him off to Tesla's location, that we **wanted** him to take the disk drive.
That it contained one of Tesla's patented highly undetectable viruses.
And that it would let Lex know in no uncertain terms that this cat doesn't play games.
HMMPH. WELL DONE, SELIN MY DEAR. UNTIL NEXT TIME...
AND THERE **WILL** BE A NEX TIME.

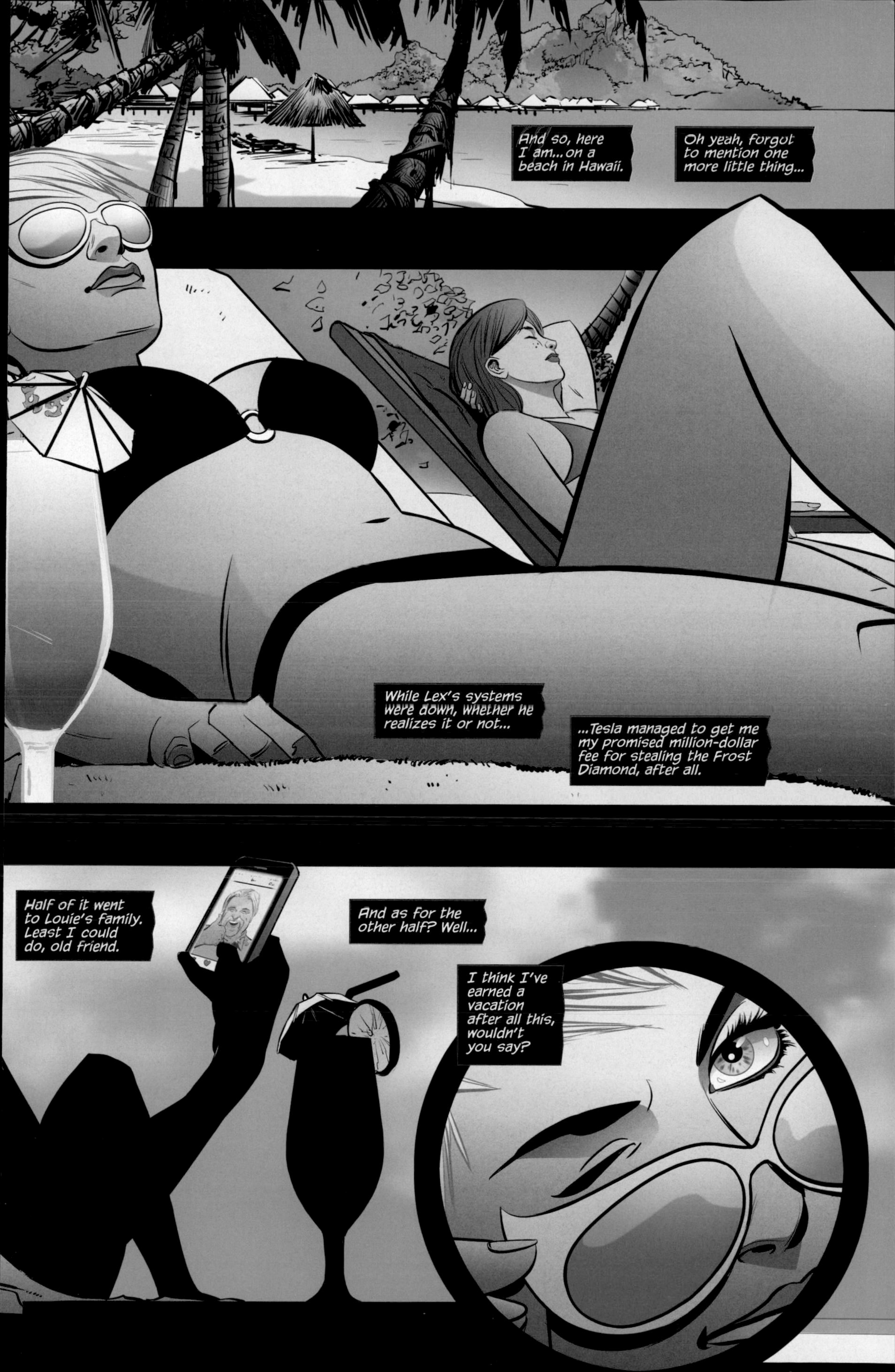
And so, here I am...on a beach in Hawaii.
Oh yeah, forgot to mention one more little thing...
While Lex's systems were down, whether he realizes it or not...
...Tesla managed to get me my promised million-dollar fee for stealing the Frost Diamond, after all.
Half of it went to Louie's family. Least I could do, old friend.
And as for the other half? Well...
I think I've earned a vacation after all this, wouldn't you say?

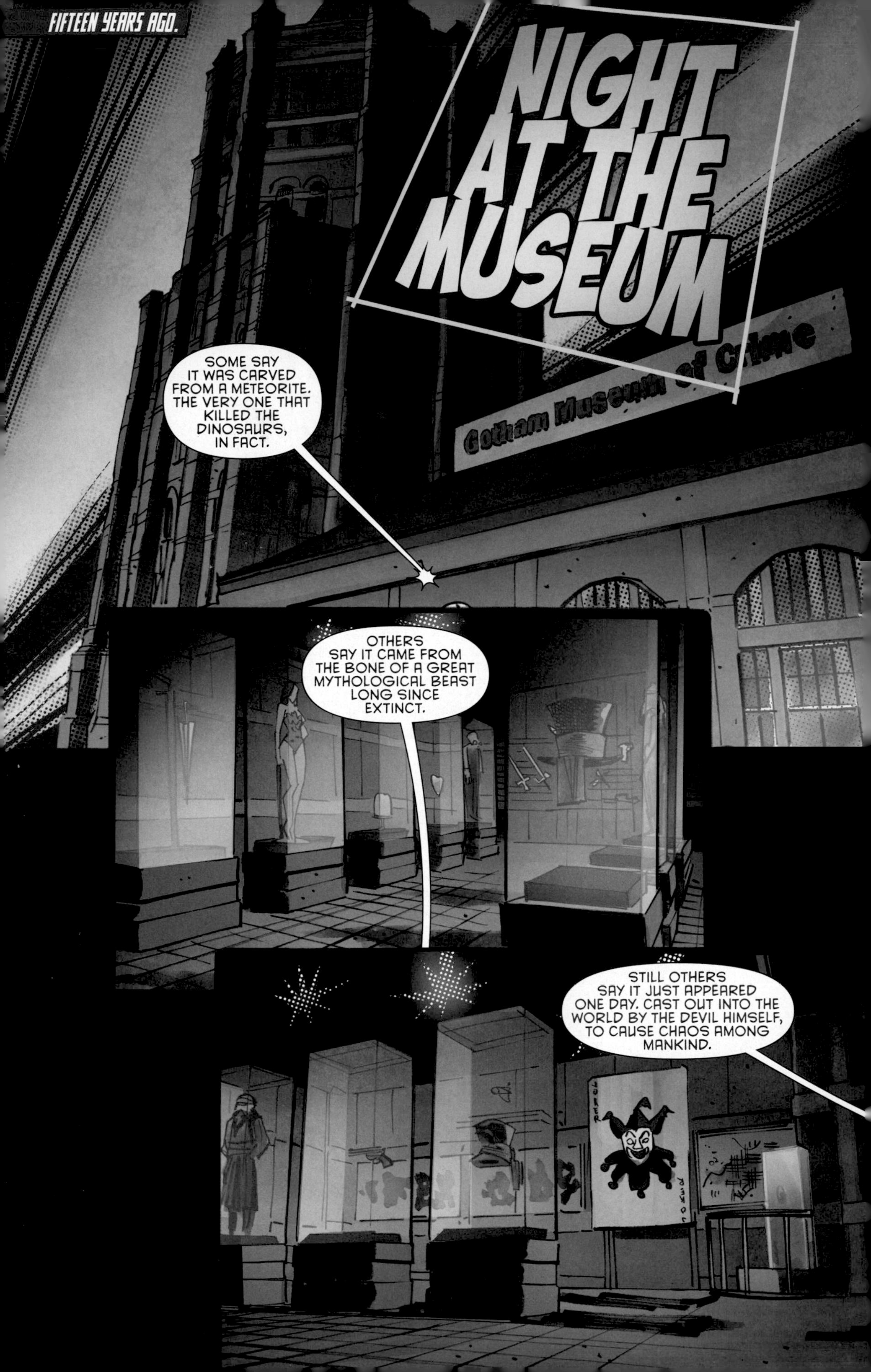
FIFTEEN YEARS AGO.
NIGHT AT THE MUSEUM
Gotham Museum of Crime
SOME SAY IT WAS CARVED FROM A METEORITE. THE VERY ONE THAT KILLED THE DINOSAURS, IN FACT.
OTHERS SAY IT CAME FROM THE BONE OF A GREAT MYTHOLOGICAL BEAST LONG SINCE EXTINCT.
STILL OTHERS SAY IT JUST APPEARED ONE DAY. CAST OUT INTO THE WORLD BY THE DEVIL HIMSELF, TO CAUSE CHAOS AMONG MANKIND.
JOKER

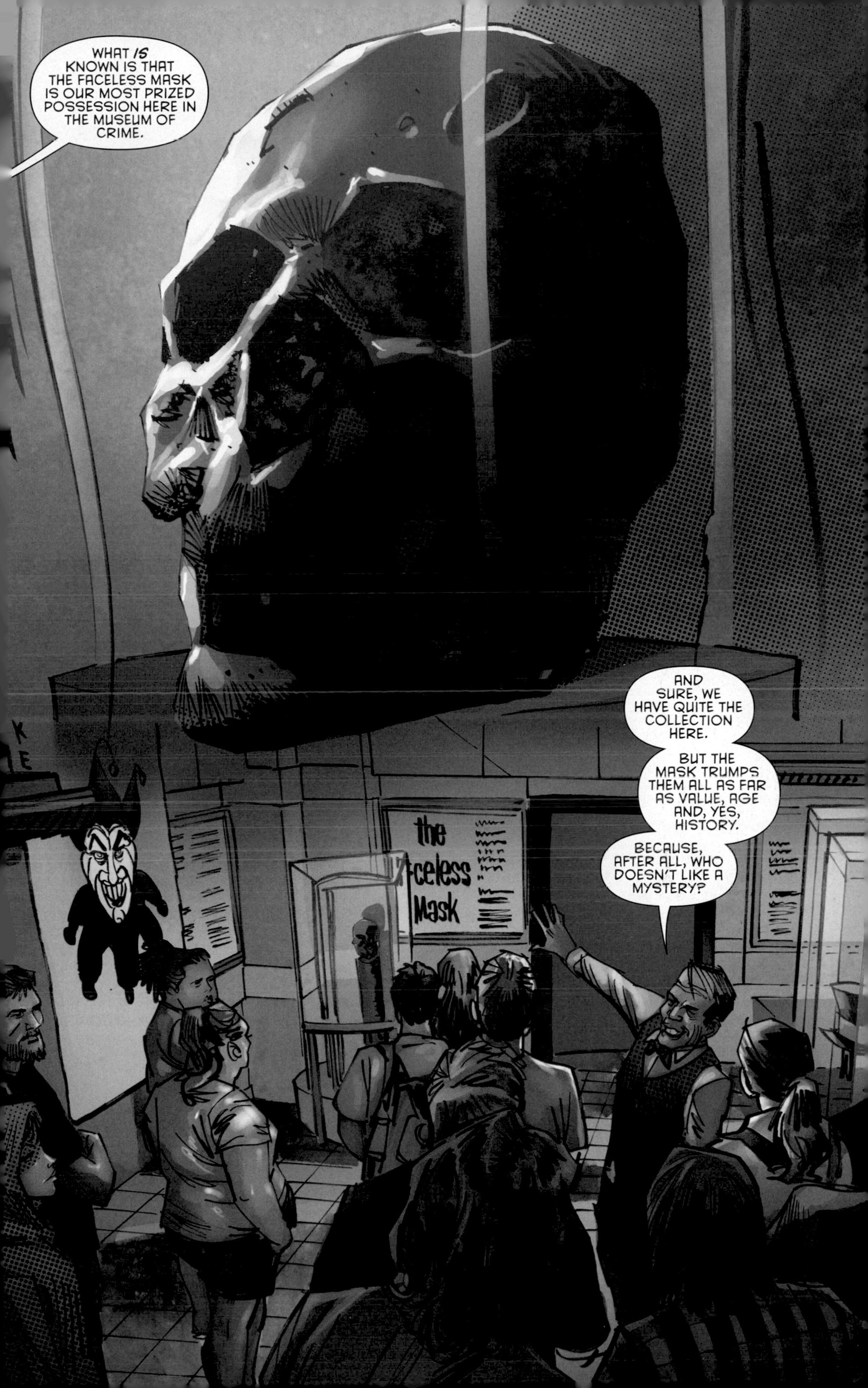
WHAT *IS* KNOWN IS THAT THE FACELESS MASK IS OUR MOST PRIZED POSSESSION HERE IN THE MUSEUM OF CRIME.
AND SURE, WE HAVE QUITE THE COLLECTION HERE.
BUT THE MASK TRUMPS THEM ALL AS FAR AS VALUE, AGE AND, YES, HISTORY.
BECAUSE, AFTER ALL, WHO DOESN'T LIKE A MYSTERY?
Mask

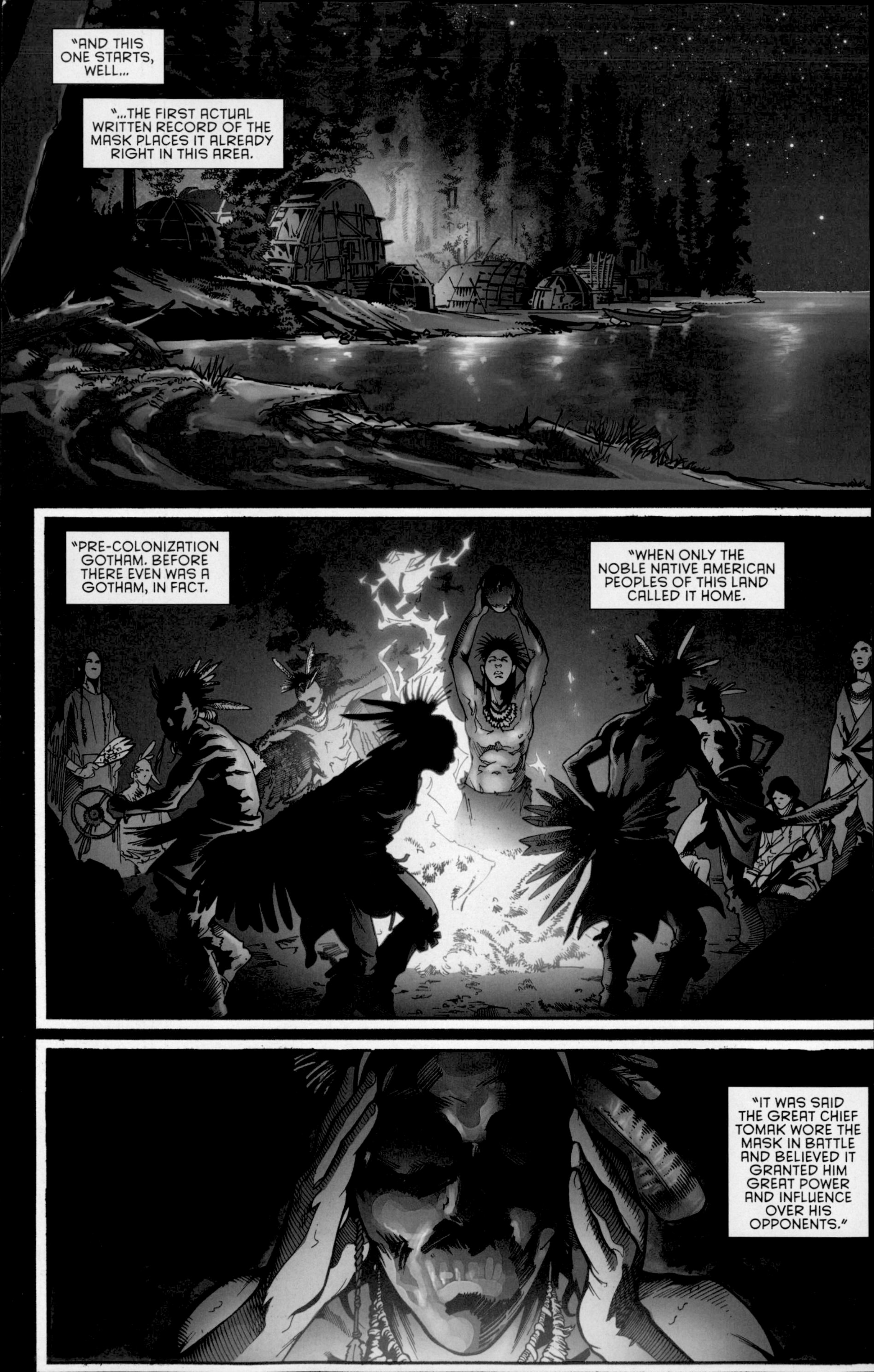
"AND THIS ONE STARTS, WELL...
"...THE FIRST ACTUAL WRITTEN RECORD OF THE MASK PLACES IT ALREADY RIGHT IN THIS AREA.
"PRE-COLONIZATION GOTHAM. BEFORE THERE EVEN WAS A GOTHAM, IN FACT.
"WHEN ONLY THE NOBLE NATIVE AMERICAN PEOPLES OF THIS LAND CALLED IT HOME.
"IT WAS SAID THE GREAT CHIEF TOMAK WORE THE MASK IN BATTLE AND BELIEVED IT GRANTED HIM GREAT POWER AND INFLUENCE OVER HIS OPPONENTS."

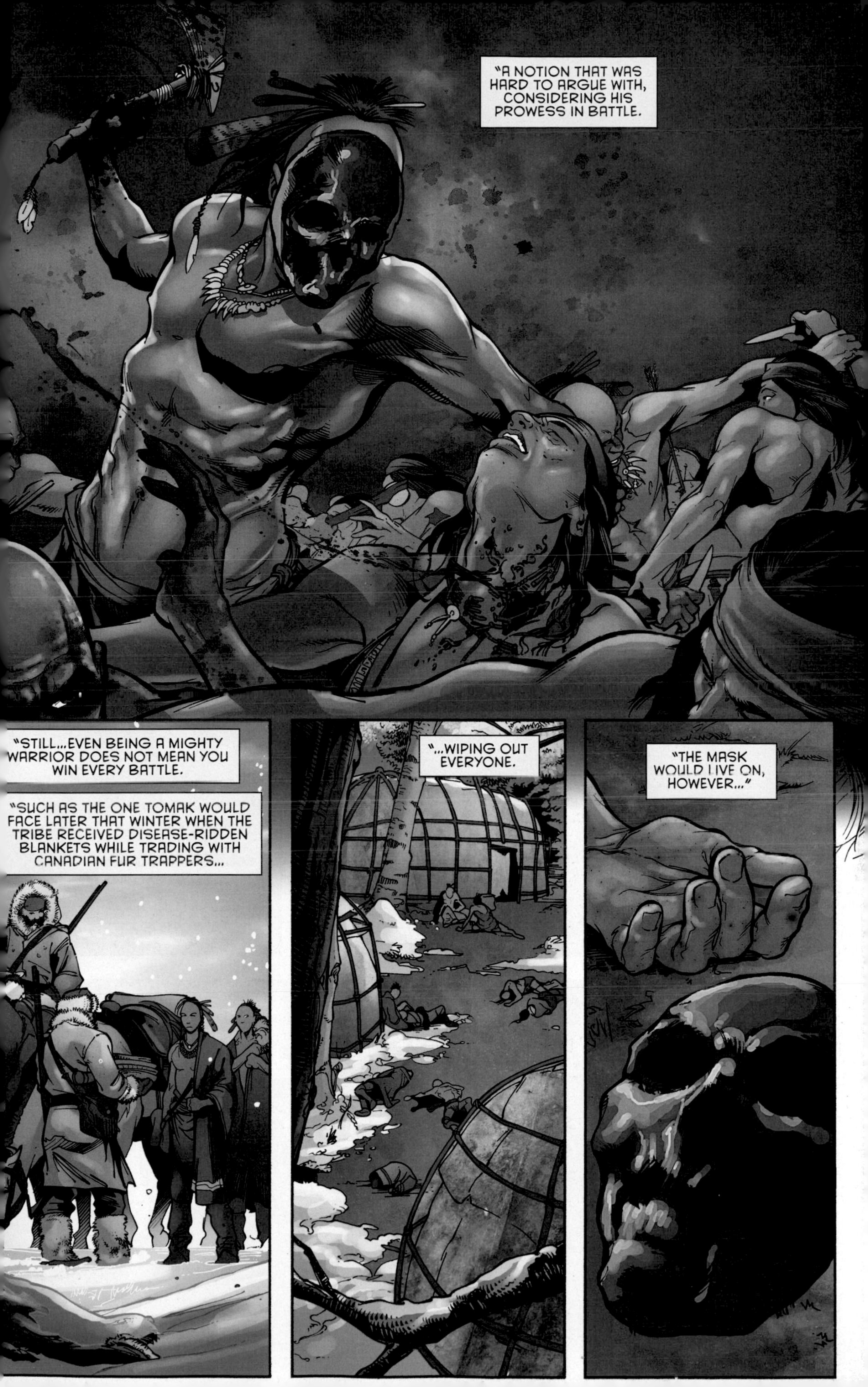
"A NOTION THAT WAS HARD TO ARGUE WITH, CONSIDERING HIS PROWESS IN BATTLE.
"STILL...EVEN BEING A MIGHTY WARRIOR DOES NOT MEAN YOU WIN EVERY BATTLE.
"SUCH AS THE ONE TOMAK WOULD FACE LATER THAT WINTER WHEN THE TRIBE RECEIVED DISEASE-RIDDEN BLANKETS WHILE TRADING WITH CANADIAN FUR TRAPPERS...
"...WIPING OUT EVERYONE.
"THE MASK WOULD LIVE ON, HOWEVER..."

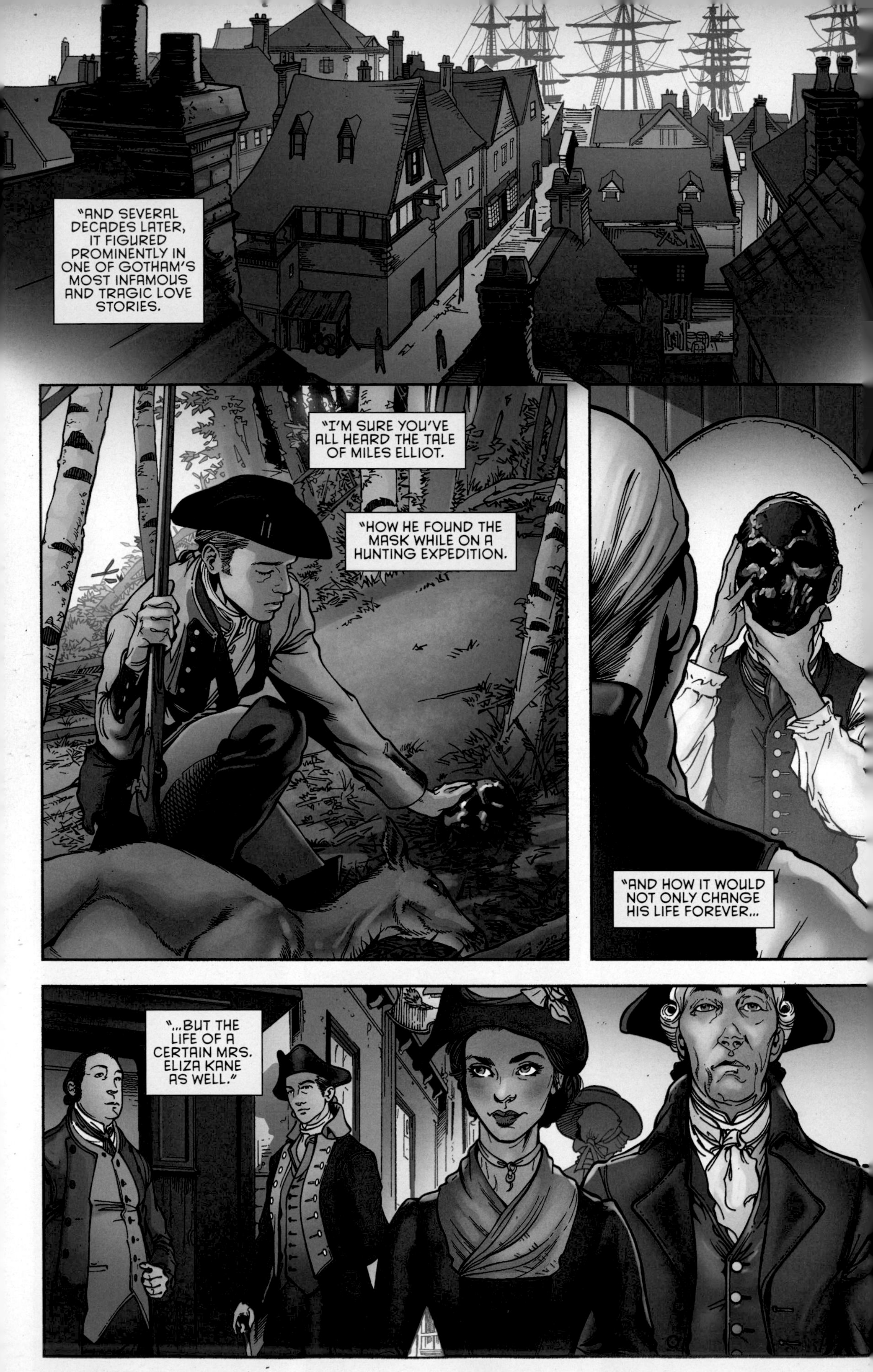
"AND SEVERAL DECADES LATER, IT FIGURED PROMINENTLY IN ONE OF GOTHAM'S MOST INFAMOUS AND TRAGIC LOVE STORIES.
"I'M SURE YOU'VE ALL HEARD THE TALE OF MILES ELLIOT.
"HOW HE FOUND THE MASK WHILE ON A HUNTING EXPEDITION.
"AND HOW IT WOULD NOT ONLY CHANGE HIS LIFE FOREVER...
"...BUT THE LIFE OF A CERTAIN MRS. ELIZA KANE AS WELL."

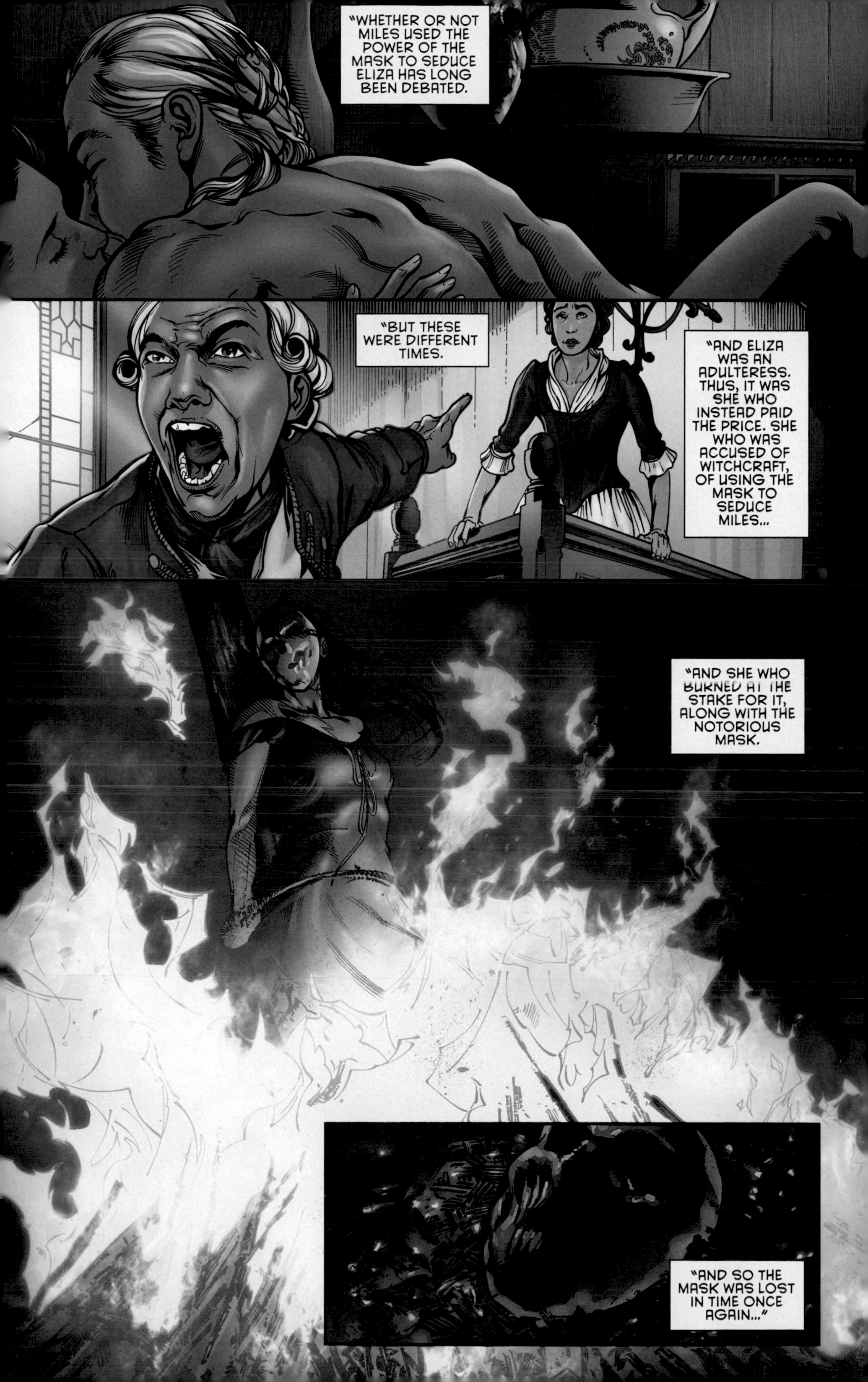
"WHETHER OR NOT MILES USED THE POWER OF THE MASK TO SEDUCE ELIZA HAS LONG BEEN DEBATED.
"BUT THESE WERE DIFFERENT TIMES.
"AND ELIZA WAS AN ADULTERESS. THUS, IT WAS SHE WHO INSTEAD PAID THE PRICE. SHE WHO WAS ACCUSED OF WITCHCRAFT, OF USING THE MASK TO SEDUCE MILES...
"AND SHE WHO BURNED AT THE STAKE FOR IT, ALONG WITH THE NOTORIOUS MASK.
"AND SO THE MASK WAS LOST IN TIME ONCE AGAIN..."

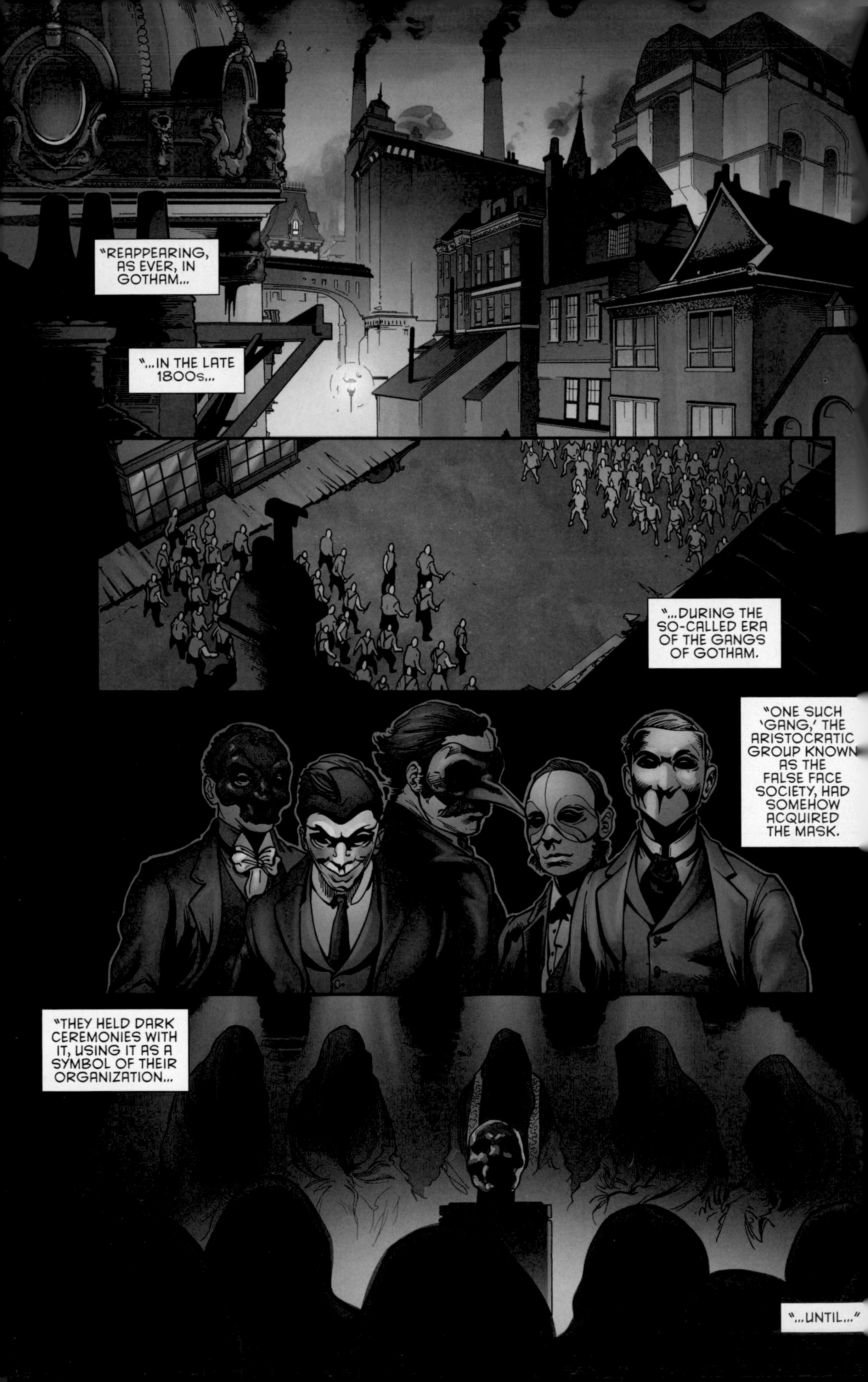
"REAPPEARING, AS EVER, IN GOTHAM...
"...IN THE LATE 1800s...
"...DURING THE SO-CALLED ERA OF THE GANGS OF GOTHAM.
"ONE SUCH 'GANG,' THE ARISTOCRATIC GROUP KNOWN AS THE FALSE FACE SOCIETY, HAD SOMEHOW ACQUIRED THE MASK.
"THEY HELD DARK CEREMONIES WITH IT, USING IT AS A SYMBOL OF THEIR ORGANIZATION...
"...UNTIL..."

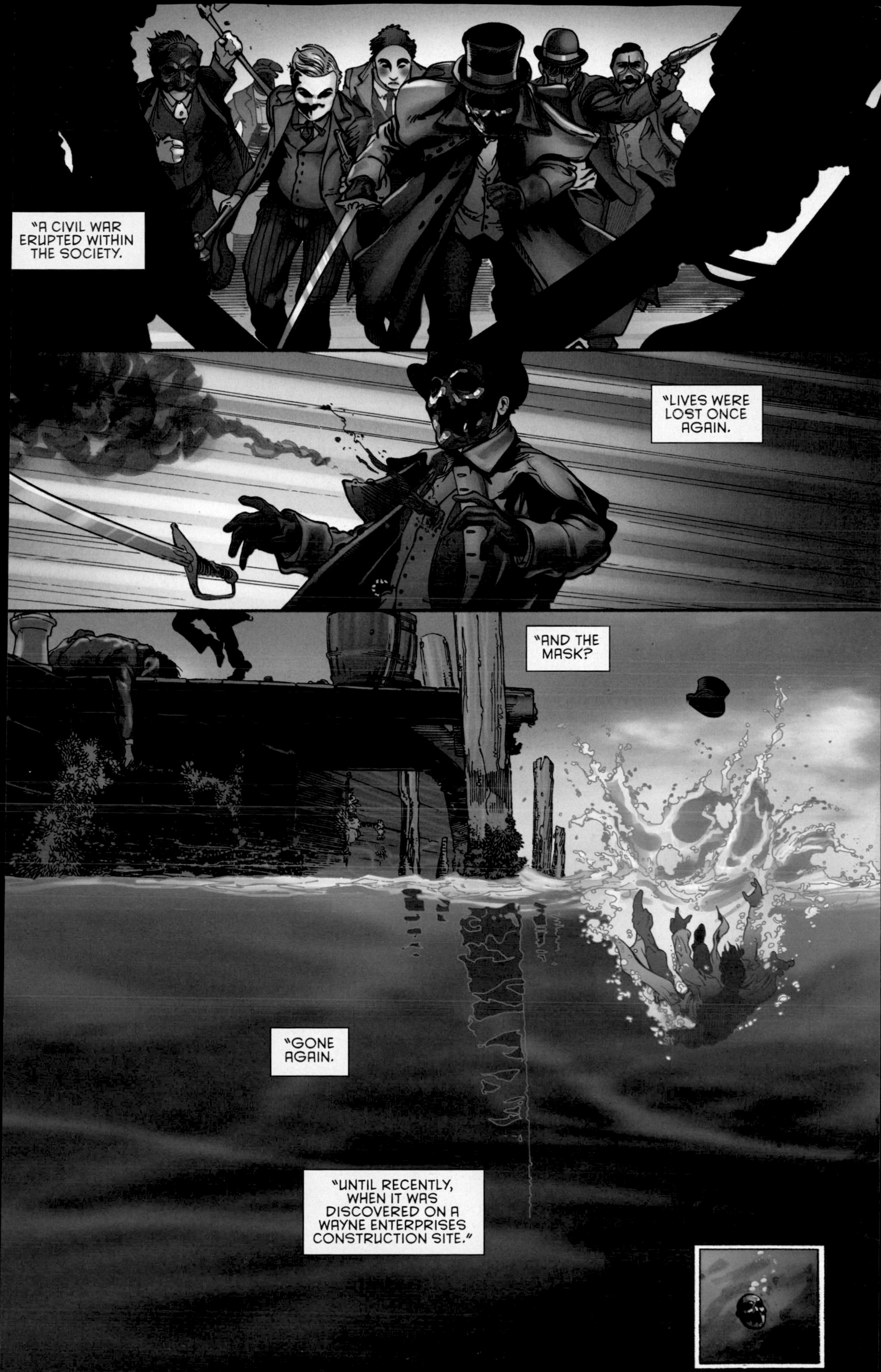
"A CIVIL WAR ERUPTED WITHIN THE SOCIETY.
"LIVES WERE LOST ONCE AGAIN.
"AND THE MASK?
"GONE AGAIN.
"UNTIL RECENTLY, WHEN IT WAS DISCOVERED ON A WAYNE ENTERPRISES CONSTRUCTION SITE."

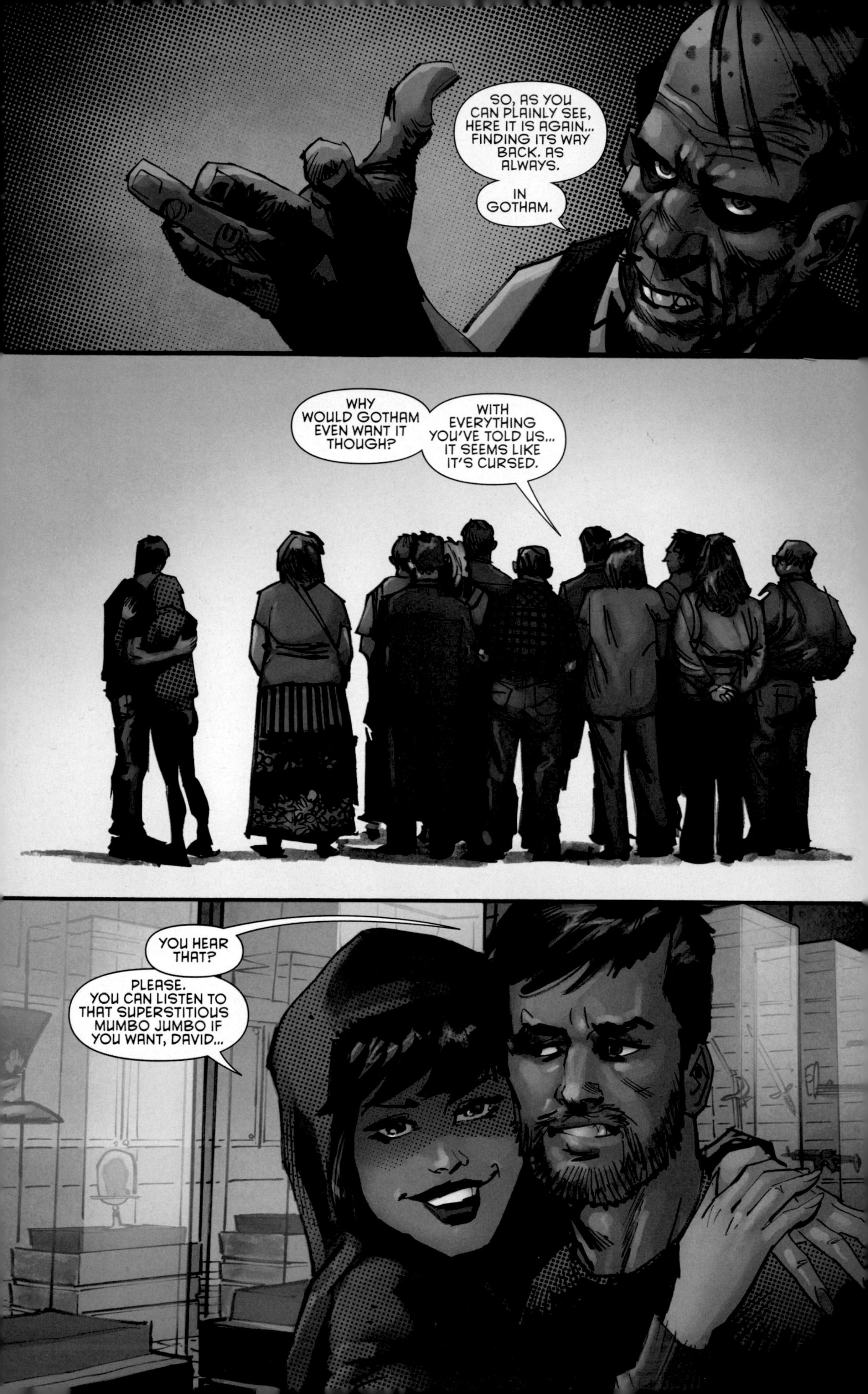
SO, AS YOU CAN PLAINLY SEE, HERE IT IS AGAIN... FINDING ITS WAY BACK. AS ALWAYS.
IN GOTHAM.
WHY WOULD GOTHAM EVEN WANT IT THOUGH?
WITH EVERYTHING YOU'VE TOLD US... IT SEEMS LIKE IT'S CURSED.
YOU HEAR THAT?
PLEASE. YOU CAN LISTEN TO THAT SUPERSTITIOUS MUMBO JUMBO IF YOU WANT, DAVID...

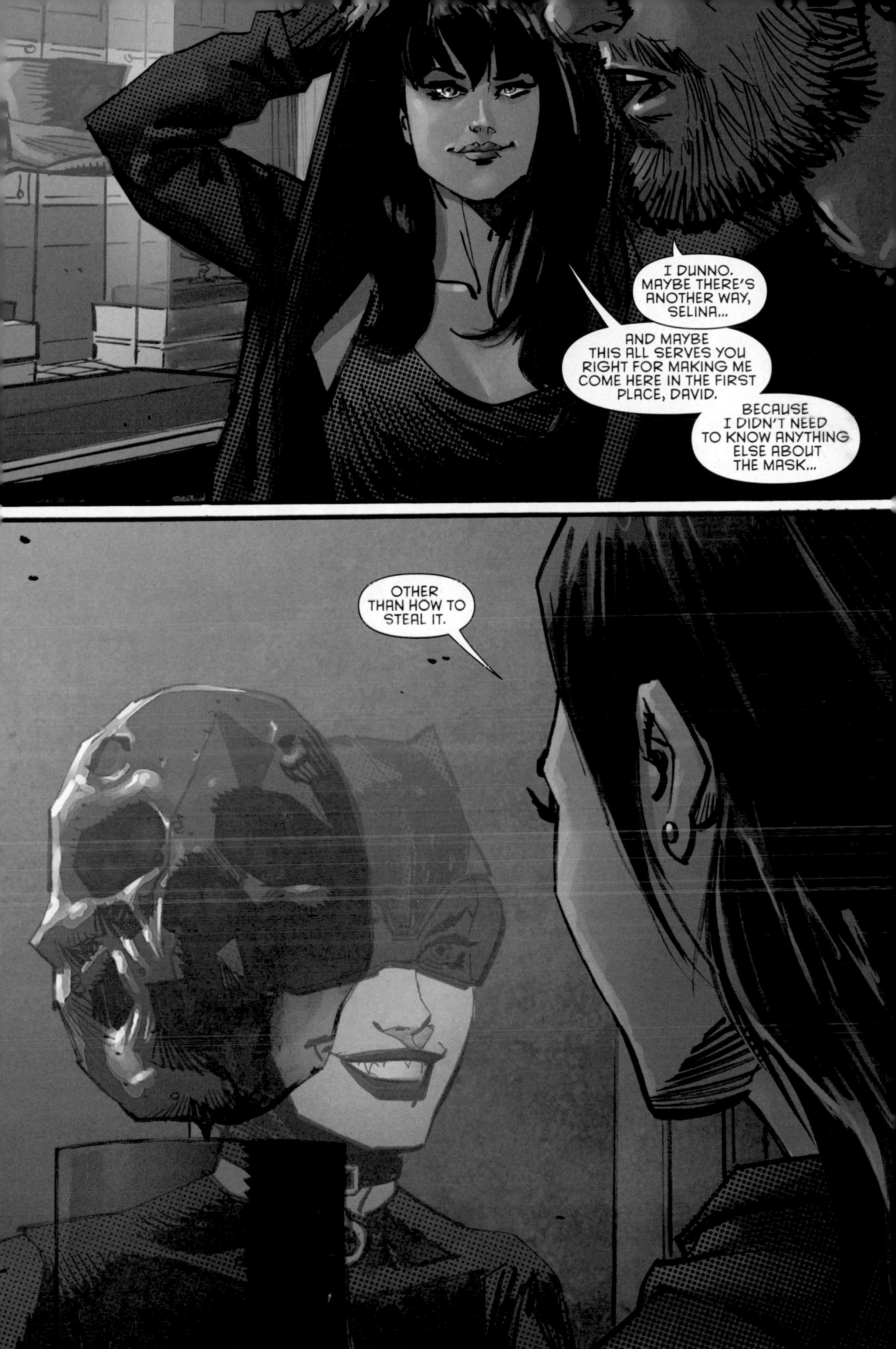
I DUNNO. MAYBE THERE'S ANOTHER WAY, SELINA...
AND MAYBE THIS ALL SERVES YOU RIGHT FOR MAKING ME COME HERE IN THE FIRST PLACE, DAVID.
BECAUSE I DIDN'T NEED TO KNOW ANYTHING ELSE ABOUT THE MASK...
OTHER THAN HOW TO STEAL IT.

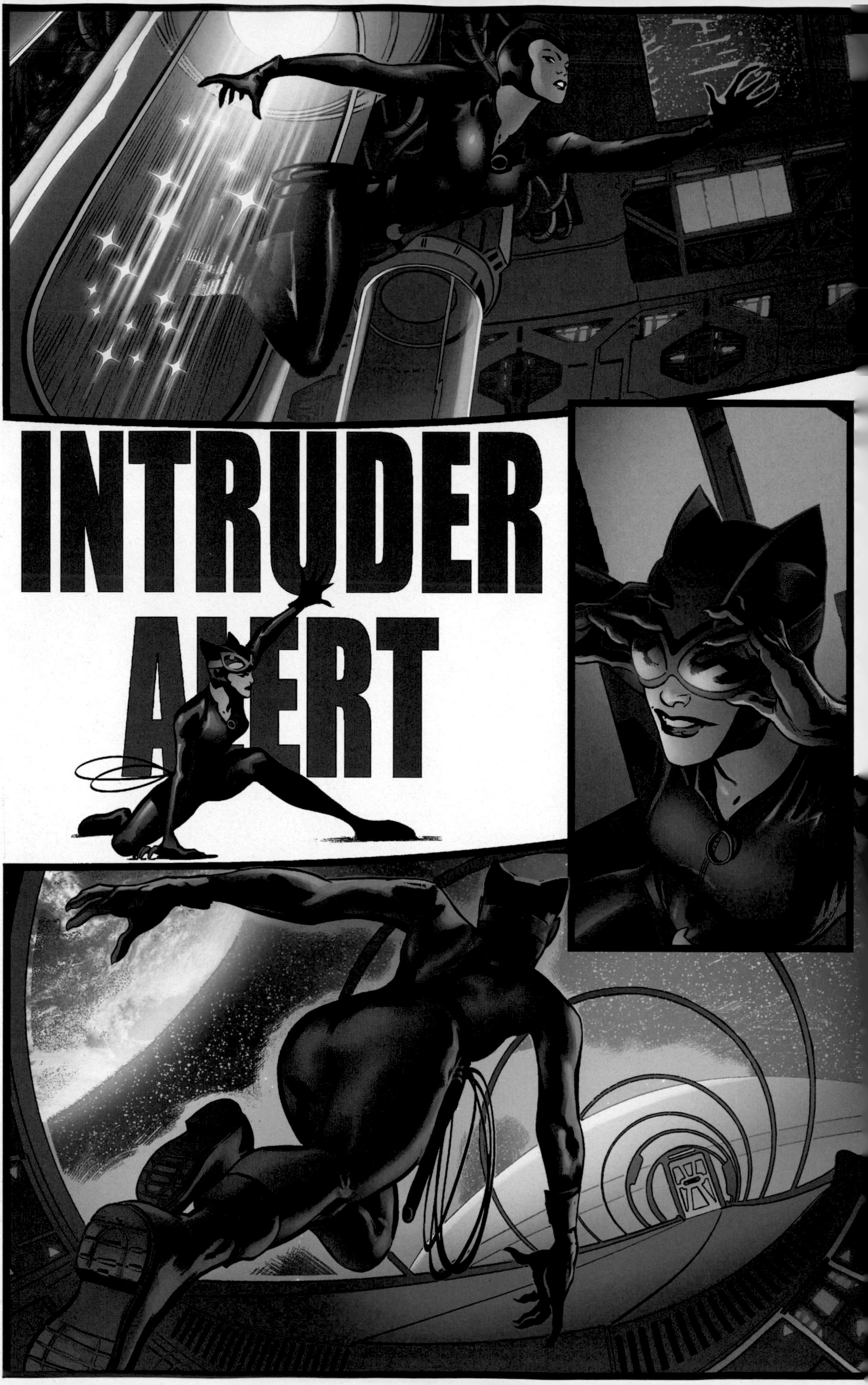
INTRUDER
ALERT

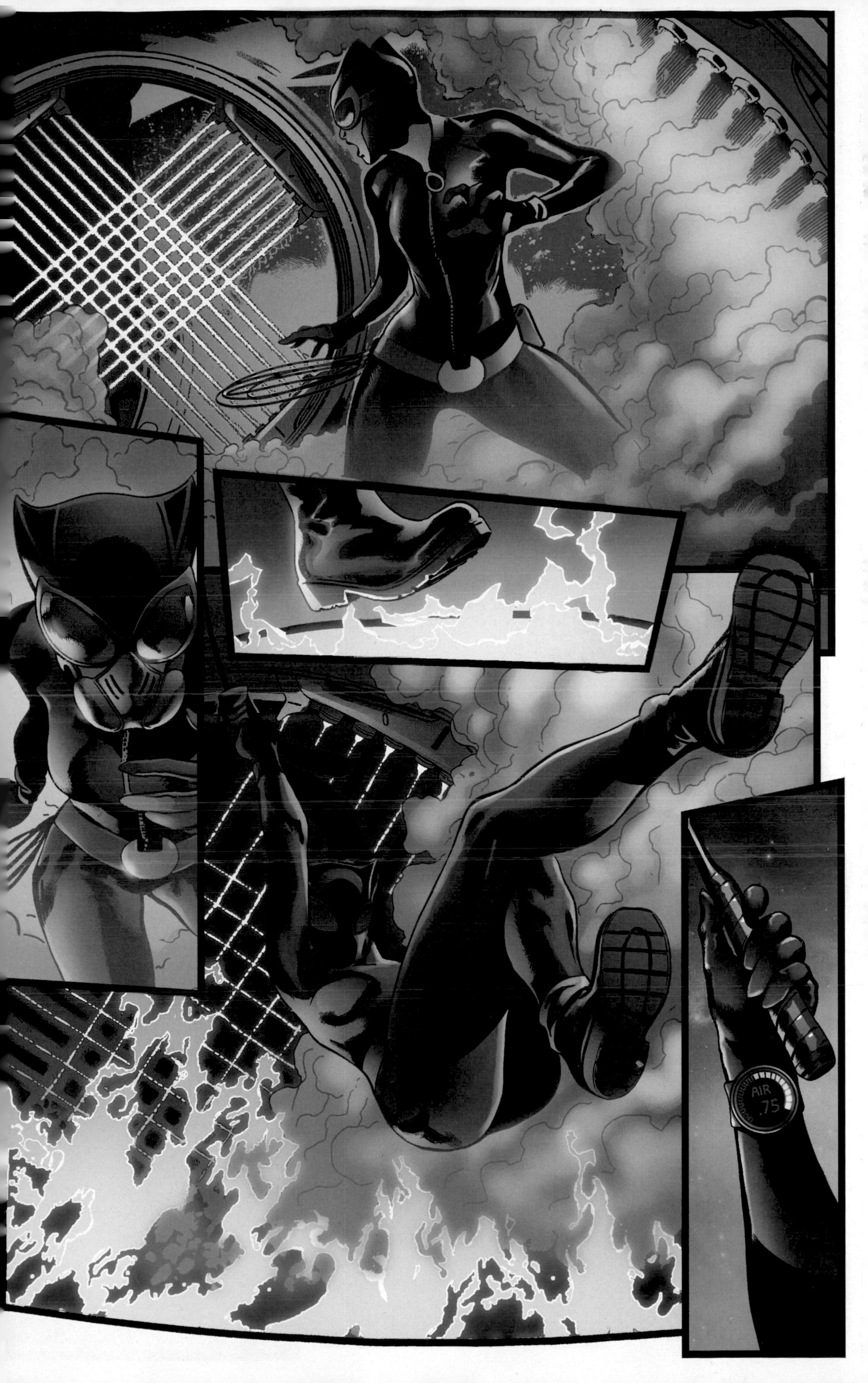
AIR
.75

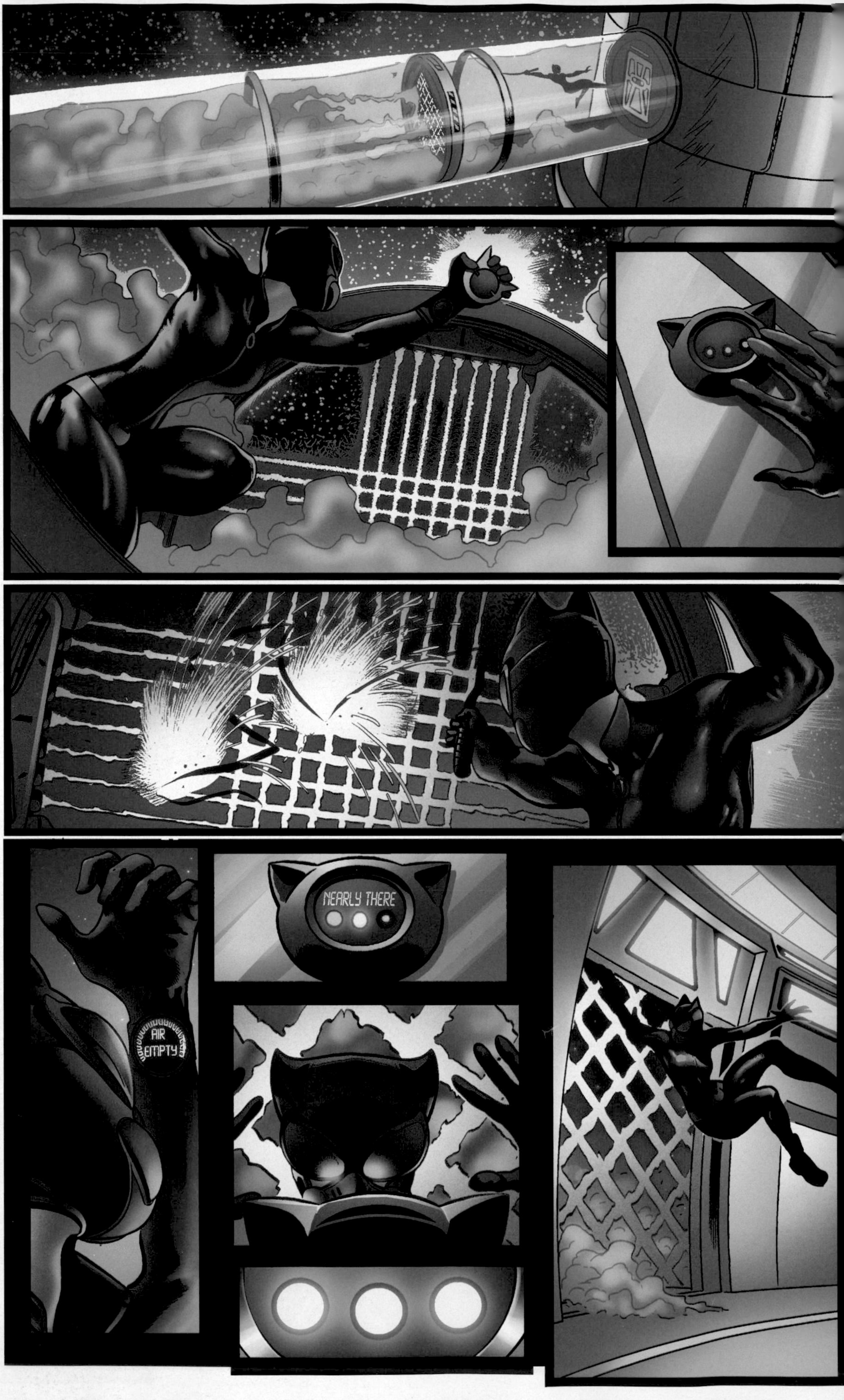
AIR
EMPTY
NEARLY THERE

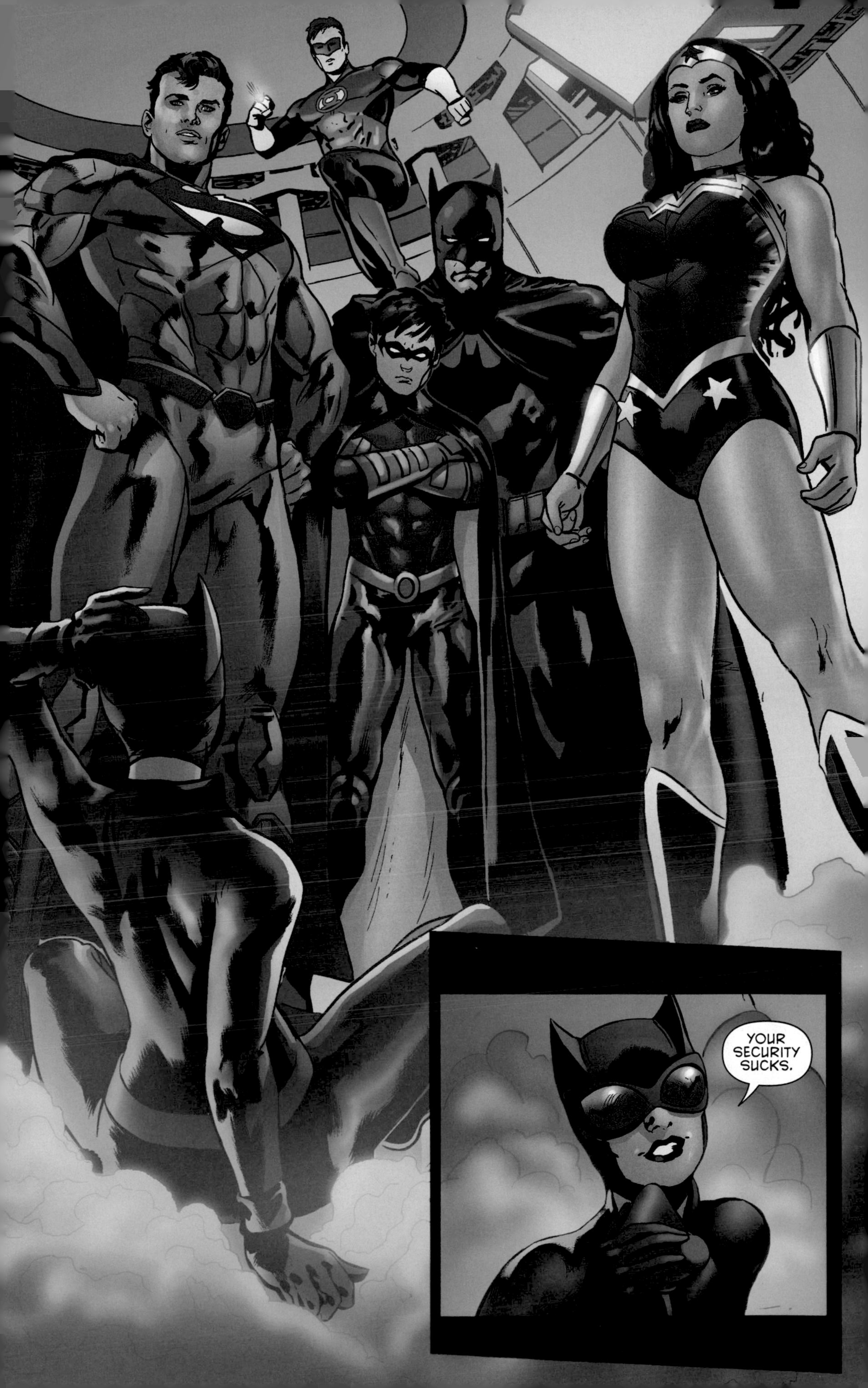
YOUR SECURITY SUCKS.

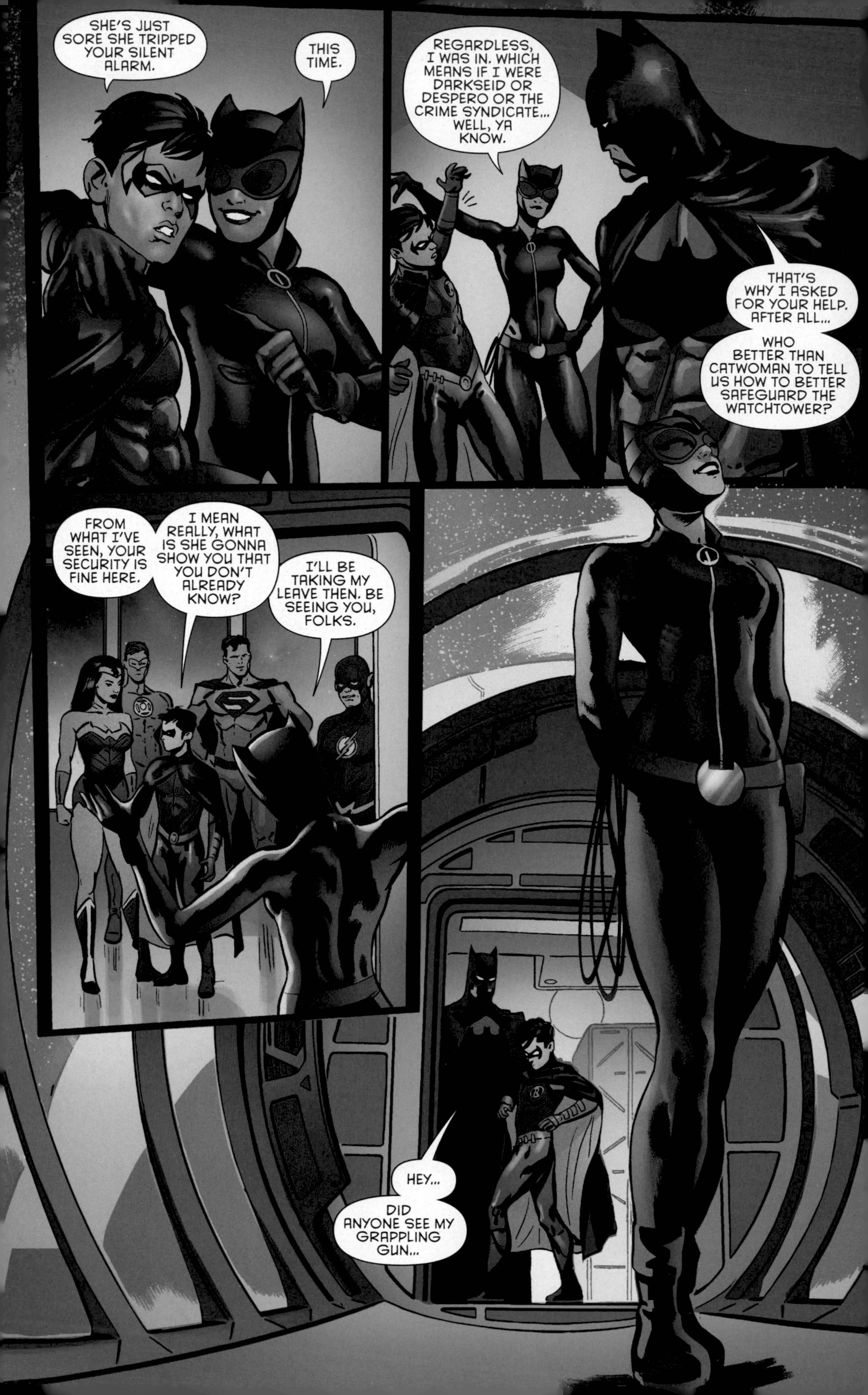
SHE'S JUST SORE SHE TRIPPED YOUR SILENT ALARM.
THIS TIME.
REGARDLESS, I WAS IN. WHICH MEANS IF I WERE DARKSEID OR DESPERO OR THE CRIME SYNDICATE... WELL, YA KNOW.
THAT'S WHY I ASKED FOR YOUR HELP. AFTER ALL...
WHO BETTER THAN CATWOMAN TO TELL US HOW TO BETTER SAFEGUARD THE WATCHTOWER?
FROM WHAT I'VE SEEN, YOUR SECURITY IS FINE HERE.
I MEAN REALLY, WHAT IS SHE GONNA SHOW YOU THAT YOU DON'T ALREADY KNOW?
I'LL BE TAKING MY LEAVE THEN. BE SEEING YOU, FOLKS.
HEY...
DID ANYONE SEE MY GRAPPLING GUN...

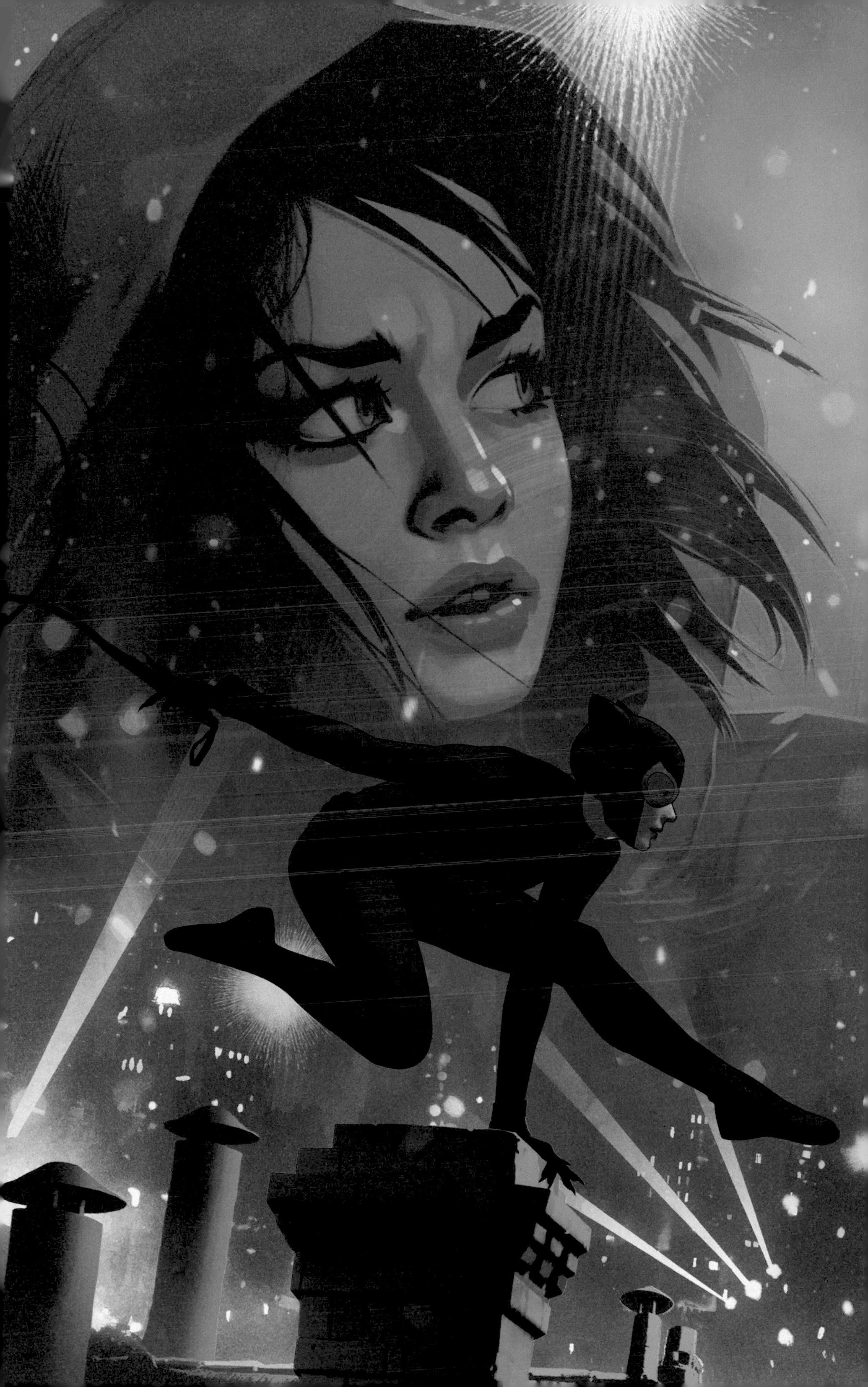

FACELESS, PART ONE

FRANK TIERI writer INAKI MIRANDA & ELIA BONETTI artists EVA DE LA CRUZ colorist TRAVIS LANHAM letterer JOSH MIDDLETON cover

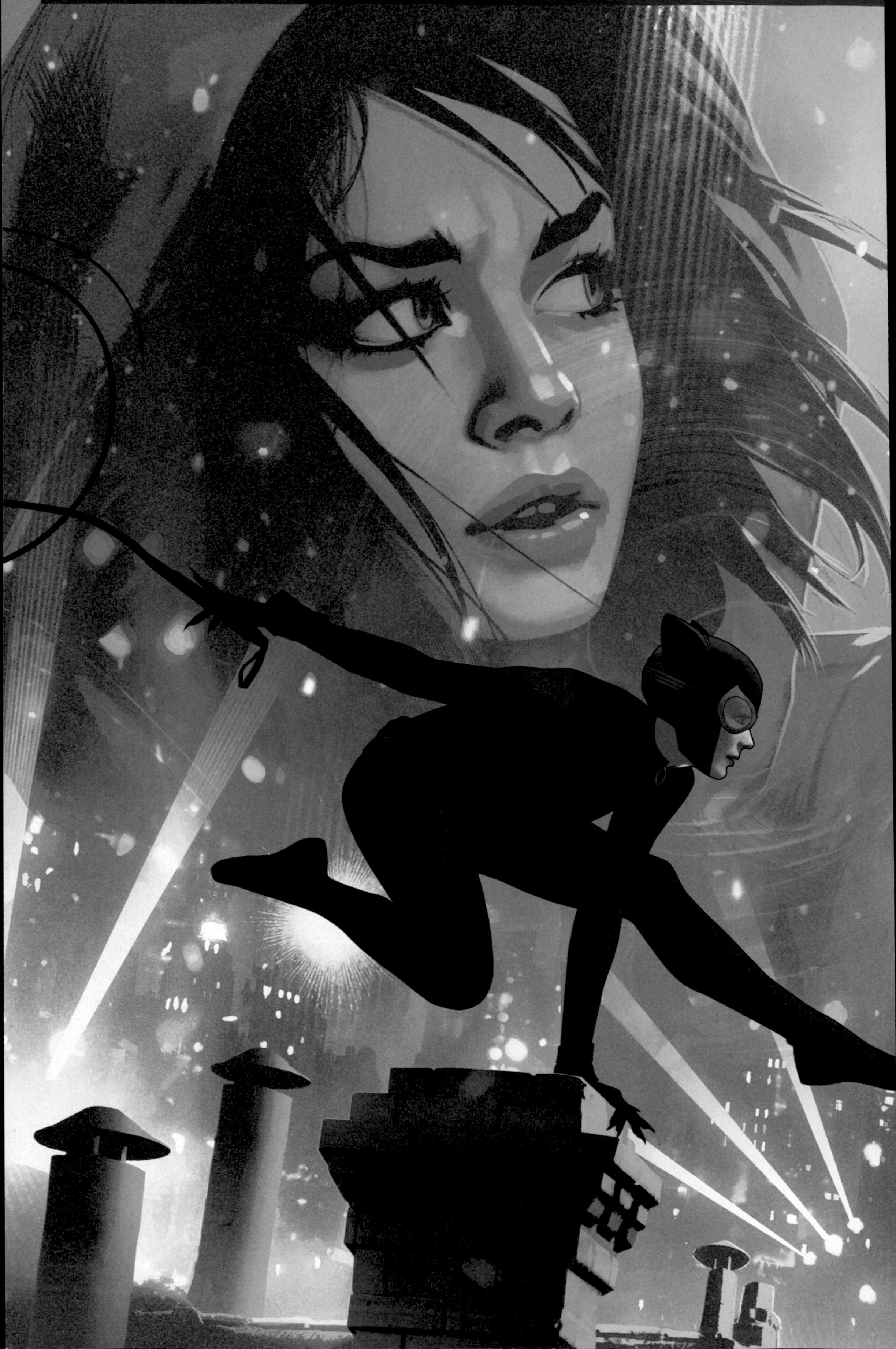

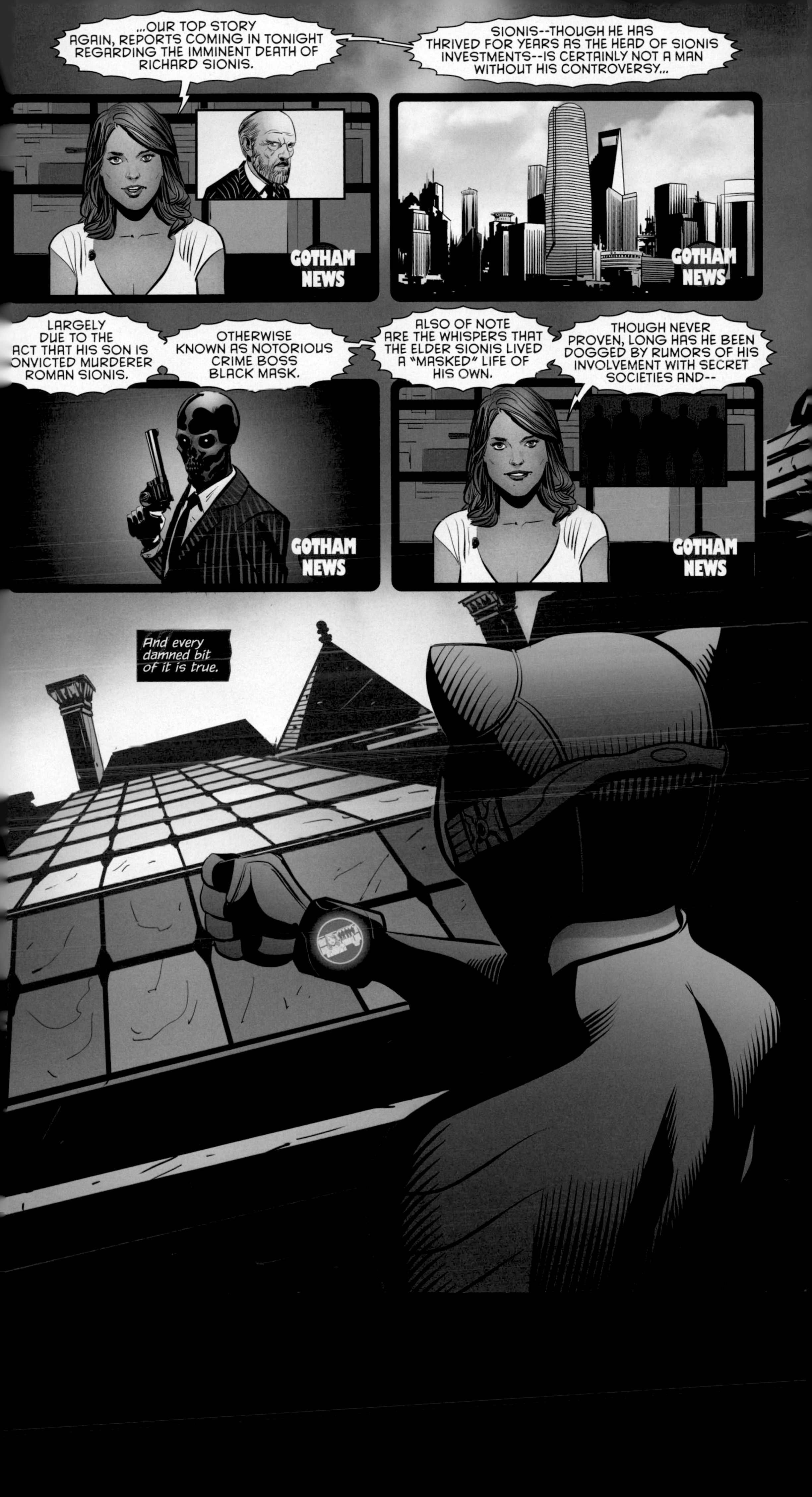
...OUR TOP STORY AGAIN, REPORTS COMING IN TONIGHT REGARDING THE IMMINENT DEATH OF RICHARD SIONIS.
SIONIS--THOUGH HE HAS THRIVED FOR YEARS AS THE HEAD OF SIONIS INVESTMENTS--IS CERTAINLY NOT A MAN WITHOUT HIS CONTROVERSY...
GOTHAM NEWS
GOTHAM NEWS
LARGELY DUE TO THE ACT THAT HIS SON IS ONVICTED MURDERER ROMAN SIONIS.
OTHERWISE KNOWN AS NOTORIOUS CRIME BOSS BLACK MASK.
ALSO OF NOTE ARE THE WHISPERS THAT THE ELDER SIONIS LIVED A "MASKED" LIFE OF HIS OWN.
THOUGH NEVER PROVEN, LONG HAS HE BEEN DOGGED BY RUMORS OF HIS INVOLVEMENT WITH SECRET SOCIETIES AND--
GOTHAM NEWS
GOTHAM NEWS
And every damned bit of it is true.

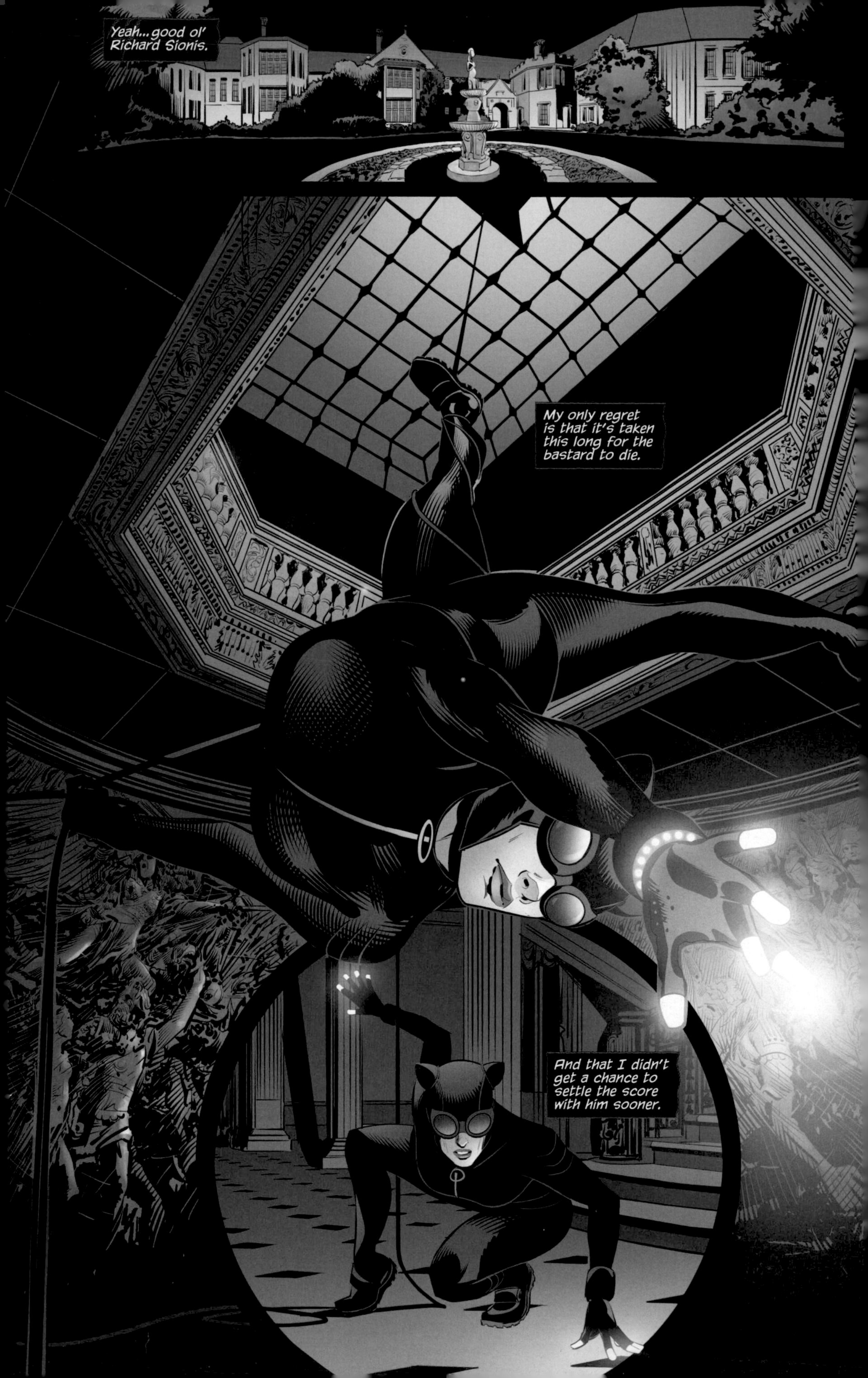
Yeah...good ol' Richard Sionis.
My only regret is that it's taken this long for the bastard to die.
And that I didn't get a chance to settle the score with him sooner.

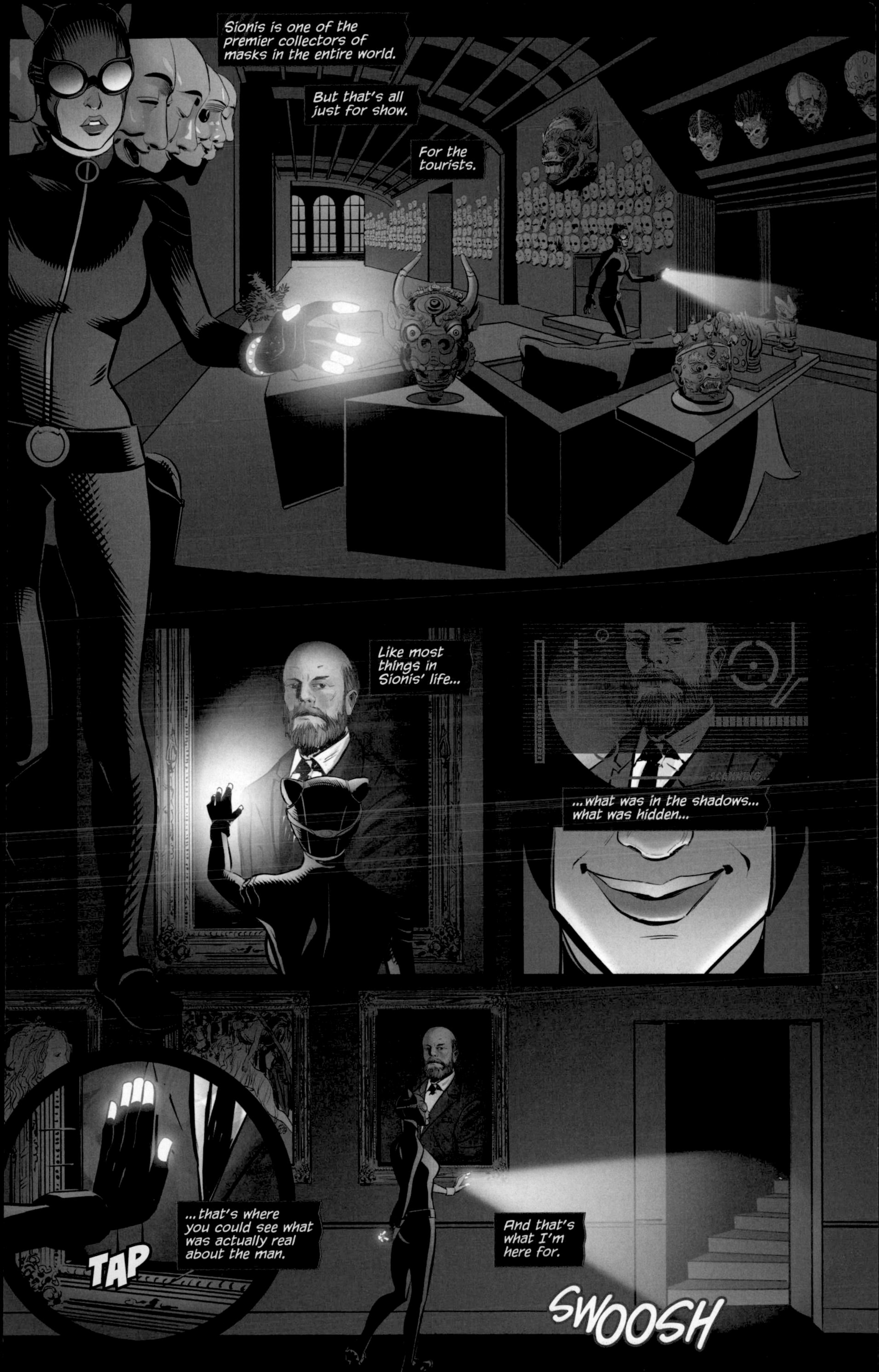
Sionis is one of the premier collectors of masks in the entire world.
But that's all just for show.
For the tourists.
Like most things in Sionis' life...
...what was in the shadows... what was hidden...
...that's where you could see what was actually real about the man.
TAP
And that's what I'm here for.
SWOOSH

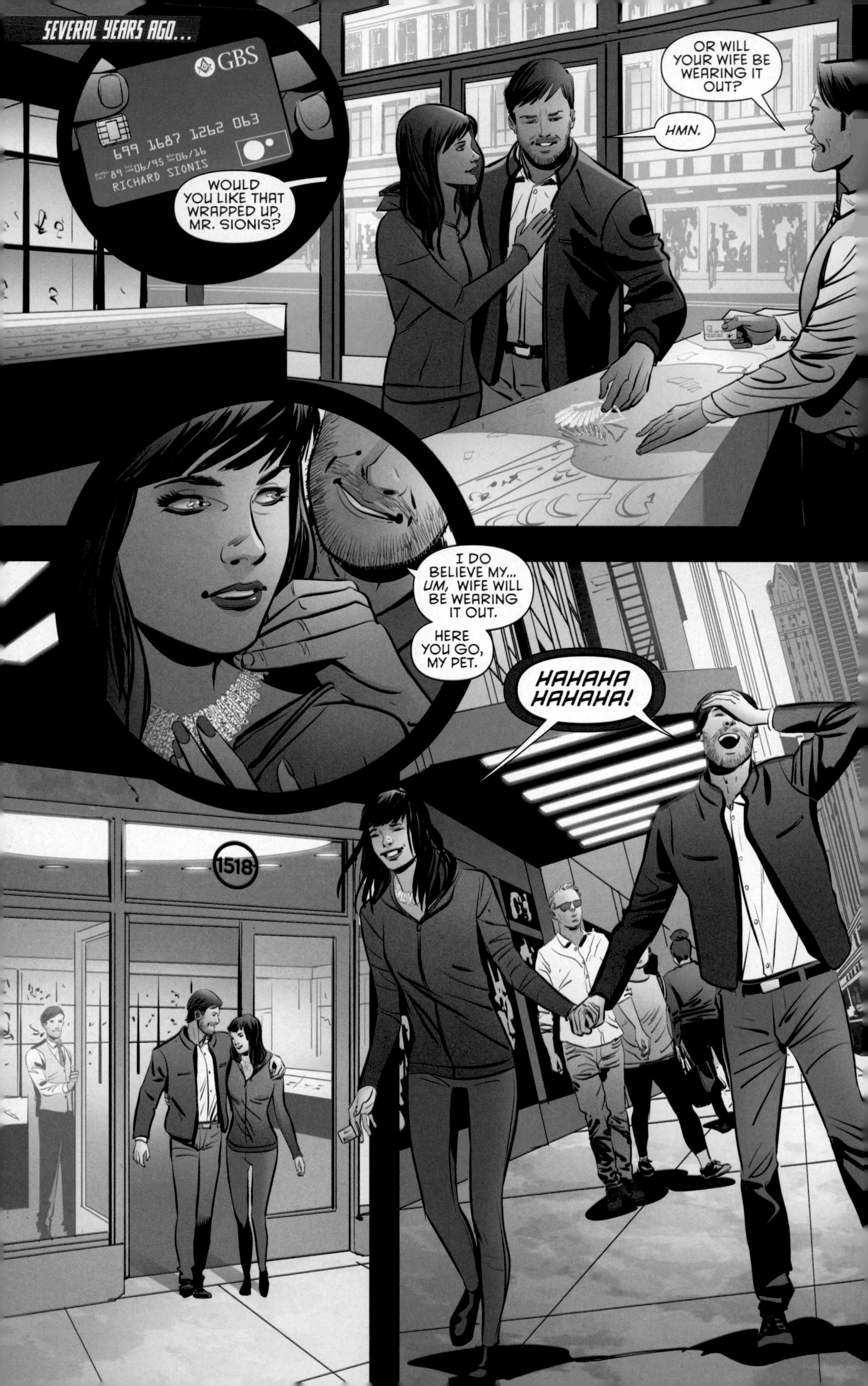
SEVERAL YEARS AGO...
GBS
699 1687 1262 063
89 06/95 06/16
RICHARD SIONIS
WOULD YOU LIKE THAT WRAPPED UP, MR. SIONIS?
OR WILL YOUR WIFE BE WEARING IT OUT?
HMN.
I DO BELIEVE MY... UM, WIFE WILL BE WEARING IT OUT.
HERE YOU GO, MY PET.
HAHAHA HAHAHA!
1518

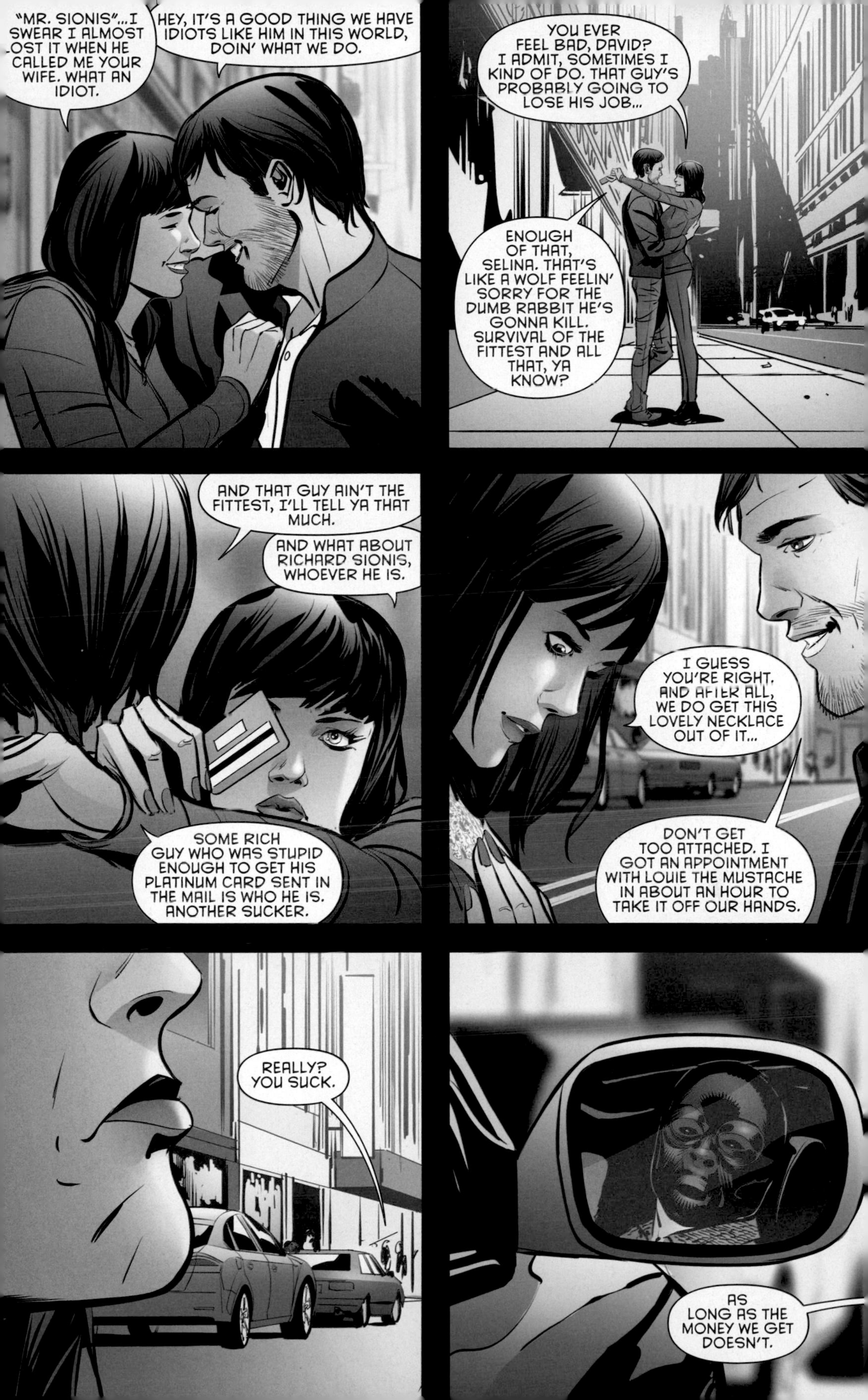
"MR. SIONIS"...I SWEAR I ALMOST LOST IT WHEN HE CALLED ME YOUR WIFE. WHAT AN IDIOT.
HEY, IT'S A GOOD THING WE HAVE IDIOTS LIKE HIM IN THIS WORLD, DOIN' WHAT WE DO.
YOU EVER FEEL BAD, DAVID? I ADMIT, SOMETIMES I KIND OF DO. THAT GUY'S PROBABLY GOING TO LOSE HIS JOB...
ENOUGH OF THAT, SELINA. THAT'S LIKE A WOLF FEELIN' SORRY FOR THE DUMB RABBIT HE'S GONNA KILL. SURVIVAL OF THE FITTEST AND ALL THAT, YA KNOW?
AND THAT GUY AIN'T THE FITTEST, I'LL TELL YA THAT MUCH.
AND WHAT ABOUT RICHARD SIONIS, WHOEVER HE IS.
SOME RICH GUY WHO WAS STUPID ENOUGH TO GET HIS PLATINUM CARD SENT IN THE MAIL IS WHO HE IS. ANOTHER SUCKER.
I GUESS YOU'RE RIGHT. AND AFTER ALL, WE DO GET THIS LOVELY NECKLACE OUT OF IT...
DON'T GET TOO ATTACHED. I GOT AN APPOINTMENT WITH LOUIE THE MUSTACHE IN ABOUT AN HOUR TO TAKE IT OFF OUR HANDS.
REALLY? YOU SUCK.
AS LONG AS THE MONEY WE GET DOESN'T.

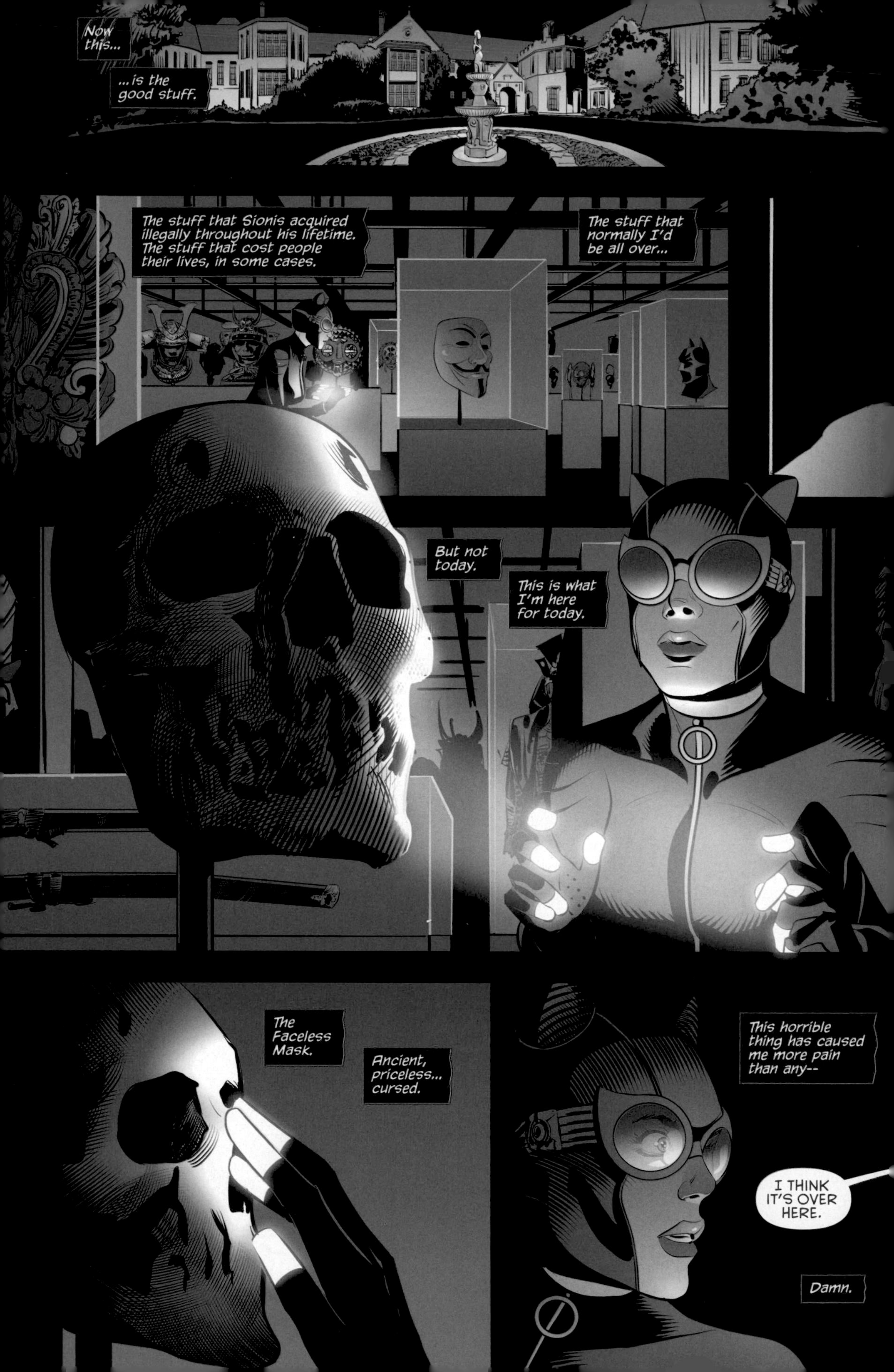

Now this...
...is the good stuff.
The stuff that Sionis acquired illegally throughout his lifetime. The stuff that cost people their lives, in some cases.
The stuff that normally I'd be all over...
But not today.
This is what I'm here for today.
The Faceless Mask.
Ancient, priceless... cursed.
This horrible thing has caused me more pain than any--
I THINK IT'S OVER HERE.
Damn.

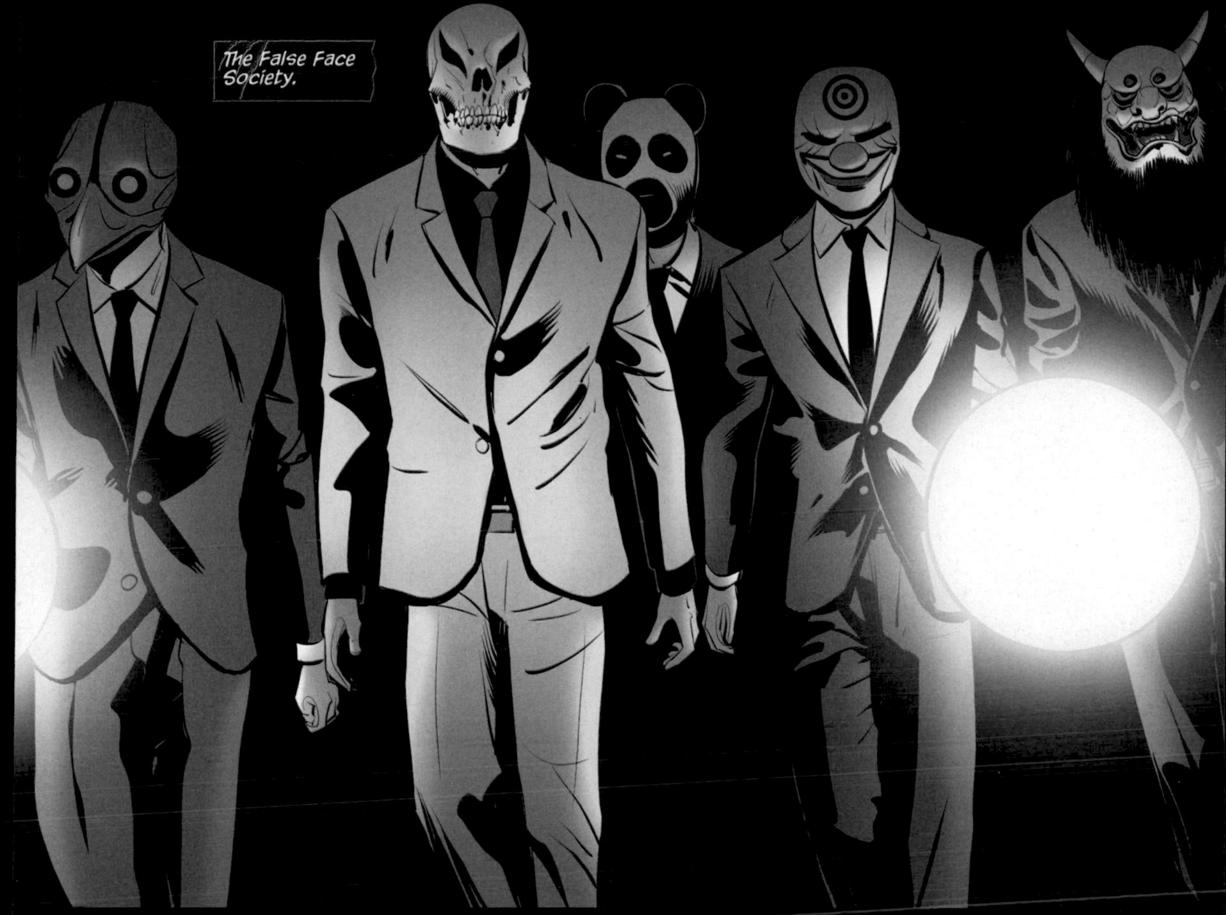
The False Face Society.

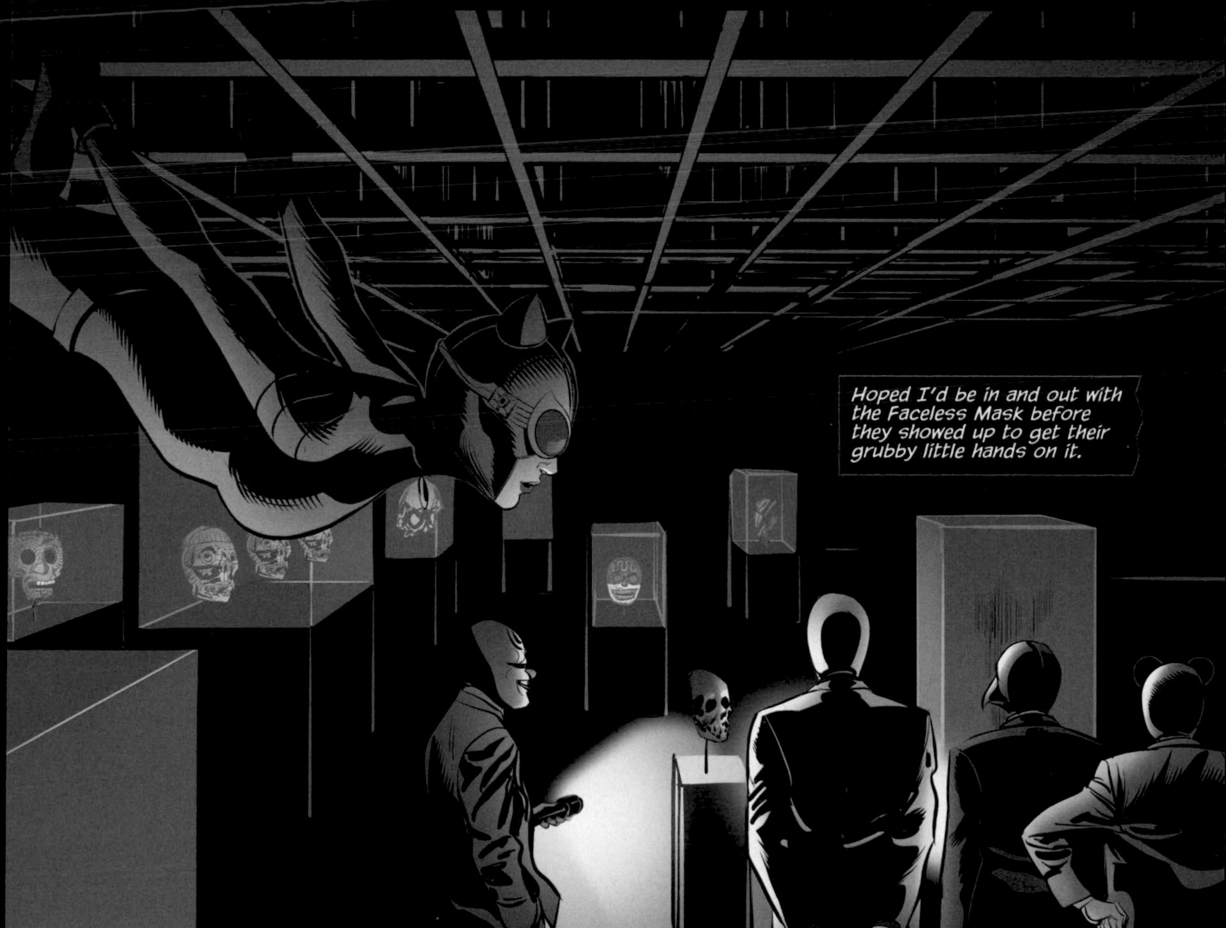
Hoped I'd be in and out with the Faceless Mask before they showed up to get their grubby little hands on it.

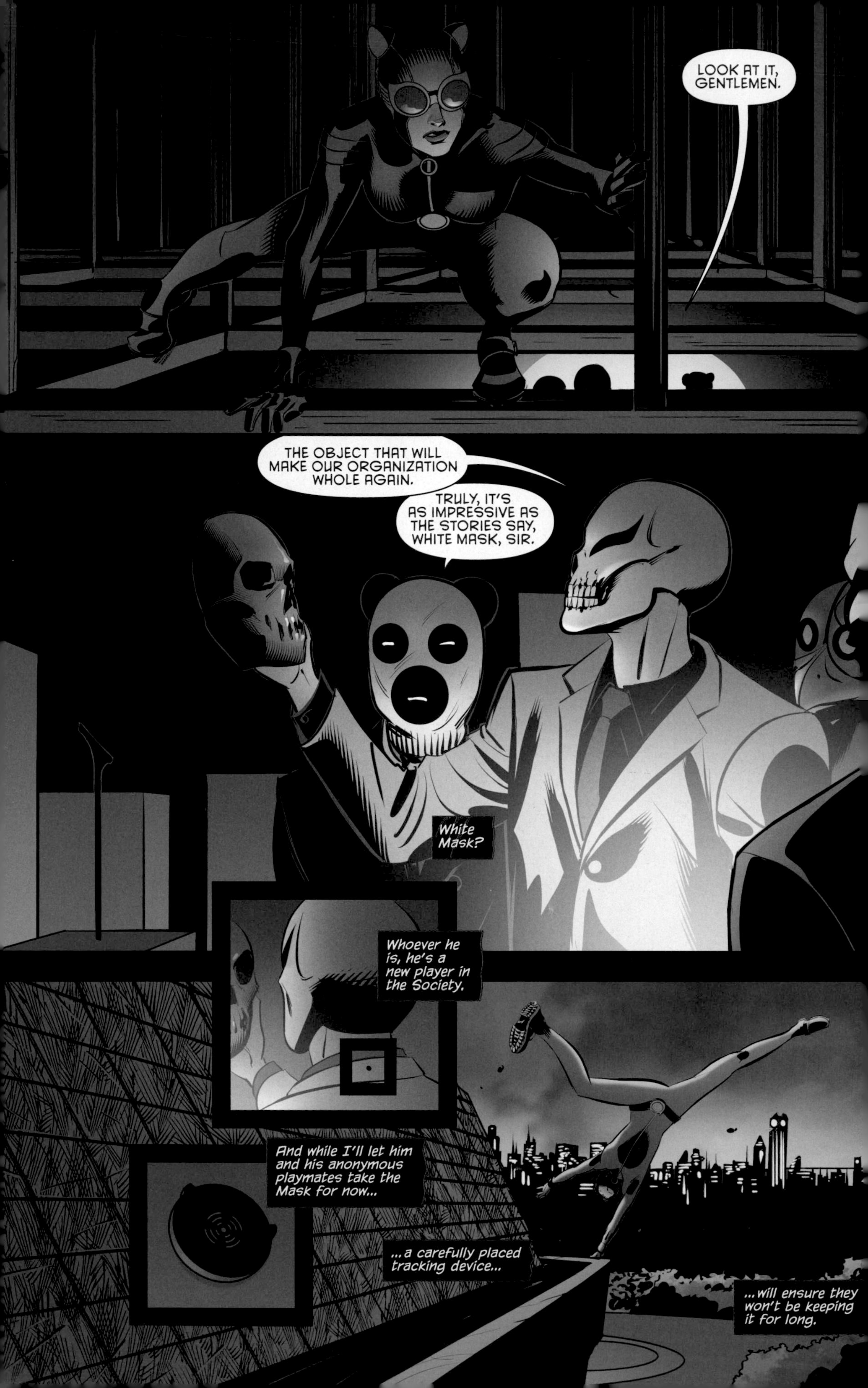
LOOK AT IT, GENTLEMEN.
THE OBJECT THAT WILL MAKE OUR ORGANIZATION WHOLE AGAIN.
TRULY, IT'S AS IMPRESSIVE AS THE STORIES SAY, WHITE MASK, SIR.
White Mask?
Whoever he is, he's a new player in the Society.
And while I'll let him and his anonymous playmates take the Mask for now...
...a carefully placed tracking device...
...will ensure they won't be keeping it for long.

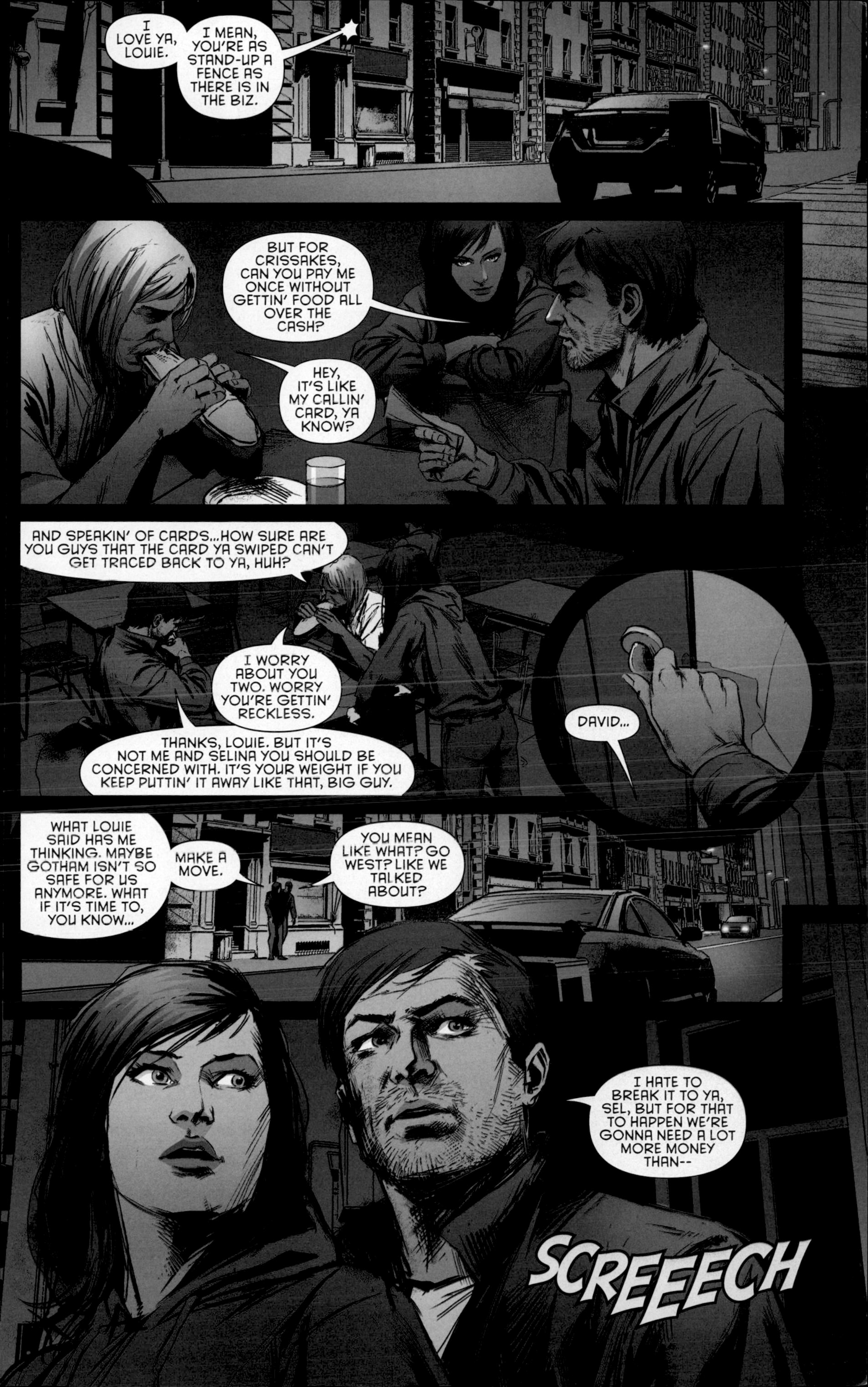
I LOVE YA, LOUIE.
I MEAN, YOU'RE AS STAND-UP A FENCE AS THERE IS IN THE BIZ.
BUT FOR CRISSAKES, CAN YOU PAY ME ONCE WITHOUT GETTIN' FOOD ALL OVER THE CASH?
HEY, IT'S LIKE MY CALLIN' CARD, YA KNOW?
AND SPEAKIN' OF CARDS...HOW SURE ARE YOU GUYS THAT THE CARD YA SWIPED CAN'T GET TRACED BACK TO YA, HUH?
I WORRY ABOUT YOU TWO. WORRY YOU'RE GETTIN' RECKLESS.
THANKS, LOUIE. BUT IT'S NOT ME AND SELINA YOU SHOULD BE CONCERNED WITH. IT'S YOUR WEIGHT IF YOU KEEP PUTTIN' IT AWAY LIKE THAT, BIG GUY.
DAVID...
WHAT LOUIE SAID HAS ME THINKING. MAYBE GOTHAM ISN'T SO SAFE FOR US ANYMORE. WHAT IF IT'S TIME TO, YOU KNOW...
MAKE A MOVE.
YOU MEAN LIKE WHAT? GO WEST? LIKE WE TALKED ABOUT?
I HATE TO BREAK IT TO YA, SEL, BUT FOR THAT TO HAPPEN WE'RE GONNA NEED A LOT MORE MONEY THAN--
SCREEECH

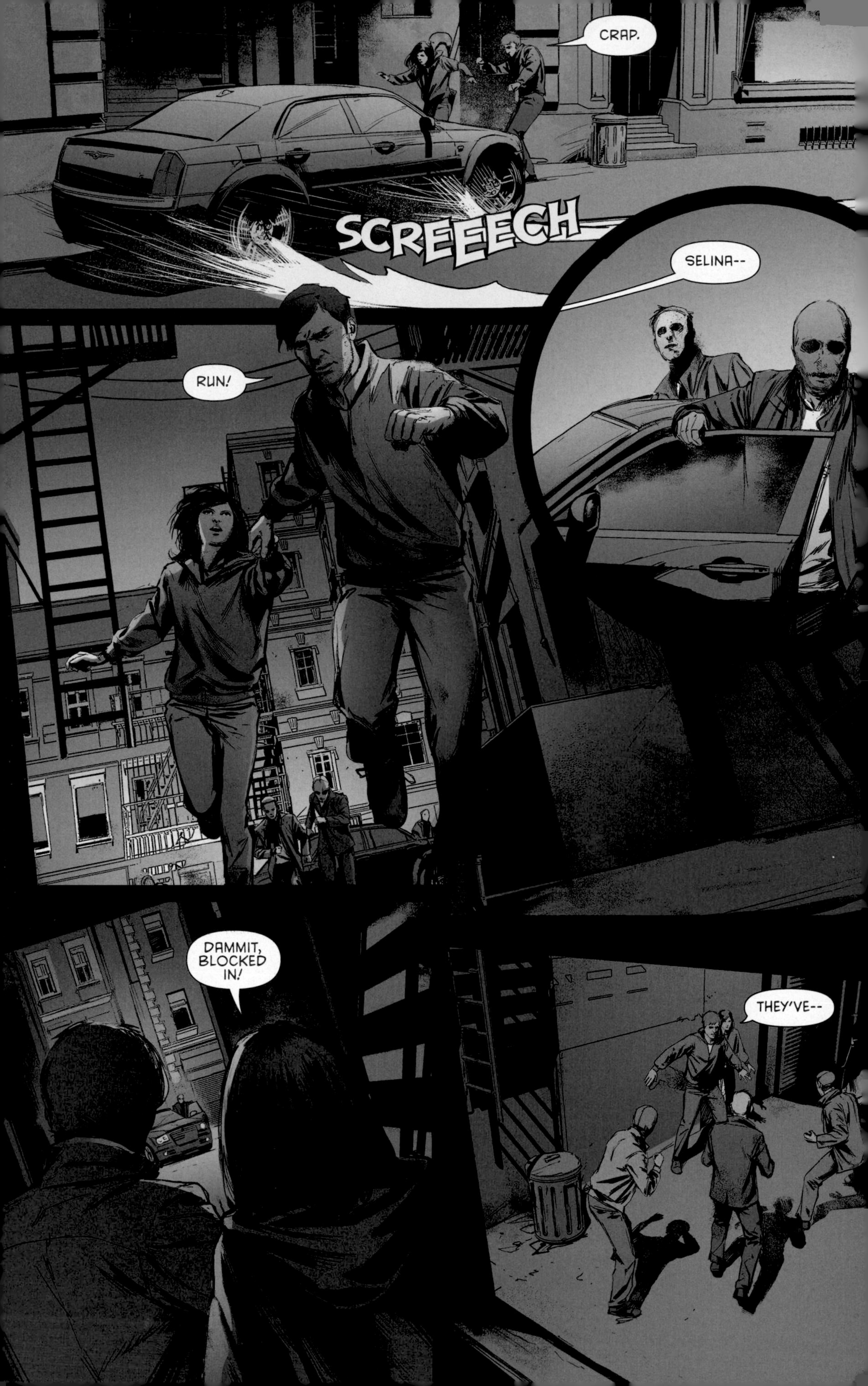
CRAP.
SCREEECH
SELINA--
RUN!
DAMMIT, BLOCKED IN!
THEY'VE--

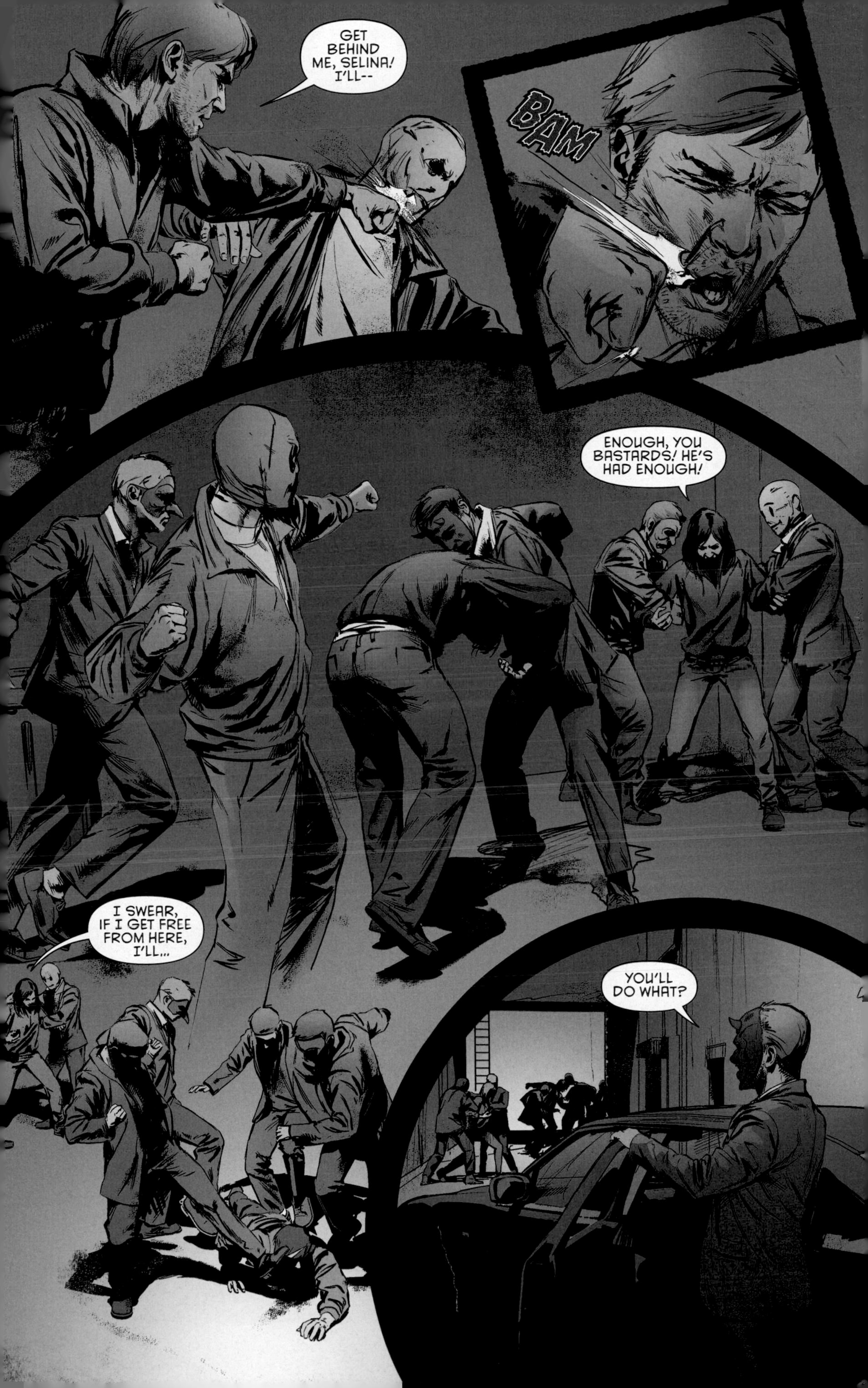
GET BEHIND ME, SELINA! I'LL--
BAM
ENOUGH, YOU BASTARDS! HE'S HAD ENOUGH!
I SWEAR, IF I GET FREE FROM HERE, I'LL...
YOU'LL DO WHAT?

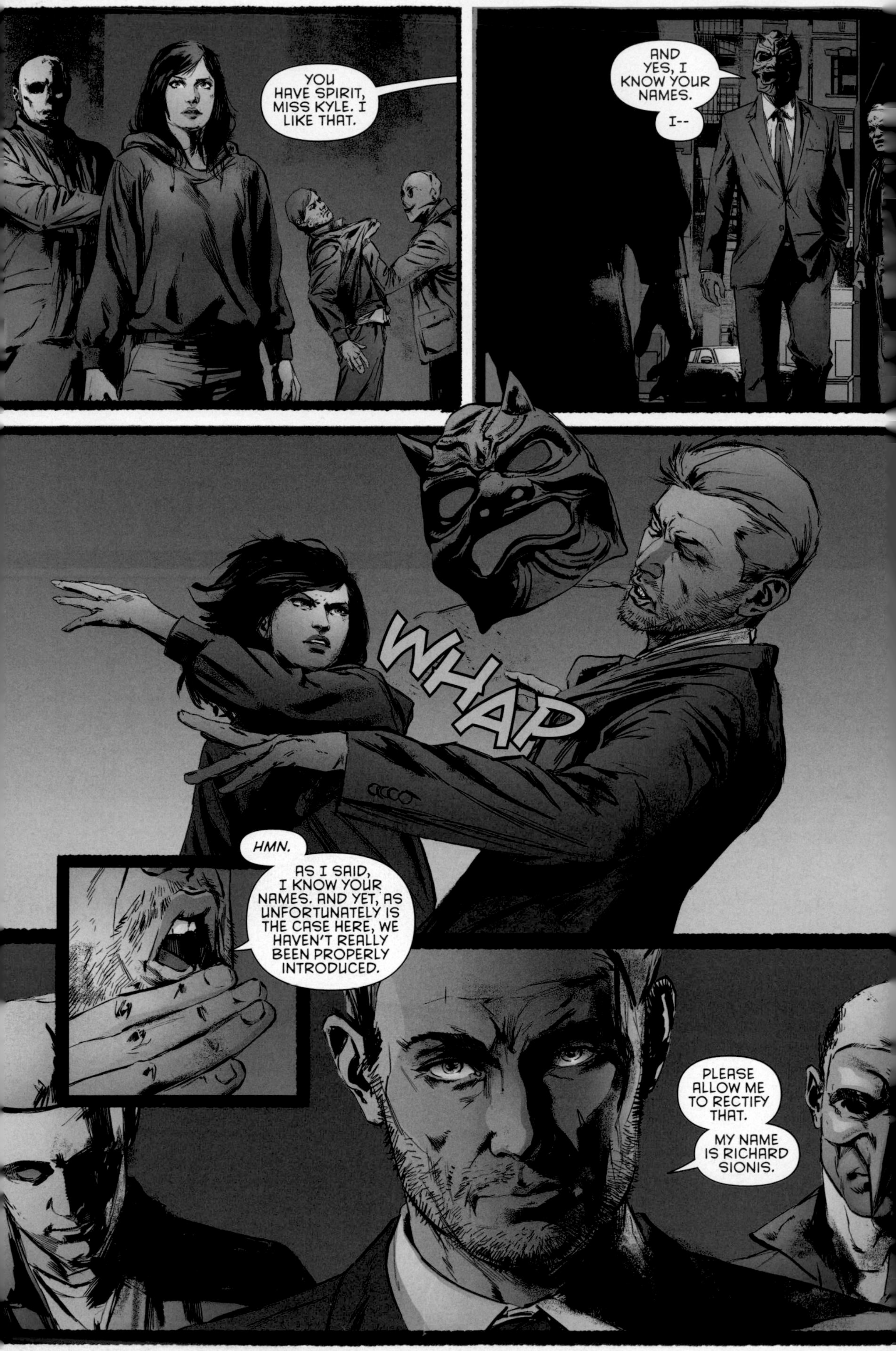
YOU HAVE SPIRIT, MISS KYLE. I LIKE THAT.
AND YES, I KNOW YOUR NAMES.
I--
WHAP
HMN.
AS I SAID, I KNOW YOUR NAMES. AND YET, AS UNFORTUNATELY IS THE CASE HERE, WE HAVEN'T REALLY BEEN PROPERLY INTRODUCED.
PLEASE ALLOW ME TO RECTIFY THAT.
MY NAME IS RICHARD SIONIS.

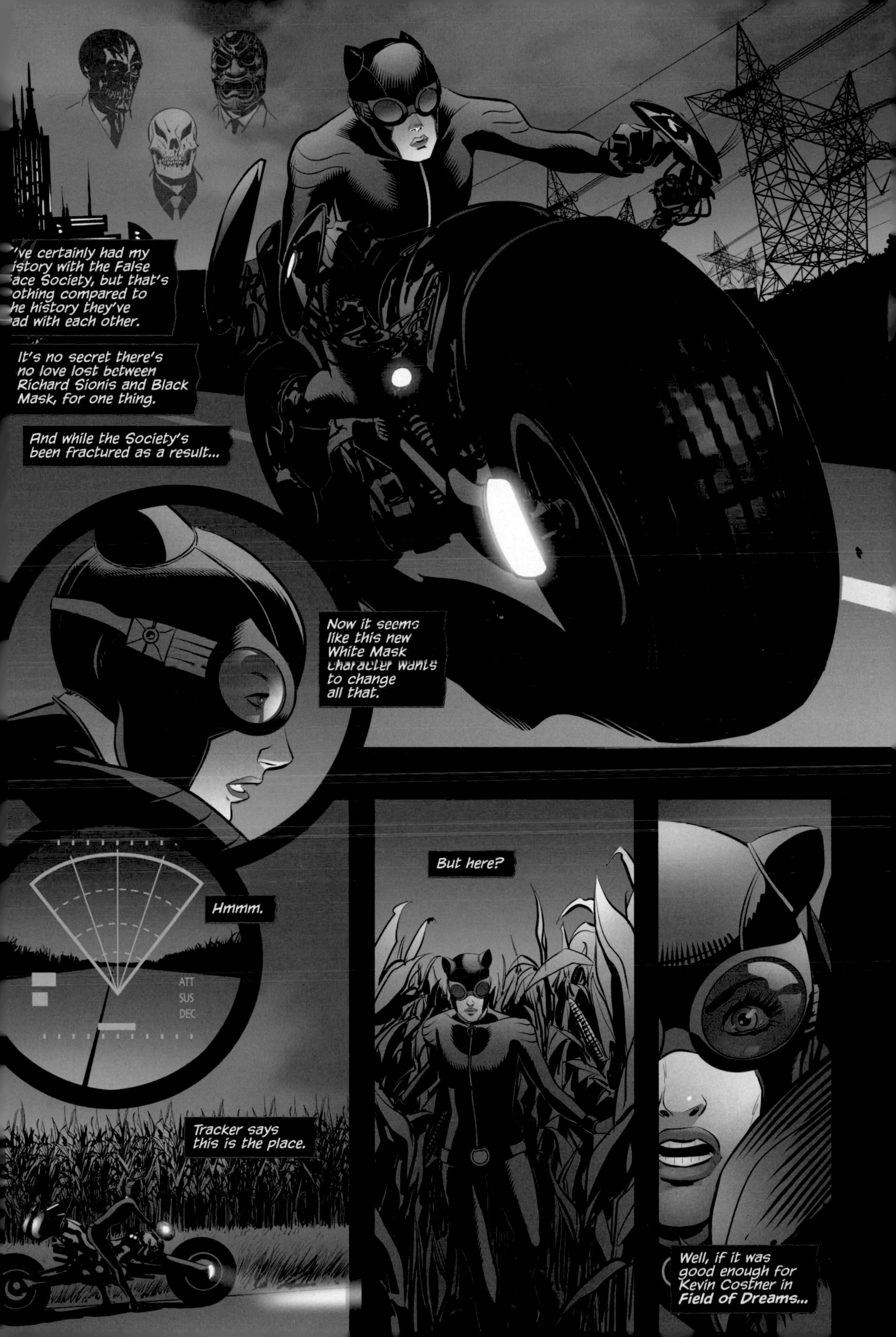
've certainly had my
istory with the False
ace Society, but that's
othing compared to
he history they've
ad with each other.
It's no secret there's no love lost between Richard Sionis and Black Mask, for one thing.
And while the Society's been fractured as a result...
Now it seems like this new White Mask character wants to change all that.
Hmmm.
ATT
SUS
DEC
Tracker says this is the place.
But here?
Well, if it was good enough for Kevin Costner in Field of Dreams...

I guess it's good enough for these creepy masked weirdos now.

Add to that the fact that this all is taking place in the middle of nowhere, they probably also figured they'd only need armed guards in the front...

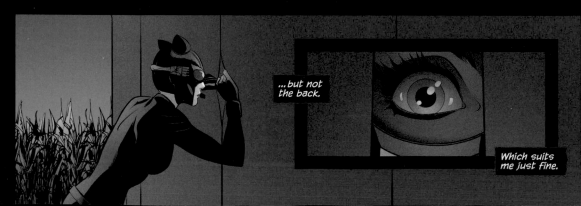

...but not the back.

Which suits me just fine.

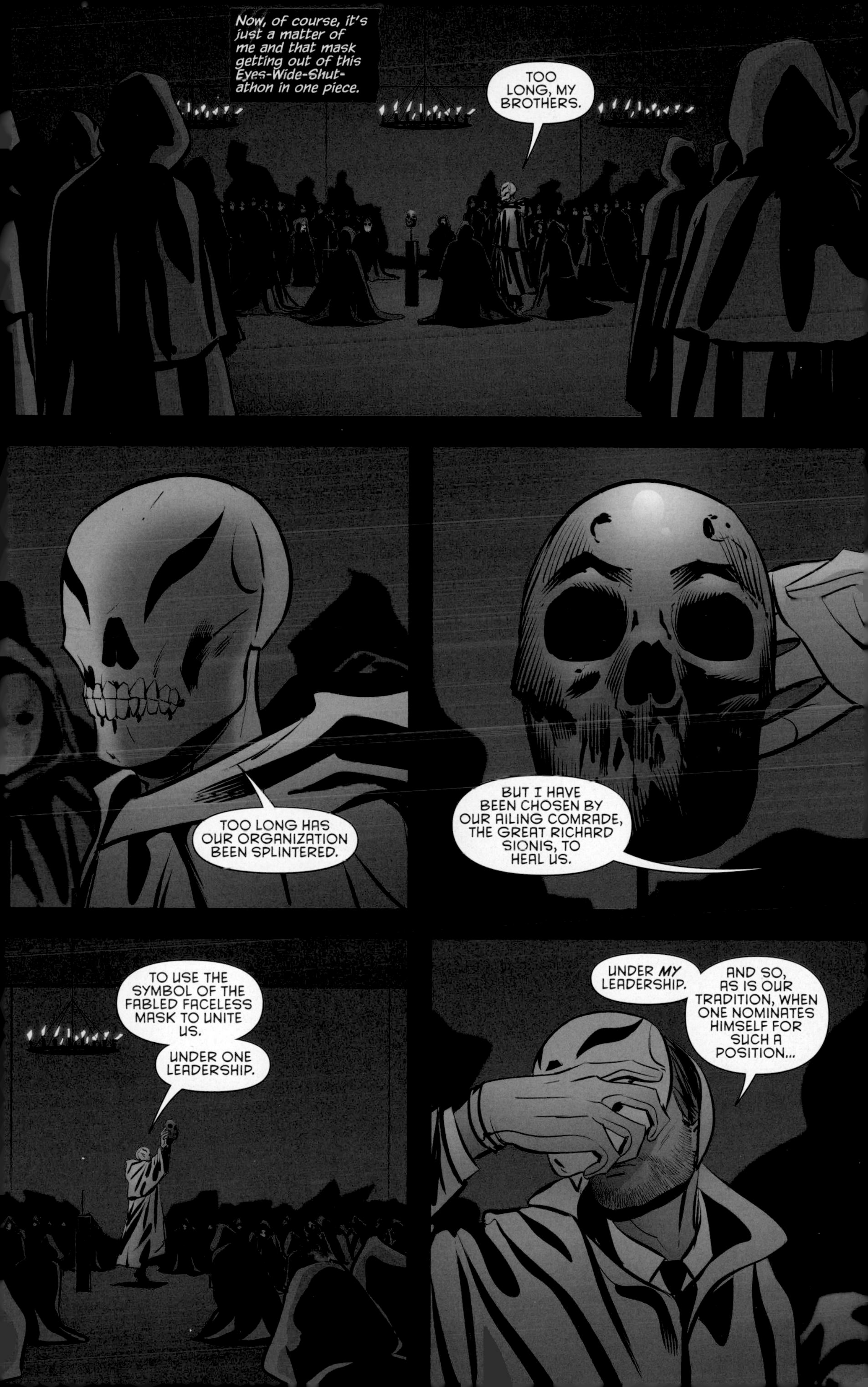
Now, of course, it's just a matter of me and that mask getting out of this Eyes-Wide-Shut-athon in one piece.
TOO LONG, MY BROTHERS.
TOO LONG HAS OUR ORGANIZATION BEEN SPLINTERED.
BUT I HAVE BEEN CHOSEN BY OUR AILING COMRADE, THE GREAT RICHARD SIONIS, TO HEAL US.
TO USE THE SYMBOL OF THE FABLED FACELESS MASK TO UNITE US.
UNDER ONE LEADERSHIP.
UNDER MY LEADERSHIP.
AND SO, AS IS OUR TRADITION, WHEN ONE NOMINATES HIMSELF FOR SUCH A POSITION...

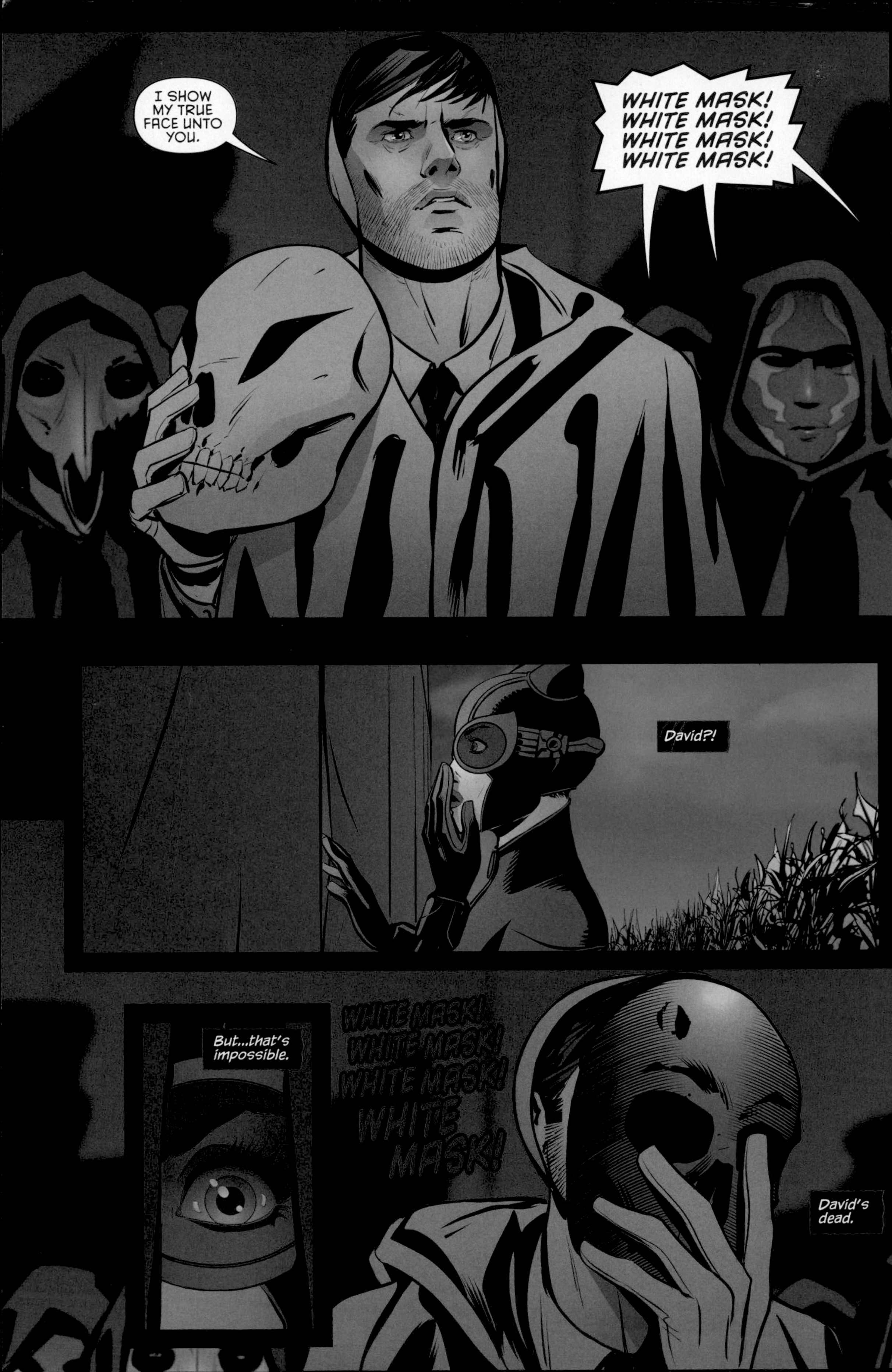
I SHOW MY TRUE FACE UNTO YOU.
WHITE MASK! WHITE MASK! WHITE MASK! WHITE MASK!
David?!
But...that's impossible.
WHITE MASK! WHITE MASK! WHITE MASK! WHITE MASK!
David's dead.

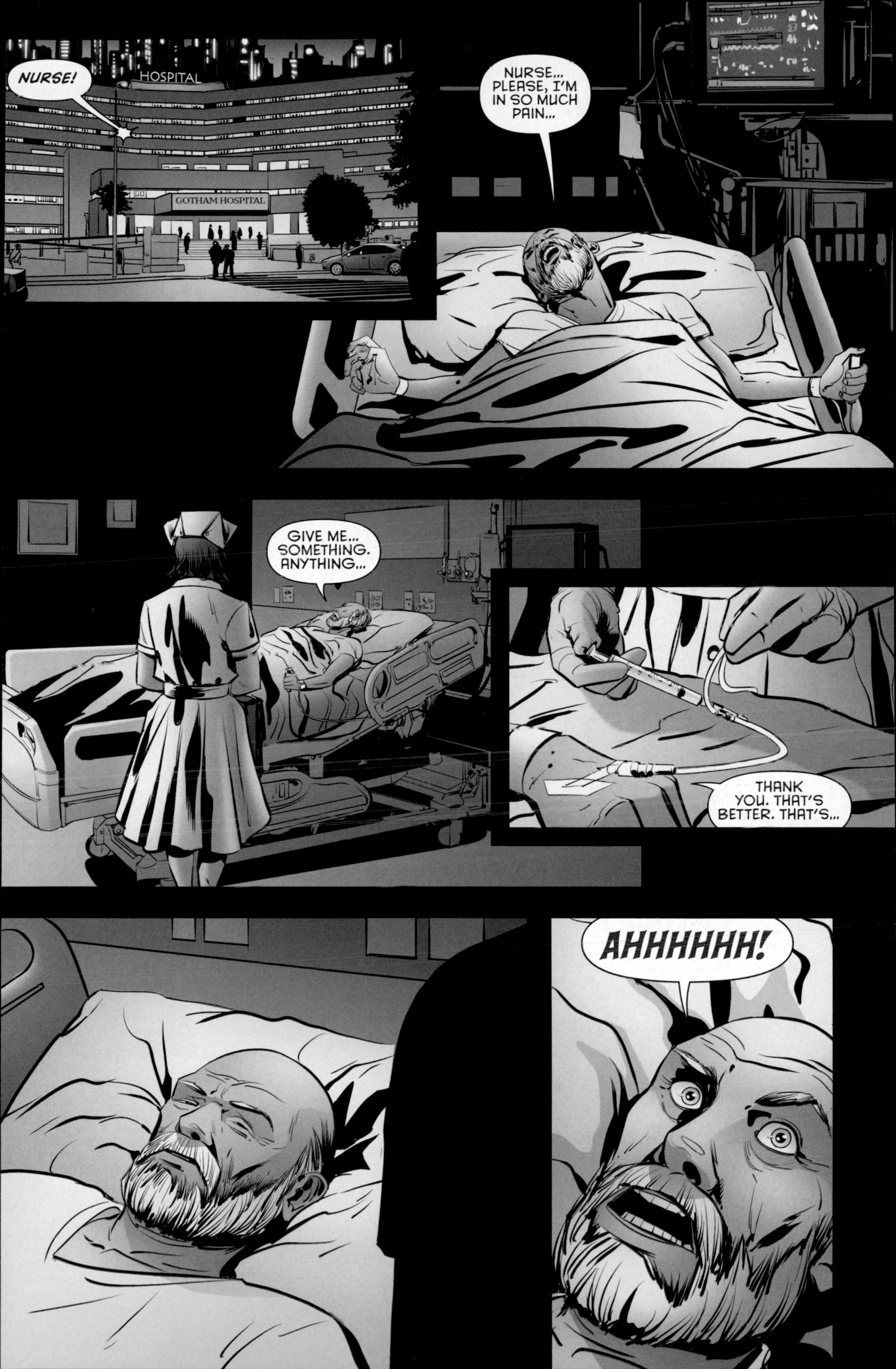
HOSPITAL
NURSE!
GOTHAM HOSPITAL
NURSE... PLEASE, I'M IN SO MUCH PAIN...
GIVE ME... SOMETHING. ANYTHING...
THANK YOU. THAT'S BETTER. THAT'S...
AHHHHHH!

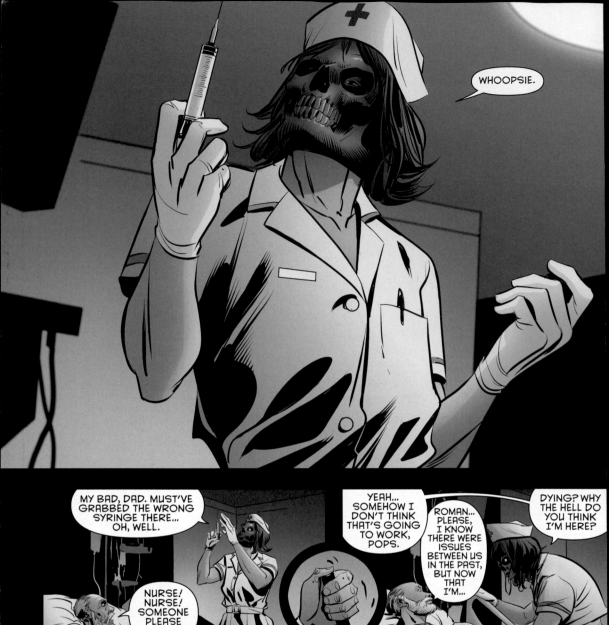

WHOOPSIE.

MY BAD, DAD. MUST'VE GRABBED THE WRONG SYRINGE THERE... OH, WELL.

NURSE! NURSE! SOMEONE PLEASE HELP ME!

YEAH... SOMEHOW I DON'T THINK THAT'S GOING TO WORK, POPS.

ROMAN... PLEASE, I KNOW THERE WERE ISSUES BETWEEN US IN THE PAST, BUT NOW THAT I'M...

DYING? WHY THE HELL DO YOU THINK I'M HERE?

TO MAKE SURE I'M HERE FOR YOUR LAST DYING BREATH, YOU OLD SON OF A BITCH.

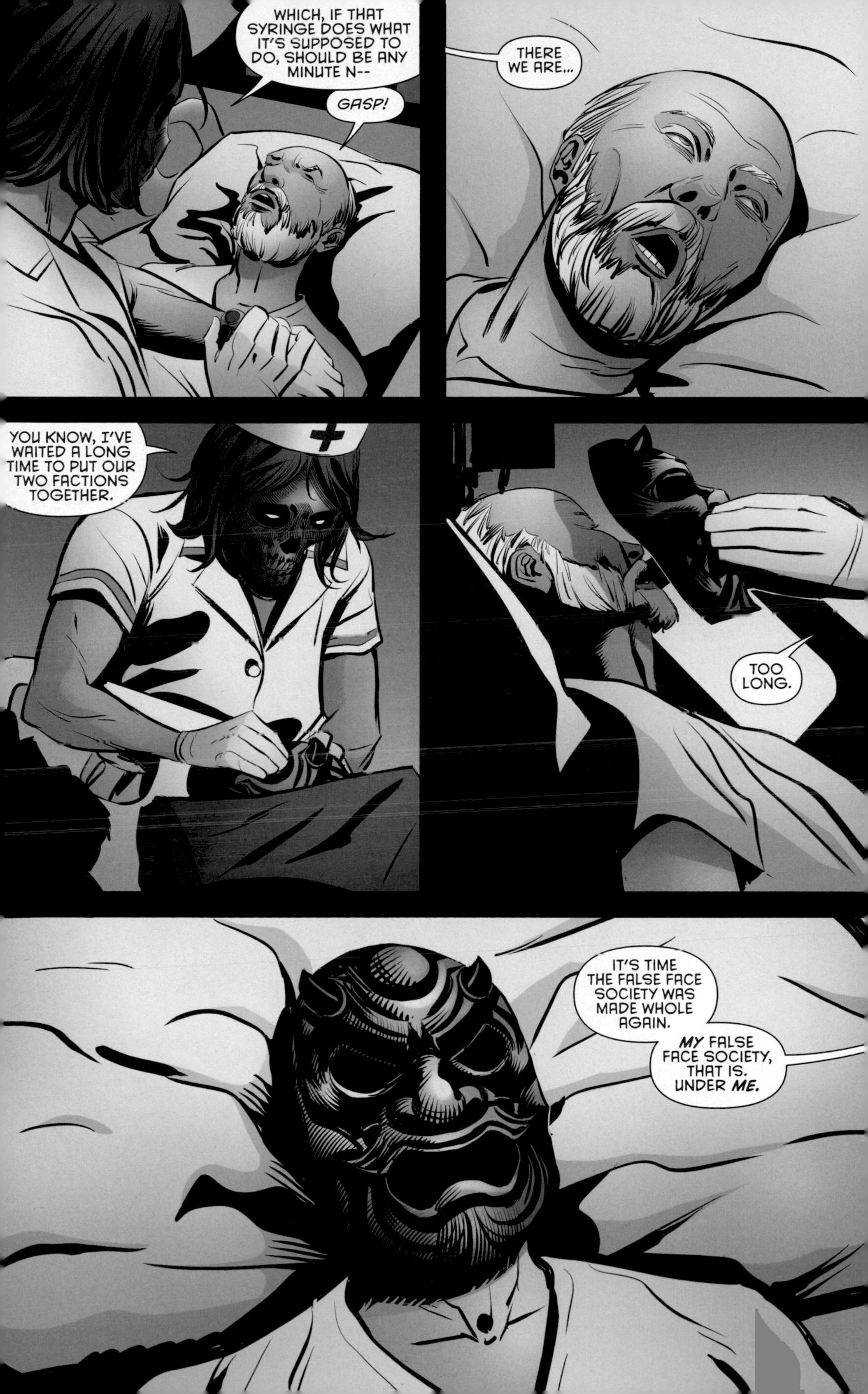
WHICH, IF THAT SYRINGE DOES WHAT IT'S SUPPOSED TO DO, SHOULD BE ANY MINUTE N--
GASP!
THERE WE ARE...
YOU KNOW, I'VE WAITED A LONG TIME TO PUT OUR TWO FACTIONS TOGETHER.
TOO LONG.
IT'S TIME THE FALSE FACE SOCIETY WAS MADE WHOLE AGAIN.
MY FALSE FACE SOCIETY, THAT IS. UNDER *ME.*

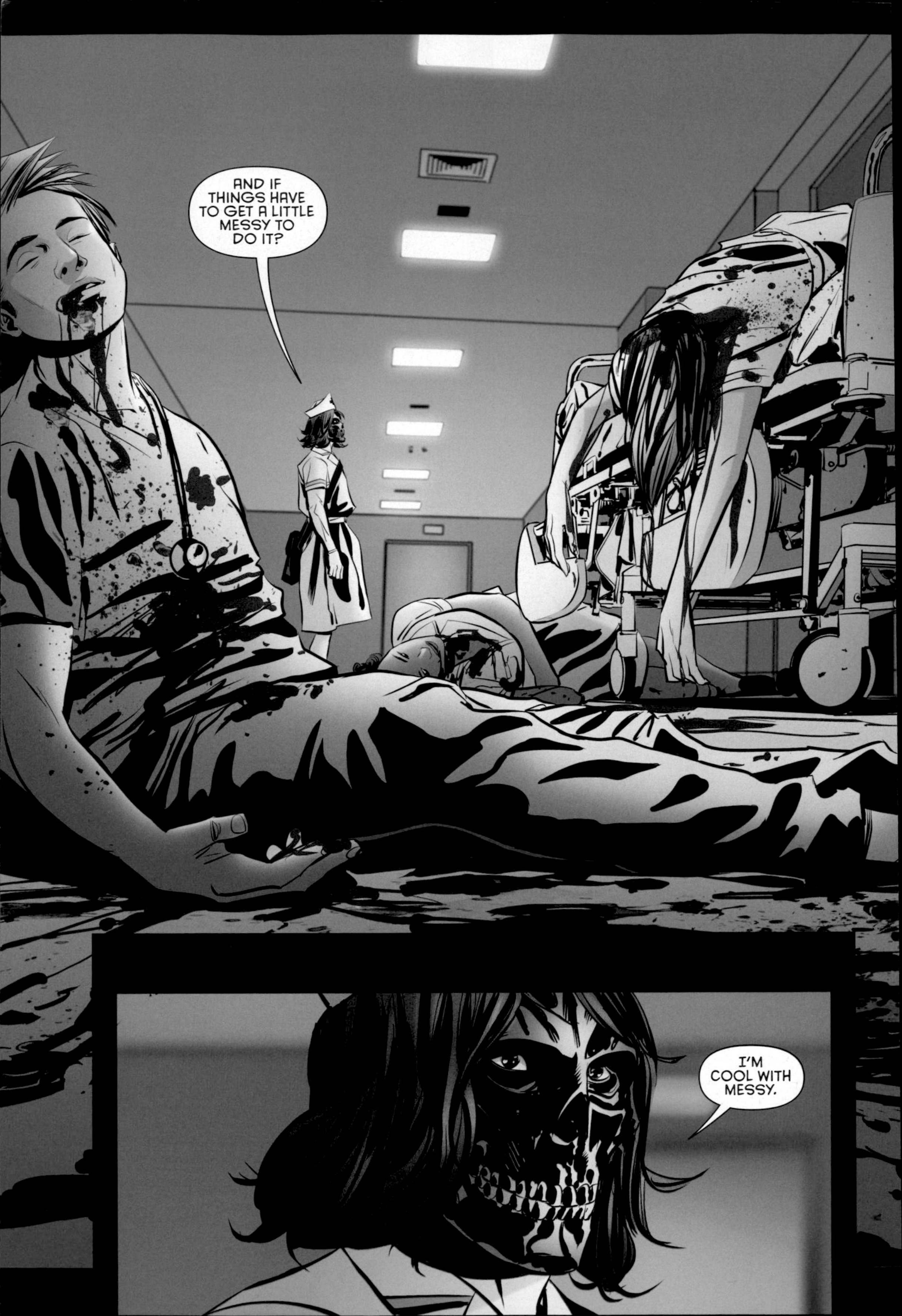
AND IF THINGS HAVE TO GET A LITTLE MESSY TO DO IT?
I'M COOL WITH MESSY.

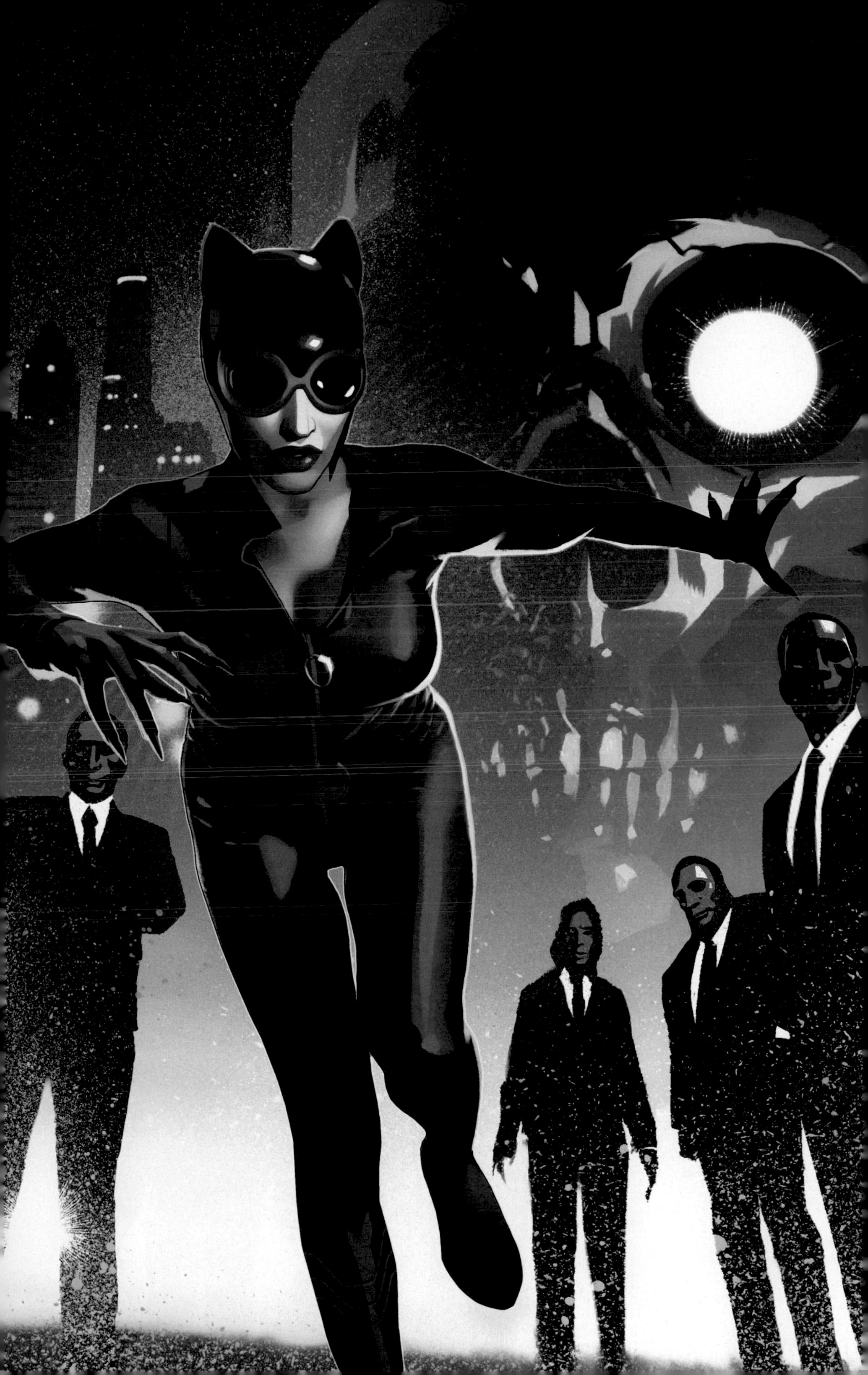

FACELESS, PART TWO

FRANK TIERI writer **INAKI MIRANDA, POP MHAN & GIUSEPPE CAFARO** artists **EVA DE LA CRUZ, BETH SOTELO & JOHN STARR** colorists **TRAVIS LANHAM** letterer
JOSH MIDDLETON cover

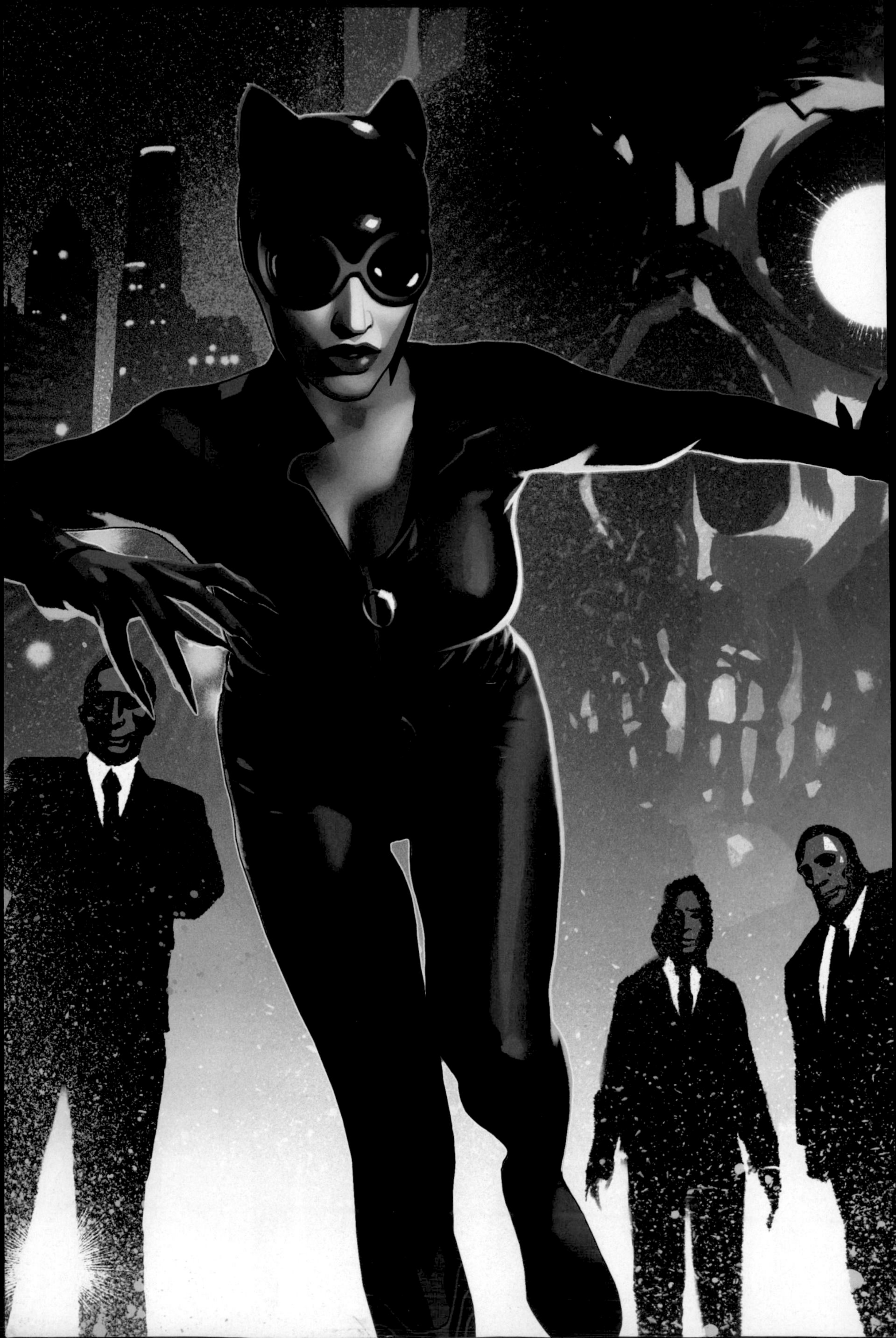

NOTHING ON WHITE MASK.
NOTHING ON DAVID FRANCO.
SORRY, SEL, I'VE GOT WELL...
NOTHING.
EH, IT'S NOT SURPRISING YOU COULDN'T FIND ANYTHING, TESLA.
Especially considering one is supposed to be six feet under and the other is his secret creepo society I.D.
So if in fact a False Face Society civil war is about to happen and my one-time-presumed-dead boyfriend is leading the charge...
I guess I'll have to find out what's going on the old-fashioned way.
NOW IF YOU'LL EXCUSE ME...

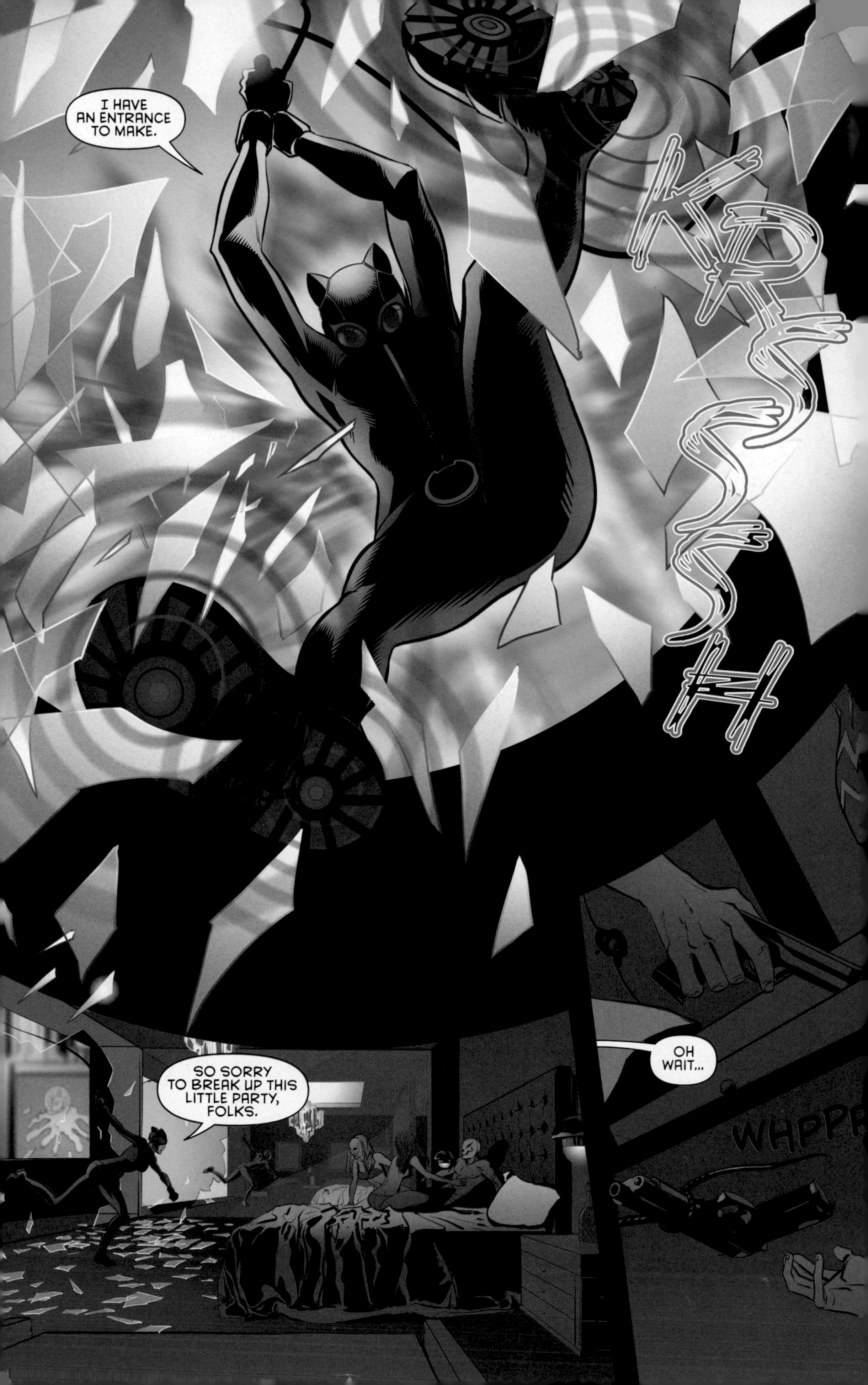
I HAVE AN ENTRANCE TO MAKE.
KRSSSHH
SO SORRY TO BREAK UP THIS LITTLE PARTY, FOLKS.
OH WAIT...
WHPPF

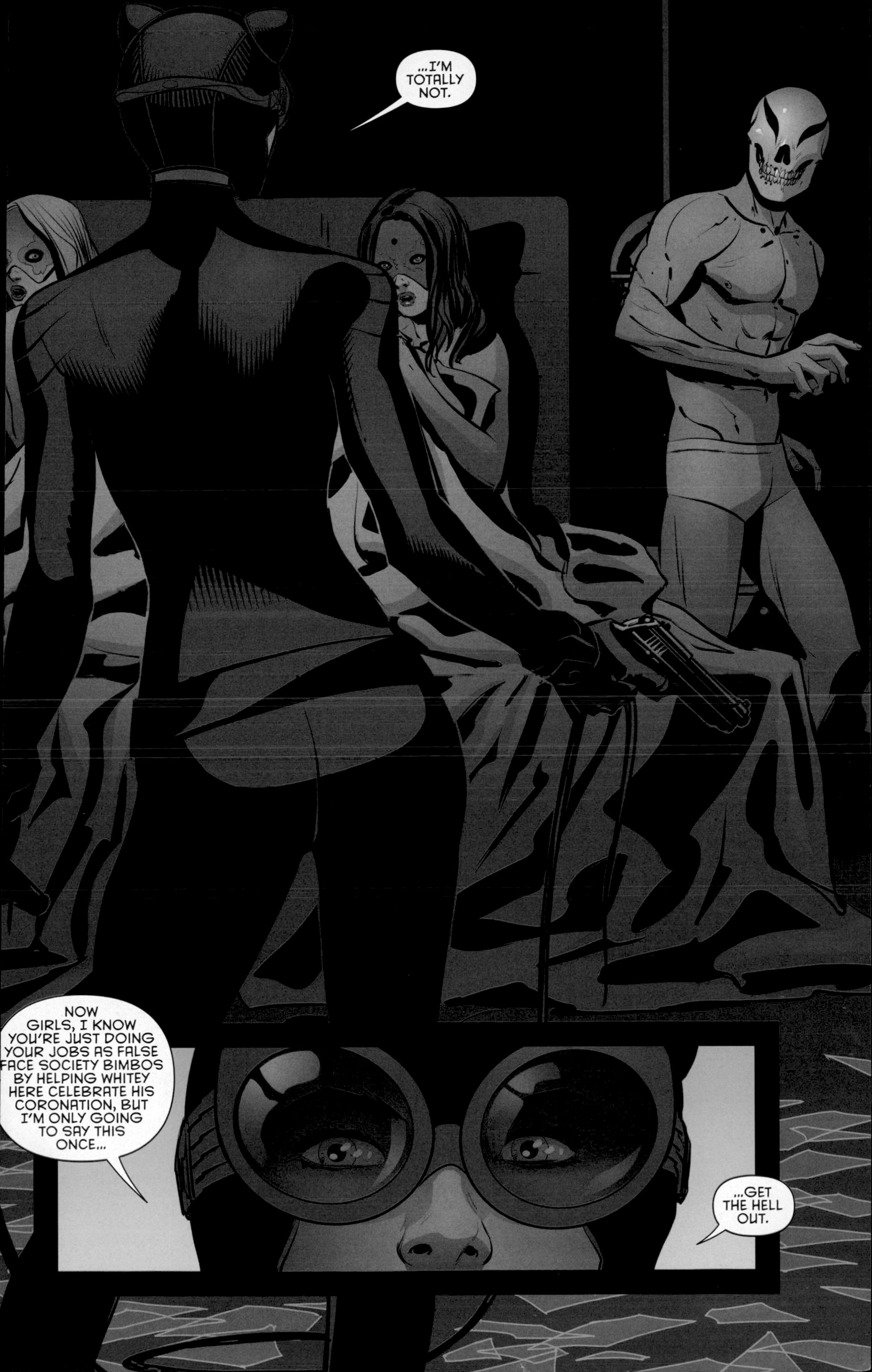
...I'M TOTALLY NOT.
NOW GIRLS, I KNOW YOU'RE JUST DOING YOUR JOBS AS FALSE FACE SOCIETY BIMBOS BY HELPING WHITEY HERE CELEBRATE HIS CORONATION, BUT I'M ONLY GOING TO SAY THIS ONCE...
...GET THE HELL OUT.

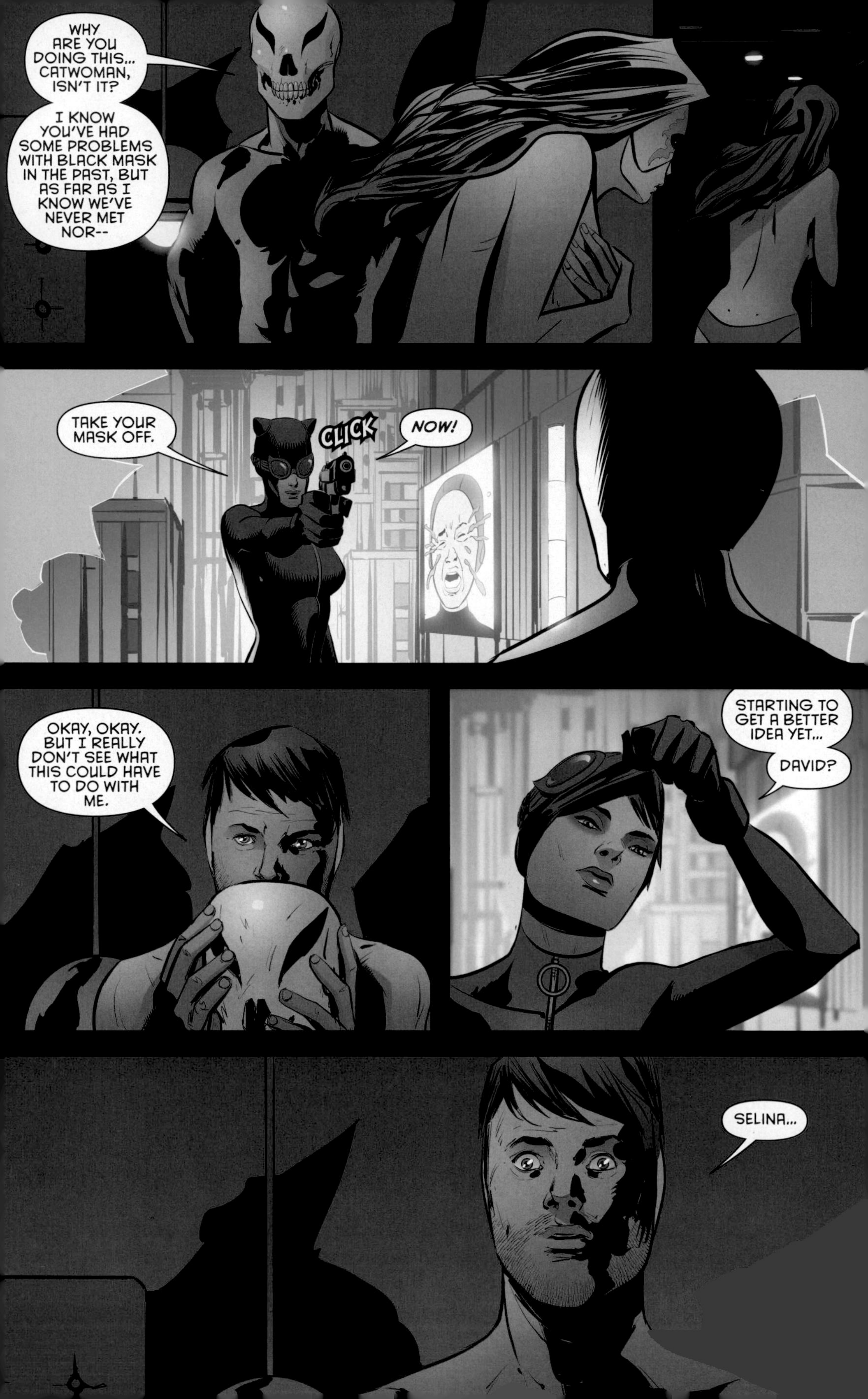
WHY ARE YOU DOING THIS... CATWOMAN, ISN'T IT?
I KNOW YOU'VE HAD SOME PROBLEMS WITH BLACK MASK IN THE PAST, BUT AS FAR AS I KNOW WE'VE NEVER MET NOR--
TAKE YOUR MASK OFF.
CLICK
NOW!
OKAY, OKAY. BUT I REALLY DON'T SEE WHAT THIS COULD HAVE TO DO WITH ME.
STARTING TO GET A BETTER IDEA YET...
DAVID?
SELINA...

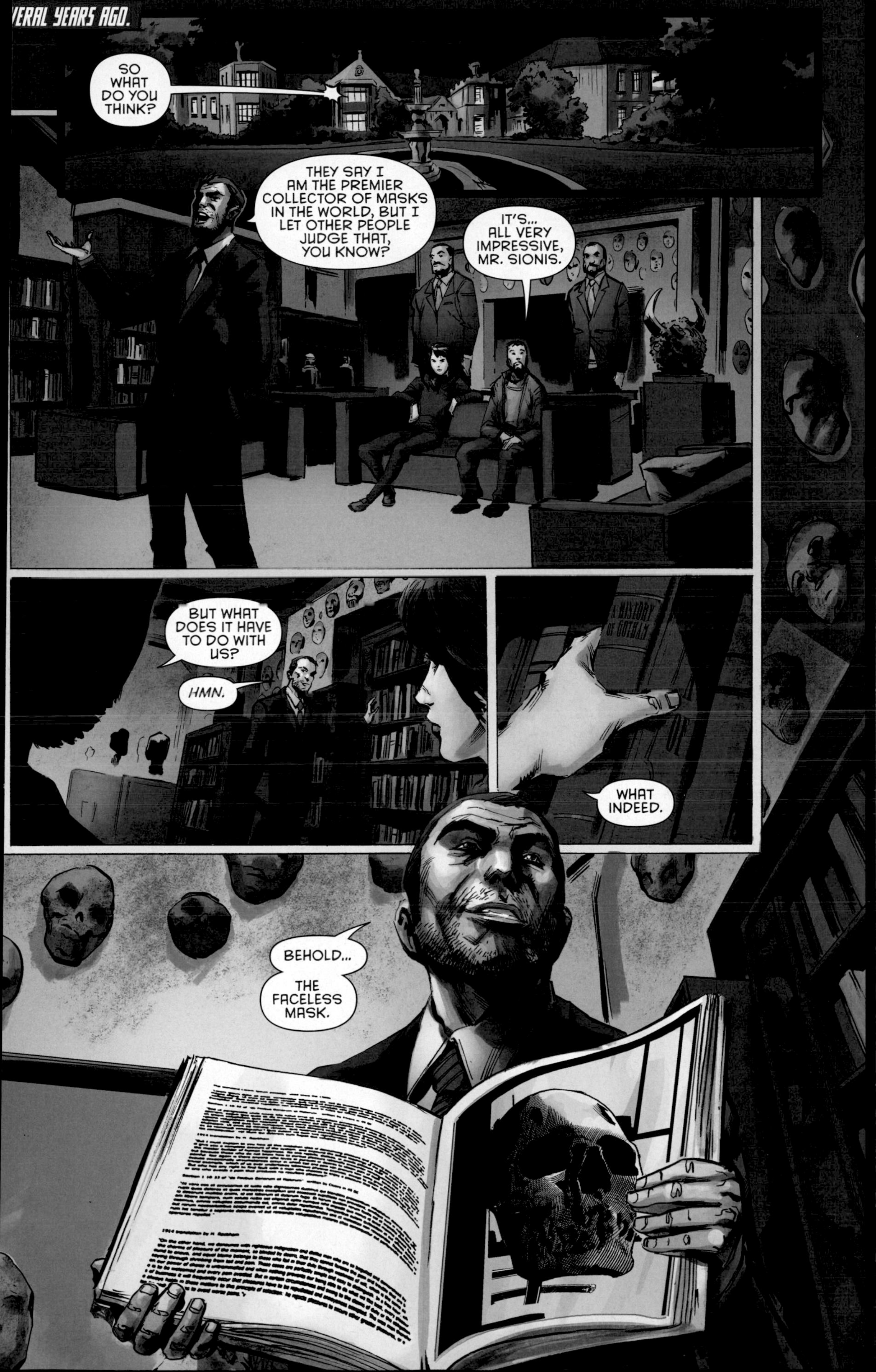

ERAL YEARS AGO.
SO WHAT DO YOU THINK?
THEY SAY I AM THE PREMIER COLLECTOR OF MASKS IN THE WORLD, BUT I LET OTHER PEOPLE JUDGE THAT, YOU KNOW?
IT'S... ALL VERY IMPRESSIVE, MR. SIONIS.
BUT WHAT DOES IT HAVE TO DO WITH US?
HMN.
A HISTORY OF GOTHAM
WHAT INDEED.
BEHOLD...
THE FACELESS MASK.

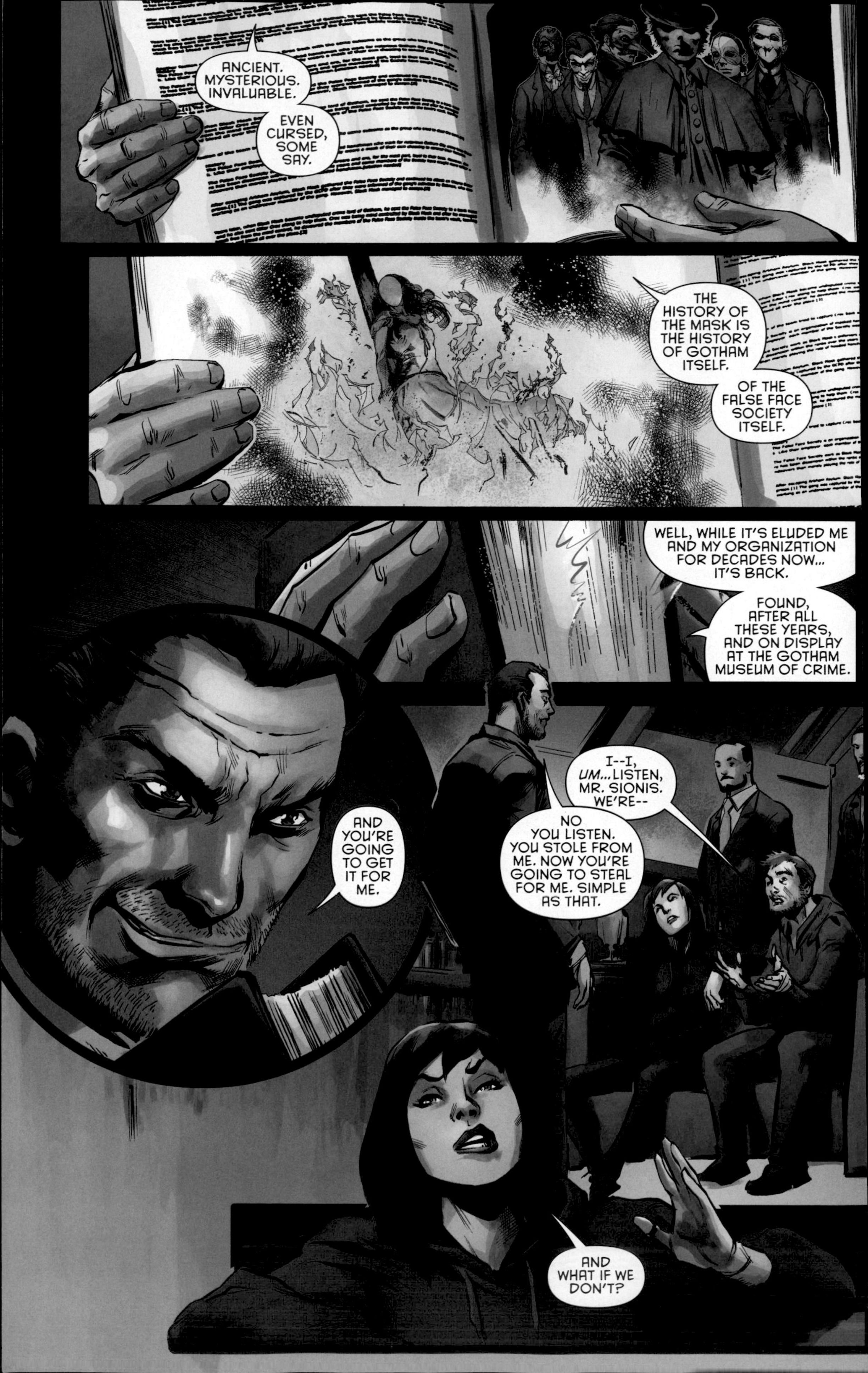
ANCIENT. MYSTERIOUS. INVALUABLE.
EVEN CURSED, SOME SAY.
THE HISTORY OF THE MASK IS THE HISTORY OF GOTHAM ITSELF.
OF THE FALSE FACE SOCIETY ITSELF.
WELL, WHILE IT'S ELUDED ME AND MY ORGANIZATION FOR DECADES NOW... IT'S BACK.
FOUND, AFTER ALL THESE YEARS, AND ON DISPLAY AT THE GOTHAM MUSEUM OF CRIME.
AND YOU'RE GOING TO GET IT FOR ME.
I--I, UM... LISTEN, MR. SIONIS. WE'RE--
NO YOU LISTEN. YOU STOLE FROM ME. NOW YOU'RE GOING TO STEAL FOR ME. SIMPLE AS THAT.
AND WHAT IF WE DON'T?

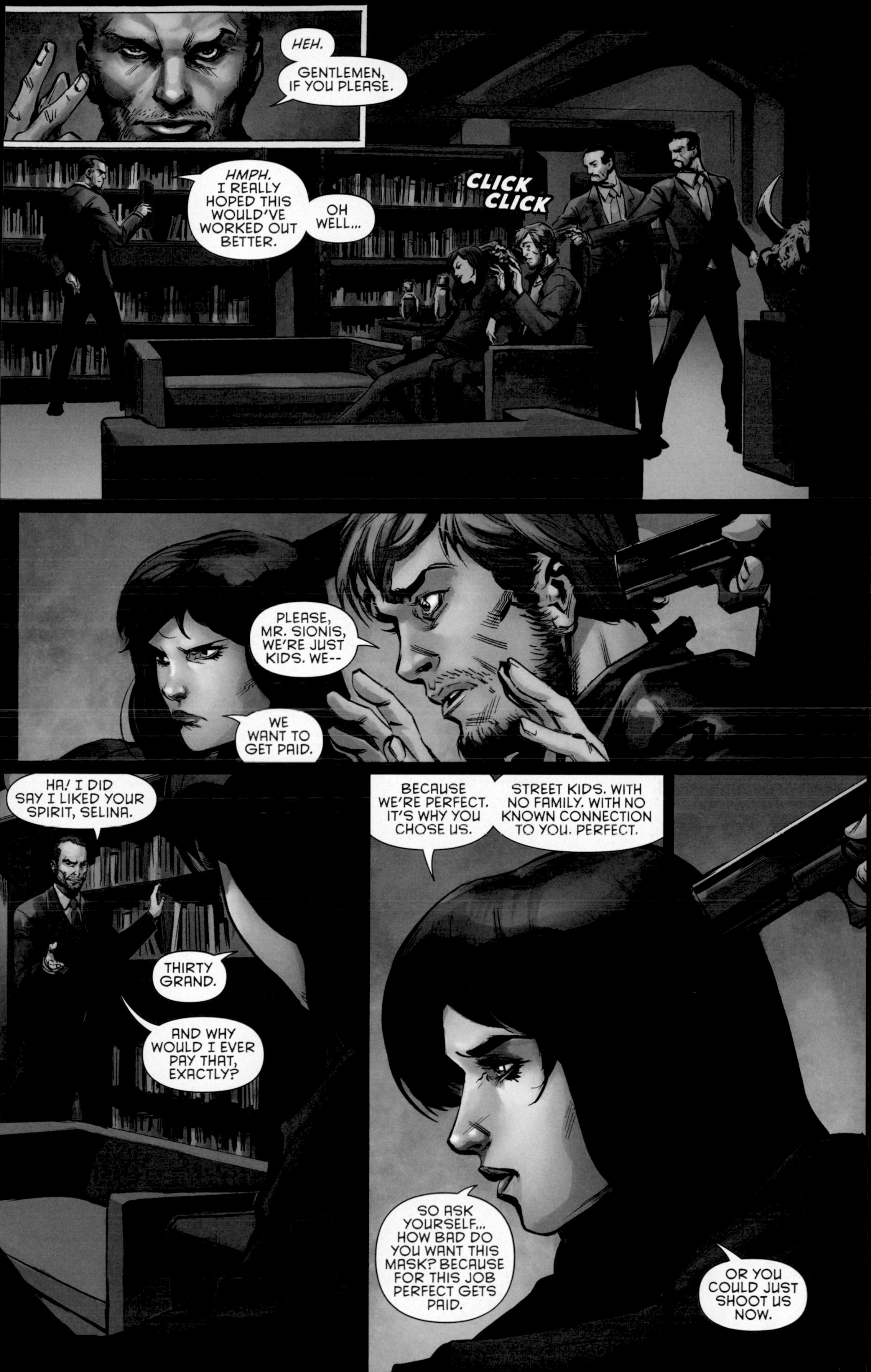
HEH.
GENTLEMEN, IF YOU PLEASE.
HMPH. I REALLY HOPED THIS WOULD'VE WORKED OUT BETTER.
OH WELL...
CLICK CLICK
PLEASE, MR. SIONIS, WE'RE JUST KIDS. WE--
WE WANT TO GET PAID.
HA! I DID SAY I LIKED YOUR SPIRIT, SELINA.
THIRTY GRAND.
AND WHY WOULD I EVER PAY THAT, EXACTLY?
BECAUSE WE'RE PERFECT. IT'S WHY YOU CHOSE US.
STREET KIDS. WITH NO FAMILY. WITH NO KNOWN CONNECTION TO YOU. PERFECT.
SO ASK YOURSELF... HOW BAD DO YOU WANT THIS MASK? BECAUSE FOR THIS JOB PERFECT GETS PAID.
OR YOU COULD JUST SHOOT US NOW.

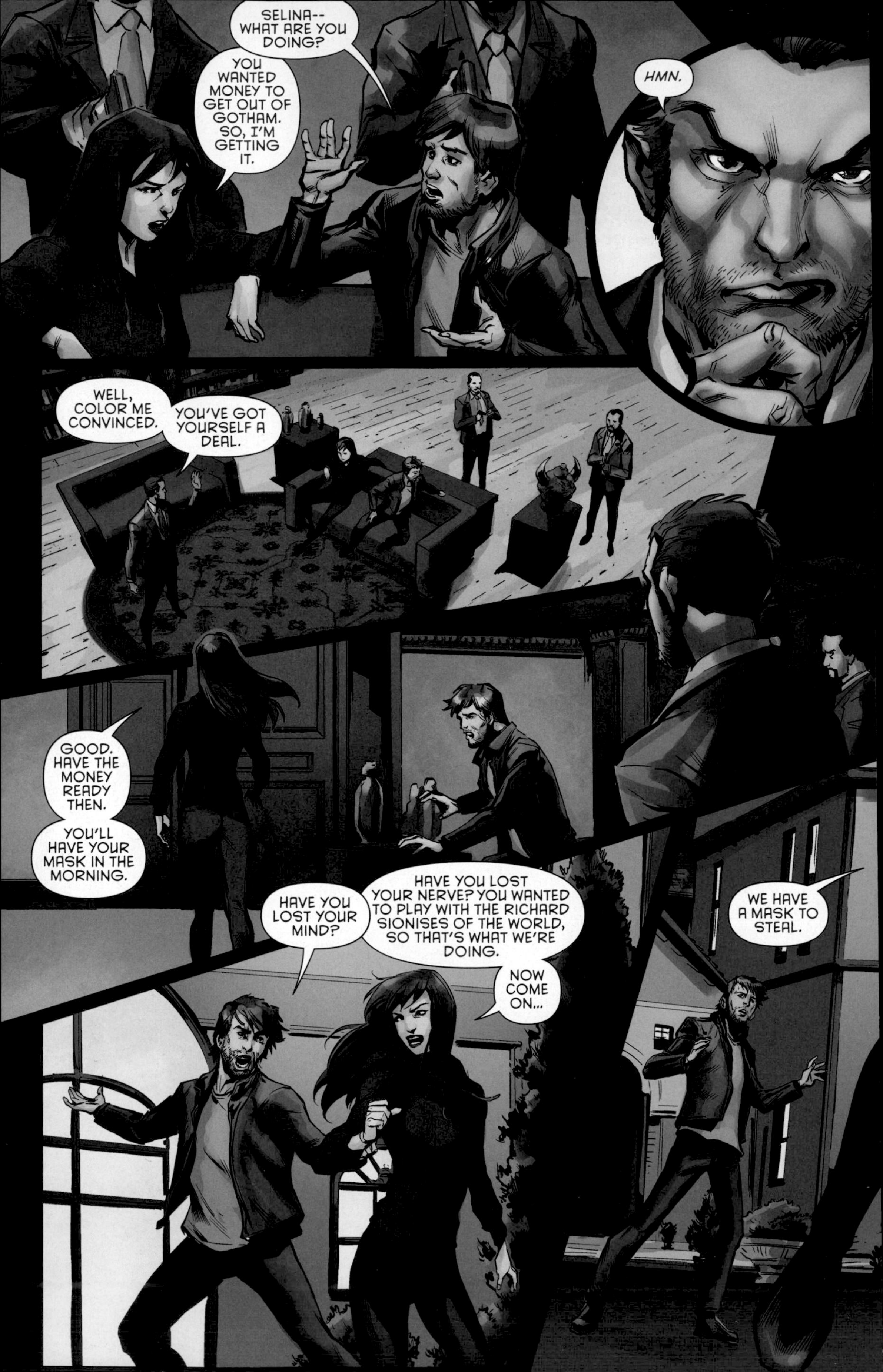
SELINA-- WHAT ARE YOU DOING?
YOU WANTED MONEY TO GET OUT OF GOTHAM. SO, I'M GETTING IT.
HMN.
WELL, COLOR ME CONVINCED.
YOU'VE GOT YOURSELF A DEAL.
GOOD. HAVE THE MONEY READY THEN.
YOU'LL HAVE YOUR MASK IN THE MORNING.
HAVE YOU LOST YOUR MIND?
HAVE YOU LOST YOUR NERVE? YOU WANTED TO PLAY WITH THE RICHARD SIONISES OF THE WORLD, SO THAT'S WHAT WE'RE DOING.
NOW COME ON...
WE HAVE A MASK TO STEAL.

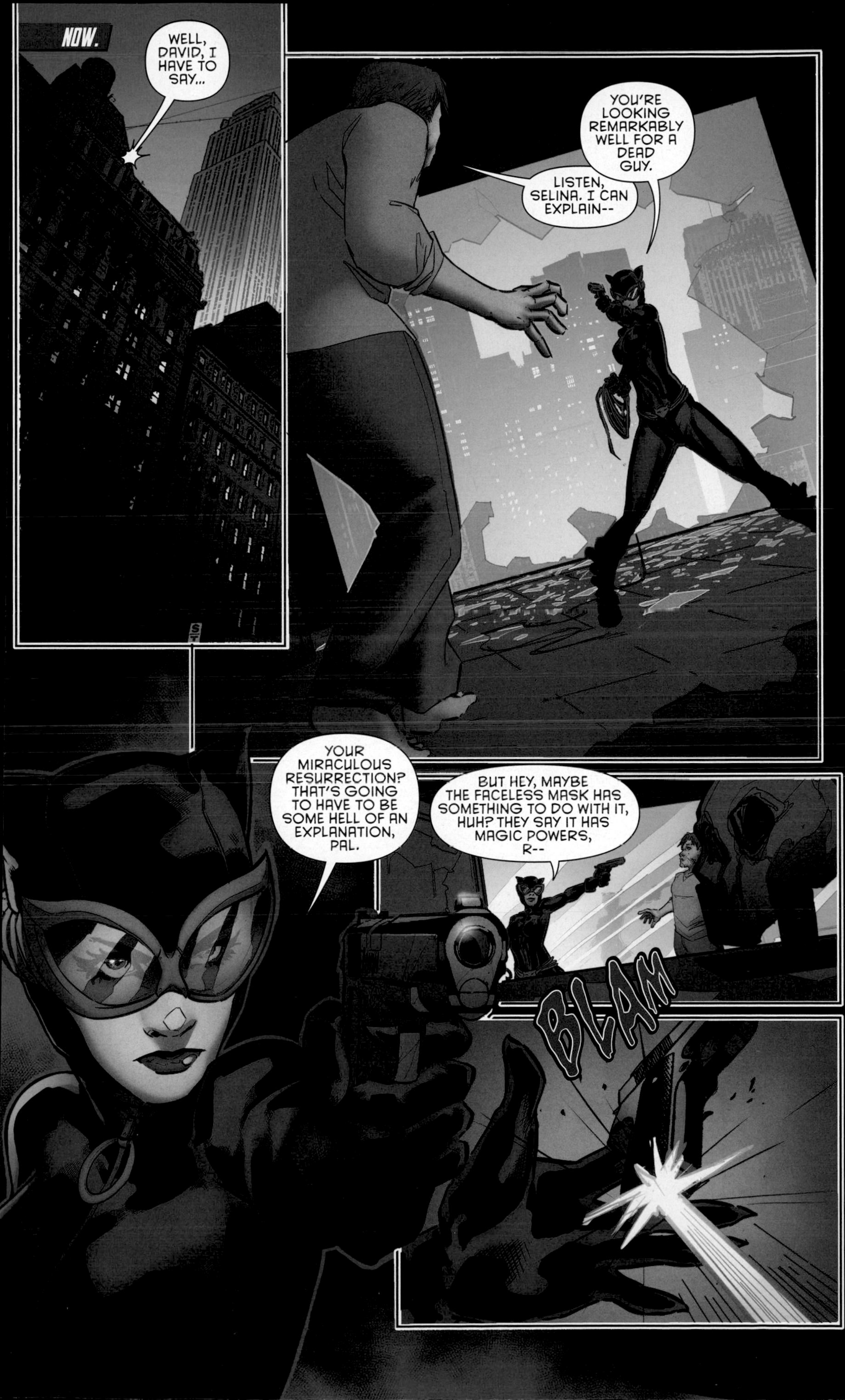
NOW.
WELL, DAVID, I HAVE TO SAY...
YOU'RE LOOKING REMARKABLY WELL FOR A DEAD GUY.
LISTEN, SELINA. I CAN EXPLAIN--
YOUR MIRACULOUS RESURRECTION? THAT'S GOING TO HAVE TO BE SOME HELL OF AN EXPLANATION, PAL.
BUT HEY, MAYBE THE FACELESS MASK HAS SOMETHING TO DO WITH IT, HUH? THEY SAY IT HAS MAGIC POWERS, R--
BLAM

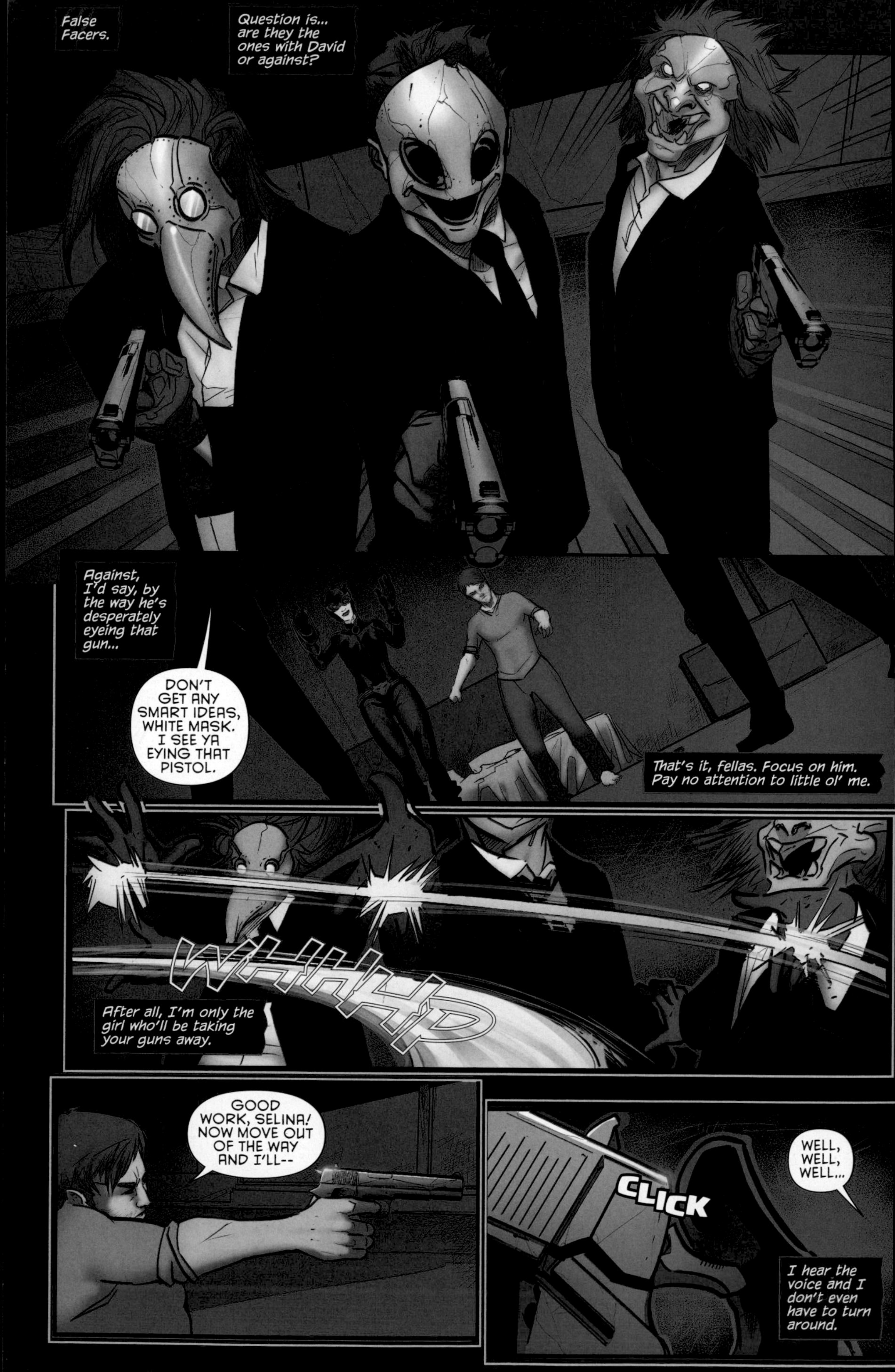

False Facers.
Question is... are they the ones with David or against?
Against, I'd say, by the way he's desperately eyeing that gun...
DON'T GET ANY SMART IDEAS, WHITE MASK. I SEE YA EYING THAT PISTOL.
That's it, fellas. Focus on him. Pay no attention to little ol' me.
WHHHIP
After all, I'm only the girl who'll be taking your guns away.
GOOD WORK, SELINA! NOW MOVE OUT OF THE WAY AND I'LL--
CLICK
WELL, WELL, WELL...
I hear the voice and I don't even have to turn around.

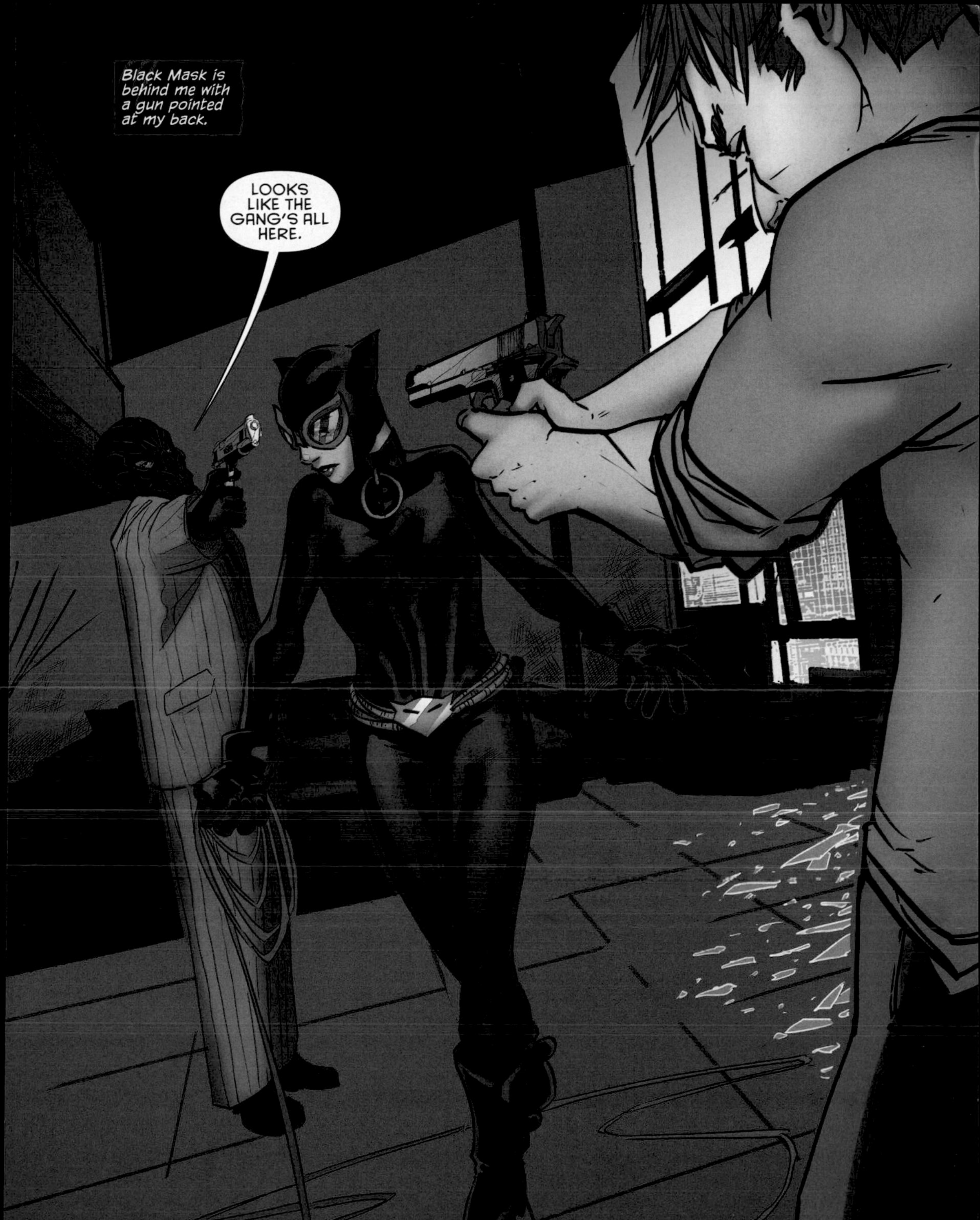
Black Mask is behind me with a gun pointed at my back.
LOOKS LIKE THE GANG'S ALL HERE.
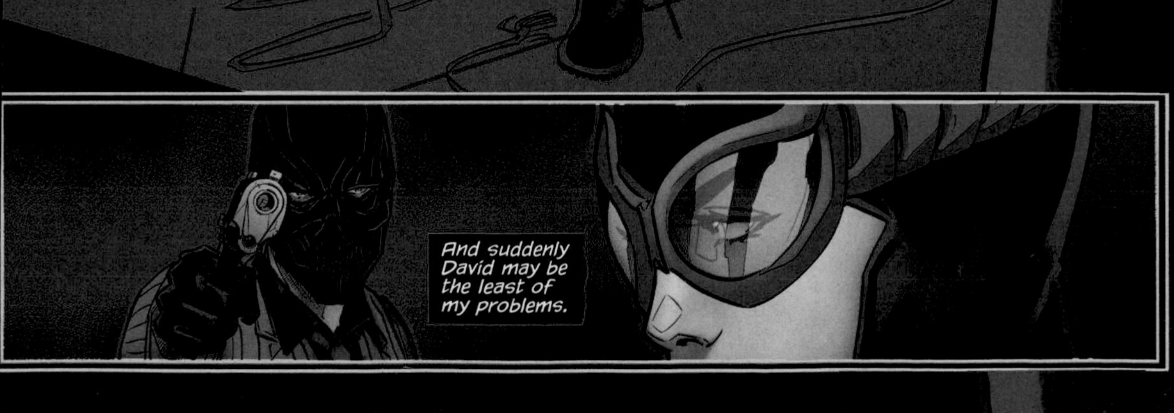
And suddenly David may be the least of my problems.

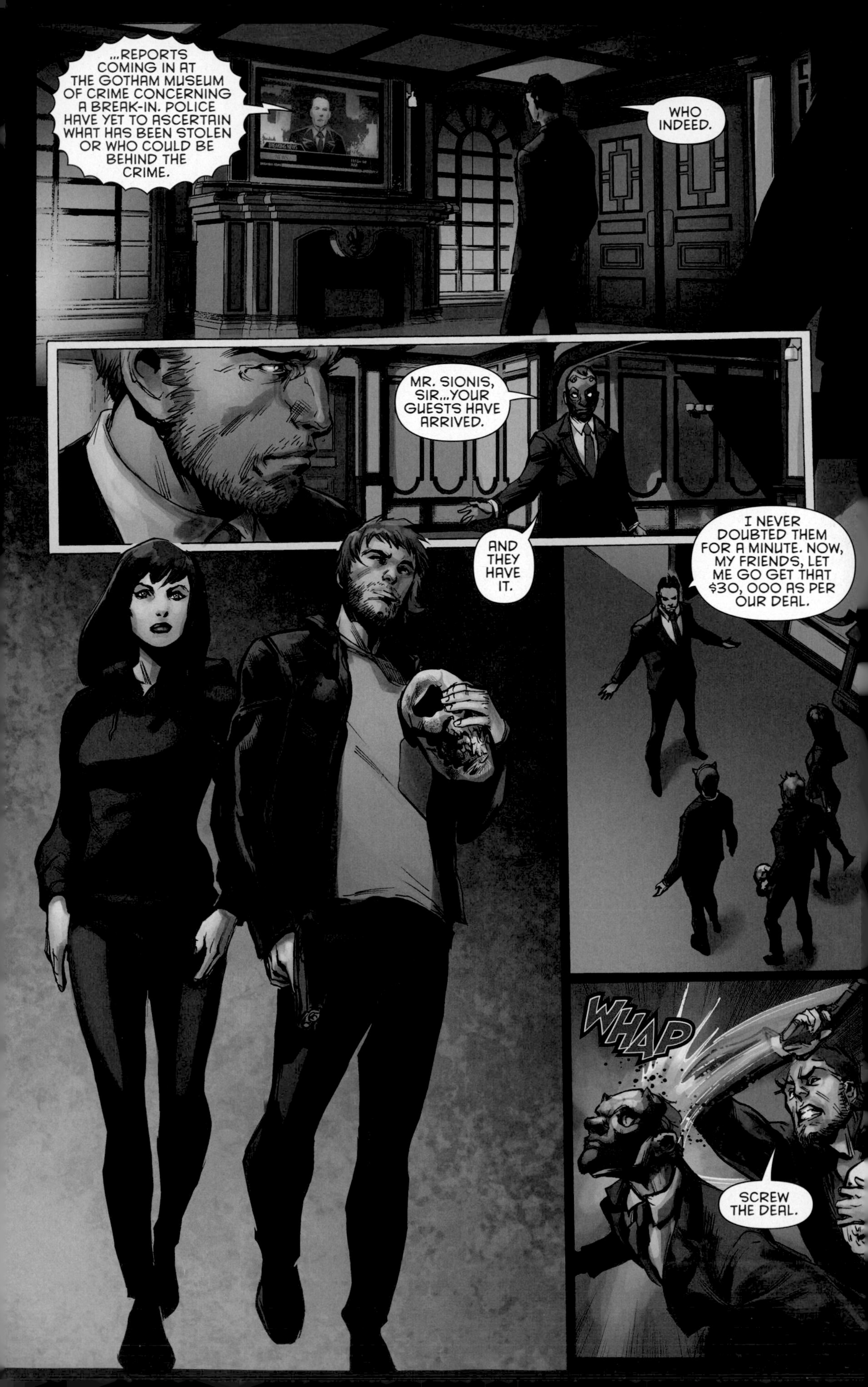
...REPORTS COMING IN AT THE GOTHAM MUSEUM OF CRIME CONCERNING A BREAK-IN. POLICE HAVE YET TO ASCERTAIN WHAT HAS BEEN STOLEN OR WHO COULD BE BEHIND THE CRIME.
WHO INDEED.
MR. SIONIS, SIR...YOUR GUESTS HAVE ARRIVED.
AND THEY HAVE IT.
I NEVER DOUBTED THEM FOR A MINUTE. NOW, MY FRIENDS, LET ME GO GET THAT $30, 000 AS PER OUR DEAL.
WHAP
SCREW THE DEAL.

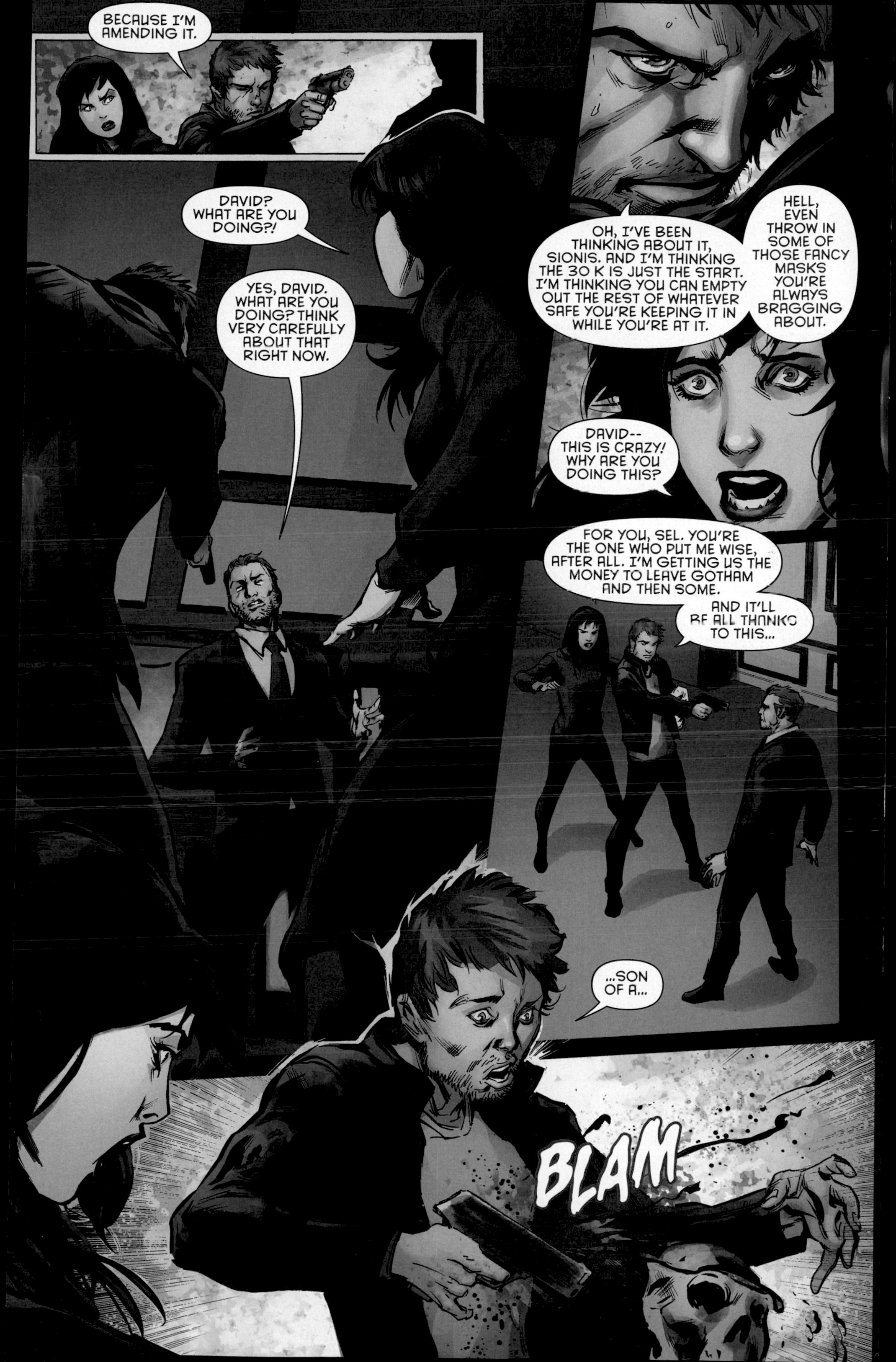
BECAUSE I'M AMENDING IT.
DAVID? WHAT ARE YOU DOING?!
YES, DAVID. WHAT ARE YOU DOING? THINK VERY CAREFULLY ABOUT THAT RIGHT NOW.
OH, I'VE BEEN THINKING ABOUT IT, SIONIS. AND I'M THINKING THE 30 K IS JUST THE START. I'M THINKING YOU CAN EMPTY OUT THE REST OF WHATEVER SAFE YOU'RE KEEPING IT IN WHILE YOU'RE AT IT.
HELL, EVEN THROW IN SOME OF THOSE FANCY MASKS YOU'RE ALWAYS BRAGGING ABOUT.
DAVID-- THIS IS CRAZY! WHY ARE YOU DOING THIS?
FOR YOU, SEL. YOU'RE THE ONE WHO PUT ME WISE, AFTER ALL. I'M GETTING US THE MONEY TO LEAVE GOTHAM AND THEN SOME.
AND IT'LL BE ALL THANKS TO THIS...
...SON OF A...
BLAM

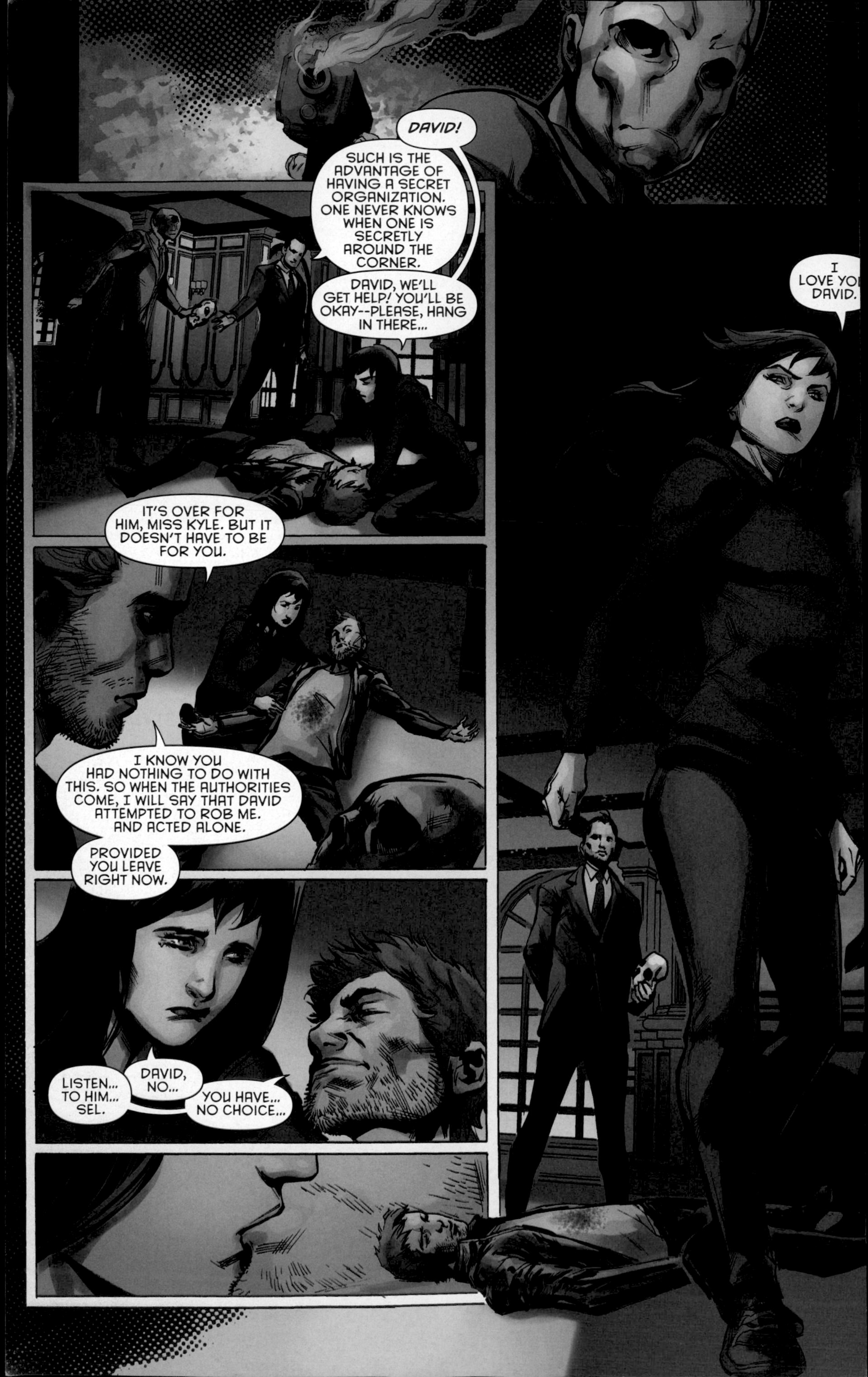
DAVID!
SUCH IS THE ADVANTAGE OF HAVING A SECRET ORGANIZATION. ONE NEVER KNOWS WHEN ONE IS SECRETLY AROUND THE CORNER.
DAVID, WE'LL GET HELP! YOU'LL BE OKAY--PLEASE, HANG IN THERE...
IT'S OVER FOR HIM, MISS KYLE. BUT IT DOESN'T HAVE TO BE FOR YOU.
I KNOW YOU HAD NOTHING TO DO WITH THIS. SO WHEN THE AUTHORITIES COME, I WILL SAY THAT DAVID ATTEMPTED TO ROB ME. AND ACTED ALONE.
PROVIDED YOU LEAVE RIGHT NOW.
DAVID, NO...
LISTEN... TO HIM... SEL.
YOU HAVE... NO CHOICE...
I LOVE YO DAVID.

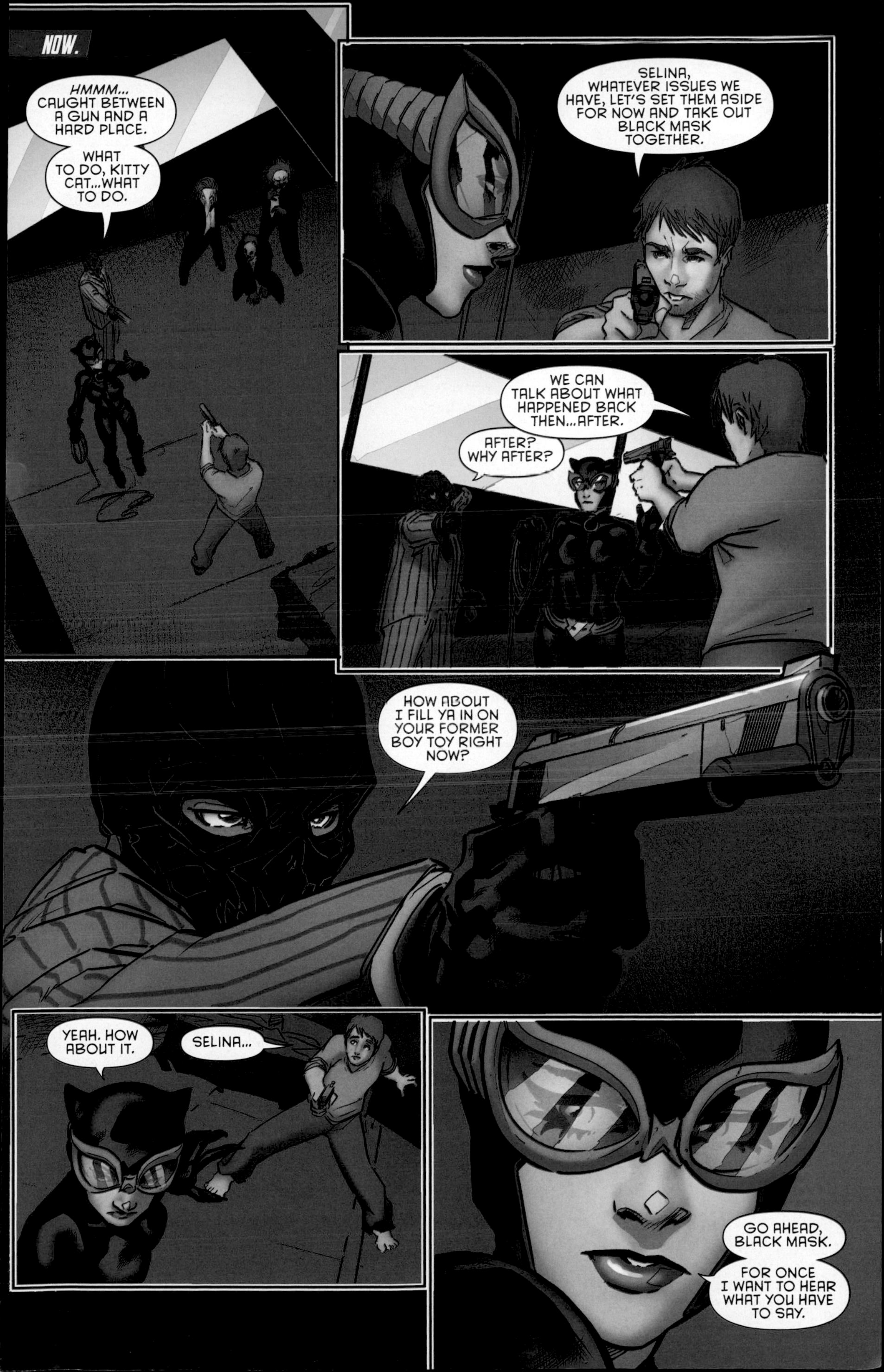
NOW.
HMMM... CAUGHT BETWEEN A GUN AND A HARD PLACE.
WHAT TO DO, KITTY CAT...WHAT TO DO.
SELINA, WHATEVER ISSUES WE HAVE, LET'S SET THEM ASIDE FOR NOW AND TAKE OUT BLACK MASK TOGETHER.
WE CAN TALK ABOUT WHAT HAPPENED BACK THEN...AFTER.
AFTER? WHY AFTER?
HOW ABOUT I FILL YA IN ON YOUR FORMER BOY TOY RIGHT NOW?
YEAH. HOW ABOUT IT.
SELINA...
GO AHEAD, BLACK MASK.
FOR ONCE I WANT TO HEAR WHAT YOU HAVE TO SAY.

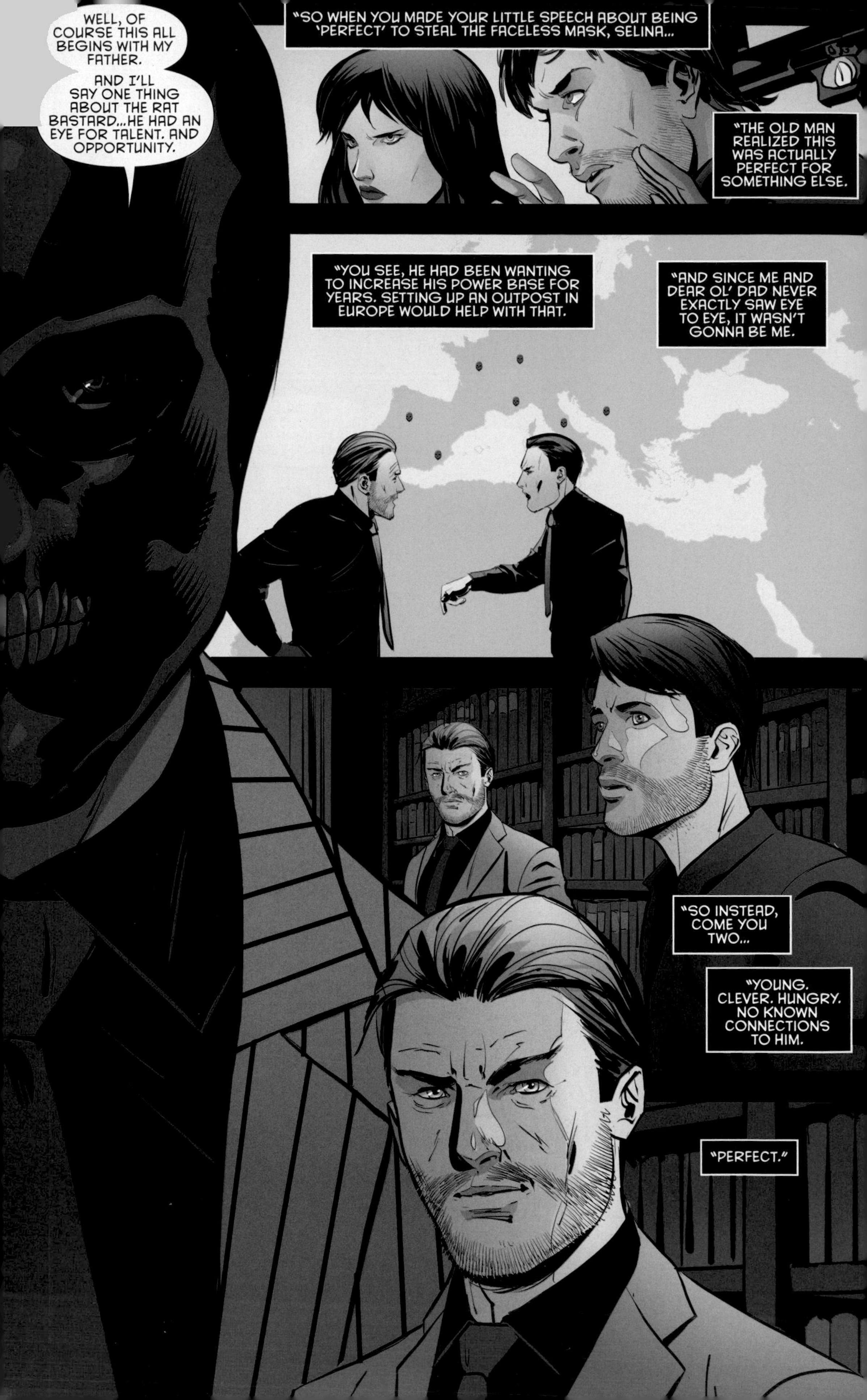
WELL, OF COURSE THIS ALL BEGINS WITH MY FATHER.
AND I'LL SAY ONE THING ABOUT THE RAT BASTARD...HE HAD AN EYE FOR TALENT. AND OPPORTUNITY.
"SO WHEN YOU MADE YOUR LITTLE SPEECH ABOUT BEING 'PERFECT' TO STEAL THE FACELESS MASK, SELINA...
"THE OLD MAN REALIZED THIS WAS ACTUALLY PERFECT FOR SOMETHING ELSE.
"YOU SEE, HE HAD BEEN WANTING TO INCREASE HIS POWER BASE FOR YEARS. SETTING UP AN OUTPOST IN EUROPE WOULD HELP WITH THAT.
"AND SINCE ME AND DEAR OL' DAD NEVER EXACTLY SAW EYE TO EYE, IT WASN'T GONNA BE ME.
"SO INSTEAD, COME YOU TWO...
"YOUNG. CLEVER. HUNGRY. NO KNOWN CONNECTIONS TO HIM.
"PERFECT."

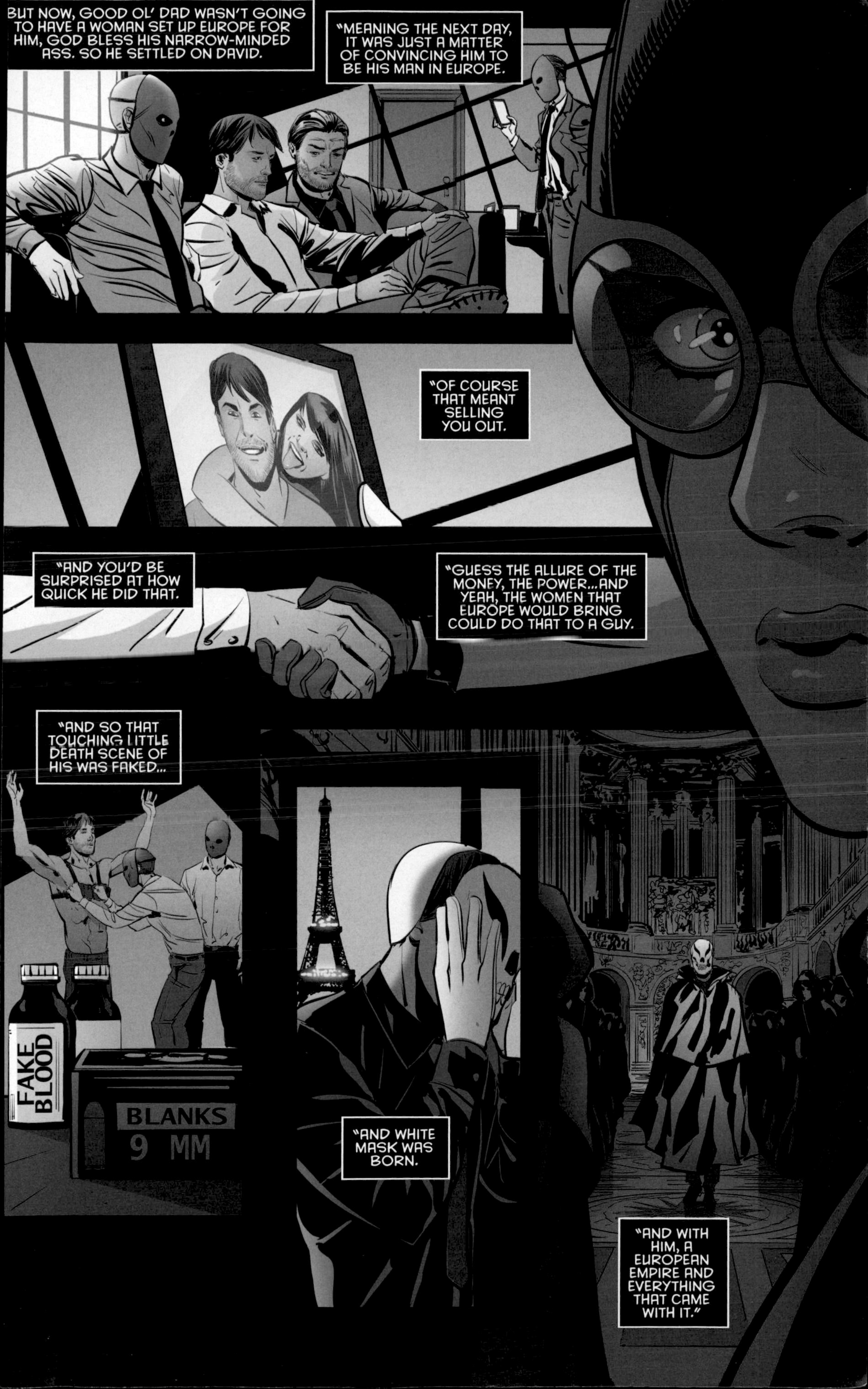
BUT NOW, GOOD OL' DAD WASN'T GOING TO HAVE A WOMAN SET UP EUROPE FOR HIM, GOD BLESS HIS NARROW-MINDED ASS. SO HE SETTLED ON DAVID.
"MEANING THE NEXT DAY, IT WAS JUST A MATTER OF CONVINCING HIM TO BE HIS MAN IN EUROPE.
"OF COURSE THAT MEANT SELLING YOU OUT.
"AND YOU'D BE SURPRISED AT HOW QUICK HE DID THAT.
"GUESS THE ALLURE OF THE MONEY, THE POWER...AND YEAH, THE WOMEN THAT EUROPE WOULD BRING COULD DO THAT TO A GUY.
"AND SO THAT TOUCHING LITTLE DEATH SCENE OF HIS WAS FAKED...
FAKE BLOOD
BLANKS 9 MM
"AND WHITE MASK WAS BORN.
"AND WITH HIM, A EUROPEAN EMPIRE AND EVERYTHING THAT CAME WITH IT."

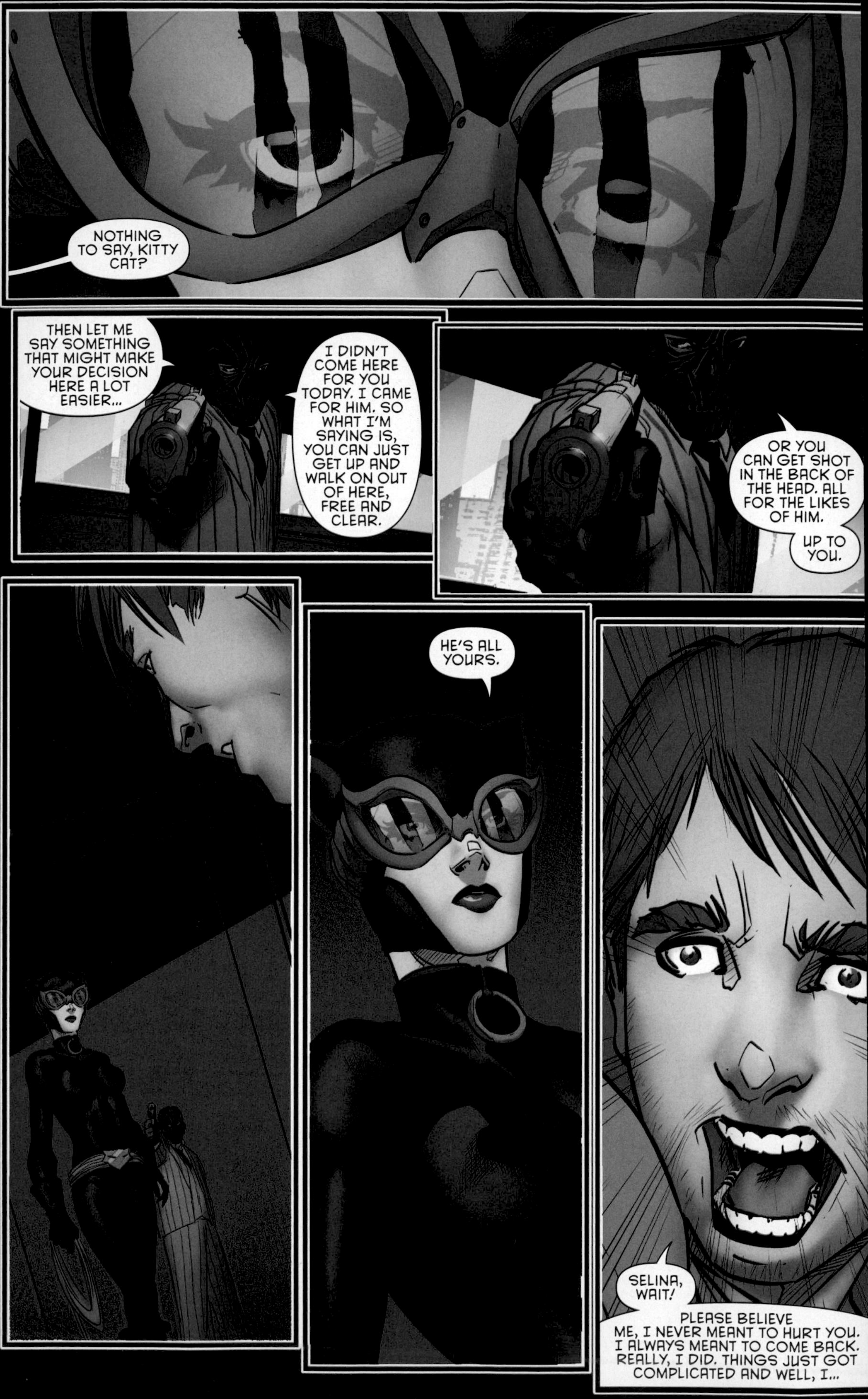
NOTHING TO SAY, KITTY CAT?
THEN LET ME SAY SOMETHING THAT MIGHT MAKE YOUR DECISION HERE A LOT EASIER...
I DIDN'T COME HERE FOR YOU TODAY. I CAME FOR HIM. SO WHAT I'M SAYING IS, YOU CAN JUST GET UP AND WALK ON OUT OF HERE, FREE AND CLEAR.
OR YOU CAN GET SHOT IN THE BACK OF THE HEAD. ALL FOR THE LIKES OF HIM.
UP TO YOU.
HE'S ALL YOURS.
SELINA, WAIT!
PLEASE BELIEVE ME, I NEVER MEANT TO HURT YOU. I ALWAYS MEANT TO COME BACK. REALLY, I DID. THINGS JUST GOT COMPLICATED AND WELL, I...

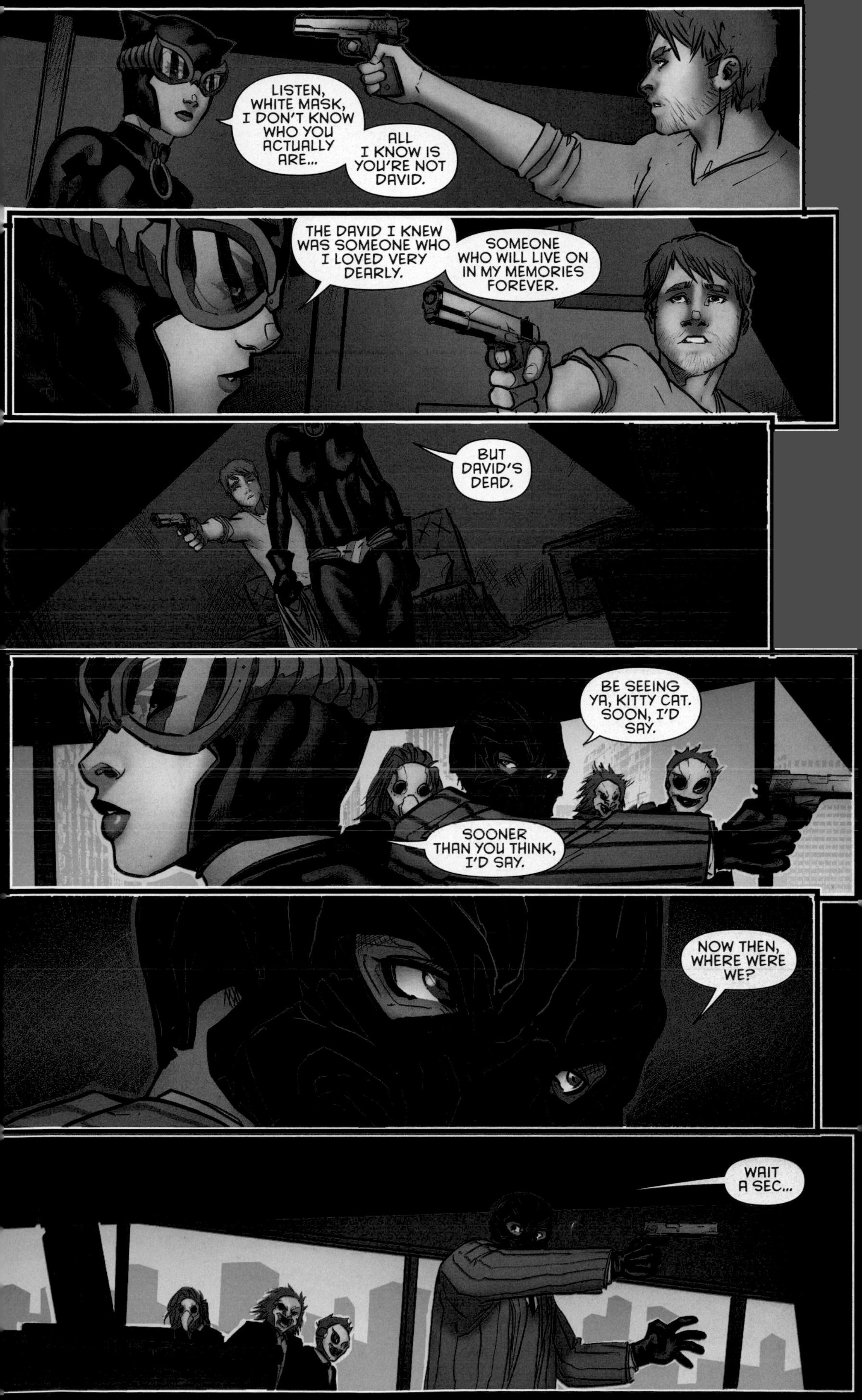
LISTEN, WHITE MASK, I DON'T KNOW WHO YOU ACTUALLY ARE...
ALL I KNOW IS YOU'RE NOT DAVID.
THE DAVID I KNEW WAS SOMEONE WHO I LOVED VERY DEARLY.
SOMEONE WHO WILL LIVE ON IN MY MEMORIES FOREVER.
BUT DAVID'S DEAD.
BE SEEING YA, KITTY CAT. SOON, I'D SAY.
SOONER THAN YOU THINK, I'D SAY.
NOW THEN, WHERE WERE WE?
WAIT A SEC...

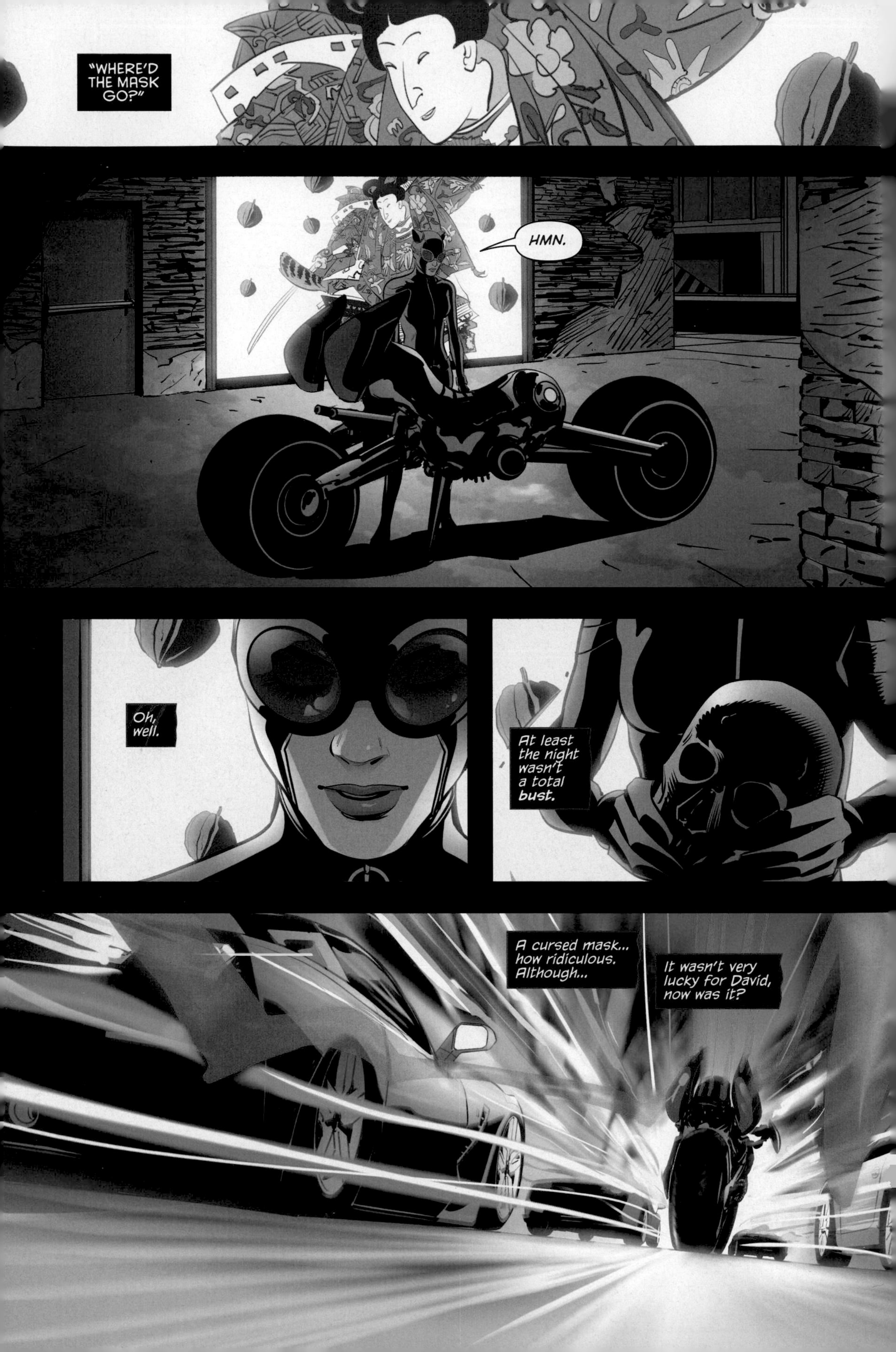
"WHERE'D THE MASK GO?"
HMN.
Oh, well.
At least the night wasn't a total **bust.**
A cursed mask... how ridiculous. Although...
It wasn't very lucky for David, now was it?

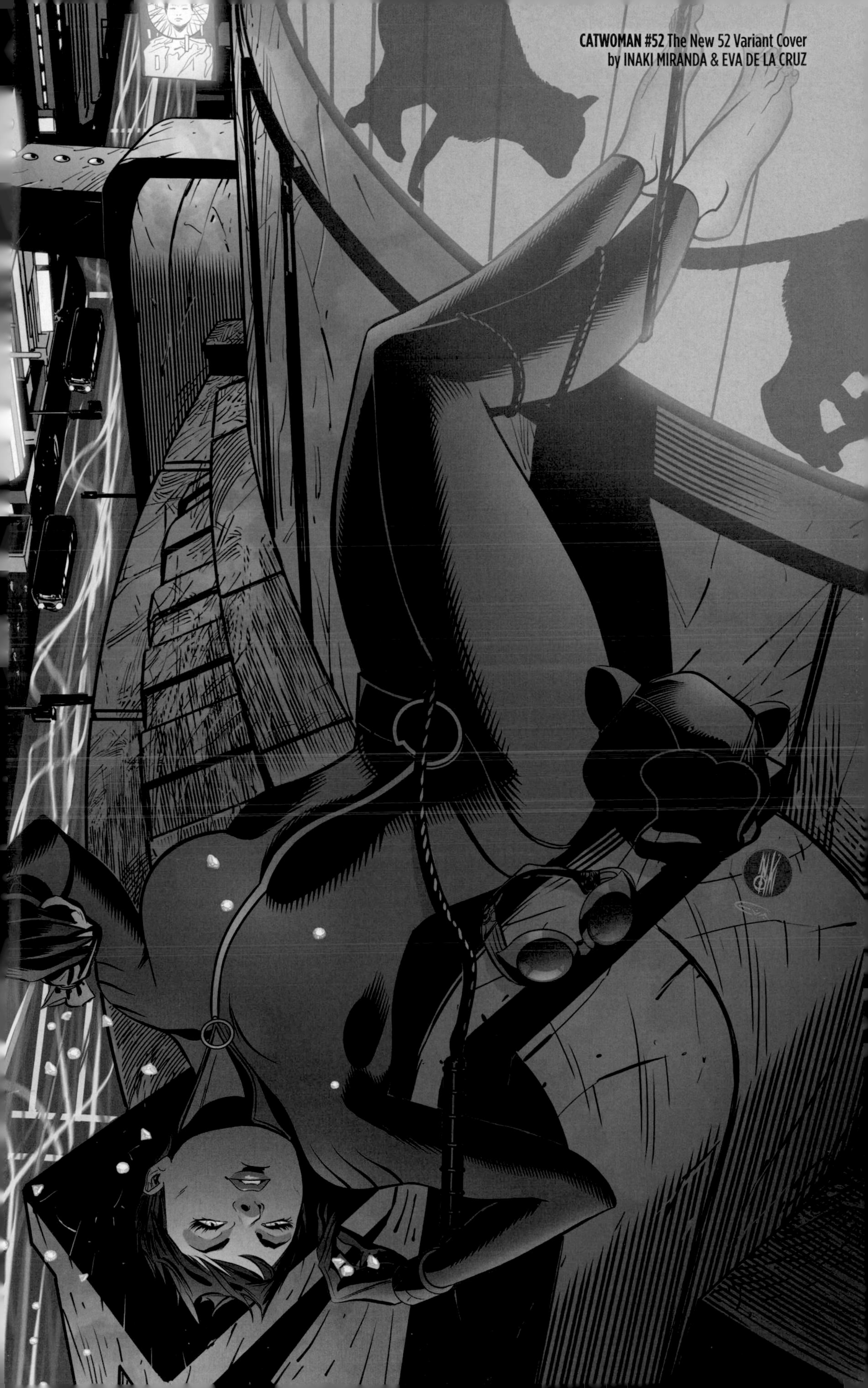

CATWOMAN #52 The New 52 Variant Cover
by INAKI MIRANDA & EVA DE LA CRUZ

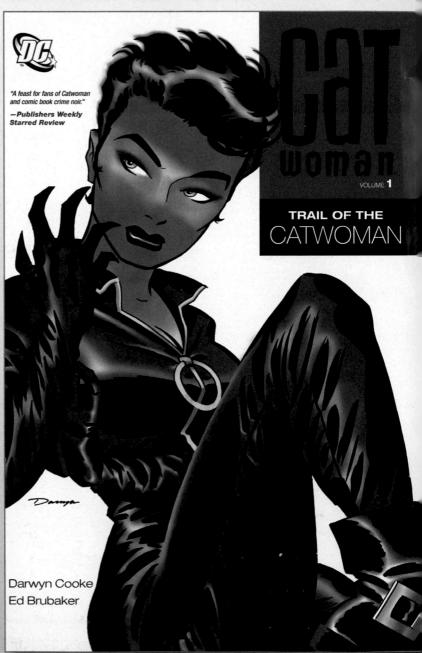

HARLEY QUINN
VOLUME 1: HOT IN THE CITY

SUICIDE SQUAD VOL. 1: KICKED IN THE TEETH

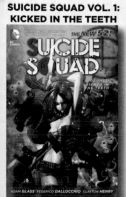

with ADAM GLASS and FEDERICO DALLOCCHIO

HARLEY QUINN: PRELUDES AND KNOCK-KNOCK JOKES

with KARL KESEL and TERRY DODSON

BATMAN: MAD LOVE AND OTHER STORIES

with PAUL DINI and BRUCE TIMM

DC COMICS™

"THE LONG HALLOWEEN is more th
a comic book. It's an epic traged
—Christopher Nolan (director of BATMAN BEGIN
THE DARK KNIGHT and THE DARK KNIGHT RISE

"THE LONG HALLOWEEN is the preemine
influence on both movies [BATMAN BEGINS a
THE DARK KNIGHT
—David Goyer (screenwriter
THE DARK KNIGHT RISE

FROM THE AWARD-WINNING TEAM BEH
SUPERMAN: FOR ALL SEASONS

JEPH LOEB & TIM SALE

BATMAN:
DARK VICTORY

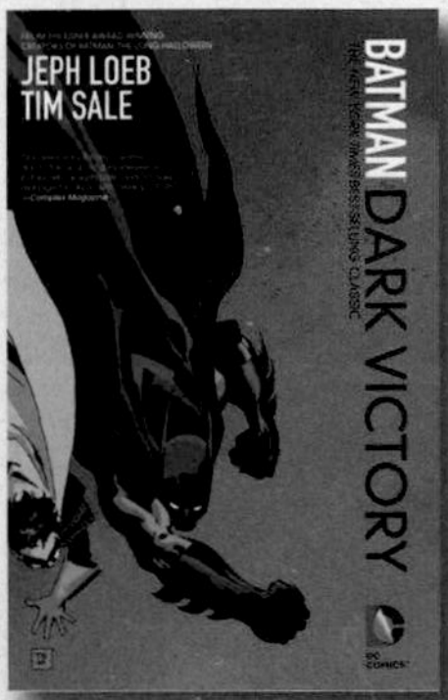
JEPH LOEB
TIM SALE
BATMAN DARK VICTORY

BATMAN:
HAUNTED KNIGHT

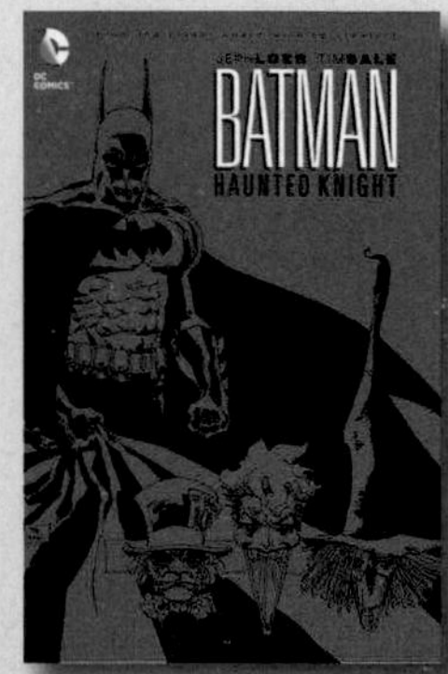
BATMAN
HAUNTED KNIGHT

CATWOMAN:
WHEN IN ROME

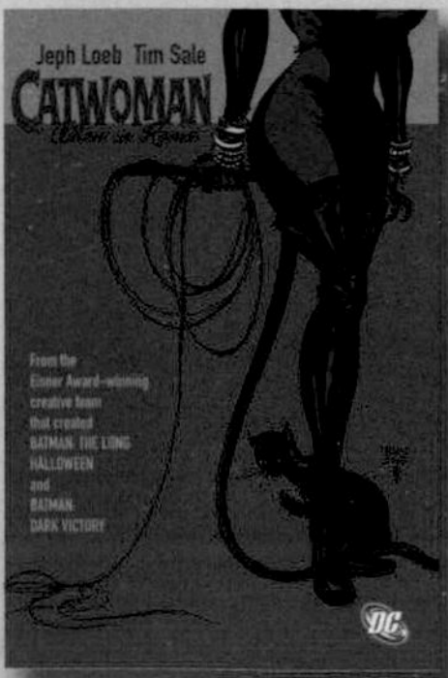
Jeph Loeb Tim Sale
CATWOMAN

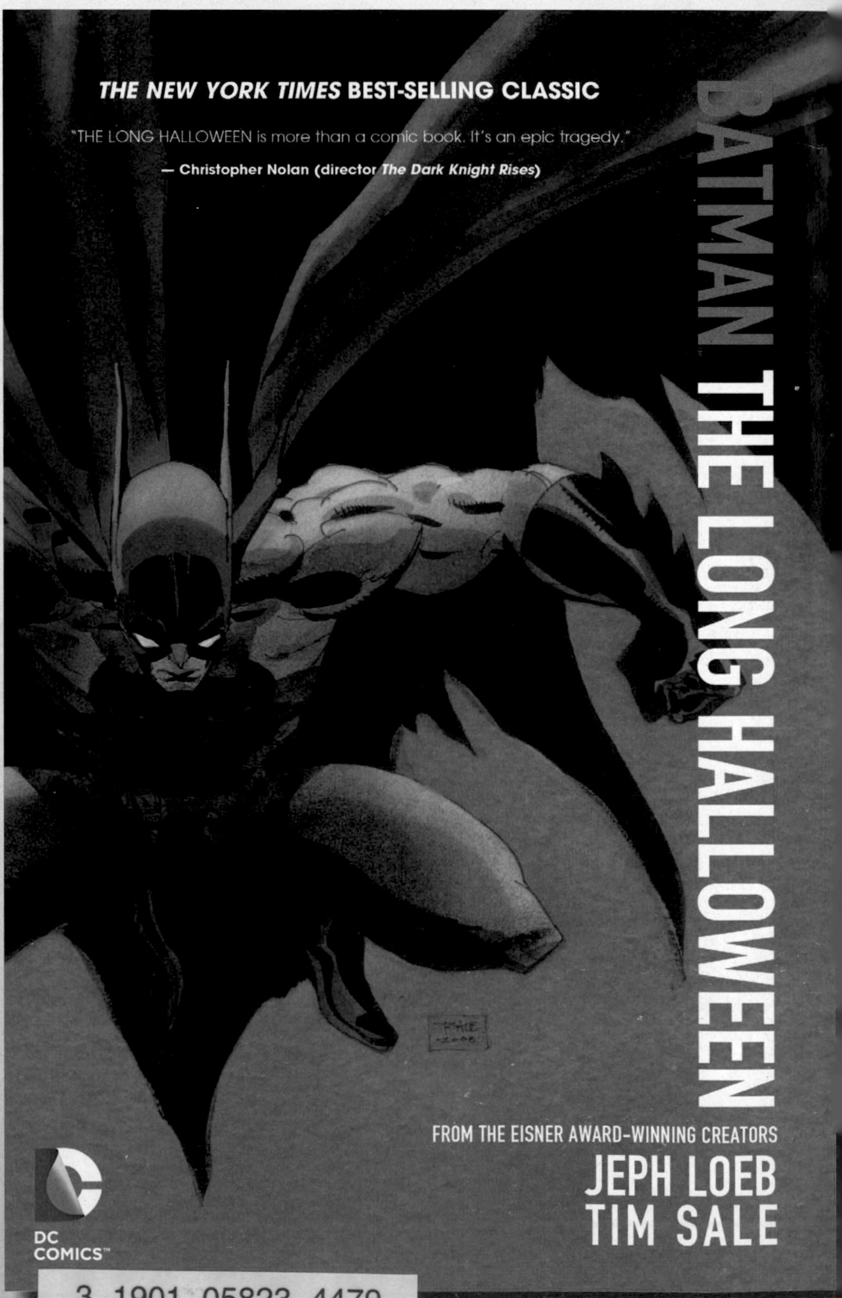
THE NEW YORK TIMES BEST-SELLING CLASSIC
"THE LONG HALLOWEEN is more than a comic book. It's an epic tragedy."
— Christopher Nolan (director The Dark Knight Rises)
BATMAN THE LONG HALLOWEEN
FROM THE EISNER AWARD-WINNING CREATORS
JEPH LOEB
TIM SALE
DC COMICS™

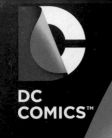